International Labour Conference
86th Session   1998

Report VI (1)

Child labour

Targeting the intolerable

Sixth item on the agenda

International Labour Office   Geneva

ILO
Child labour: Targeting the intolerable
Geneva, International Labour Office, 1996

/Child labour/, /role of ILO/, /developed country/, /developing country/. 14.02.2
ISBN 92-2-110328-5

Also published in Arabic, Chinese, French, German, Russian and Spanish

Cover photograph © Ron Giling/Panos Pictures

ILO Cataloguing in Publication Data

Contents

Introduction

The world community is calling for an end to the intolerable: the persistent exploitation of children in slave-like and bonded conditions, in hazardous and arduous work, in prostitution, pornography and other unspeakable situations.

As part of its campaign to eliminate child labour, the International Labour Organization is proposing the adoption of new international legal instruments to combat the worst forms of child labour, supplemented by recommendations for practical action and assistance. The proposal, put forward by its three constituent groups — governments, and employers' and workers' organizations — seeks the commitment of member States to ban and prevent child labour in hazardous work and to remove children without delay from such work.

Drawing on ILO action against child labour, including the experience of the ILO's International Programme on the Elimination of Child Labour and other initiatives, this report chronicles the exploitation and abuse of working children, surveys international and national law and practice, and points the way toward effective practical action to remove children from debt bondage, prostitution and hazardous occupations and activities. It is accompanied by a questionnaire (Report VI (1): *Questionnaire*) which seeks the views of governments, in consultation with employers' and workers' organizations, on the possible scope and content of the proposed international legal instruments.

The problem

1

The world context

Child labour remains a serious problem in the world today. According to revised estimates by the ILO's Bureau of Statistics, the number of working children between the ages of 5 and 14 is at least 120 million. As may be expected given the prevailing economic conditions, the overwhelming majority of these are in developing countries in Africa, Asia and Latin America. But pockets of child labour also exist in many industrialized countries. Numerous children work in occupations and industries which are plainly dangerous and hazardous. They are found in mines, in factories making glass bangles, matches and fireworks, in deep-sea fishing, in commercial agriculture and so on. The list is endless, as are the dangers and hazards and the consequences:

— Working children suffer significant growth deficits compared with children in school: they grow up shorter and lighter, and their body size continues to be smaller even in adulthood.[1]

— Both anecdotal evidence and statistical surveys indicate that far too many working children are exposed to hazardous conditions which expose them to chemical and biological hazards. For example, according to one large-scale ILO national survey in the Philippines, more than 60 per cent of working children are exposed to such hazards and, of these, 40 per cent experience serious injuries or illnesses including amputations and loss of body parts.

— Large numbers of working children work under conditions which expose them to substances with long latency periods — for example, asbestos — which increases the risk of contracting chronic occupational diseases such as asbestosis or lung cancer in young adulthood. A World Health Organization (WHO) report on a district in India attributes epidemic epilepsy to chronic exposure to the pesticide benzine hexachloride, which is used as a food preservative.[2]

— In rural areas, more children are believed to die of exposure to pesticide than from the most common childhood diseases put together, according to a study on occupational health in developing countries.[3]

— Children in certain occupations are especially vulnerable to particular types of abuse. For example, many studies confirm that child domestic workers are victims of verbal and sexual abuse, beating or punishment by starvation.

Child labour is simply the single most important source of child exploitation and child abuse in the world today.

But there are grounds for optimism. The world we now know is radically different from what it was some 15 years ago. It offers new opportunities and possibilities and there is an emerging consensus that the world community has the duty and the obligation to combat especially those intolerable forms of child labour that still persist in much of industry, agriculture and services and in conditions of bondage and serfdom.

One of the most striking developments in the last decade and a half is the emergence of a worldwide movement against child labour. This is reflected in the remarkable changes in attitudes and perceptions as well as in the number and range of actors involved in the cause of children and child workers.

Until very recently, child labour was not an issue of major concern, at either the national or the international level:

— There were few institutions active in child labour, say, before the mid-1980s. For all practical purposes, the ILO was one of the few international organizations and ILO Conventions the only international instruments directly focused on and committed to the elimination of child labour.

— Until a few years ago, child labour was viewed with a mixture of indifference, apathy and even cynicism. It was so widely practised that it was accepted by many as part of the natural order of things. For others, child labour was equated with child work, excused with the argument that work is good for children and a means of helping families.

At the policy level, therefore, a major difficulty facing the ILO was getting member States to admit or recognize the problem. The position was one of denial — denial by governments, by employers and by parents. For most governments child labour was illegal, and therefore what did not exist in law did not prevail in practice. For employers the illegality of child labour meant that children could be employed only clandestinely. For destitute parents trapped in poverty the employment of their children was considered the only option left and its prohibition a nuisance and even a portent of economic catastrophe. Even for the donor community child labour was almost nowhere on its list of priorities. There was thus a silence born out of necessity and opportunism which kept the problem hidden, making remedial action virtually impossible.

This is no longer the case. Today, child labour is one of the dominant issues of our time:

— There is an explosion in the literature on child labour and in the coverage of child labour abuses and violations in the international print and electronic media.

— Today, there is a large number of distinguished institutions at the forefront of the struggle against child labour. In 1986 UNICEF gave impetus to the cause through its programme on children in especially difficult circumstances. The body of international law and ILO instruments was given added momentum with the adoption, in 1989, of the United Nations Convention on the Rights of the Child. Perhaps less well known, but important too, was the increasingly central place that child labour was given in the deliberations of the subcommittees of the Geneva-based United Nations Commission on Human Rights.

— Thanks to the commitment of thousands of concerned individuals and groups, the cause of child rights has been given a further boost by the emergence of numerous non-governmental organizations (NGOs) which have carried the torch and transformed what was at best a fledgling local concern into a formidable worldwide movement.

Perhaps the best illustration of the long distance we have travelled is the fact that child labour has now shot to the top of the global agenda and consumer concerns in both developing and industrialized countries. Corporations are reacting to consumer and other pressure in rich countries demanding corporate responsibility from manufacturers to respect human rights, including the ILO's Conventions on workers' rights and child labour. World-renowned manufacturers such as Levi Strauss, Reebok, Sears and others in the sporting goods industry are now looking into the conditions under which their products are being produced. In Europe a number of established stores have decided not to sell products such as carpets unless they are certified as being made without child labour. Some have agreed to establish a code of conduct to help abolish child labour. The world's football governing body, the International Federation of Association Football (FIFA) has agreed upon the content of a code of labour practice for production of goods licensed by FIFA with the International Confederation of Free Trade Unions (ICFTU), the International Textile, Garment and Leather Workers' Federation (ITGLWF), and the International Federation of Commercial, Clerical, Professional and Technical Employees (FIET). The Code contains a specific provision prohibiting the use of child labour in producing FIFA-licensed goods; only workers above the age of 15 years are allowed, in accordance with ILO Convention No. 138.

These very powerful movements by consumers and manufacturers alike have been accompanied by perhaps even more powerful efforts on the legislative and trade fronts:

— The European Union (EU) has reached agreement on a new Generalized System of Preferences (GSP). The GSP, while providing reduced tariffs on the import of many products from developing countries, requires a ban on goods produced by prison and slave labour, respect for trade union rights and the prohibition of child labour, as defined by ILO Conventions. Countries which provide proof of compliance will receive privileged access to EU markets.

— The United States also has introduced provisions into its legislation linking the granting of trade privileges to foreign countries with their respect for minimum workers' rights. The Generalized System of Preferences (GSP) includes references to workers' rights in the exporting country. In the United States, Senator Tom Harkin has introduced a bill, not yet enacted, banning the import of products from industries using child labour.

— At the international level, there has been considerable discussion as to whether global competition rules should require the implementation of certain basic international labour standards, including the progressive elimination of child labour. In the ILO, the question of linkage of trade and labour standards has been the subject of sharply divergent views. But there has been wide agreement on the need for intensified action against child labour with an immediate attack on the worst abuses.

This change in attitude has led to some remarkable changes in the behaviour of the major actors, particularly governments. In the past, the illegality of child labour and the political sensitivity of governments were such a barrier to national action that there was not one single technical cooperation project which the ILO could implement. This is no longer so.

Many governments have embarked on a review and updating of national legislation on child labour and have adopted practical policies and programmes on child labour (Brazil, India, Indonesia, Kenya, Nepal, Pakistan, Philippines, United Republic of Tanzania, Thailand, Zimbabwe). The ILO's International Programme on the Elimination of Child Labour (IPEC) is now operational in more than 25 countries.

The nature and magnitude of the problem

Child labour today

Much has been achieved, but there is still so far to go.

Statistics on child labour are elusive not only because of the special and practical difficulties involved in the design and implementation of child surveys but also because of differences in perception about what constitutes a child, or child work, or child labour. Even so, the evidence reveals a problem found throughout the world, and especially in Africa, Asia and Latin America.

Earlier estimates based on very limited statistical information obtained from about 100 countries indicated that there were 73 million working children between 10 and 14 years of age in these countries in 1995. However, recent experimental surveys carried out by the ILO's Bureau of Statistics in a number of countries indicate that this figure is a gross underestimation. They further indicate that even children below 10 years of age are at work in substantial numbers. The Bureau now estimates that, in the developing countries alone, there are at least 120 million children between the ages of 5 and 14 who are fully at work, and more than twice as many (or about 250 million) if those for whom work is a secondary activity are included. Of these, 61 per cent are found in Asia, 32 per cent in Africa, and 7 per cent in Latin America. Although Asia has the largest number of child workers, Africa has the highest incidence at around 40 per cent of children between 5 and 14 years old. Though primarily a developing country problem, child labour also exists in many industrialized countries and is emerging in many East European and Asian countries which are in transition to a market economy.

There are, of course, considerable national differences in the incidence of child labour. A recent ILO survey of child labour in Ghana,

India, Indonesia and Senegal[4] found that 25 per cent of all children between 5 and 14 years of age had been engaged in an economic activity and that around 33 per cent of the children did not attend school.

"Everyone", says the Universal Declaration of Human Rights, "has the right to education. Education shall be free, at least in the elementary and fundamental stages. Elementary education shall be compulsory." Today, lack of education is especially damaging because both individual and societal well-being increasingly depend on literacy, numeracy and intellectual competence. A child working is therefore a future denied.

Working children are disadvantaged in other ways as well, and there is evidence that the early involvement of children in work can have serious health and developmental consequences.[5] A comparative study carried out over a period of 17 years in India on both school-going children and working children in agriculture, small-scale industries and the service sector showed that working children grow up shorter and lighter than schoolchildren.[6] In studies carried out in Bombay the health of children working in hotels, restaurants, construction and elsewhere was found to be considerably inferior to that of a control group of children attending school. Symptoms included muscular, chest and abdominal pain, headaches, dizziness, respiratory infections, diarrhoea and worm infection.[7] Similar findings were observed in the carpet-weaving industry in Mirzapur, India. Poor sanitation, overcrowding, inadequate ventilation and extreme temperatures in the working environment are aggravated by poor conditions and malnutrition in the living environment, thus making working children more susceptible to infectious diseases, injuries and other workplace-related ailments.

Most statistical surveys cover only children aged 10 and above. But many children begin work at an earlier age. Rural children, in particular girls, tend to begin their economic activity at an early stage, at 5, 6 or 7 years of age. In some countries, children under 10 years of age are estimated to account for 20 per cent of child labour in the rural areas and around 5 per cent in urban centres. Their number can be much higher in certain occupations and industries, for example, in domestic service and home-based industries. Children are also conspicuously present in scavenging and rag-picking or in marginal economic activities in the streets and are exposed to drugs, violence, criminal activities, physical and sexual abuse in many cities around the world.

Child labour, then, is a denial of the right to education and of the opportunity to reach full physical and psychological development. Worse still, many millions of children are found working throughout the world, trapped in forced labour, debt bondage, prostitution, pornography, and other kinds of work which cause lasting damage and immediate dangers. Clearly, therefore, the design of a national policy aimed at the effective abolition of child labour must focus on a priority basis on the most vulnerable children and on the most intolerable forms of child labour.[8]

Children in hazardous work

The most common situation in which children are vulnerable is when they work in hazardous occupations and industries.

Health and safety hazards in the working environment can be related to the nature of the work (for example, whether or not the work involves intrinsically hazardous processes), to their exposure to hazardous substances and agents or to their exposure to poor working conditions.[9] Chemical, physical, biological and psychological hazards are often found in combination in the workplace. Often, too, their adverse effects are not only cumulative but magnified through their synergic interaction. It is not easy to isolate one single source or cause of an occupational hazard.

Children are susceptible to all of the dangers that are faced by adults when placed in the same situation, and survival and physical integrity are of course as important to them as to older people. However, work hazards that affect adults affect children even more strongly. Children differ biologically from adults in their anatomical, physiological, and psychological characteristics. These differences make them more susceptible to occupational hazards. The health effects can be more devastating for them, causing irreversible damage to their physical and physiological development, resulting in permanent disabilities, with serious consequences for their adult lives. For example, carrying heavy loads or being forced to adopt unnatural positions at work can permanently distort or disable growing bodies. There is evidence that children suffer more readily from chemical hazards and radiation than do adults, and that they have less resistance to disease. They are much more vulnerable to psychological and physical abuse than are adults, and suffer more devastating psychological damage from living and working in an environment in which they are denigrated or oppressed. When speaking of children, therefore, it is necessary to go beyond the relatively limited concept of "work hazard" as applied to adults, and expand it to include the developmental aspects of childhood. Because children are still growing, they have special characteristics and needs that must be taken into consideration when defining workplace risks to them.

Children are found working in manifestly hazardous industries and exposed to different types of risks. For example, studies in India describe how children are exposed to intrinsically dangerous processes such as firing ceramics and drawing molten glass. In the brassware industry in Moradabad, Uttar Pradesh, they work under exposure to extremely high temperature while rotating the wheel furnace, and use sharp and heavy hand tools.[10] In Pakistan also, children are found working in a wide range of industries, including construction-related industries such as brick-making, under arduous and hazardous conditions. Muro-ami fishing, which is common in many countries in Asia, involves deep-sea diving without the use of protective equipment. This is notoriously hazardous, resulting in drowning, ruptured eardrums and death from decompression illness.[11] In slate-making and metalwork, children are exposed to, and are sometimes victims of, unguarded and poorly maintained machinery, and inappropriate and unsafe hand tools.

There are various other hazards in the physical working environment of children. Exposure to organic dusts is widespread in farms and plantations. According to data from Sri Lanka, mortality from pesticides poisoning is greater than from a combination of other childhood diseases such as malaria, tetanus, diphtheria, polio and whooping cough.[12] Children working in repair shops, woodwork and construction suffer from constant exposure to dust and fumes, as has been reported by various studies from Egypt, the Philippines and Turkey. Ergonomic problems are serious in work where children have to squat for long hours such as in carpet making and in subcontracted garment work. Poor housekeeping contributes to accumulation of dusts and wastes causing respiratory troubles and accidents, as observed in artisanal work in Kenya, the United Republic of Tanzania and the Philippines.

Several work situations expose children to dangerous substances including toxic and carcinogenic substances. Asbestos is probably one of the best known of the human carcinogens. Children should not work in mining, construction, brake repair, or anywhere asbestos is used, nor in jobs with exposure to silica or coal dust. Aniline dyes are also known human carcinogens and children should not be involved in the dying of wool for carpets or leather for shoes if aniline dyes are used.

Exposure to solvents and glues causes neurotoxicity. Children should thus not be involved in work with these substances, for example in the leather industry. Many metals contain lead and mercury. Children are particularly sensitive to lead exposure which is frequent in construction, glass works and repair of automobile radiators. Children would incur high mercury exposure in gold-mining and therefore need to be removed immediately from such an occupation.

Benzene is another established human carcinogen. It is used as solvent for glues, rubber, paints and oils. Even at low levels, exposure can give rise to toxic symptoms; long-term exposure can result in blood disorders ranging from anaemia to leukaemia. Children are found in garage work and gasoline stations where exposure to benzene is a definite risk.

For all the reasons outlined above, the exposure of children to hazardous substances and agents should be avoided. Any work that involves exposure to known human carcinogens, neurotoxins, heavy metals, and substances which sensitize skin or lungs should be banned for children.

Children working in hazardous employment handle hazardous materials and use inappropriate tools. As evidenced above, they are exposed to ergonomic hazards, toxic chemicals and hazardous physical and biological agents such as noise and anthrax spores. Exposure limits established for adult workers are not protective enough for children. Children using hand tools designed for adults run a higher risk of fatigue and injury. When personal protective equipment does not fit children they have to work without it or use alternative devices, such as handkerchiefs to cover their nose and mouth, which do not provide real protection. Children who use seats and work benches designed for adults may develop musculoskeletal disorders.

Children undertaking heavy work, carrying heavy loads and maintaining awkward body positions for a long time, can develop deformation of the spinal column and sometimes of the pelvis because excessive stress may be placed on the bones before the epiphysis has fused and may result in skeletal damage or impaired growth. Heavy work at an early age also has direct consequences on the child's physical and mental development. Physically, children are not suited to long hours of strenuous and monotonous work. Their level of concentration is also lower than that of adults. Their bodies suffer the effects of fatigue faster than adults due to excessive energy expenditure, and most suffer from malnutrition, which lowers their resistance to disease.

Even if most child labourers work side by side with adults, the conditions of work of children and of adult workers may not be the same. Children may be more exposed to an occupational hazard than adult workers in the same trade because of the type of task they carry out. In many cases, children tend to be given the most menial jobs which might involve exposure to solvents, strong alkalis and a variety of toxic substances, with which they are often unfamiliar. Children are especially vulnerable to accidents because they have neither the awareness of the dangers nor knowledge of the precautions to be taken at work. It is often found that children and young workers tend to have more serious accidents than adults.

If child workers in general are vulnerable to work-related hazards, very young children and girls are of course even more so. Children starting work at an early age have a longer period of exposure to cumulative hazards. In certain enterprises, children are hired because adult health has already been compromised, as for example in limestone, slate and glass industries. Exposure in early life to substances with long latency periods such as asbestos increases the possibility of contracting chronic diseases such as lung cancer in young adulthood instead of at a later age. Children have a lower heat tolerance than adults and are therefore more subject to heat stress, just as young workers are more susceptible to induced hearing loss from noise exposure. For these reasons, maximum permitted heat and noise levels for adults may not be stringent enough for children. Ionizing radiation, too, is likely to be particularly harmful for children since their injurious effects on growing tissues are well known and the risk is cumulative.

Because some kinds of work tend to be performed mostly by girls and others by boys, there are sexual differences in the exposure of children to work hazards. Boys predominate in construction work, and girls in domestic service. There is some evidence that girls, as a group, work longer hours than boys, which largely reflects their concentration in household tasks. This is one important reason why girls receive less schooling than do boys. They are also much more vulnerable than boys to sexual abuse and its consequences, such as social rejection, psychological trauma and unwanted motherhood. Boys, on the other hand, tend to suffer more injuries resulting from carrying weights too heavy for their age and stage of physical development.

Some examples of occupational hazards in specific occupations and industries are set out below:

Agriculture: Children work in agriculture throughout the world and are subject to occupational hazards such as exposure to machinery, biological and chemical agents. They can be found mixing, loading and applying pesticides, fertilizers or herbicides, some of which are highly toxic and potentially carcinogenic. Pesticides exposure poses a considerably higher risk to children than adults and has been linked to an increased risk of cancer, neuropathy, neuro-behavioural effects and immune system abnormalities.

Mines: Child labour is used in small-scale mines in many countries in Africa, Asia and Latin America. The children work long hours, without adequate protective equipment, clothing and training, and are exposed to high humidity levels and extreme temperatures. Hazards include exposure to harmful dusts, gases and fumes which cause respiratory diseases that can develop into silicosis, pulmonary fibrosis, asbestosis, and emphysema after some years of exposure. Child miners also suffer from physical strain, fatigue and musculoskeletal disorders, as well as serious injuries from falling objects. Those involved in gold-mining are endangered by mercury poisoning.

Ceramics and glass factory work: Child labour in this industry is common in Asia but can also be found in other regions as well. Children carry molten loads of glass dragged from tank furnaces at a temperature of 1,500-1,800°C. They work long hours in rooms with poor lighting and little or no ventilation. The temperature inside the factories, some of which operate only at night, ranges from 40°C to 45°C. Floors are covered with broken glass and in many cases electric wires are exposed. The noise level from glass-pressing machines can be as high as 100db or more, causing hearing impairment. The main hazards in this industry are: exposure to high temperatures leading to heat stress, cataracts, burns and lacerations; injuries from broken glass and flying glass particles; hearing impairment from noise; eye injuries and eye strain from poor lighting; and exposure to silica dust, lead and toxic fumes such as carbon monoxide and sulphur dioxide.

Matches and fireworks industry: The production of matches normally takes place in small cottage units or in small-scale village factories where the risk of fire and explosion is present all the time. Children as young as 3 years of age are reported to be involved in the production of matches in unventilated rooms where they are exposed to dust, fumes, vapours and airborne concentrations of hazardous substances — asbestos, potassium chlorate, antimony trisulphide, amorphous red phosphorous mixed with sand or powdered glass, tetraphosphorus trisulphide. Intoxication and dermatitis from these substances are frequent.

Deep-sea fishing: Muro-ami fishing, which involves deep-sea diving without the use of protective equipment, is common in Asia, particularly in Burma, Indonesia, the Philippines and Thailand. It relies on children who bang on coral reefs to scare the fish into nets. Each fishing ship employs up to 300 boys between 10 and 15 years old recruited from poor neighbourhoods. Divers reset the net several times a day, and therefore children are in the water for up to 12 hours. Dozens of young swimmers die or are injured each year. They can be attacked by predatory fishes (needle-fish, sharks, barracudas, poisonous sea snakes) or suffer from drowning, ruptured eardrums, decompression illness or other fatal accidents due to exposure to high atmospheric pressure.

Child domestic workers

Violence and sexual abuse are among the most serious and frightening hazards facing children at work. It is of course almost inevitable that children growing up in such an environment will be permanently damaged both psychologically and emotionally.

Among the groups subject to such abuse are child domestic workers. Child domestic service is a widespread practice in many developing countries, with employers in urban areas often recruiting children from rural villages through family, friends and contacts. While most child domestic workers come from extremely poor families, many have been abandoned, are orphaned or come from single parent families. (A survey of child domestic workers in Togo found that 24 per cent of child domestic workers were orphans.)

We do not know how many children are employed in domestic service because of the "hidden" nature of the work but the practice, especially in the case of girls, is certainly extensive. For example, studies in Indonesia estimate that there are around 400,000 child domestic workers in Jakarta and up to 5 million in Indonesia as a whole, and about 500,000 in Sri Lanka. In Brazil 22 per cent of working children are employed in services, of which domestic service is the main occupation, and in Venezuela 60 per cent of the girls working between 10 to 14 years of age are employed as domestic workers.

The majority of child domestic workers tend to be between 12 and 17 years old, but some surveys have identified children as young as 5 or 6 years old. For example, a Bangladesh survey of child domestic workers found that 38 per cent were 11 to 13 years old, and nearly 24 per cent were 5 to 10 years old. Other surveys found that 11 per cent of child domestic workers were 10 years old in Kenya; 16 per cent were 10 years old or less in Togo; around 5 per cent were less than 11 years old, and 29 per cent were between 11 and 15 years old in Greater Santiago; and 26 per cent were less than 10 years old in Venezuela.

Hours of work tend to be long. The Domestic Workers Union in Zimbabwe reports as much as 10-15 hours of work per day; a survey in Morocco found that 72 per cent of the children started their working day before 7 a.m. and 65 per cent went to bed after 11 p.m. There is also alarming evidence of physical, mental and sexual abuse of adolescents and young women working as domestics.

Slavery and forced child labour

Slavery is not dead. Societies are loath to admit to still harbouring it but, as can be surmised from cases reported to the ILO Committee of Experts on the Application of Conventions and Recommendations, numerous children are trapped in slavery in many parts of the world. Of all working children, surely these are the most imperilled.

Some bondage practices are virtually indistinguishable from chattel slavery of 200 years ago, except that the markets are not so open. Children are sold outright for a sum of money. Sometimes landlords buy child workers from their tenants or, in a variant of the system, labour "contractors" pay an advance sum to rural families in order to take their children away to work in carpet-weaving, in glass manufacture, in prostitution. Child slavery of this type has long been reported from South and South-East Asia and West Africa, and despite vigorous official denial of its existence it is both common and well-documented.

One of the most common forms of bondage is family bondage, where children work to help pay off a loan or other obligation incurred by the family. The lenders, who are often landlords, usually manipulate the situation in such a way that it is difficult or impossible for the family to pay off its debt, thereby assuring essentially free labour indefinitely. A family may thus remain bonded through generations, with children replacing their aged or infirm parents in an inter-generational bondage arrangement. Perhaps most widespread of all are informal bondage agreements under which impoverished parents surrender their children to outsiders simply to work in exchange for their upkeep, on the assumption that they will be better provided for as unremunerated servants in an affluent household than they could be in their own families.

Bondage arrangements, it must be emphasized, are illegal in nearly every country, including in the countries where they are most prevalent. They fall foul not only of child labour laws, but also of international conventions of which virtually all countries are signatories.

Prostitution and trafficking of children

The commercial sexual exploitation of children has in recent years become an issue of global concern, and the indications are that it is on the rise. Children are increasingly being bought and sold across national borders by organized networks.

There are believed to be five such international networks trafficking in children from Latin America to Europe and the Middle East; from South and South-East Asia to northern Europe and the Middle East; a European regional market; an associated Arab regional market; and a West Africa export market in girls. In Eastern Europe today, the traffic generally moves from East to West, girls from Belarus, Russia and Ukraine being transported to Hungary, Poland and the Baltic States, or on to Western European capitals. There is also a traffic in Romanian prostitutes to Italy, Cyprus and Turkey. Several well-defined child trafficking routes have been identified in South-East Asia: Myanmar to Thailand; internally within Thailand; from Thailand and other countries to China, Japan, Malaysia and the United States; from the Philippines and Thailand to Australia, New Zealand and Taiwan, China; from Bangladesh and Nepal to India; from South-East Asia to Hawaii and Japan via Hong Kong; from India and Pakistan to the Middle East.

According to the 1996 report of the United Nations Special Rapporteur on the Sale of Children, Child Prostitution and Child Pornography, about 1 million children in Asia are victims of the sex trade.[13] Reports in the media and from NGOs indicate that trafficking of young girls between Thailand and neighbouring countries is on the rise, that girls from Cambodia, China, Laos, Myanmar and Viet Nam are being sold to brothels in Thailand and that the problem is also becoming visible in Bangladesh, India, Nepal, the Philippines and Sri Lanka.[14] In Latin America a large number of children work and live on the streets, where they can easily become victims of commercial sexual exploitation. A report published by the International Catholic Child Bureau revealed that the problem exists in Argentina, Bolivia, Brazil, Chile, Colombia and Peru. In Africa, too, a number of countries including Burkina Faso, Côte d'Ivoire, Ghana, Kenya, Zambia and Zimbabwe are faced with rising child prostitution. The increase in the child sex trade in Africa, Asia and Latin America is no doubt largely due to the internationalization of sex tourism, together with the false perception by many that there is less danger of infection from AIDS with younger partners.

At the root of the commercial sexual exploitation of children in many countries lies poverty, the inability of rural and urban families to support and educate their children. In some cases ethnic origin, cultural practices and social discrimination render children from indigenous populations, minority groups and the lower castes especially vulnerable. They may not speak the same language, they may not have rights to citizenship and education and, once forced into this situation, they are isolated and unable to communicate with the outside world.

Commercial sexual exploitation is one of the most brutal forms of violence against children. Child victims suffer extreme physical, psychosocial and emotional abuse which have lifelong and life-threatening consequences. They risk early pregnancy, maternal mortality and sexually transmitted diseases. Case-studies and testimonies of child victims speak of a trauma so deep that many are unable to re-enter or return to a normal way of life. Many others die before they reach adulthood.

The causes

Factors affecting the supply of child labour

The available data on the causes of child labour normally relates to the phenomenon in general, and a great deal remains to be learnt about the causes of child labour in hazardous work as distinct from non-hazardous occupations. However, poverty is the most important reason why children work. Poor households need the money which their children can earn, and children commonly contribute around 20-25 per cent of family income.[15] Since by definition poor households spend the bulk of their income on food (the poverty line in a relatively poor country such as India is defined as only 20 per cent more than the income required for purchasing the minimum nutritional needs for a family) it is clear that the income provided by working children is critical to their survival.

It cannot, however, be said that poverty necessarily causes child labour. The picture varies, and in many poor households some children at least are singled out to attend school. Similarly, there are regions in poor countries where child labour is extensively practised while in other equally poor regions it is not. Kerala State in India for example, though poor, has virtually abolished child labour. At the international level again, countries may be equally poor and yet have relatively high or relatively low levels of child labour.

Other supply factors affecting child labour are also important for understanding not only why child labour exists but also why children from certain families, areas and countries are more likely to be available for hazardous work. Certain areas and certain families have a tradition of children following in their parents' footsteps. If the family has a tradition of engaging in a hazardous occupation such as leather tanning, then there is every likelihood that the children will be caught up in the same process. In industries and occupations where payment is on a piece-rate basis, children are frequently called upon to "help" the other members of the family, for example, in construction sites in many parts in the world and in home-based work such as bidi-making.

Finally, child labour in hazardous conditions is most prevalent in the most vulnerable families, those whose low income allows them little margin to cope with the injury or illness of an adult member of the household or the distress and disruption resulting from abandonment or divorce. Not only do poor households have few financial assets, but in many cases they are in debt. Whatever the reason, debt or the threat of debt is very often at the root of hazardous and bonded child labour, children being in effect sold to pay off the family debt.

Demand for child labour

Research on the causes of child labour tend to concentrate on the supply factors, both because of a justifiable preoccupation with the victims, the children, and because of the commonly shared view that poverty is the driving force. But the demand for child labour plays a critical role in determining the involvement of children in hazardous work.

There are a number of reasons why employers hire child labour, commonest explanations that are given being the lower cost and the irreplaceable skills afforded by children (the "nimble fingers" argument). In fact, however, these two claims are often unsustainable, and there are many other and more telling reasons why children are hired.

To take the "nimble fingers" argument first (that only children with small fingers have the ability to make fine hand-knotted carpets, for example) ILO studies and a workshop on hazardous work in India recently concluded that this argument was entirely fallacious in a number of hazardous industries, including carpet-making, glass factories, the mining of slate, limestone and mosaic chips, lock-making and gem and diamond polishing. In all these industries most of the activities performed by children are also performed by adults working side by side with the children in unskilled work. Obviously, then, adults could take their place. Moreover, virtually all the tasks carried out almost exclusively by children, such as carrying and packing, are unskilled and require little physical strength. Here again, it is clear that child labour is replaceable. Even in the hand-knotting of carpets, which calls for considerable dexterity, an empirical study of over 2,000 weavers found that children were no more likely than adults to make the finest knots. Some of the best carpets, with the greatest density of small knots, are in fact woven by adults, and if a child's "nimble fingers" are not essential in such demanding work, it is difficult to imagine in which trades the claims might be valid.

So much for the "nimble fingers" argument. But what of the argument of children's economic irreplaceability? The fact is that it fares only a little better. That child workers are paid less than their adult counterparts is indeed true in most cases. But the lower wages and other advantages claimed for child labour are not always as clear and compelling as is said. Recent ILO studies conducted in India[16] suggest that, as a portion of the final price of carpets or bangles to the consumer, any labour-cost savings realized through the employment of children are surprisingly small — less than 5 per cent for bangles and between 5 and 10 per cent for carpets. At this level, it is likely that sellers and buyers could between them easily absorb the added cost of hiring adults only. Given this extremely small difference, why then does the industry hire children, especially in the face of growing international resistance to products involving the use of child labour? The answer lies in *where* the gains from using child labour occur. In the carpet industry, for example, it is the loom owners who supervise the weaving who benefit directly. Many in number, they are themselves usually poor, small contractors (most with only one or two looms) who work to a very slim profit margin and who can as much as double their meagre income by utilizing child workers. Yet, their income is so modest that a very small levy on the consumer price would be sufficient to subsidize the cost to the loom owner of using exclusively adult labour if the payments were properly targeted.[17]

The implication from this is that children are not in fact economically necessary for the carpet industry to survive in the market, and that relatively minor changes in the financial arrangements between loom owners, exporters and importers could reduce the incentive to employing child labour. These findings from an extremely competitive, labour-intensive industry, thought by some to be among those most dependent on child workers, raise serious doubts that any industry at all has to depend on child workers in order to be competitive, and surely puts the burden of proof on those who would make such a claim. Nevertheless, in a free global market in which countries compete in producing similar products, abolishing child labour in one country could have the effect of simply transferring business to others that still employ it. Again, the example of handwoven carpets is instructive. A survey of carpet importers in a United States city found that, if the price of carpets in India rose by more than about 15 per cent, the importers would stop buying them from the country.[18] In such cases the demand for child labour is effectively international, and action to discourage it needs to encompass all the major producers so as to avoid "beggar-thy-neighbour" competition.

Since the children do not have irreplaceable skills and are often not much less costly than adults, a major important explanation for hiring children seems to be non-economic. There are many non-pecuniary reasons but the most important seems to be the fact that children are less aware of their rights, less troublesome and more willing to take orders and to do monotonous work without complaining (indeed, children often engage in work activities which are considered too menial by many adults), more trustworthy, less likely to steal, and less likely to be absent from work. Children's lower absentee rate is especially valuable for employers in informal sector industries where workers are employed on a daily, casual basis and a full contingent of workers must therefore be found each day.

Priorities for action

Clearly, the problem of child labour is quite enormous and there is an urgent need for action. But where does one begin? Not all countries are institutionally or financially equipped to attack all forms of child labour at once. Choices must be made about where to concentrate available human and material resources. The most logical and humane strategy must therefore be to focus scarce resources first on the most intolerable forms of child labour such as slavery, debt bondage, child prostitution and work in hazardous occupations and industries, and the very young especially girls. This approach has the additional advantage that policies designed to reach the children in most need are likely to benefit other working children and that focusing on the most socially repugnant examples can help maintain the necessary social commitment and consensus.

A second important point to note is the need to address the problem relating to the invisibility of endangered children. One reason why modern societies and governments have not been more active in curbing the most harmful forms of child labour is that working children are often not readily visible. It is a matter of "out of sight, out of mind".

Any effort to protect children from workplace hazards must therefore begin by making the invisible visible, bringing to light and public consciousness both the children who work and the dangers they face. A starting-point would be to carry out a survey of the child labour situation. In diagnosing and analysing the results, priority should be given to identifying those children whose work constitutes a serious threat to their lives or to their physical, mental and social development.

But by what criteria is it possible to set priorities according to risk? It is certainly helpful to start with lists of industries, occupations and working conditions known to place children in jeopardy, but generic information of this sort does not automatically address the most vexing questions. How does one decide whether one kind of work is more detrimental to children than another? How can one rank injurious effects of different types? Is vision loss worse than lung disease? How much physical risk equates with how much psychosocial jeopardy? How should short- and long-term effects be compared? In setting priorities, such questions are inescapable, but there are no easy or universal answers to them and the process of deciding whom to consider most at risk necessarily involves an element of subjective judgement.

Experience shows that questions of this sort have no purely technical solution and must be resolved by agreement rather than by formula. What is important is that concrete, feasible decisions be made about which child work problems require the most urgent attention, and that these decisions enjoy at least a modicum of social credibility and legitimacy. Fortunately, the task of designating children at high risk usually turns out to be easier in practice than in theory. Within a given place, the most dangerous forms of work and the children affected tend to stand out when adequate information is available. Knowledgeable people of different institutions and perspectives seem able to agree on who are the most threatened child workers.

Notes

[1] World Health Organization: *Children at work: Special health risks*, Technical Report Series No. 756 (Geneva, 1987); K. Satyanarayan et al.: "Effect of early childhood under-nutrition and child labour on growth and adult nutritional status of rural Indian boys around Hyderabad", in *Human nutrition: Clinical nutrition*, No. 40 C, 1986.

[2] N. Senanayake and G. C. Román: "Epidemiology of epilepsy in developing countries", in *Bulletin of the World Health Organization*, Vol. 71(2), 1993, pp. 247-258.

[3] J. Jeyaratnam: "1984 and occupational health in developing countries", in *Scandinavian Journal on Working Environment and Health*, No. II, 1985.

[4] International Labour Organization: *Child labour surveys: Results of methodological experiments in four countries, 1992-93* (Geneva, 1996).

[5] For an extensive discussion of the health and safety hazards facing working children, see V. Forastieri: *Danger: Children at work* (Geneva, ILO, forthcoming).

[6] Satyanarayan et al., op. cit.

[7] U. Naidu and S. Parasuman: *Health situation of working children in Greater Bombay* (Bombay, Unit for Child and Youth Research, Tata Institute of Social Sciences, 1985, mimeographed).

[8] For an extensive treatment of forced and hazardous child work and policy and programme experiences, see A. Bequele and W. Myers: *First things first in child labour: Eliminating work detrimental to children* (Geneva, ILO, 1995).

[9] For a detailed review and analysis, see Forastieri, op. cit.

[10] E. S. Naidu and K. R. Kapadia (eds.): *Child labour and health, problems and prospects* (Bombay, Tata Institute of Social Sciences, 1984), and *Child labour in the brassware industry of Moradabad* (Ghaziabad, India, National Labour Institute, July 1992).

[11] Rialp, op. cit.

[12] J. Jeyaratnam: "Planning for the health of the worker", in *Bull pesticides and the third world poor: A growing problem* (Oxford, Oxfam Public Affairs Unit, 1982).

[13] United Nations Commission on Human Rights: *Rights of the child: Report of the Special Rapporteur on the Sale of Children, Child Prostitution and Child Pornography* (Doc. No. E/CN.4/1996/100, 17 Jan. 1996), p. 7.

[14] For more detailed information, see M. Black: *In the twilight zone: Child workers in the hotel, tourism and catering industry* (Geneva, ILO, 1995); S. W. E. Goonesekere: *Child labour in Sri Lanka: Learning from the past* (Geneva, ILO, 1993); V. Rialp: *Children and hazardous work in the Philippines* (Geneva, ILO, 1993).

[15] R. Anker and H. Melkas: *Economic incentives for children and families to eliminate or reduce child labour* (Geneva, ILO, 1996).

[16] Originally begun in 1992, this research concluded with a seminar in India (26-28 July 1995), with the main publication forthcoming. See R. Anker and S. Barge: *Economics of child labour in Indian industries* (Geneva, ILO, forthcoming).

[17] D. Levison, R. Anker, S. Ashraf and S. Barge: *Is child labour really necessary in India's carpet industry?*, Labour Market Paper No. 15 (Geneva, ILO, 1996).

[18] ibid.

International law and child labour   2

One of the most important tools available to the ILO for improving the legislation and practice of its member States in the fight against child labour is the adoption and supervision of international labour Conventions and Recommendations. Several international labour standards have been adopted to prohibit child labour in different sectors and under different conditions. ILO Conventions of more general applicability, such as safety and health Conventions, also include provisions specific to the work of children. Additionally, serious problems of the exploitation of children through debt bondage and other "contemporary forms of slavery", such as child prostitution, are examined by ILO supervisory bodies[1] in the framework of the ILO's Forced Labour Convention, 1930 (No. 29).

Concern about child labour is also expressed in instruments of the United Nations, most recently the United Nations Convention on the Rights of the Child. To understand how a new instrument on child labour would fit into this existing system and to avoid the possible incompatibility of proposed new instruments with existing provisions, it is instructive to examine some of the most relevant international standards concerning child labour and their application.

ILO Conventions and Recommendations

The ILO adopted its first Convention on child labour in 1919, the year of its foundation. The Minimum Age (Industry) Convention, 1919 (No. 5), prohibits the work of children under the age of 14 in industrial establishments. Subsequently, nine sectoral Conventions on the minimum age of admission to employment were adopted applying to industry, agriculture, trimmers and stokers, maritime work, non-industrial employment, fishing and underground work. Numerous other

23

TABLE 1.   MINIMUM AGES IN ACCORDANCE WITH CONVENTION NO. 138

General minimum age (Article 2)	Light work (Article 7)	Hazardous work (Article 3)
In normal circumstances:		
15 years or more	13 years	18 years
(not less than compulsory school age)		(16 years conditionally)
Where economy and educational facilities are insufficiently developed:		
14 years	12 years	18 years
		(16 years conditionally)

ILO standards contain provisions setting minimum ages for various activities.

The most recent and comprehensive ILO instruments on child labour are the Minimum Age Convention, 1973 (No. 138), and Recommendation (No. 146). Convention No. 138 is a consolidation of principles that had been gradually established in various earlier instruments and applies to all sectors of economic activity, whether or not the children are employed for wages.

The Convention obliges ratifying States to fix a minimum age for admission to employment or work and undertake to pursue a national policy designed to ensure the effective abolition of child labour and to raise progressively the minimum age for admission to employment or work to a level consistent with the fullest physical and mental development of young persons.[2] The Convention was not intended as a static instrument prescribing a fixed minimum standard but as a dynamic one aimed at encouraging the progressive improvement of standards and of promoting sustained action to attain the objectives.

Recommendation No. 146, which supplements Convention No. 138, provides the broad framework and essential policy measures for both the prevention of child labour and its elimination.

Fixing the minimum age for admission to employment or work remains a basic obligation of ratifying States within the framework of national policy. But rather than speak of one minimum age, it is more appropriate to speak of various minimum ages depending on the type of employment or work (see table 1).

The first principle is that the minimum age should not be less than the age for completing compulsory schooling and in no event less than age 15 and that the minimum age should be progressively raised to a level consistent with the fullest physical and mental development of young persons. For countries whose economy and educational facilities are insufficiently developed the age can be set initially at 14. Employers' and workers' organizations must be consulted to fix the age for admission to employment at age 14. Recommendation No. 146 recommends raising the minimum age to 16 and calls for the minimum age to be fixed at the same level for all sectors of economic activity.[3]

Convention No. 138 sets a higher minimum age of 18 for hazardous work, "which by its nature or the circumstances in which it is carried out is likely to jeopardize the health, safety or morals of young persons". Because this provision refers to work "likely" to jeopardize the safety, health or morals of young persons and not only work which is recognized as having that effect, it is necessary to examine both the nature of the work and the circumstances in which it is carried out. Certain types of activities which are not in themselves hazardous may become so in certain circumstances, and the competent authorities are to take this into account.

The Convention also provides that the types of employment or work concerned shall be determined by national laws or regulations or by the competent authority, leaving it to the individual countries to determine the content of these activities. Whatever the method chosen, it is necessary that a determination be made, and for this purpose prior consultations must be held with the organizations of employers and workers concerned, if they exist in the country.

The Recommendation gives guidance on the criteria which should be applied to the determination of hazardous employment or work. It states the need to take full account of relevant international labour standards and to pay special attention to dangerous substances, agents or processes (including ionizing radiations), the lifting of heavy weights and underground work. It further states that a periodic review of the types of employment or work designated as hazardous should be undertaken, particularly in the light of advancing scientific and technological knowledge, and in consultation with employers' and workers' organizations.

The minimum age for the types of work described is 18 years. The Recommendation reinforces this by stating that when the minimum age is still below 18 years, immediate steps should be taken to raise it to that level. However, the Convention provides that a lower age of 16 may be authorized if (a) the health, safety and morals of the young persons concerned are fully protected and (b) they have received adequate specific instruction or vocational training in the relevant branch of activity. Both these conditions must be fulfilled to allow such a lower age, as well as consultation with the employers' and workers' organizations concerned beforehand.

Although Convention No. 138 requires a minimum age for employment or work and is, in principle, to be applied to all sectors of activity whether or not children are employed for wages, flexibility is built in to allow for progressive implementation. For example, a country whose economy and educational facilities are insufficiently developed can initially specify a general minimum age of 14 years of age instead of 15, which lowers the minimum age for light work to 12 instead of 13. There is no corresponding exception, however, concerning dangerous work, which is consistent with the principle that the level of development is no excuse for allowing children to be exposed to work which is likely to jeopardize their health, safety or morals.

In addition, Convention No. 138 contains provisions intended to make it flexible concerning economic sectors or activities covered. It permits the exclusion of limited categories of employment or work which raise special and substantial problems of application, though these are not further defined. During the preparatory work, however, reference was made to employment in family undertakings, domestic service in private households and some types of work carried out without the employer's supervision, for example, home work.[4] These exclusions were foreseen mainly because of the practical difficulties of enforcing laws in the categories in question, not because of the absence of possible exploitation or abuse in these situations.

The Convention also gives a developing country the possibility of limiting initially the scope of its application by specifying the branches of activity or types of undertakings to which the Convention will apply. It none the less requires that the following seven sectors be covered: mining and quarrying; manufacturing; construction; electricity, gas and water; sanitary services; transport, storage and communication; and plantations and other agricultural undertakings (excluding family and small-scale holdings mainly producing for local consumption and not regularly employing hired workers).

Several other provisions allow for exceptions — for example, the exclusion of work done in specified schools or training institutions and the participation of children in artistic performances — and for setting the minimum age for apprenticeship at 14. In the context of hazardous work, the care needed in applying these provisions cannot be underestimated. For example, work in artistic performances can present a risk of serious damage to the health or morals of young persons. As a result, some countries prohibit work in night clubs, cabarets and circuses, for example. Such work can also lead children into situations of sexual exploitation. Training relationships can be subterfuges to enable employers to demand heavy and continuous work from children below the minimum age. Supervisory and inspection activities are thus essential to ensure that young people receive training in proper conditions and are not exposed to hazardous work.

The Convention requires the competent authority to take all necessary measures, including the provision of appropriate penalties, to ensure the effective enforcement of the provisions of the Convention. Penalties, here, mean those to be defined in national legislation for violations of national law giving effect to the Convention.

Another ILO Convention that is crucial in protecting children against some of the worst forms of exploitation is the Forced Labour Convention, 1930 (No. 29), which aims at suppressing the use of forced or compulsory labour — defined as "work or service which is exacted from any person under the menace of any penalty and for which the said person has not offered himself voluntarily". This Convention is one of the fundamental Conventions of the ILO and one of the most widely ratified. Since it applies to everyone, whatever age, it protects children from forced or compulsory labour and is applicable to some of the most intolerable forms of child labour, such as children in bondage and their exploitation in prostitution and pornography. Indeed, the Committee of Experts and the Conference Committee on the Application of Standards have been dealing extensively with the problem of the forced or compulsory labour of children in relation to the application of the Convention by several member States.

In 1994 the Committee of Experts expressed its grave concern about forced child labour, and particularly the exploitation of children for prostitution and pornography. It has stated on several occasions that forced labour exploitation of children is one of the worst forms of forced labour, which must be fought energetically and punished severely. The Committee has called for action not only by the States in which such exploitation of children occurs, but also by other countries to assist in the eradication of these practices, especially exploitation by tourists and visitors from outside. The United Nations Working Group on Contemporary Forms of Slavery too has come to classify the sale and sexual exploitation of children as contemporary forms of slavery, and the ILO's Committee of Experts observed in 1995 that the nature of child labour often brings it within the meaning of forced or compulsory labour. Countries which have not ratified child labour Conventions but have ratified forced labour Conventions are therefore being held accountable under the latter.

In view of this, it might seem that new instruments would overlap with the forced labour Convention. But a new Convention which explicitly covered forced child labour would in no way reduce the importance of Convention No. 29, nor the obligations of States which have ratified it. A new Convention would add specificity and focus on the worst forms and most hazardous types of child labour, including slavery, servitude, forced labour, bonded labour and serfdom, and on the measures to be taken to eradicate them. The principles of application established by ILO supervisory bodies concerning forced child labour under Convention No. 29 would also be relevant to the new Convention. The practice of the supervisory bodies in the case of Conventions covering the same subject is to examine the matter under the most recent or more specific instrument.

Ratification of relevant Conventions

There is then a wide range of Conventions that bear on the problem of forced and hazardous child labour. The great majority of the ILO's member States (133 out of 173) have ratified at least one of the 11 ILO Conventions concerning the minimum age of admission to employment or work and thus have made a formal commitment to undertake measures concerning some aspects of child labour or child labour in certain branches of activity. To date, 49 countries have ratified Convention No. 138 (see table 2 and appendix), a fairly high score compared to that of the other Conventions adopted between 1970 and 1974. But only 21 developing countries have ratified Convention No. 138, and these do not include any in Asia where over half of all working children are found. Convention No. 138 is one of the fundamental Conventions of the ILO. It remains a key instrument of a coherent strategy against child labour at the national level. None the less, it is the Office's experience that an obstacle to ratification has been that some member States view the text as too complex and too difficult to apply it in detail. The Office intends to take more vigorous action to promote ratification by providing technical advisory services and a better explanation of the provisions of this instrument and the possibilities of applying its flexibility clauses. But it is generally thought that ratification would still be difficult for many countries and that there is a need for a new instrument focusing on extreme forms of child labour and one which will complement Convention No. 138.

TABLE 2.   RATIFICATION OF ILO CONVENTIONS ON MINIMUM AGE AND FORCED LABOUR (AS AT 15 AUGUST 1996)

Convention No.	Title of Convention	Total of ratifications[1]
5	Minimum Age (Industry), 1919	72 [23]
59	Minimum Age (Industry) (Revised), 1937	36 [17]
7	Minimum Age (Sea), 1920	53 [23]
58	Minimum Age (Sea) (Revised), 1936	52 [21]
10	Minimum Age (Agriculture), 1921	54 [23]
15	Minimum Age (Trimmers and Stokers), 1921	70 [27]
33	Minimum Age (Non-Industrial Employment), 1932	25 [8]
60	Minimum Age (Non-Industrial Employment) (Revised), 1937	11 [10]
112	Minimum Age (Fishermen), 1959	30 [17]
123	Minimum Age (Underground Work), 1965	42 [10]
138	Minimum Age, 1973	49
29	Forced Labour, 1930	49[2]
105	Abolition of Forced Labour, 1957	118[3]

[1] The figures in brackets are the total of denunciations following ratification of revised Conventions. In most cases, the ratification of a new Convention implies the automatic denunciation of the earlier Convention on the same subject.

[2] List of countries with specified minimum age:

[14] El Salvador, Equatorial Guinea, Guatemala, Honduras, Nicaragua, Niger, Rwanda, Togo, Venezuela (9 countries).

[15] Belgium, Bosnia and Herzegovina, Costa Rica, Croatia, Cuba, Dominica, Finland, Germany, Greece, Iraq, Ireland, Israel, Italy, Libyan Arab Jamahiriya, Luxembourg, Mauritius, Netherlands, Norway, Poland, Slovenia, Spain, Sweden, Uruguay, Yugoslavia, Zambia (25 countries).

[16] Algeria, Antigua and Barbuda, Azerbaijan, Belarus, Bulgaria, France, Kenya, Kyrgyzstan, Malta, Romania, Russian Federation, San Marino, Tajikistan, Tunisia, Ukraine (15 countries).

[3] Malaysia and Singapore have denounced this Convention.

Other international treaties

A good number of international treaties are relevant to child labour and the protection of children from its most intolerable forms. Foremost among these is the United Nations Convention on the Rights of the Child, 1989 (entry into force: 2 September 1990; 187 ratifications as at 31 July 1996). This Convention is the most comprehensive treaty on the rights of children, whom it defines as persons under the age of 18, unless the age of majority is attained earlier. It seeks to protect a wide range of children's rights, including the right to be protected from economic exploitation and from performing any work that is likely to be hazardous or to interfere with their education, or to be harmful to their health or physical, mental, spiritual, moral or social development. It requires States Parties to take legislative, administrative, social and educational measures to ensure implementation and, in particular, to provide for (a) a minimum age or minimum ages for admission to employment, (b) appropriate regulation of the hours and conditions of employment, and (c) appropriate penalties or other sanctions to ensure the effective enforcement of its provisions. The International Labour Office regularly sends information relating to the application of the relevant provisions of the instrument to the pre-sessional working group of the Committee on the Rights of the Child, which examines the reports of States Parties concerning the application of the Convention.

The United Nations Convention also contains several articles bearing on other extreme forms of child labour, such as sexual exploitation and sexual abuse, the abduction of, sale of or traffic in children for any purpose or in any form, and all other forms of exploitation prejudicial to any aspects of the child's welfare. It calls on States to take all appropriate measures to promote physical and psychological recovery and social reintegration of a child victim of neglect, exploitation or abuse. The right of the child to education is also recognized under this Convention, which provides that primary education should be compulsory, available and free to all.

The other major international instruments relevant to child labour include the International Covenant on Economic, Social and Cultural Rights (entry into force: 3 January 1976; 133 ratifications), some of whose provisions relate to compulsory free primary education, the International Covenant on Civil and Political Rights (entry into force: 23 March 1976, 132 ratifications) which deals with the prohibition of slavery, servitude and forced or compulsory labour and the protection of minors, the Supplementary Convention on the Abolition of Slavery, the Slave Trade, and Institutions and Practices Similar to Slavery (entry into force: 30 April 1957; 114 ratifications) which refers to debt bondage of children, and the Convention for the Suppression of the Traffic in Persons and of the Exploitation of the Prostitution of Others (entry into force: 25 July 1951; 70 ratifications).

Notes

[1] The supervisory bodies referred to in this chapter are the Committee of Experts on the Application of Conventions and Recommendations (referred to as the Committee of Experts) and the tripartite Committee on the Application of Standards of the International Labour Conference (referred to as the Conference Committee). The Committee of Experts is a body of independent experts entrusted with the technical examination of reports supplied by governments to the ILO, as well as other relevant information, concerning the application of ILO standards. The report of the Committee of Experts is discussed by the Conference Committee which reports to the Conference.

[2] This was the first time the phrase on national policy had been used in a minimum age Convention.

[3] In the preparatory work on these instruments, it was explained that this provision was "intended to prevent, as far as possible, situations in which children ineligible for employment in a well regulated sector are employed in sectors covered by lower standards with the result that the child labour is merely transferred rather than reduced or abolished".

[4] The Home Work Convention (No. 177) adopted in 1996 calls for the promotion of equality of treatment between homeworkers and other wage-earners in relation to minimum age, among other things; the Home Work Recommendation (No. 184) suggests programmes to eliminate child labour in home work.

Basic minimum age

3

Almost all countries have enacted legislation prohibiting the employment of children below a certain age and, where they are legally permitted to work, specifying the conditions under which they may work. Many have set higher minimum ages for hazardous work that legally ban certain work for persons under age 18. There are still shortcomings, however, especially in the coverage of many of these laws and in their application in practice. Legislative commitments often lie dormant, sometimes due to lack of resources for effective monitoring and enforcement, sometimes due to lack of political will, but often simply because the authorities do not know how to tackle the problem of eliminating child labour given the invisibility of so many child workers and the fact that the poverty, discrimination and cultural attitudes that foster it are so deeply entrenched in society.

Setting a minimum age for work

A review of the legislation of 155 ILO member States shows that, although virtually all countries have enacted legislation setting a basic minimum age for admission to employment, many have not established a single minimum age for admission to *any employment or work* as required by Convention No. 138; only 33 (or one-fifth of the countries) have done so, and only in Europe is this common practice. The usual practice is to prescribe a basic minimum age but to limit it to specified sectors or occupations. Another approach, followed in about one-quarter of all countries surveyed, is to prescribe different minimum ages according to the sector of economic activity while totally excluding from coverage certain sectors or occupations.

Most of the countries surveyed conform to the spirit of Convention No. 138: some 45 set the minimum age for admission to employment or work at 15, and 37 at 14. The age of 15 tends to be the age in Europe and

14 in the rest of the world. In 23 countries the basic minimum age is 16, while four others have age limits between 15 and 16. In other words, at least 122 countries have legislation prohibiting work for children below the age of 14, at least in some sectors.

On the other hand, in 30 countries it is legally acceptable for children below 14 to work, and in six the basic minimum age is 12. The greatest spread in minimum age limits is in Africa and Asia where they range from 12 to 16, as opposed to Europe where they range from 14 to 16.

The minimum age may not be applicable in certain sectors of economic activity but no country excludes industry. On the other hand, agriculture is commonly excluded, and about a quarter (38) of the countries examined have done so — most of them in Asia. Commerce is excluded from general rules on minimum age in 17 countries, and in 13 other exceptions can be enacted by the competent authority.

Sometimes, certain types of undertaking or categories of work are excluded. One of the most common exclusions from coverage, found in some 60 countries, concerns family undertakings, defined with different degrees of rigour. Another category widely excluded is domestic service. Among the other categories excluded from coverage in various countries are undertakings employing fewer than a specified number of workers (often 10); apprentices, self-employed persons, homeworkers and temporary or casual workers. Finally, in the great majority of countries — some 135 — exceptions from general rules may be granted by the competent authority.

There are two main exceptions to the generally prescribed minimum ages provided for in Convention No. 138: a lower minimum age for "light work", and a higher minimum age for hazardous employment or work. Although the focus of this report is on hazardous work, it is relevant to see how national laws and regulations interpreted the term "light work".

In approximately half the countries examined certain types of light work are permitted for children below the generally prescribed minimum age (see table 3 for a summary of provisions in national legislation on light work). While 13 countries exclude certain types of light work from any limitations, the majority fix 12, 13 or 14 years as the minimum. One country, Lebanon, sets the minimum age at age 8 for children performing certain unspecified non-arduous work "suitable to their age". Regionally, the 12-year minimum age for light work dominates in the Americas and in Africa, while it is more common in Europe to allow 13- or 14-year-old children to perform light work.

Only about 20 countries which waive the basic minimum age for light work subject such exceptions to all of the conditions laid down in Convention No. 138, namely that the work should not be harmful to the child's health or development, should not interfere with school instruction, should not take place during school hours and should not be for more than specifically prescribed hours of work. A frequent condition in national law is that work only be permitted in a family undertaking or under parental supervision. Thirty-four countries allow light work of any type, while 21 lower the minimum age for light agricultural, horticultural or plantation work — the large majority to 12 years, three countries to 13, and seven to any age. Light work of a non-industrial nature is permitted for children in 17 countries.

While 43 countries exclude domestic service from their legislation, 15 considered it as "light work"; six set limits on the hours of work and three stipulate that the work must not interfere with education. Eight countries subject such work to the authorization of a competent authority.

Difficulties relating to the type of work classified as "light" for the purpose of minimum age regulation or to the conditions under which such work is permitted constitute, in the view of many governments, a major obstacle to the ratification of Convention No. 138.

Compulsory education

Compulsory education has historically been one of the most effective instruments for eliminating child labour in practice. It is evident that children in school are less likely to be in full-time or close to full-time employment or work. Conversely, children who are not obliged to attend school or who realistically do not have access to education have little alternative to working or falling into begging, delinquency or worse. Child labour legislation, in addition to protecting children from unsuitable work or working conditions, is aimed at ensuring that their education and development are not jeopardized. Thus, compulsory education laws and minimum age laws are interdependent; the enforcement of one contributes to the enforcement of the other. That is why Convention No. 138 explicitly links the minimum age for admission to employment with the age of completion of compulsory schooling.

This link is reflected in the legislation of most industrialized countries, which fix substantially the same ages for both purposes or in

TABLE 3.   LEGISLATIVE PROVISIONS ON LIGHT WORK

Definition of light work	Min. age	Country
General, i.e. not restricted to any particular sectors	15	Bulgaria,[1, 9, 13, 14] Mongolia [1]
	14	Antigua and Barbuda, Botswana,[1, 2, 10, 11, 12, 19] Chile,[1, 2, 9 or 15, 17] Finland,[8, 13, 14, 20] France,[20] Hungary,[20] Iceland, Portugal, Tunisia,[1, 2, 5, 7] Zaire [1, 2, 23]
	13	Cyprus,[11, 15] Equatorial Guinea,[1, 2] Germany,[1, 8, 17, 21] Latvia,[2, 9] Norway,[1, 2, 15] Sweden,[1, 2] Turkey [1, 2]
	12	Albania,[2, 20] Brazil,[1, 2] Burundi,[1, 2, 12, 15, 16] Colombia,[9, 15, 23] Cyprus,[6, 11, 15] France,[1, 2, 11] Malawi,[15] Seychelles,[2] Singapore,[13] Somalia,[1, 22] Uganda [15]
	None	Algeria, Republic of Korea,[2] Malaysia,[7, 11, 12] Philippines [1, 2]
Light work of a non-industrial nature	15	Netherlands [2]
	14	Ireland,[2] Italy [1, 2]
	13	Denmark,[1, 2, 5, 7, 8, 14, 26] Switzerland,[1, 2, 6, 8] Tunisia,[1, 2] United Kingdom [1, 2, 6, 8]
	12	Chad,[9, 15] Central African Republic,[9, 13, 15] Congo,[9, 15] Japan,[2, 7, 9] Mali,[15, 23] Thailand,[16] Uruguay [15, 17, 18]
	8	Lebanon
	None	Jamaica,[11] Niger,[2, 6, 7, 15] Solomon Islands [11, 15]
Non-agricultural work, occasional, light assistance, of short duration and not equivalent to that of an employee	12	Austria,[1, 2, 5, 6, 7, 8, 9] Seychelles
Light agricultural, horticultural or plantation work	13	Denmark,[1, 2, 5, 7, 8, 14] Germany,[2, 8, 9, 24, 25] Netherlands [6]
	12	Benin, Burkina Faso, Burundi,[1, 2, 9, 12, 16] Cape Verde, Central African Republic,[9, 13, 15] Costa Rica,[2, 27] Congo,[1, 9, 15] Côte d'Ivoire,[9, 23] Equatorial Guinea,[15] Fiji,[4] Guinea-Bissau, Mali,[15, 23] Niger,[2, 6, 7] Nigeria,[11, 15] Panama,[2, 15] Paraguay,[1, 2, 7, 9, 13, 15, 23] Sao Tome and Principe, United Republic of Tanzania [8, 11, 15, 23]
	None	Belize,[4] Ghana,[11] Jamaica,[11] Saint Lucia,[4] Sierra Leone,[6, 8, 11, 15] Sri Lanka,[4, 11] United Kingdom [1, 2, 6, 8]
Domestic service	14	Botswana,[1, 12] Italy [1, 2, 4]
	12	Belize, Benin, Burkina Faso, Burundi,[1, 2, 9, 12] Central African Republic,[9, 13, 15] Chad,[9, 15] Congo,[9, 15] Costa Rica,[2] Côte d'Ivoire, Haiti,[15] Jamaica,[11] Mali,[15, 23] Niger,[2, 6, 7] Nigeria,[11, 15] Panama [2, 15]
	None	Sierra Leone [6, 8, 11, 15]

Definition of light work	Min. age	Country
Excluded from coverage by legislation		Afghanistan, Algeria, Antigua and Barbuda, Argentina, Bahamas, Bahrain, Bangladesh, Barbados, Belgium, Comoros, Costa Rica, Dominica, Ecuador, Egypt, Iceland, India, Indonesia, Japan, Jordan, Kenya, Kuwait, Lebanon, Lesotho, Libyan Arab Jamahiriya, Malawi, Nepal, Nicaragua, Pakistan, Peru, Qatar, Sao Tome and Principe, Saudi Arabia, Switzerland, Swaziland, Syrian Arab Republic, United Republic of Tanzania, Tunisia, Turkey, United Arab Emirates, United States, Venezuela, Yemen, Zambia
Shop assistants, work in laundries, ticketing goods, kiosks, bakeries, greengrocers, packing and sorting light articles, newspaper sale and delivery	15 13	Netherlands [2, 5] Denmark,[1, 2, 5, 7, 8, 14] Thailand [1, 16]
Seasonal and intermittent work	15 14 12	Poland [15] Russian Federation, San Marino Senegal [9]

[1] Work must not expose the minor to risk of accident, endanger physical or mental health or development, or jeopardize morals.   [2] Work must not interfere with school instruction/not during school hours.   [3] Not in industry, commerce or commercial agriculture.   [4] Only on parents' or guardians' lands, gardens or plantation.   [5] No work on weekly rest day or religious or statutory holidays.   [6] Work must not exceed two hours a day.   [7] Combined school and work hours must not exceed seven in any day.   [8] No work between 20:00 and 08:00/19:00 and 06:00, or similar time periods.   [9] Consent of a parent or guardian is required.   [10] Domestic service only where suitable accommodation is provided.   [11] Work allowed if performed for a member of the family, in a family undertaking or under parental supervision.   [12] No more than six hours a day or 30 hours a week.   [13] Medical examination required, either before acceptance for employment or on a regular basis during employment.   [14] Must have an interruption of at least 12 or 14 hours between days of work.   [15] Work must be authorized by the labour inspector or appropriate authority.   [16] Weight limits imposed for loads which may be lifted by minors.   [17] Provided compulsory schooling has been completed.   [18] Work is essential to the existence of the family.   [19] Child must return each night to parents' or guardians' residence.   [20] Work to be done only during school holidays and for a restricted time during the holidays.   [21] Light work up to seven hours a day and 35 hours a week.   [22] Work must be essential to the learning of the trade/apprenticeship.   [23] Work must not exceed four or four-and-a-half hours a day.   [24] No work before school on school days.   [25] Work must not exceed three hours a day.   [26] In individual cases, and subject to a decision for each occasion, children under 13 years may take professional part in certain public performances, including sport activities, theatre, concerts, circus performances, radio and TV performances and film production.   [27] Work must not exceed five hours a day and 30 hours a week except for domestic service.

Source: This table is an updated version of Annex 2, of Part II "National legislation on the minimum age for admission to employment or work", in ILO: *Conditions of Work Digest*, Vol. 10, No. 1: *Child labour: Law and practice* (Geneva, 1991), pp. 46-47.

some other way condition access to employment on completion of compulsory education. Enforcement techniques can also gain from such a link. Some countries, for example, require employers to maintain work permits for children of a certain age, which can only be issued by the school authorities after taking into account school attendance and other relevant regulations. In other cases, the labour administration may be responsible for issuing the permit, but with the approval of parents and school authorities. Establishing and monitoring a link between labour and school authorities is crucial to ensuring that both societal goals of universal education and the elimination of child labour are met. An important dimension of compulsory education laws is that they place an obligation on parents to send their children to school.

Of course, compulsory education laws are meaningless if adequate schools are not available or if, because of cost or other practical difficulties, they are not accessible to poorer families. Thus any serious endeavour to attack the problem of child labour as a whole must include the commitment of sufficient resources to provide free and compulsory schooling to all children up to the age at which they become eligible to enter employment or work.

An overview of the existing legal position by region may be found in table 4, which presents a comparison of compulsory school ages with minimum ages for admission to employment.

TABLE 4. COMPULSORY EDUCATION AGES AND MINIMUM AGE FOR
ADMISSION TO EMPLOYMENT BY REGIONS OF THE WORLD

Africa

Country	Age limits for compulsory education	Minimum age for work		
		Basic minimun age	Light work	Dangerous/ hazardous work
Algeria	6-15	16	None; authorization necessary[2]	16 to 18[1]
Angola	7-15	14	—	18
Benin	6-11	14	12	18
Botswana	—	15	14	15 to 18[3]
Burkina Faso	7-14	14	12	16 to 18[4]
Burundi	7-13	16	12	18
Cameroon	6-12	14	—	18
Cape Verde	7-13	14 to 15[5]	12	16 to 18
Central African Republic	6-14	14	12	16 to 18
Chad	6-14	12 to 14[6]	12	16 to 18
Comoros	7-16	15	—	—[7]
Congo	6-16	16	12	16 to 18
Côte d'Ivoire	7-13	14	12	18
Djibouti	6-12	14	—	16 to 18
Egypt	6-11	12	—	15 to 17
Equatorial Guinea	6-14	14	12 to 13	16
Eritrea	7-13	—	—	—
Ethiopia	7-13	14	—	14 to 18
Gabon	6-16	16	—	18
Gambia	—	—	—	—
Ghana	6-14	15	No limit	18
Guinea	7-13	16[8]	—	—
Guinea-Bissau	7-13	14[9]	—	18
Kenya	6-14	16[10]	—	16
Lesotho	6-13	15[11]	13 (apprentice)	18 (16 for male apprentice)
Liberia	7-16	14 to 16 (by sector)[12]	—	18
Libyan Arab Jamahiriya	6-15	15	—	18
Madagascar	6-13	14 to 15 (by sector)[13]	—	16 to 18
Malawi	6-14	14 to 15 (by sector)[14]	12	18
Mali	8-15	14	12	16 to 18
Mauritania	—	14 to 15 (by sector)[13]	—	18
Mauritius	5-12	15	—	18

Country	Age limits for compulsory education	Minimum age for work		
		Basic minimun age	Light work	Dangerous/ hazardous work
Morocco	7-13	12	—	16
Mozambique	7-13	15	—	18
Namibia	6-16	14	—	15 to 16
Niger	7-15	14	12	16 to 18
Nigeria	6-12	12 to 15 (by sector)[15]	No limit	16 to 18
Rwanda	7-13	14	—	—
Sao Tome and Principe	7-14	14 to 15	12	16 to 18
Senegal	7-13	14 to 15 (by sector)[13]	12	16 to 18
Seychelles	6-15	15	12	18
Sierra Leone	—	12 to 16 (by sector)[16]	No limit[17]	16 to 18
Somalia	6-14	15	12	16 to 18
South Africa	7-16	15	—	16
Sudan	7-12	12	—	18
Swaziland	6-13	13 to 15 (by sector)[18]	—	18
Tanzania, United Republic of	7-13	12 to 15 (by sector)[19]	12	18
Togo	6-12	14	—	18
Tunisia	6-16	13 to 15 (by sector)[20]	13 to 14	18
Uganda	—	—[21]	12	16 to 18
Zaire	6-12	16	14	18
Zambia	7-14	14[10]	—	18
Zimbabwe	7-15	—	—	17[1]

[1] 16 for work that is dangerous, unhealthy or detrimental to morals. 18 for work in the maritime industry. [2] Determined by the competent authority. [3] 15 for work involving lifting, carrying or moving anything heavy; 18 for underground work and dangerous or harmful work. [4] General minimum age for hazardous work is 16 years; 18 for work exceeding strength and harmful to morality. [5] Minimum age of 14 for contract as a permanent worker; 15 for work in industry. [6] General minimum age is 14 years; 12 years for specified agricultural work. [7] Age limits and nature of work prohibited to adolescents to be determined by ministerial decision. [8] Applies only to industry and contractual employment. [9] Or upon completion of compulsory schooling. [10] Basic minimum age applies only to industry. [11] Basic minimum age applies only to commerce and industry. [12] General minimum age is 14 years; 15 for work on fishing vessels and on school ships; 16 for work in industry, agriculture and on ships. [13] General minimum age is 14 years; 15 for work at sea. [14] Minimum age of 14 for work in industry; 15 for work at sea. [15] General minimum age is 12 years, 15 for work in industry and shipping (except family undertakings). [16] General minimum age is 12 years; 15 for work in industry and at sea; 16 for work in mines. [17] Authorized only where the work is not harmful to the child. Authorization for light work is subject to approval by the competent authority. [18] Minimum age of 13 in commercial undertakings; 15 in industrial undertakings. [19] General minimum age is 12 years; 15 for work in industry. [20] 13 years for work in agriculture; 15 for work in industry, fishing and work at sea. [21] A person under the apparent age of 18 shall not be employed other than as provided for by decree.

Americas

Country	Age limits for compulsory education	Minimum age for work		
		Basic minimun age	Light work	Dangerous/ hazardous work
Antigua and Barbuda	5-16	16[1]	14	—
Argentina	6-14	14	—	18
Bahamas	5-14	14[2]	—	16 to 18
Barbados	5-16	15 to 16[3]	—	18
Belize	5-14	12 to 15 (by sector)[4]	No limit	16 to 18
Bolivia	6-13	14	—	18
Brazil	7-14	14[5]	—	18 to 21[6]
Canada	6-16			
Federal		—[7]	—	17[8]
Provinces		Various[9]	—	16 to 18
Chile	6-13	15	14	18 to 21[10]
Colombia	6-12	14	12	18
Costa Rica	6-15	12 to 15[11]	12	18
Cuba	6-11	15 to 17	—	17 to 18
Dominica	5-15	15[12]	—	18
Dominican Rep.	7-14	14	—	18
Ecuador	6-14	14	—	18
El Salvador	7-15	14	—	18
Grenada	5-16	—	—	—
Guatemala	7-14	14	—	16
Guyana	6-14	14	—	16 to 18
Haiti	6-12	12 to 15	—	18
Honduras	7-13	14	—	16
Jamaica	6-12	12 to 15 (by sector)[13]	No limit	16 to 17[13]
Mexico	6-14	14	—	16 to 18
Nicaragua	7-12	14[2]	—	18
Panama	6-15	14 to 16[14]	12	18
Paraguay	7-12	15	12	18
Peru	6-16	12 to 16 (by sector)	—	18
Saint Kitts and Nevis	5-17	—	—	—
Saint Lucia	5-15	12 to 14 (by sector)[15]	No limit	14 to 16
Saint Vincent and the Grenadines	—	—	—	—
Suriname	6-16	14	—	18

41

Country	Age limits for compulsory education	Minimum age for work		
		Basic minimun age	Light work	Dangerous/ hazardous work
Trinidad and Tobago	6-12	12 to 16 (by sector)[16]	—	14 to 18
United States (Federal)	7-16	16	—	16 to 18
Uruguay	6-14	15	12	18 to 21
Venezuela	5-15	14	—	18

[1] Minimum age applies only to agriculture and industrial undertakings and for work on ships. [2] Minimum age applies only to industrial undertakings. [3] Minimum age applies only to industrial undertakings or ships, including work in mines and quarries, construction, transportation. Minimum age of 15 only if compulsory schooling is finished. [4] General minimum age is 12 years; 14 for work in industry, mines and quarries, construction, transportation, etc.; 15 for work at sea. [5] Except apprentices above the age of 12. [6] Minimum age of 21 for stevedoring and underground work. [7] The Canada Labour Code does not set an absolute minimum age for employment. It provides that an employer may employ a person under 17 years in (a) occupations as may be specified by regulation, and (b) subject to the conditions and at a wage of not less than the minimum wage prescribed, and (c) provided that persons under 17 years are not required by provincial law to be in attendance at school (the youngest age for leaving school as provided by the provinces is 15). (Branches and undertakings governed by federal jurisdiction include communications, international and national transport, broadcasting, banking, uranium extraction and nuclear energy, and also certain branches declared by Parliament to be of interest to the nation. Federal legislation covers 10 per cent of the active population.) [8] Persons under 17 years cannot be employed in specified jobs or at night. [9] According to province, or territory, and sector. In certain provinces and territories, the employment of young persons is prohibited for various sectors only during school hours. [10] Minimum age of 21 for work in cabarets, etc., presenting live performances and offering alcoholic beverages. [11] Minimum age of 12 only if compulsory schooling has been completed or work does not prevent its completion, and not for more than five hours a day. Minimum age of 15 to 18 for work not exceeding seven hours a day. [12] Minimum age applies only to industrial undertakings, including mining, manufacturing, shipbuilding, electrical utilities, construction and transportation. [13] General minimum age is 12 years; 15 for work in industry, mines and quarries, construction, transportation, and work at sea. [14] General minimum age is 14 years; 15 years where the child has not yet finished school; 16 for work on ships. [15] General minimum age is 12 years; 14 for work in industry and on ships. No work may be performed during school hours, if the child is still completing schooling. [16] General minimum age is 12 years; 14 for work in industry; 16 for work on ships.

Asia

Country	Age limits for compulsory education	Minimum age for work		
		Basic minimun age	Light work	Dangerous/ hazardous work
Afghanistan	7-13	15	—	18
Armenia	—	—	—	—
Australia	6-16	Varies according to province and sector[1]	—	16 to 18
Azerbaijan	6-17	—	—	—
Bahrain	6-17	14	—	16
Bangladesh	6-10	12 to 15 (by sector)[2]	—	16 to 18[3]
Cambodia	6-12	16	—	18
China	7-16	16	—	18
Fiji	—	12 to 15 (by sector)[4]	No limit	16 to 18
India	6-14	14[5]	—	18
Indonesia	7-13	14[6]	—	18
Iran, Islamic Rep. of	6-10	15	—	18
Iraq	6-12	15	—	18
Japan	6-15	15	12	18
Jordan	6-15	13[7]	—	15
Kazakstan	6-18	—	—	—
Korea, Rep. of	6-15	13	13, with permission	18
Kuwait	6-14	14	—	18
Lao, People's Dem. Rep.	6-15	15	—	18
Lebanon	—	13	8	13 to 16
Malaysia	6-16	14	No limit	16
Mongolia	8-16	16	15	18
Myanmar	5-10	—	—	—
Nepal	6-11	14	—	16
New Zealand	6-16	15[8]	—	15 to 21
Oman	—	—	—	—
Pakistan	—	14 to 15 (by sector)[9]	—	15 to 21
Papua New Guinea	—	14 to 16	—	16
Philippines	7-13	15	No limit	18
Qatar	—	12	—	—
Saudi Arabia	—	13	—	18
Singapore	—	12 to 14 (by sector)	12	16 to 18

Country	Age limits for compulsory education	Minimum age for work		
		Basic minimun age	Light work	Dangerous/ hazardous work
Solomon Islands	—	12 to 15 (by sector)[10]	No limit	16 to 18
Sri Lanka	5-15	14 to 15 (by sector)[11]	No limit	16 to 18
Syrian Arab Rep.	6-11	12 to 13 (by sector)[12]	—	15
Tajikistan	7-17	—	—	—
Thailand	6-11	13	13 to 15	15 to 18
United Arab Emirates	6-12	15[13]	—	18
Uzbekistan	—	—	—	—
Viet Nam	6-11	15	—	18
Yemen	7-14	15	—	—

[1] Regulations cover only work at sea (16 years). Certain states and territories impose a minimum age in certain sectors; others merely prohibit the employment of young persons during school hours. [2] Minimum age of 12 for work in shops and on tea plantations; 14 for work in factories; and 15 for work at sea. [3] 16 for work in factories with machinery in motion; 17 for mining; 18 for work at sea as trimmers and stokers. [4] General minimum age is 12 years; 15 for work in industry. [5] Minimum age applies only to designated occupations. [6] Children below 14 may work with the permission of parents or guardians up to four hours a day. [7] Legislation in factories applies only to those employing at least ten workers. The competent authority may authorize the exclusion of any region or establishment from the scope of legislation concerning commerce. [8] Minimum age applies only to factories, work at sea, fishing and railways. [9] Minimum age of 14 for work in factories, shops and commerce, and work at sea; 15 for work in mines and on railways. [10] General minimum age is 12 years; 15 for work in industry and at sea. [11] General minimum age is 14 years; 15 for work at sea. [12] General minimum age is 12 years; 13 for work in industry. Applies only to undertakings with more than 10 employees. [13] Minimum age applies only to undertakings with more than five employees.

Europe

Country	Age limits for compulsory education	Minimum age for work		
		Basic minimun age	Light work	Dangerous/ hazardous work
Albania	6-14	16	12	16 to 18
Austria	6-15	15	12	16 to 18
Belarus	6-17	16	12	18
Belgium	6-18	14[1]	13 to 14[2]	16 to 21
Bosnia and Herzegovina	—	—	—	—
Bulgaria	7-16	16	15	18
Croatia	7-15	15	—	Generally no
Cyprus	6-15	15	No limit	16 to 18
Czech Republic	6-15	15	—	18
Denmark	7-15	15	13	15 to 18
Estonia	7-17	—	—	—
Finland	7-15	15[1]	14	16 to 18
France	6-16	16[1]	12 to 14	16 to 18
Georgia	—	—	—	—
Germany	6-18	15[3]	13	18
Greece	6-15	15	—	16 to 18
Hungary	6-16	15[1]	14	16 to 18
Iceland	7-15	15[4]	14	18 to 19
Ireland	6-15	15[1]	14	18
Israel	5-16	15	—	16 to 18
Italy	6-13	14 to 15 (by sector)[5]	14	15 to 18
Kyrgyzstan	—	—	—	—
Latvia	7-15	15	13	18
Lithuania	7-16	—	—	—
Luxembourg	6-15	15[1]	—	18
Malta	5-16	15 to 16 (by sector)[6]	—	18
Moldova, Rep. of	6-17	—	—	—
Netherlands	5-16	15	13 to 15	18
Norway	7-15	15 to 16 (by sector)[7]	13	18
Poland	7-14	15	15	18
Portugal	6-15	16	14	18
Romania	6-14	14 to 16	—	16 to 18
Russian Federation	7-17	15	14	18
San Marino	6-13	16	14	—
Slovakia	6-15	15	—	18
Slovenia	7-15	15	—	18
Spain	6-15	16	—	18
Sweden	7-15	16	13	18

Country	Age limits for compulsory education	Minimum age for work		
		Basic minimun age	Light work	Dangerous/ hazardous work
Switzerland	7-15	15	13	16 to 18
Turkey	6-14	15	13	18
Turkmenistan	7-15	—	—	—
The former Yugoslav Republic of Macedonia	7-15	—	—	—
Ukraine	7-15	15 to 16	—	17 to 18
United Kingdom	5-16	13 to 16 (by sector)[8]	—	16 to 18
Yugoslavia	7-15	15	—	18

[1] Provided compulsory schooling has been completed.   [2] Determined by the competent authorities on condition that well-being, safety and health are not endangered.   [3] Child must have completed compulsory schooling. Minimum age applies not only to employment relationships, but to all work, including the self-employed.   [4] Minimum age applies only to factories and transport. The child must have also completed compulsory schooling.   [5] General minimum age is 15 years; 14 for work in agriculture or to assist the family.   [6] General minimum age is 16 years; 15 for work on ships.   [7] General minimum age is 15 years and the completion of compulsory schooling; 16 to work in merchant shipping.   [8] General minimum age is 13 years; 16 for work in industry. Children below the age of 16 may not work during school hours or for more than two hours a day.

Source: UNESCO: *Statistical Yearbook*, 1995; and ILO: *Conditions of Work Digest*, op. cit.

National legislation on hazardous work

4

Prohibiting child labour in hazardous activities

The ILO's Minimum Age Convention, 1973 (No. 138), sets a minimum age of 18 for employment or work which by its nature or the circumstances in which it is carried out is likely to jeopardize the health, safety or morals of young persons. That is the sense in which the term "hazardous" work is used in this report, and that is the main target of the urgent and concentrated action being proposed by the ILO.

Effective laws and regulations are fundamental to underpin action against child labour. Where violations are particularly egregious, as is often the case where children are working in hazardous occupations and conditions, legal remedies and penalties might be the only effective way of putting an immediate stop to the practice and compensating the victims. Therefore, an essential first element in national legislative action against child labour in hazardous work is the fixing, unambiguously, of the minimum age for admission to hazardous work which, under the ILO's Minimum Age Convention, 1973 (No. 138), should not be less than age 18.

Another important aspect of legislation is the designation of work considered hazardous. As seen in Chapter 1, work hazards have various dimensions. They can be obvious and immediate, as in the case of physical hazards — for example, the risks associated with construction work or in glass factories. They can be imperceptible and may appear only after a long time of exposure, as in the case of work involving the use of chemicals or radiation agents. Or the hazards may be of a psychological nature linked to various forms of abuse, as occurs in domestic service. Again, the hazards may have far-reaching physical and moral consequences, as in the case of children working in bars and places of entertainment where the job overlaps with prostitution. In short, the dangers are diverse and numerous, and often have multiple sources.

Just as the hazards and dangers to which children are exposed vary from one sector, industry and occupation to another, so the focus for action will vary from country to country and even within countries. In a mineral-producing country (Colombia), the priority may be child labour in mines, in an island economy (the Philippines), deep-sea fishing, in a very poor country (Bangladesh, Sri Lanka, Togo), domestic service, elsewhere (Thailand, Mexico, Kenya), the entertainment industry. Consequently, one of the first steps must be to identify the occupations that are manifestly hazardous and where the employment of children should therefore be prohibited. For this, there must be a mechanism for consulting government, employers, workers, community groups, relevant professional groups, non-governmental organizations and religious groups. Moreover, the list of hazardous occupations and industries must be monitored and reviewed in the light of new technologies and processes, industrial development and the identification of work-related risks and dangers.

The following review of the decisions being taken by legislators on what constitutes hazardous work for children is based on the legislation of 155 member States.

The universal recognition of the imperative need to protect children from hazardous work is demonstrated by the fact that all but a handful of the countries examined have enacted national laws or regulations imposing stringent restrictions on work by children in hazardous work.

The majority of countries (76) view 18 as the appropriate minimum age for certain hazardous activities. A fair number fix age limits of 16 or 17 years. A few countries set the limit higher, up to 21 years, whereas in a few others children of 14 or 15 may engage in certain hazardous occupations. Five countries appear to have no rules on the subject.

Convention No. 138 does not itself specify the types of work considered hazardous because any such text in a binding international instrument could be limitative and quickly fall out of date. But the Convention does require national laws or regulations of the competent authority, after consultation with employers' and workers' organizations, to make the necessary determination.

In national law and practice there is considerable variety in the restrictions on dangerous work by young persons. In some cases, the definition merely refers to "dangerous, dirty, unhealthy or detrimental to morals" in general, or is left to separate regulations; in others, hazardous

Hazardous industries, occupations, activities and agents most frequently cited in national legislation on child labour

Prohibited industries and occupations	No. of countries
Mining, quarries, underground work	101
Maritime work (trimmers and stokers)	57
Machinery in motion (operating, cleaning, repairs, etc.)	57
Weights and loads	40
Construction/and or demolition	37
Circular saws and other dangerous machinery	35
Lead/zinc metallurgy	34
Transportation, operating vehicles	33
Entertainment	32
Alcohol production and/or sale	29
Cranes/hoists/lifting machinery	23
Crystal and/or glass manufacture	22
Welding and smelting of metals	20
Agriculture (specified tasks only)	14
Abattoirs and meat rendering	14
Underwater work	13
Street trades	12
Production of pornographic material	10
Tanneries	12
Textile industry (specified tasks)	5
Metal and wood handicraft (different tasks inc. carpentry, slate-pencil production, precious stone work)	7
Forestry	6
Brick manufacture	5

Prohibited agents	
Explosives (manufacturing and handling)	50
Fumes, dust, gas and other noxious substances	35
Radioactive substances or ionizing radiation	29
Chemicals, general provisions for exposure to	26
Pathogenic agents, exposure to (hospital work, city cleaning, work related to sewers, handling of corpses)	18
Electricity	15
Paints, solvents, shellac, varnish, glue or enamel	9
Asbestos	8
Benzene	5

activities are listed in detail. As can be seen in the box, underground work, maritime work (especially trimmers and stokers), work with machinery that is in motion, work with explosives or noxious substances and work in lead or zinc metallurgy are most commonly singled out for prohibition or a higher minimum age.

A few countries define dangerous or hazardous work in their principal legislation. For example, in Mexico, it is work which, on account of its nature or the physical, chemical or biological conditions of the environment in which it is performed or the composition of the raw materials used, is liable to affect the life, development and physical and mental health of young persons. Slovenia prohibits work which can have a harmful influence on and seriously endanger children's health or development, and Sweden work that involves a risk of accidents, excessive strain or any other effect detrimental to their health or development. Saint Lucia introduces the notion of education and prohibits any occupation likely to be injurious to life, limb, health or education.

Some countries define dangerous and unhealthy work separately. For example, the Labour Code of El Salvador defines "unhealthy work" as work that "is capable by its nature of being detrimental to the worker's health or of causing injury by virtue of the type of substance used or produced, including toxic materials, harmful gases, vapours or effluvia and dangerous or noxious dust, and any other type of work specified in relevant laws, regulations, collective agreements, individual contracts or work rules", while "dangerous work" is defined as work which is "capable of causing death or immediate physical injury, because of its nature, the substances used or residues produced, or because of the need to handle or store corrosive, inflammable or explosive substances". The Labour Code of Honduras has a similar provision.

Usually, however, hazardous work is referred to in general terms as posing danger to the *health, safety or morals* of children, as indicated in Convention No. 138. A few countries qualify it as work which is *particularly* dangerous, or work *likely* to be dangerous to safety, health or morals. The definition of "oppressive child labour" in the United States, for example, is employment in any occupation found by the Department of Labor to be particularly hazardous for the employment of children between the ages of 16 and 18 or detrimental to their health or well-being.

Reference is also frequently made (33 countries) to work which is physically arduous for young persons or out of proportion to their strength.

The concept of hazardous work may extend to situations where inexperience or lack of mature judgement could present risks to the safety of others. For example, in Finland work which puts unreasonable pressure or responsibility on a young person or which implies responsibility for another person's safety is prohibited for those below the age of 18. The same age limit is set in Germany for work which involves a risk of accidents due to a young person's lack of safety consciousness or experience.

A list of general prohibitions is given in table 5.

Another approach is to define hazards in the physical environment which children may not be exposed to (see table 6). These include provisions relating to light, sound, vibration and humidity levels, as well as air pressure. A few countries refer to ergonomic hazards which are specifically dangerous for children. In China, for example, it is prohibited for persons under 18 to do work which involves maintaining a body position (lowered head, stooping, squatting) for a long time, or to repeat the same action more than 50 times.

Very few countries rely entirely on general prohibitions, however, and the overwhelming majority of countries include more or less detailed listings of agents or products that children may not be exposed to (see table 7). In India, a list of hazardous occupations and provisions is included in a schedule which can be modified by the Government with proper notice; the law also provides for a Child Labour Technical Advisory Committee to advise the Government on occupations or processes to be added. Some European Union countries complement listings of harmful agents with references to relevant EU directives, or to regulations implementing such directives.

The largest category of specific legislative prohibitions is the listing of industries, occupations or activities prohibited for children. Again, some countries leave the designation of occupational limitations to administrative decision. The United States Department of Labor, for example, has issued 17 Hazardous Occupations Orders under the Federal Fair Labor Standards Act for youth in non-farm work under the age of 18; separate rules apply to farm work. The complexity of some of these listings is exemplified by the Order of the Department of Labor and Employment in the Philippines, which specifies nine occupational groupings and numerous specific occupations which are prohibited for young persons.

The industries where hazardous work is most commonly prohibited are: mining, maritime work, work with machinery in motion, work involving heavy weights and loads, construction and demolition work, transportation and entertainment (see table 8).

TABLE 5. GENERAL PROHIBITION OF HAZARDOUS WORK BY CHILDREN

General prohibitions	Min. age	Country
Dangerous to safety	18	Argentina, Barbados, Belarus, Botswana, Brazil, Bulgaria, Chile, Costa Rica, Ecuador, El Salvador, Equatorial Guinea, Ethiopia, Lesotho, Mali, Mozambique, Norway, Panama, Romania, Sudan, Swaziland, Tajikistan, United Republic of Tanzania, Togo, Uganda, Ukraine, Viet Nam
	17	Canada (federal)
	16-18	Madagascar
	16	Lebanon, Morocco
Likely to endanger safety	18	Norway
	17	Canada (federal)
Dangerous to health	21	Uruguay
	18	Afghanistan, Albania, Argentina, Barbados, Belarus, Belgium, Belize, Bolivia, Brazil, Bulgaria, Chile, Costa Rica, Croatia, Cuba, Czech Republic, Ecuador, El Salvador, Ethiopia, Greece, Haiti, Islamic Republic of Iran, Iraq, Republic of Korea, Lao People's Democratic Republic, Latvia, Lesotho, Luxembourg, Mozambique, Nigeria, Romania, Slovakia, Sudan, Swaziland, United Republic of Tanzania, Uganda, Ukraine
	16-18	Equatorial Guinea
	16	Algeria, France, Papua New Guinea, Singapore
Particularly dangerous (dangerous to life)	18	Gabon, Venezuela
	16	France
Dangerous to morals	18	Barbados, Belgium, Bolivia, Botswana, Burundi, Chad, Chile, Costa Rica, El Salvador, Equatorial Guinea, Gabon, Islamic Republic of Iran, Iraq, Republic of Korea, Latvia, Lesotho, Luxembourg, Mali, Mauritania, Panama, Swaziland
	16-18	Madagascar
	16	Algeria, France, Morocco, Sao Tome and Principe, Senegal
Likely to be harmful to morals	18	Congo, Guinea, Mali, Nigeria, Sudan
Seriously dangerous to morals	18	Ecuador
Dangerous to the development (physical, intellectual or moral) of a child	18	Angola,[1] Brazil, Czech Republic, Denmark, Ecuador, Greece, Luxembourg, Norway, Poland,[1] Venezuela

General prohibitions	Min. age	Country
Physically arduous	18	Afghanistan, Argentina, Belarus, Belgium, Bolivia, Brazil, Bulgaria, Mongolia, Mozambique, Romania, Slovenia, Sudan, Ukraine, Viet Nam
Too arduous	18	Albania, Cameroon, Chile, China, Croatia, Germany, Greece, Guinea-Bissau, Haiti, Islamic Republic of Iran, Iraq, Lao People's Democratic Republic, Luxembourg, Mali, Mauritania, Panama, Poland,[1] Venezuela
	16-18	Madagascar
Particularly hazardous or detrimental to health or well-being	18	United States

[1] Except for apprenticeships.

Source: ILO: *Conditions of work digest on child labour: Law and practice*, Vol. 10, No. 2 (Geneva, 1991), pp. 48-54.

TABLE 6. GENERAL PROHIBITIONS RELATING TO THE PHYSICAL ENVIRONMENT

General prohibitions	Min. age	Country
Thermal stress (heat and/or cold)	20	Uruguay
	18	Austria, Bolivia, China, Colombia,[1] Denmark,[1] Germany,[1] Japan, Luxembourg, Poland,[1] Switzerland, Thailand
	16	Bahrain
	15	Egypt
Vibration and noise	18	Austria,[1] Bolivia, China, Colombia,[1] Denmark,[1] Germany,[1] Japan, Poland,[1] Thailand
Ventilation (inadequate)	18	Colombia,[1] Denmark [1]
Light (lack of, or at abnormal level)	18	Poland,[1] Thailand
Air pressure (increased or decreased)	18	Belarus, China, Denmark,[1] Poland,[1] Portugal
Ergonomic hazards	18	China, Poland [1]
	16	France
Accident hazards	18	Netherlands, Slovakia

[1] Except for apprenticeships.

Source: ILO: *Conditions of work digest on child labour: Law and practice*, Vol. 10, No. 2 (Geneva, 1991), pp. 48-54.

TABLE 7.   PROHIBITION OF SPECIFIC AGENTS OR PRODUCTS

Agent or product	Minimum age	Country
Alcohol production and/or sale	21	Chile
	18	Argentina, Australia (Victoria), Bolivia, Brazil, Burundi, Cameroon, Colombia, Costa Rica, Dominican Republic, Ecuador, Equatorial Guinea, Haiti, Italy, Luxembourg, Mexico, Panama, Peru, Portugal, Spain,[1] Swaziland, Venezuela, Zaire
	17	Egypt
	16	Guatemala, Honduras, Mexico
	15	Jamaica, Thailand
Asbestos	18	Cyprus, Luxembourg, Portugal, Singapore, United Kingdom
	16	Australia (Victoria), Bahrain
	14	India
Benzene	21	Uruguay
	18	Iraq, Netherlands, Portugal
	14	India
Bleaching and chlorine	18	Cameroon, Portugal
Cadmium	18	Portugal
	14	India
Cement	18	Angola,[2] Cameroon, Colombia[2]
	14	India
	15	Egypt
	12	Bangladesh
Chemicals, general provisions for exposure to	18	Angola,[2] Austria, Bolivia,[6] Cameroon, Chad, China, Colombia,[2] Congo, Cyprus, Denmark,[2] France, Germany, Guinea, Lao People's Democratic Republic, Philippines, Poland,[2] Portugal, Spain,[1] Sudan, Thailand, Togo, United Kingdom
	16	Bahrain, Honduras, Mexico
	15	Egypt
Chromium	18	Portugal, United Kingdom
	14	India
Compressed air/gas	18	Cameroon, Denmark,[1] Sweden
	16	Bahrain
	15	Egypt
Electricity	18	Angola,[2] Cameroon, Colombia,[2] Denmark,[1] France, Panama, Poland,[2] Portugal, Sweden, Uruguay, Zaire
	16	Bahrain, Mexico

Agent or product	Minimum age	Country
	15	Dominica, Jamaica
	14	Belize
Explosives	18	Angola,[2] Austria, Belgium, Bolivia, Burundi, Cameroon, Chad, China, Colombia,[2] Congo, Costa Rica, Côte d'Ivoire, Cyprus, Denmark,[2] Djibouti, Ecuador, El Salvador, Equatorial Guinea, Guinea, Finland, France, Japan, Lao People's Democratic Republic, Luxembourg, Madagascar, Mali, Netherlands, Panama, Peru, Philippines, Portugal, Senegal, Spain,[1] Sweden, Switzerland, Thailand, Togo, United Kingdom, United States, Zaire
	17	Canada (federal), Egypt
	16	Bahrain, Dominican Republic, Honduras, Mexico, Morocco
	14	India, Pakistan
Fumes, dust, gas and other noxious substances	18	Angola,[2] Austria,[2] Bolivia, China, Chad, Colombia,[2] Congo, Denmark,[2] Ecuador, El Salvador, France, Germany,[2] Japan, Lao Peoples' Democratic Republic, Luxembourg, Madagascar, Netherlands, Nicaragua, Peru, Poland,[2] Portugal, Spain,[1] Sudan, Sweden, Switzerland, Thailand, Togo
	17	Cuba
	16	Bahrain,[3] Honduras, Mexico, Morocco, United Kingdom
	14	India
Infra-red and ultraviolet rays, laser, radio-frequency emissions	18	Austria, Colombia,[2] Poland
Lead/zinc metallurgy, white lead, lead in paint	21	Uruguay
	18	Australia (Queensland, Victoria), Austria, Barbados, Belgium, Bolivia, Cameroon, Colombia,[2] Cyprus, Denmark,[2] Djibouti, Ecuador, France, Gabon, Germany, Ireland, Madagascar, Malta, Norway, Portugal, Sudan, Sweden, Syrian Arab Republic, Togo, United Kingdom,[7] Zaire
	17	Egypt
	16	Bahrain, Cyprus, Greece, Honduras, Mexico, United Kingdom
	15	Syrian Arab Republic
	14	India
Manganese	18	Portugal
	14	India

Agent or product	Minimum age	Country
Marble, stone and gypsum	18 16	Angola,[2] Cameroon, Spain[1] Bahrain
Mercury	18 17 15 14	Portugal, Sudan Egypt Syrian Arab Republic India
Paints, solvents, shellac varnish, glue, enamel	18 16 14	Angola,[2] Bolivia, Cameroon, Colombia,[2] Ecuador Cyprus, Mexico India, Pakistan
Pathogenic agents, exposure to (hospital work, city cleaning, work related to sewers, handling corpses, etc.)	18 17	Austria, Bangladesh, Colombia, Ethiopia, Finland, Lao People's Democratic Republic, Luxembourg, Madagascar, Netherlands, Panama, Poland,[2, 4] Portugal, Spain,[1] Switzerland, Thailand, Turkey, Uruguay Israel[5]
Potassium and sodium	18	Cyprus
Radioactive substances or ionizing radiation	18 17 16	Argentina, Austria,[2] Belgium, Colombia,[2] China, Denmark,[2] Finland, France, Germany, India, Lao People's Democratic Republic, Luxembourg, Malta, Netherlands, Panama, Philippines, Poland,[2] Portugal, Slovenia, Sudan, Thailand, United Kingdom, United States Canada (federal) Bahrain, Guyana, Honduras, Switzerland, United Kingdom
Rubber	18 17 16	Angola[2] Egypt Cyprus, Mexico
Tar, asphalt, bitumen	18 17 15	Angola,[2] Luxembourg Egypt Syrian Arab Republic
Tobacco (inc. bidi and cigarette making)	16 15 14	Cameroon Syrian Arab Republic India, Pakistan

[1] Minimum age of 18 for men, 21 for women.   [2] Except for apprenticeships.   [3] Work connected with materials or components provided for in schedule for occupational diseases attached to Social Insurance Law.   [4] Risk of contagious diseases generally.   [5] Applies only to work involving contact with tuberculosis, leprosy or mental patients.   [6] Exceptions possible under specified conditions for 15-year-olds.   [7] Specific tasks.

Source: ILO: *Conditions of work digest on child labour: Law and practice*, Vol. 10, No. 2 (Geneva, 1991), pp. 48-54.

TABLE 8. PROHIBITED HAZARDOUS INDUSTRIES,
OCCUPATIONS OR ACTIVITIES

Industry, occupation or activity	Minimum age	Country
Abattoirs and meat rendering	18	Central African Republic, Congo, Denmark,[1] Finland, Gabon, Guinea, Luxembourg,[1] Thailand, Togo, United States, Zaire
	17	Egypt
	16	Bahrain, Lebanon [2]
Aluminium industry	16	Bahrain, Cyprus
Agriculture	21	Uruguay
	18	Colombia,[1, 3] Costa Rica,[3] France,[3] Spain,[3, 4]
	17	Australia (Queensland),[5] Ukraine
	16 or 18	France[3, 6]
	16	Denmark,[3] United Kingdom,[3] United States[3, 5]
	15	Syrian Arab Republic[5]
	14	India,[3] Pakistan[3]
Airport runways	18	Portugal
Animals, work with dangerous or wild	18	Denmark,[1] Netherlands
Archaeological excavations	18	Iraq
	16	Mexico
Bakery	21	Uruguay
	18	United States
Brick manufacture	18	Austria,[1] Colombia,[1] United States
	16	Bahrain, Cameroon
Cable laying	18	Turkey
Care for mentally disturbed persons	18	Finland
Carpet weaving	14	India
	12	Bangladesh
Catering at railway stations	14	India
Cinderpicking, clearing an ashpit	14	India
Circular saws and other dangerous machines	18	Argentina, Australia (Victoria), Austria, Bolivia, Cameroon,[1] China, Colombia,[1] Congo, Côte d'Ivoire, Denmark,[1] Djibouti, Ecuador, France, Gabon, India, Luxembourg, Madagascar, Mali,[35] Mauritius, Peru, Saudi Arabia, Spain, Thailand, Trinidad and Tobago, United Kingdom,[1] United States, Zaire

Industry, occupation or activity	Minimum age	Country
	17	Pakistan
	16	Burkina Faso, Chad, Central African Republic, Guinea, Malaysia,[1] Senegal
Construction and/or demolition	18	Austria, Bolivia, Burundi, Colombia,[1, 7] El Salvador, France, Gabon,[8] Luxembourg,[7] Madagascar,[7] Netherlands, Peru,[7] Spain,[7] Turkey,[10] United States
	16	Bahrain, Barbados, Burkina Faso,[7] Cameroon,[7] Central African Republic,[9] Chad, Congo, Côte d'Ivoire,[7] Djibouti,[7] France, Guinea,[8] Kenya, Mali, Morocco, Senegal,[7] Somalia, United States,[7] United Kingdom
	15	Dominica, Jamaica
	14	Belize, Cyprus, India
Cranes/hoists/lifting machinery	18	Argentina, Austria, Canada, Central African Republic, Chad, Colombia,[1] Congo, Cyprus, Denmark,[1] Gabon, Guinea, Japan, Luxembourg, Madagascar, Mauritius, Netherlands, Thailand, United Kingdom, United States, Zaire
	16	Bahrain, Denmark, France, Israel[11]
Crystal and/or glass manufacture	18	Angola,[1] Argentina, Austria, Bolivia, Cameroon, Colombia,[1] Côte d'Ivoire, Cyprus,[12] Denmark,[1] Djibouti, Ecuador, Ireland, Madagascar, Mali,[35] Portugal, Senegal
	17	Austria,[3] Egypt
	16 to 18	France[3, 6]
	16	Bahrain
	15	Syrian Arab Republic
	14	Pakistan
Domestic service	16	Denmark
Entertainment (night clubs, bars, casinos, circuses, gambling halls)	21	Chile, Seychelles, Uruguay
	18	Angola,[1] Austria, Bolivia, Brazil, Burundi, Cameroon, Colombia, Costa Rica,[13] Ecuador, El Salvador, Italy, Latvia, Luxembourg, Madagascar, Panama, Peru, Philippines, Seychelles, Switzerland,[14] Thailand
	17	Egypt
	16	Djibouti, France, Honduras, Mali
	15	Thailand
	14 to 18	Dominican Republic[15]
	14	Nicaragua, Republic of Korea

Industry, occupation or activity	Minimum age	Country
Excavation	18	Central African Republic, United States
Fire brigades and gas rescue services	18	Austria[1]
Forestry	18	China, Netherlands, Philippines, United States
	16 to 18	Spain
Machinery in motion (operation, cleaning, repairs, etc.)	21	Uruguay
	18	Argentina, Austria,[1] Bolivia, Burundi, Cameroon, Central African Republic, Colombia,[1] Chad, Congo, Côte d'Ivoire, Cyprus, Denmark,[1] Djibouti, Dominica, Dominican Republic, El Salvador, Equatorial Guinea, France,[16] Gabon, Greece, Guinea, India, Ireland, Japan, Luxembourg, Madagascar, Malawi, Mali, Malta, Mauritius, Myanmar, Netherlands, Peru, Saudi Arabia, Spain, Sweden, Switzerland, Thailand, Zaire, Zambia
	17	Egypt, Pakistan
	16	Bahrain, Bangladesh, Djibouti, France,[16] Guyana, Jamaica, Malaysia,[1] Morocco, Nigeria, Saint Lucia, Senegal, Singapore, United Kingdom
	15	Italy,[17] Syrian Arab Republic
Matches, manufacture of	16	Cameroon
	14	India, Pakistan
Maritime work (trimmers and stokers, stevedoring)	21	Brazil[18]
	19	Denmark[1] (stokers), Iceland
	18	Algeria, Argentina, Australia, Austria, Bahamas,[19] Bangladesh,[20] Belgium, Belize,[21] Burundi, Cameroon, China, Colombia,[1] Congo, Costa Rica, Côte d'Ivoire, Denmark[1] (trimmers), Djibouti, Ecuador, El Salvador, Fiji, Gabon, Iraq, Ireland,[1] Japan, Kenya, Liberia, Luxembourg, Malawi, Malta, Myanmar, Nigeria,[21] Pakistan,[21] Papua New Guinea, Peru, Philippines, Romania, Sierra Leone,[21] Singapore, Solomon Islands, Somalia, Sri Lanka, Sudan, United Republic of Tanzania, Trinidad and Tobago, Tunisia, United Kingdom,[22] Yugoslavia, Zaire
	17	Canada (federal), Cuba[18]
	16	Denmark,[23] Finland,[23] Singapore[24]
	15	Kenya[25]
	14	India, Pakistan[26]

Industry, occupation or activity	Minimum age	Country
Mining, quarries, underground work	21	Brazil
	18	Afghanistan, Albania, Angola,[1] Argentina, Australia (South and Western), Austria,[1] Belarus, Belgium, Belize,[1] Bolivia, Botswana, Burundi, Cambodia,[1] Cameroon,[1] Cape Verde, Central African Republic, Chad, Chile, China, Colombia,[1] Congo, Croatia, Cuba, Cyprus,[27] Czech Republic, Denmark,[1] Djibouti, Dominican Republic, Ecuador, Egypt, El Salvador, Equatorial Guinea, Fiji, France, Gabon, Germany,[1] Ghana,[28] Greece, Guinea, Guinea-Bissau, India, Indonesia, Iraq, Ireland, Israel, Italy, Japan, Jordan, Lao People's Democratic Republic, Lesotho,[1] Luxembourg, Mongolia, Nicaragua, Panama, Peru, Philippines, Poland,[1] Portugal, Sao Tome and Principe, Saudi Arabia, Slovenia, Somalia, South Africa, Sudan, Swaziland, Switzerland, Tajikistan, United Republic of Tanzania, Thailand, Tunisia, Turkey,[10] United Kingdom, United States, Venezuela, Zaire, Zambia
	17	Australia (Victoria), Bangladesh, Canada (federal), Jamaica, Myanmar,[29] Pakistan
	16	Bahrain, Barbados, Burkina Faso, Côte d'Ivoire, Hungary, Kenya, Mali, Mexico, Nicaragua, Nigeria, Sierra Leone,[2] Singapore, Solomon Islands,[2] Uganda
	15	Dominica, Syrian Arab Republic
	14	Belize, Cyprus[27]
Oil prospecting/work with petroleum	18	China, Sudan
	16	Bahrain, Mexico
	15	Egypt
Oxyacetylene blowpipes	16	Australia (all States), Bahrain
Paper/printing	18	Spain,[4] United States
	14	Pakistan
Pedal/crank operated equipment	16	Cameroon,[12] Congo, Djibouti,[12] Mali
Pornographic material, production of or work at premises handling	18	Bolivia, Brazil, Cameroon, Colombia, Côte d'Ivoire, Djibouti, Ecuador, Honduras,[30] Uruguay, Zaire
Salt and brine processes	18	Cyprus[12]

Industry, occupation or activity	Minimum age	Country
Shipbuilding	16	Cyprus
Soap manufacture	14	Bangladesh, India, Pakistan
Steam engines or equipment (work with)	18	Côte d'Ivoire, France, Sudan
	16	Cameroon, Djibouti, Mali
Street trades	18	Austria, Bolivia, Brazil, Peru[4]
	16	Burkina Faso, Cyprus, Djibouti,[12] Dominican Republic, Italy, United Kingdom
	15	Costa Rica[17]
	14 to 18	Ecuador[31]
	14	Sri Lanka
Sugar mill	16	Jamaica
Tanneries	18	Chad, France, Gabon, Guinea, Zaire
	17	Austria, Egypt
	16	Dominican Republic, Mexico
	15	Syrian Arab Republic
	14	India, Pakistan
	12	Bangladesh
Textile industry (specific tasks)	21	Uruguay
	18	Spain[4]
	16	Bahrain
	15	Egypt
	12	Bangladesh
Transportation, operating vehicles	18	Argentina, Austria, Bolivia, Burundi, Central African Republic, Chad, Congo, Denmark,[1] Ecuador,[32] Equatorial Guinea, Gabon, Guinea, Pakistan,[33] Panama, Peru, Philippines, Portugal, Spain,[4] United States, Zaire
	17	Egypt
	16	Barbados, Dominican Republic, Israel, Kenya, Senegal,[34] United Kingdom
	15	Dominica, Jamaica
	14	Belize, Cyprus, India
Underwater work	18	Austria, China, Colombia,[1] Croatia, El Salvador, Lao People's Democratic Republic, Poland,[1] Sudan, Sweden, Thailand, Turkey[10]
	16	Dominican Republic, Mexico
Water and gas industry	18	Spain[4]

Industry, occupation or activity	Minimum age	Country
Weights and loads	14 to 18	Afghanistan, Australia (Victoria), Bahrain, Belarus, Belgium, Belize, Bolivia, Botswana, Burkina Faso, Burundi, Cameroon, Central African Republic, Chad, China, Colombia,[1] Congo, Costa Rica, Côte d'Ivoire, Cuba, Cyprus, Denmark,[1] Djibouti, Ecuador, Egypt, Gabon, Guinea, India, Israel, Italy, Latvia, Mali, Netherlands, Niger, Poland,[1] Saint Lucia, Spain, Switzerland, Ukraine, Uruguay, Zaire
Welding and smelting of metals, metal working	18	Argentina, Australia (all States), Austria,[1] Bolivia, Cameroon, Colombia,[1] Cyprus,[12] Denmark,[1] Ecuador, Luxembourg, Portugal, Spain,[4] Sudan, Sweden, Thailand, United States, Venezuela
	17	Egypt
	16	Bahrain, Mexico
	15	Syrian Arab Republic
Work alone if it involves a risk of accidents or criminal acts	18	Finland
Work at courts, prisons or as probation officers	18	Seychelles

[1] Except for apprenticeships. [2] Medical certificate required. [3] For specified tasks only. [4] Minimum age of 18 for men, 21 for women. [5] Application or manufacture of agricultural chemicals. [6] Different minimum age depending on the type of work. [7] Applies only to work on scaffolding. [8] Except finishing work that does not include scaffolding. [9] Not requiring scaffolding. [10] Applies to men, women generally prohibited. [11] Including signalling for these operations. [12] Women only. [13] Work during daytime (a general limit of 18 is imposed for all night work). [14] 16 is minimum age for work in hotels, restaurants and cafes, and 18 for work in other types of entertainment. [15] Prior authorization required. [16] Depending on the type of machinery. [17] Minimum age of 15 for men, 18 for women (applies to street trades in Costa Rica for unmarried women only). [18] Applies only to stevedoring. [19] 16 if medically fit according to certificate presented. [20] Exceptionally 16. [21] Where a person over 18 is unavailable for a trimmer and stoker position, this position may be filled by two 16-year-olds. [22] Offshore mining. [23] Except in family undertakings not using dangerous equipment. [24] Except on family vessels. [25] Concerns employment on any vessel unless it is a training ship. a family vessel or unless a medical certificate has been obtained. [26] Concerns only fishing. [27] Minimum age of 18 for underground work; 14 for other work in mines, quarries, etc. [28] Apparently 18. [29] Minimum age of 17 for underground work; 15 for other work in mines, quarries, etc. [30] Minimum age 16 for men and 18 for women. [31] Authorization for men between 14 and 18 and for women between 14 and 21 only if necessary for the subsistence of the minor. [32] Only transportation of substances in a state of incandescence. [33] Minimum age of 21 in road transport services requiring the driving of a vehicle. [34] Piloting ships. [35] The competent authority may grant certain exceptions.

Source: ILO: *Conditions of work digest on child labour: Law and practice*, Vol. 10, No. 2 (Geneva, 1991), pp. 48-54.

Prohibiting forced and bonded labour

Most countries in the world prohibit forced labour in their constitution or general labour legislation; two, India and Pakistan, have adopted legislation specifically outlawing bonded labour.

The Constitutions of most countries contain provisions relating to fundamental rights which include such injunctions as "no person shall be held in slavery or servitude" and "no person shall be required to perform forced or compulsory labour" or to the effect that no person shall be compelled to perform work or render personal services without his or her full consent and/or without fair compensation. Some constitutions deal with forced labour under general provisions on the right to work, stipulating that everyone has the right to freedom of labour and that involuntary labour is prohibited, or that work is an obligation for every citizen but that no one may be unlawfully forced into a specific occupation.

The Constitution of India prohibits a form of forced labour known as *begar*, which is "labour or service exacted by government or a person in power without remuneration". Honduras appears to be the only country in which the Constitution itself deals specifically with children in bondage: "Every child must be protected against every form of abandonment, cruelty and exploitation. No child shall be the object of any type of bondage". Penalties are provided for by law for those who violate the provision.

Many countries devote a section of their labour legislation to forced or compulsory labour. Definitions are often in conformity with the ILO's Forced Labour Convention, 1930 (No. 29), which defines "forced or compulsory labour" as "all work or service which is exacted from any person under the menace of any penalty and for which the said person has not offered himself voluntarily" — other than in the performance of military service, normal civil obligations or any work exacted as a consequence of a conviction in a court of law or in cases of emergency.

Though most legislation prohibits forced or compulsory labour in general terms, certain provisions are more detailed. Some, for example, provide for the prosecution of any person who exacts or imposes forced labour or causes or permits forced labour to be exacted or imposes such labour for his benefit or for the benefit of any other person, while others prohibit public officers from putting any constraint upon the population under their charge or upon any individual member of the population to work for any private individual, company or association.

In about half of the countries where the prohibition of forced labour is provided for in general labour legislation, there are specific penalties for the illegal exaction of work or any form of illegal constraint. In others, such provisions are found under general or penalty provisions of the labour legislation. Labour legislation typically declares that any person who imposes or permits the imposition of forced labour is guilty of an offence and liable to a fine of a certain amount of money and/or to imprisonment for some months or years. For example, in the Republic of Korea a person violating the provisions concerning employment of workers through violence, threats, illegal confinement or any other means of unjustifiable mental or physical restraint "shall be punished by imprisonment for not more than five years or a fine not exceeding 30 million *won*"; a labour inspector who has wilfully connived at contravening the same provisions "shall be punished by imprisonment for not more than three years or suspension of civil rights for a period of not more than five years".

In some countries any public servant or person entrusted with a public service who exacts forced labour of a person in circumstances other than in the public interest is liable to imprisonment and/or a fine under the penal code. In others, the provision is more general; for example, the Bahraini Penal Code states that anyone who subjects workers to forced labour for a specific job or who withholds without due cause the whole or a part of their wages is liable to imprisonment and/or a fine.

Specific legislation for the abolition of bonded labour was adopted in India and Pakistan in 1976 and 1992 respectively.

In India *begar* has flourished in various states in invisible forms. Efforts to abolish the practice date back to an 1843 law concerning the prohibition of forced labour, since when various government resolutions and declarations have been adopted on the subject, culminating in the *Bonded Labour System (Abolition) Act, 1976.*

The Act provides that the bonded labour system shall stand abolished and every bonded labourer shall stand freed and discharged from any obligation to render any bonded labour. The law provides for the establishment of vigilance committees which include members of scheduled castes or scheduled tribes and social workers. The committees advise on proper implementation of the Act, provide for economic and social rehabilitation of the freed labourers, coordinate the functions of rural banks and cooperative societies with a view to providing adequate credit to the freed labourers, and defend any suit instituted against a freed bonded labourer for the recovery of bonded debt. Under the Bonded

Labour System (Abolition) Rules, 1976, the registers maintained by the vigilance committees must include the names and addresses of the freed bonded labourers and details of the benefits which they receive, including benefits in the form of land, inputs in agriculture, training in handicrafts and allied occupations, and loans. Under the Act's enforcement measures, "compulsion to render bonded labour, advancement of bonded debt, enforcement of any custom, tradition, contract, agreement or other instrument requiring any service to be rendered under the bonded labour system are punishable with imprisonment for up to three years and a fine". The Act also provides for various measures to be taken by state authorities to ensure punishment of offenders.

Similarly, in Pakistan, the Bonded Labour System (Abolition) Act, 1992, declares the abolition of the bonded labour system and states that every bonded labourer is to be freed and discharged from any obligation to render any bonded labour. No suit or other proceeding can lie in any civil court, tribunal or before any other authority for the recovery of any bonded debt or any part thereof. The Act provides for special enforcement measures, including the setting up of vigilance committees at district level. These committees comprise elected representatives of the area, representatives of the district administration, bar associations, press, recognized social services, and labour departments of federal and provincial governments. Their functions include advising the district administration on matters relating to the effective implementation of the law, helping in the rehabilitation of freed bonded labourers, monitoring application of the law, and providing bonded labourers with the necessary assistance to achieve the objectives of the law. The Bonded Labour System (Abolition) Rules, 1995, provide that provincial governments are to establish one or more authorities to deal with the restoration of the property of bonded labourers, and confer upon every district magistrate the power to inspect workplaces where a system of bonded labour is suspected to operate. Provincial governments are also to establish vigilance committees to enforce the Act, as well as a fund to finance programmes to assist bonded labourers. Compulsion to render bonded labour or extracting bonded labour under the bonded labour system is punishable with imprisonment from two to five years or with a fine of 50,000 rupees, or both.

Attacking child prostitution, sex tourism, sale and trafficking of children, and child pornography

Child prostitution, child pornography and the sale and trafficking of children are crimes of violence against children. They must be treated as crimes and attacked as the most serious crimes are attacked. Such repellent abuses are so far removed from any normal notion of work or labour that it seems strange to focus on them in an ILO report. Yet while they are crimes they are also forms of economic exploitation akin to forced labour and slavery. Any new international standards on the most extreme forms of child labour must therefore specifically aim at abolishing the commercial sexual exploitation of children.

The problem is as complex as it is grave. Some forms of child abuse may not have a clear or direct economic or commercial dimension. But there is undeniably a strong link between paedophilia or sexual abuse in general and the use of children to pander to these vices for commercial gain. Hence, effective action to protect children requires the concerted application, nationally and internationally, of a range of legal measures going well beyond the sphere of labour legislation.

This section describes the various approaches pursued by governments to combat the victimization of children through prostitution, sex tourism, sale and trafficking, and pornography.

The predominant approach to combating child prostitution[1] is to rely on the repressive and deterrent effect of criminal law.

In most countries of the world, criminal law seeks to protect children from prostitution, though child prostitution as such is not usually singled out as a criminal offence. General laws prohibiting prostitution will also apply to children though they do not necessarily distinguish between adult prostitution and child prostitution. It is common, however, to provide higher penalties for involving persons below given ages.

Some countries have enacted specific provisions on child prostitution or on sexual exploitation and abuse which cover prostitution. For example, Sri Lanka recently amended its Penal Code to include sexual exploitation of children and trafficking (see box). The recent law against child abuse, exploitation and discrimination in the Philippines devotes a special part to child prostitution and other sexual abuse (see box). Another example is the St. Kitts and Nevis' Child Welfare Board Act 1994 (No. 6 of 1994), which provides that "child abuse means ... and includes ... the involvement of any child in activities of a sexual nature to which they cannot give consent, including fondling, kissing, engaging in prostitution, the photographing or depiction of any

---

Republic Act No. 7610 of the Philippines

(Stronger deterrence and special protection against child abuse, exploitation and discrimination.)

Article III

Child prostitution and other sexual abuse

Sec. 5 — Children whether male or female, who for money, profit or any other consideration or due to the coercion or influence of any adult, syndicate or group, indulge in sexual intercourse or lascivious conduct, are deemed to be children exploited in prostitution and other sexual abuse.

The penalty of reclusion temporal in its medium period to reclusion perpetua shall be imposed upon the following:

(a) Those who engage in or promote, facilitate or induce child prostitution which include, but are not limited to the following:

— Acting as a procurer of child prostitute;

— Inducing a person to be a client of a child prostitute by means of written or oral advertisements or other similar means;

— Taking advantage of influence or relationship to procure a child prostitute;

— Threatening or using violence towards a child to engage him as prostitute; or

— Giving monetary consideration, goods or other pecuniary benefit to a child in prostitution.

---

child for indecent or pornographic purposes or a course of sexual conduct that causes or is likely to cause the health or welfare of the child to be harmed or threatened."

Most countries criminalize sexual relations with minors, often under 16 or 15 years of age. Some countries define the crime in terms of committing indecent acts with or corrupting minors. In Thailand, for example, the main recourse against child prostitution is to charge perpetrators with an "indecent act on a child" under age 16 whether or not the child consents. The laws of Costa Rica and Colombia criminalize the act of inducing a child under 16 into "perverted and premature sexual acts". In Costa Rica, however, this provision only protects minors who have not already become "corrupted". Offenders may also be guilty of crimes such as rape and indecent assault. The Nepalese Penal Code *(Muluki Ain)* considers intercourse with a child under 14 years of age to be rape. Similarly, in the Philippines, perpetrators are prosecuted for rape or lascivious conduct when a child exploited in prostitution is under 12 years of age.

Penal Code, Sri Lanka

Section 360B.

(1) Whoever:

— knowingly permits any child to remain in any premises, for the purposes of causing such child to be sexually abused or to participate in any form of sexual activity or in any obscene or indecent exhibition or show;

— acts as a procurer of a child for the purposes of sexual intercourse or for any form of sexual abuse;

— induces a person to be a client of a child for sexual intercourse or for any form of sexual abuse, by means of print or other media, oral advertisements or other similar means;

— takes advantage, of his influence over, or his relationship to a child, to procure such child for sexual intercourse or any form of sexual abuse;

— threatens, or uses violence towards, a child to procure such child for sexual intercourse or any form of sexual abuse;

— gives monetary consideration, goods or other benefits to a child or his parents with intent to procure such child for sexual intercourse or any form of sexual abuse;

commits the offence of "sexual exploitation of children" and shall on conviction be punished with imprisonment of either description for a term not less than five years and not exceeding 20 years and may also be punished with fine.

(2) In this section "child" means a person under 18 years of age.

The enticement of children into sexual acts, the procurement of children for prostitution and/or the drawing of economic benefit from the sexual activities involving children may also, with a varying degree of detail, be prohibited as separate crimes. One such example is Sweden where a sexual relation with a child under 15 (and with a dependant under 18) is prohibited as one type of crime. Adult prostitution *per se* is not criminalized, but the act of procuring for prostitution as well as the drawing of economic benefit from (any) sexual activities of another person is criminalized independently. Enticing anyone under 18 to have sex is also criminalized.

Comprehensive laws to protect children, inspired by the UN Convention on the Rights of the Child, are another source of law to address child prostitution and child pornography. Recently adopted children's statutes in Brazil, Mauritius, Myanmar and Nepal, as well as the comprehensive programme against sexual exploitation and abuse of children launched by the Philippines under the new law mentioned above, illustrate this trend. For example, the Children's Act 1992 of Nepal regulates the welfare of children in many areas including the exploitation of children in immoral activities (including prostitution and pornography) and work. Violations are all sanctioned with imprisonment and fines. Damages are also provided for injuries resulting from actions in contravention of the law. Further, these issues can all be heard by a juvenile court instituted under the Act.

National laws concerning child prostitution identify and pursue different groups of actors. Some countries hold parents, guardians or others with legal authority over a child, accountable for failure to supervise the activities of the children effectively. It is not usual for a child to be considered as committing a crime when engaged in prostitution but this does appear to be the case in a few countries. However, the need to distinguish between the perpetrator and the victim is increasingly being recognized. Thus, in Iceland, section 206 of the Penal Code at present provides that it is punishable by up to two years' imprisonment to engage in prostitution for one's living. A draft bill is being discussed which will focus specifically on, inter alia, child prostitution, and in which the child will be defined as a victim and not as a perpetrator.

It is general practice to criminalize two main aspects of child prostitution. One is based on using the helplessness of the child to "force" the child to engage in sexual activities (with or without economic benefit for the child), i.e. the act of luring, enticing or tricking (coercing may constitute an independent crime) a child. The other aspect is to derive economic benefit from the sexual activities of the child. Sometimes the law identifies those who derive economic benefit, while in other cases "any" person who does so may be penalized. There are wide variations in national laws along these lines, but most countries criminalize such action.

Whether accepting the sexual services offered by a child is a crime can depend on the age of the child. A number of countries prohibit the acceptance of sexual services offered by a child, and define a child as a person under the age of 18. Among the countries that have recently introduced 18 years as the age limit are Belgium, Mauritius, the Philippines, Spain, Sri Lanka and Ukraine.

In many countries the law prescribes a lower age limit than 18 on the theory that above a certain age — normally after puberty — a child is deemed to be capable of consenting to have sexual relations. In some cases, the child of that age is thus also considered as capable of voluntarily offering sexual relations. In these countries it is therefore not a crime to have sexual relations with a child or make use of sexual services offered by a child above the legally prescribed age. It is most common to define the age of consent at 16 years, although 14 and 15 are the ages in some countries. However, as mentioned above, other related acts, such as procuring or enticing into prostitution or living off proceeds from prostitution can be a separate crime no matter the age of consent, and the penalties are often higher the younger the child.

Given the importance of age in determining whether a crime has been committed, a procedurally important issue is the evidence requirements concerning the age of a child. In many countries it is a legal defence to plead that the accused had reason to believe the victim in question was above the legal age. A recent amendment in Belgian law removed the right to use such an excuse and shifted the burden of proof to the suspect, who has to demonstrate an "insurmountable error" (e.g. a false identity card used by the minor). In countries like Australia and Sweden the law states that the allegation must be reasonable under the circumstances.

In some countries the legal age for marriage may be lower than the age of consent. In these cases it is a legal defence to invoke the marriage against an allegation of sexual relations with a child below the age of consent. The recently adopted child sex tourism law in Australia provides the same, but adds the requirement that the marriage has to be a valid and genuine marriage.

While there are exceptions at both extremes, the penalties for sexual exploitation of children are quite severe and the trend is to increase them. In the Philippines a bill was filed in Congress to classify child prostitution and paedophilia as heinous crimes, which would increase the penalty from life imprisonment to death. A death penalty is also imposable in particularly grave circumstances under Chinese law. Penalties are also generally more severe where threats or violence are involved.

In addition to punishing prostitution, corruption, rape and sexual abuse of juveniles, Spain's Criminal Code increases the penalties when the guilty persons are parents, grandparents, tutors or teachers. As a result, parents or tutors can be deprived of their parental or guardianship function. Other countries which make parents, guardians or caretakers criminally liable for causing or allowing a child to engage in prostitution include the Philippines (Special Protection Act), Sri Lanka (Children and Young Persons Ordinance (1939))[2] and Uruguay (Procurement Law). In the United Kingdom the offences are aggravated if the victim is under 16 or under the care of the offender at the time.

Since child sex offenders, and in particular paedophiles, are not easily deterred from further sexual interactions with children, some countries have recently enacted laws to prohibit offenders against children from seeking or keeping employment which involves contacts with minors or provides them an opportunity to have access to children. Canadian law, for example, provides that at the time of sentencing, an order is to be considered and can be made to prohibit child sex offenders from being in places where children under age 14 congregate, or to seek or obtain employment, whether paid or as a volunteer, that involves being in a position of trust or authority towards children under age 14.

Sexual exploitation of children is a problem with international implications. Tourists who travel to engage in sexual relations with children have been observed increasingly in recent years. In view of this, an increasing number of countries have recently extended their criminal jurisdiction to cover the criminal acts of their citizens committed against children abroad and are adopting measures aimed at prohibiting the organization of travel with the intent to sexually exploit children.

One tool to combat sex tourism is to apply national criminal law to crimes committed in another country. Sex tourists from countries which do not generally extradite their nationals were able to commit crimes against children with impunity if they managed to return to their countries of origin. Extraterritorial extension of national law closes this "escape route".

The possibility of applying national criminal laws extraterritorially has existed for some time in certain countries, notably in the Scandinavian countries. Until recently, this possibility was used rather sparingly — if at all — and tended to be limited to crimes related to drug trafficking or economic crimes. Norway led the way in 1990 by applying Norwegian law to crimes committed abroad. This innovative approach encouraged a number of countries which were home to sex tourists to amend their laws to allow for extraterritorial application of criminal laws relevant to child sex tourism. These include: Germany (September 1993), France (February 1994), Australia (July 1994), United States (September 1994), Belgium (March 1995) and New Zealand (July 1995).

A common condition for applying a criminal law extraterritorially is that the crime in question also be punishable in the country where the crime is committed. The laws in Belgium and France evidence a new trend, however, in that they do not require that the act to be prosecuted under national law be punishable in the country where it was committed.

Investigating a crime in a country other than where the crime is committed can, however, be both procedurally complicated and expensive. If the act is not a crime in the country in which it is committed, law enforcement would not normally be involved. Securing evidence may also prove to be cumbersome when local police authorities cannot be relied upon. The Australian law addresses some of these concerns by providing that, under certain circumstances, courts may direct that evidence from witnesses outside Australia be given by video link. For example, this could be done if attendance of the witness at court would cause unreasonable expense or inconvenience, would cause the witness psychological harm or unreasonable distress or cause the reliability of the witness to be reduced because of intimidation or distress.

Obtaining evidence from a child or other witnesses in another country also might depend upon formal and informal mutual assistance agreements between the countries concerned, as well as cooperation between law enforcement officials. The Extradition Act and Mutual Legal Assistance in Criminal Matters Act in Thailand allow the Attorney General to provide assistance in criminal matters to foreign States. The Embassy of the Federal Republic of Germany issues verbal notes explaining the extraterritorial application of its Criminal Act. For example, it has requested the Kingdom of Thailand to inform the competent German criminal prosecution authorities about all cases of relevant criminal offences committed by German citizens, even if they already fled Thailand. The attachment of any evidence found would be helpful for the prosecution and therefore be much appreciated.

Another approach is to penalize sex tours. In the United States, under new legislation on sex tourism, a person can be prosecuted as soon as detailed plans are made for the journey; a paedophile does not have to be caught having sexual relations with a minor — a detailed travel plan and air tickets are enough to prove the existence of sex tourism. In the United Kingdom, advertising and marketing tours which offered opportunities for sexual activity with children have been officially identified as serious criminal offences under the Criminal Law Act of 1977. Information on the law was announced and circulated among travel agencies. New Zealand criminalizes the promotion and organization of child sex tours from within New Zealand.

While not specifically aimed at sex tourism, several provisions of Canada's criminal law could apply to aspects of sex tourism. The prohibition of anyone to procure, attempt to procure or solicit a person to have illicit sexual intercourse with another, whether in or out of Canada, or to procure a person to leave Canada for the purpose of prostitution would apply to tour operators and travel agents. The maximum sentence is ten years' imprisonment. Conviction of a tour operator could result in the seizure of the tour operator's enterprise as proceeds of the crime.

Cooperation and assistance among judicial and law enforcement agents is also utilized. The Government of the United Kingdom, under the Criminal Justice Act of 1990, assists law enforcement agents of foreign countries by extraditing for prosecution paedophiles suspected of committing offences abroad and the British police share information about known paedophiles with the police in other countries.

Sale and trafficking of children is dealt with by general legislation in most countries. Where particular problems have emerged there has been a tendency to adopt specific legislation to ban the sale of children.

Such legislation — the Suppression of Immoral Traffic in Women and Girls Act — was enacted by India in 1956. This was amended in 1986, and retitled the Immoral Traffic Prevention Act, to cover both sexes and increase penalties for offences involving children and minors. The Penal Code punishes both buyers and sellers of any person under the age of 18 years for the purposes of prostitution or illicit intercourse or any unlawful or immoral purpose. Specific provisions on sale and trafficking of children also exist in a number of other countries including Belgium, Brazil, Costa Rica, Cyprus, the Czech Republic, Hungary, Mauritius, Nepal, the Philippines, Rwanda and the United States. Denmark's Criminal Code focuses on the deprivation of liberty aspect of the sale of children, imposing a penalty of imprisonment for 1 to 12 years on anyone who deprives another of liberty for the purpose of gain.

There is considerable range in the severity of penalties: for example, in Brazil, five to six years in prison; in Costa Rica, eight to ten years; in Mauritius, a maximum of five years plus fines; in the Philippines, imprisonment for life; and, in the United States, a minimum of 20 years or life in prison and fines depending on the circumstances.

There are three main approaches to regulating child pornography: laws containing specific references to child pornography (found in the majority of countries); laws regulating pornography in more general terms; and laws referring to obscene or indecent publications or containing general clauses on corrupting or endangering public morals.

The definition of "child" for the purposes of regulating pornography is frequently related to the "age of consent", though there are an increasing number of countries which fix the limit at 18. In Sweden, an appellate court applied age 18 as the definition of "child", making explicit reference to the definition of child in the Convention on the Rights of the Child. Consequently, pornography depicting young persons obviously younger than 18 years of age constitutes child pornography which is illegal to distribute. In Denmark, no definition exists as regards the age of the child but the Penal Code provides that the liability to punishment of the photographer presupposes that the physical development of the photographed person corresponds to the age group under the age of 15 years, the general age of consent. In South Africa proposed legislation provides that child pornography should include publications which depict a child who "is or is depicted as being under the age of 16".

The definition of child pornography concerns both the prohibited depictions of children and the media used, but countries have taken different approaches. It is not uncommon simply to prohibit child pornography without defining the term. In some countries the criminalized types of depiction are limited to the depiction of sexual intercourse or closely related sexual behaviours. Other countries, such as the United States, include all "sexually explicit conduct".

Concerning the medium containing the image, older laws sometimes contained references to "indecent photos", but rapid technological advances, particularly in computer technology, are causing such laws to be changed. A 1994 law in the United Kingdom refers to "pseudo-photographs" such as those carried by computer.

Newer technologies also enable "constructing" child pornography from other pornographic material or even creating so called "virtual" pornography which does not rely on a depiction of a real person. Another recent disturbing trend is the use of Internet for dissemination of child pornography. Not only does it make child pornography instantly available to a global audience, but it also poses a daunting challenge for law enforcement officials who need to establish an equally functioning global net for international cooperation in this area. Only the most recently enacted laws or legal interpretations have taken these technical possibilities into consideration when defining child pornography.[3]

National laws applicable to child pornography are normally construed so as to identify different stages in the production and handling of pornography and to prohibit and penalize those responsible or involved in the different stages. It is common practice to make it a crime both to produce child pornography and to disseminate it. Commercializing such activities normally incurs higher penalties. Some countries have also criminalized possession but this is a relatively new and not yet widespread trend.

Penalties vary widely for the production, possession or dissemination of child pornography. United States legislation seems to be among the most severe, providing up to ten years' imprisonment or fines up to US$100,000. In France, as in several other countries, the penalty depends on the age of the child involved. Involvement of children aged 15-18 years old brings a maximum penalty of one year and a fine. However, for children under 15, imprisonment of up to five years is possible. In Germany, where the penalty is a minimum of six months and a maximum of five years, it is more severe if the distribution has a commercial motive but may be reduced to three months for handling child pornography for other reasons. Similarly, in the Netherlands possession is punishable by a prison sentence ranging from three months to four years, while producing for commercial purposes is punishable by six years' imprisonment. Luxembourg penalizes possession of child pornography with one year of imprisonment for children under 18, and five years for children under 15. Canadian legislation increased maximum sentences for production, sale and distribution of child pornography and possession for such purposes from two to ten years.

In addition to criminal laws, customs laws and regulations often prohibit the entry into a country of pornographic material. In Canada and the United States, for example, customs and police officers work in close cooperation to halt the trade and handling of child pornography. In the United States, the Postal Inspection Service shares responsibility with the FBI and the Customs Service to enforce child pornography laws. The Customs Service has recently announced that a Child Pornography Investigation Centre is being set up and should be operational in September or October 1996. In helping the Service attack purveyors of child pornography, it will make use of the Internet to strike against the purveyors of child pornography that use the Internet. Other countries rely mainly on customs rules: these include Australia, Ireland, Malaysia and South Africa, though Ireland, like the United States, also intervenes in distribution through the mail. In Botswana, any photographic material may be seized. A few countries mainly use censorship to repress child pornography.

An important tool for preventing and detecting crimes against children is the collection, systematizing and exchange of information. National statistics on crimes committed, categorized by age and gender and any other relevant factors, and registers of convicted offenders are of crucial importance. Internationally, the International Criminal Police Organization (Interpol) serves as a focal point for exchange of information. A concerted effort is being made to establish a register of convicted paedophiles to facilitate transparency and rapid intervention possibilities. Interpol also uses an "early warning system" to alert national authorities of the movement of known criminals, including information about the movement of paedophiles. This information is circulated to border controls, immigration and customs authorities. Focal points for national expertise and special databases also exist at the national level.

Sharing of information at the national level is equally important. In Canada, provincial and territorial governments and the police have worked to improve information sharing between authorities and NGOs to screen out known sex offenders from staff positions which involve trust of or authority over children. For example, the local police helped one NGO which worked with street children to screen out several male applicants for volunteer posts who had criminal records for procuring young girls for prostitution.

Another approach to improving the exchange of information and the detection and reporting of crimes against children is a system of liaison officers which have been set up in 64 countries. Information on training, legislation, statistics and ongoing investigations is passed on to the countries concerned and to the General Secretariat of Interpol. Training of such officers focuses on children as victims and as witnesses in investigations. Countries also post liaison officers in other countries to coordinate and facilitate investigations of crimes committed by their nationals in the other country.

Private sector initiatives have also enhanced enforcement. Information campaigns have been launched through international associations such as the Universal Federation of Travel Agents' Associations (UFTAA), the World Hotel Federation and the World Tourism Organization. These include the initiative by UFTAA in 1994 to elaborate and adopt a Child and Travel Agent Charter. Pursuant to this Charter the signatory travel agents undertake to fight against child prostitution related to sex tourism by raising awareness in the industry. To date, 60 travel agents have signed the Charter.

The breaking of child pornography rings and the effective application of extraterritorial laws also require extensive international cooperation. For example, an investigation in the Netherlands of a child pornography ring involved 15 suspects, 40 victims and three different countries over a period of 11 years. The United States postal services recently broke a major child pornography ring based in Acapulco, Mexico. At the time of reporting, 56 persons across the United States had been arrested and charged with receiving — by mail order — videotapes showing sex involving under-age boys. Thousands of videos were seized involving, according to an early estimate, some 300 children, the youngest of whom was believed to be seven years old.

The effective prosecution of defendants in their home country for crimes committed abroad often involves time-consuming procedures and relies on the goodwill and competence of foreign authorities. The difficulties are illustrated by the investigations in the first case of the extraterritorial application of Swedish criminal law. Swedish police in Thailand acted in close cooperation with the Thai police in order to detect the crime and cause the arrest of the offender. In the process of securing evidence, the victim was heard in the presence of both Thai and Swedish police. With knowledge of Swedish evidentiary requirements, the Swedish police were able to formulate questions which were submitted to the Thai police who conducted the interview with the victim. The interview was video recorded with the intention that this video recording could be used in court and the victim be spared the experience of appearing before the court in Sweden. In the end, the Swedish court found that the video recording contained certain statements which conflicted with other evidence, thus the victim had to appear before the court in Sweden. With no other possible means available for financing the travel to Sweden of the victim, an NGO paid for the ticket. The accused was finally convicted for sexual abuse of a minor, including an attempt to commit the same crime in 1995.

While informal channels are often used, special formalized procedures are required between judicial authorities. Requests for special investigation, production of evidence, release of documents and records normally have to go through diplomatic channels. Efforts are made to simplify procedures. For example, the United Nations Crime Prevention and Criminal Justice Branch has drafted a Model Treaty on Mutual Assistance which was adopted by the General Assembly in 1990. National laws can also provide for the conditions under which mutual assistance will be extended to other States in criminal matters. The law of Thailand (Act on Mutual Assistance in Criminal Matters) noted above, contains conditions under which assistance will be given to requesting States.

The Swedish aid agency, Rädda Barnen, helped to produce a card to be inserted in aeroplane tickets to Asia. One side of the card gives "the bright side" of tourism and the other "the dark side". The cards have been distributed by the Swedish Travel Agency Association. In France, the travel industry and several government ministries have joined to produce a leaflet which warns against child prostitution. More than 1 million copies have been distributed through travel agents.

The Canadian Criminal Code allows the use of electronic surveillance in investigations of child pornography. Under the legislation, a major child pornography ring was uncovered in London, Ontario. A special joint police task force was established to investigate allegations about the ring, resulting in 38 persons being charged. Another practice is to set up special toll-free telephone lines available to anyone (including, in particular, the victims themselves) to report suspected offences. The institution of ombudspersons specifically for children is yet another approach to improve investigatory methods. Originating from a Scandinavian legal tradition, ombudspersons are intended to serve as an intermediary between the individual and public authorities and normally are vested with supervisory functions over public authorities. They can have various functions such as investigating and following up on suspected violations of the rights of children. Sweden has instituted a special Children's Ombudsman specifically for these purposes. Information concerning this institution is widely spread among children mainly through campaigns at schools and day-care centres. Similar institutions have been set up in other countries.

Police officers need special expertise and sensitivity to deal with child victims. Confidentiality is one aspect. Another is ensuring that assistance is provided by those who have special expertise and can be present when the victimized child is being heard. It is vitally important to limit the trauma experienced by children in recounting their experiences to police authorities. It is also important that the evidentiary value of the child's testimony be adequately protected. In certain countries, such as in the Netherlands, special facilities have been set up specifically for this purpose, such as the immediate appointment of a curator or some other professional to assist the child through an investigation and trial. Procedures in Philippine law for dealing with victimized children include protective custody, restrictions on media and intervention of welfare authorities. In the State of Uttar Pradesh in India, some police stations have been set up with all-women staff and "rescue officers" have been posted in certain sensitive divisions to organize raids with police assistance for rescuing victims and following up court cases.

Reliable statistics on prosecutions are difficult to obtain. To the extent that reports in the press are a valid measure, more cases are being brought to trial. There are frequent reports about arrests and convictions in relation to child pornography and prostitution, and less frequently about successful actions against the sale and trafficking of children.

Notes

[1] The Special Rapporteur of the United Nations Commission on Human Rights on the Sale of Children, Child Prostitution and Child Pornography defines child prostitution as "the act of engaging or offering the services of a child to perform sexual acts for money or other consideration with that person or any other person".

[2] A person who, having the custody, charge or care of a girl under 16 years causes or encourages seduction or prostitution of such a girl or allows persons under 16 years to reside in or frequent a brothel is guilty of an offence.

[3] On 24 May 1996, two United Kingdom citizens were given prison sentences after pleading guilty to child pornography offences using the Internet computer network. The judge is reported to have ruled that images on the Internet should be treated in the same way as photographs in the eyes of the law. In the United States, the law on pornography includes reproducing, distributing or receiving prohibited visual depictions by computer.

Enforcement

5

Enforcement measures

Convention No. 138 (Article 9) and the accompanying Recommendation No. 146 (Part V) provide the international framework for enforcement of child labour laws. Convention No. 138 requires governments to take all necessary measures, including the provision of penalties, to ensure effective enforcement. It also requires employers to keep registers or other documents showing the name and ages of persons under the age of 18 who work for them. Recommendation No. 146 gives more detailed guidance such as training labour inspectors on detecting and correcting child labour abuses, focusing on hazardous work and describing measures to facilitate verification of ages.

Most national legislation contains specific measures to facilitate enforcement of minimum age and other child labour provisions, as well as machinery for enforcement. Virtually all countries have some form of labour inspection and, indeed, 118 countries have ratified the Labour Inspection Convention, 1947 (No. 81). Even so, in practice many encounter serious problems in enforcing child labour laws.

In the majority of countries the law holds the employer responsible for violations of child labour laws. However, some national legislation also explicitly holds parents or legal guardians responsible for violations concerning prohibited work or conditions. For instance, the laws of Kenya and the United Republic of Tanzania state that "any parent or guardian of a child or young person who permits such child or young person to be employed in contravention of any of the relevant provisions of the law commits an offence". Norwegian law makes any parent or guardian who allows a child or a young person to perform illegal work liable to a fine, and similar provisions are found in Belgium and Uruguay. Parents and legal guardians are more likely to be made responsible in relation to violations of compulsory schooling requirements, as in Ecuador; more recently, the Philippines has adopted a new law which places an obligation on parents or legal guardians to ensure that their children are provided with the prescribed primary and secondary education.

States have taken different approaches to record keeping. A substantial number of countries require employers to keep registers or equivalent documentation in respect of all workers employed by them, regardless of their age. In such cases, the date of birth is usually among the entries indicated in the documentation.

Many legislations, however, specifically require employers to keep records of young persons who work for them, in the form of a registry or list (Austria, Belgium, Costa Rica, Ecuador, El Salvador, Germany, Hong Kong, Japan, Republic of Korea, Lesotho, Norway, Pakistan, Peru, the Philippines, Poland, Portugal, Uruguay, Venezuela, Viet Nam, Yemen, Zaire). In some cases certain economic activities or occupations are excluded from this requirement, usually the agricultural sector. There are cases where this requirement is limited to employers of more than a specified number of workers (Mauritius) or according to duration of employment (more than two months in Finland).

In general, registers or equivalent documentation must be kept by employers at their workplace and made available for labour inspectors. The content of these registers may vary, but must usually contain name, domicile, date of birth (or the age or "apparent age", as in the case of the United Republic of Tanzania), date of commencement of work and termination, as well as the conditions and nature of employment. In some countries the law provides for an alternative recording method. In Egypt, for instance, employers must (a) notify the competent authority of the name of each young person employed; and (b) display at the entrance of the establishment a list of the young persons employed and their occupation. In China the employer must obtain a registration certificate for the young person from the competent labour department. Finally, in some countries (Pakistan, the Philippines, Portugal) the law requires the employer, in addition to keeping a register, to notify the inspector about any young employee in the establishment. It seems safe to conclude that the general trend is to conform with Convention No. 138, which requires registers and other documents concerning workers under age 18 as one measure to facilitate enforcement of child labour legislation.

While the requirement for work permits is not widespread, a good number of countries require them in a variety of activities. In some countries, such as Ecuador, Honduras, Morocco, Malta and Venezuela, permits must be obtained from the relevant authority as a prerequisite for entering employment. In Ecuador and Venezuela self-employed young persons are also required to obtain written authorization from the authorities. In Morocco the local supervisory or municipal authority issues an "employment book", containing the name, date of birth and residence of the young person; employers in commercial or industrial establishments cannot employ young workers under 16 years of age who do not have this document. In Malta workers are obliged to obtain an employment card from the competent authority, but no such card may be issued to a minor of compulsory school age except with the written permission of the Ministry of Education. Similarly, employers in Thailand must obtain a written permit from the labour inspection officer to employ a person 13 years of age by filing an application in accordance with the form prescribed. In most countries the law requires a work permit or authorization for certain activities, especially in entertainment, the film industry and television broadcasting, where the authorized working age is usually lower than for other activities (Belgium, Germany, Tunisia).

The laws in almost all countries require that children and young workers be medically examined before being employed to determine their fitness for work (Bulgaria, Cuba, Dominican Republic, Finland, Islamic Republic of Iran, Italy, Kuwait, Mexico, Nepal, Paraguay, Peru, Portugal, United States,). This requirement is sometimes applicable in general for all young workers below 18, regardless of the job. In Turkey, for instance, the Labour Code provides that before being admitted to "any employment whatsoever" children between the ages of 13 and 18 must be medically examined and that, until they have reached 18 years, they must undergo regular medical check-ups at least every six months. Germany has adopted the same approach, although the requirement does not apply to jobs of less than two months or to light work which has no adverse consequences on the young person's health. The medical certificates must be kept by the employer and produced on request of any competent labour official (Germany, Poland, Turkey). The requirement in several countries is limited to dangerous or hazardous occupations (Lebanon, Norway) or in certain occupations prescribed by law (Egypt, Tunisia).

In a few countries a medical certificate is required for children performing light work (Bulgaria, Central African Republic, Paraguay, Singapore). In some the labour administration (usually the labour inspectorate) may request a medical examination where it deems it necessary and can order the child to stop working if the examination shows that the occupation is detrimental to his or her health and development (Morocco, Tunisia). Portugal has introduced a system of free medical examinations for street vendors. Broadly speaking, the trend appears to be to include medical examinations in laws and regulations on child labour, in order to safeguard the physical, mental and moral development of minors.

In some countries the employment of children is subject to written permission by parents or legal guardians. This is the case in Viet Nam for children under the age of 15, and in Honduras for children under 16. Egypt's Labour Code provides that employers of young persons under 16 years of age must supply them with a card attesting to their employment.

In some countries the Government has taken measures to overcome the problem of determining a child's age where birth certificates and other official documents are unobtainable. In Sri Lanka it has been possible since 1981 to provide children over 16 years old with a national identity card which can be used instead of a birth certificate as proof of age. In India state governments are to be required to obtain age certificates and maintain registers of child workers.

Employers who employ young persons are often required by law to display a notice at their working place, usually at the main entrance; the notice might include abstracts or the full text of the relevant laws governing the employment of children and young workers (Germany, India, Morocco); information concerning the working conditions of young workers (Egypt, Germany); a list of their names (Egypt); and the location of the inspection office competent to supervise the working place or establishment.

Almost all countries specify penalties for violations of the legal provisions concerning the employment or work of children. The type and severity of penalties vary enormously, but generally they are in the form of money penalties only, or fines and/or imprisonment (the latter usually only in the case of repeated offences). Employers may also be penalized by revoking their licence to operate or even closing down their establishment. Finally, many countries impose fines or imprisonment on anyone who obstructs a labour inspection official in the performance of his duties (Cameroon, Viet Nam).

The laws of countries which provide for money penalties only usually establish the minimum and maximum limits. In some cases the law prescribes one specific fine for several specific violations. For instance, the Labour Code of Tunisia provides that violations of specific provisions of the Code (or of decrees or orders made pursuant to the Code), such as the prohibition of employment of children in hazardous occupations or in night work and the requirement of keeping a register and providing for medical examinations, must be sanctioned with a fine of between 500 and 2,800 dinars. The Turkish Labour Act details penalties according to the provision violated; for instance, the penalty imposed on an employer who violates the provision on young workers in prohibited or hazardous occupations is much higher than the penalty prescribed for the violation of the provision concerning medical certificates. The same is true in Cameroon. In some other countries (China, Norway, Zaire), the fine applies to all provisions or is left to the judicial or administrative authorities to determine. For repeated offences fines are generally doubled.

Imprisonment is often an additional option. In India, Japan and the Republic of Korea imprisonment is limited to specified offences, such as the employment of children in harmful and dangerous activities. Under the Labour Standards Law of the Republic of Korea, for example, employing children in any work detrimental to morality or harmful to health and in any work inside a pit is punished by imprisonment for up to three years or a fine not exceeding 20 million won.

Penalties are often cumulative for each child concerned, up to a specified sum. For example, the Federal Fair Labor Standards Act of the United States prescribes a penalty of up to US$10,000 for violation of child labour provisions for each employee who is the subject of the violation.

In addition to fines and imprisonment, various other sanctions exist. In Malta the law not only imposes a fine on an employer who employs a minor of compulsory school age without the required employment card, but also provides that the Court must, at the request of the prosecution, order the suspension or cancellation of any licence held by the offender relating to trade or business, or to any business premises where the persons are employed. Similarly, in the Philippines, in the case of repeated infringements of child labour provisions (the punishment for which may be both fines and imprisonment), the offender's licence is revoked. In Austria, if the employer is a recidivist, the administrative authorities may decide, upon recommendation by the inspector, to forbid the employer to employ young persons, on either a temporary or a permanent basis. In Côte d'Ivoire the employment authorization for the whole establishment may be revoked if it is proved that children of less than 14 years of age have been employed in activities for which they are not fit.

The United States prohibits putting goods into interstate or foreign commerce which have been produced with child labour, i.e. work by children under age 16 or work by those between the ages of 16 and 18 which is particularly hazardous or detrimental to their health or well-being.

The law in some countries explicitly provides that persons other than the competent labour inspector or authority may submit complaints (Nepal, Pakistan, the Philippines). In the Philippines they include the offended party, parents or guardians, ascendant or collateral relatives, officers, social workers or representatives of a licensed child-care institution, officers or social workers of the Department of Social Welfare and Development, or at least three concerned, responsible citizens where the violation occurred. The complaint is normally filed to the competent courts (district, magistrate or juvenile court).

Labour inspection

The State has the primary and general responsibility for enforcing provisions on child labour, which it normally does through the labour inspection system. The ILO's Labour Inspection Convention, 1947 (No. 81), specifies that among the primary duties of inspectors are the enforcement of the legal provisions relating to the employment of children and young persons. In general, labour laws contain specific clauses which give inspectors a wide range of responsibilities and which often give them a measure of discretion to decide if the conditions for employing children have been met and to authorize their work or subject it to further conditions. In many countries the labour inspectors and labour administrative authorities, are vested with the power to: (i) authorize young persons to work (Honduras); (ii) grant authorization for minors to be employed in certain activities involving light work or participation in artistic performances; (iii) request medical examinations when they deem it necessary to determine whether the work performed by young persons could be detrimental to their health or development, especially in the case of dangerous or hazardous work (Morocco); (iv) cancel an employment contract or withdraw a work permit if the work is not suitable for the child's health or physical or moral development (Croatia); and (v) enforce existing legislation during inspection visits by checking the working conditions of children and examining records of hours of work, holidays and wages and medical examinations.

Employers are often required to notify inspectors whenever they employ children or young persons or to provide them with a list of such workers. Inspectors may also be required by law to keep special registers containing the identity, date of issue of work permits and other details concerning young workers (Colombia).

Some laws or regulations include the requirement set out in Convention No. 81 that labour inspectors supply technical information and advice to employers and workers concerning the most effective means of complying with the law. The new Labour Codes of Madagascar, Nepal, Tunisia and Yemen state explicitly that inspectors are to ensure the application of the legal provisions pertaining to the employment of children and young workers, as well as supply information and advice to employers as how best to comply with the law. In the United Republic of Tanzania training has helped labour inspectors better to identify hazardous child labour situations and thus to give advice to employers before taking legal action. In the United Kingdom inspection supplemented by advice is one strategy of the labour inspectorate to reduce accidents to children in agriculture.

In some countries the education system plays an important role in the enforcement of child labour laws. In the United Kingdom, for instance, the National Health and Safety Executive is responsible for both health and safety and child employment legislation, but in non-industrial sectors the responsibility is split; local authority environmental health officials deal with health and safety matters, while education authorities enforce child employment legislation. Education authorities are empowered to go beyond national requirements concerning minimum age, hours of work and prohibited employment.

Problems and progress in enforcement

It is widely recognized that a major obstacle to effective legal protection against child labour is the weakness of enforcement mechanisms. Even countries that have progressive child labour laws commonly find it quite difficult to put them into practice. Enforcement problems are acute in the informal sector, away from main cities and in agriculture, in small businesses such as shops and hotels, in street trading, and in domestic service and home-based work. Since most working children are found in agriculture, domestic service and the informal sector, most of them work where child labour law enforcement is virtually absent. Thus, the legal tools described above have limited effectiveness in reaching much of the hazardous child work. This is true of almost all countries regardless of their level of development.

Sometimes enforcement is greatly complicated by the deficiency or complexity of the relevant laws and regulations. In Sri Lanka, for example, the law imposes so many limitations on the conditions of employment of children that it has been suggested that a total ban would be far easier to implement.

In addition, labour laws pertaining to children are found in many statutes and subsidiary regulations which are so detailed that violations cannot easily be monitored. Labour inspectors may also have difficulty determining their competencies in the face of conflicting legislation.[1]

Gaps in the law are equally detrimental to effective enforcement. Domestic work, agriculture, self-employment and the informal sector, for example, are frequently excluded from coverage of child labour laws, and thus enforcement. Even within regulated sectors there are areas, such as small workshops, that are not covered by prohibitions or regulations (Nepal). Provisions on apprenticeship can also cause problems if they are not sufficiently clear and protective of children, as apprenticeship contracts are often used to disguise exploitative and illegal forms of child labour. Sometimes, too, children are in unpaid "training positions", a problem some countries have solved by deeming a child found working in an industrial undertaking to be in employment, whether or not he or she receives wages. This method minimizes the need to establish by litigation whether an employer-employee relationship exists.

The inadequacy of penalties is another shortcoming, though it may be difficult to assess from the texts themselves. Penalties are often not well defined or are too light to serve as effective deterrents.

In an increasing number of developing countries child labour provisions are being included in new labour codes, or in special statutes and regulations (Cambodia, Cameroon, Côte d'Ivoire, Gabon, India, Republic of Korea, Laos, Lesotho, Madagascar, Malaysia, Mauritius, Myanmar, Nepal, Pakistan, Panama, the Philippines, Sao Tome and Principe). To expand coverage to excluded sectors, Ireland recently introduced legally enforceable measures in the area of agricultural safety. In the United Kingdom a code of practice was recently adopted to prevent accidents to children in agriculture; it establishes the legal duty of all the parties concerned and includes steps to ensure that areas where children are allowed to work are safe and that they are given proper instruction and supervision.

There have also been efforts to increase penalties for child labour violations in Nepal, Pakistan, Turkey and the United States. In the latter the trend among individual states is to strengthen enforcement and penalty provisions and to restrict hazardous occupations. The State of California recently increased civil penalties with a US$10,000 maximum fine for serious or wilful violations. In 1995 the State of Missouri authorized civil penalties in addition to criminal penalties,

---

Jermal operations in Indonesia

Jermals are fish traps — piles of wood implanted at the bottom of the sea with a huge fishing net attached. In the recruitment of fishermen, children are preferred to adult workers, as they are more easily managed, get low wages and work long hours.

Most of them have psychological damage caused by long isolation and separation from their families, verbal and physical abuse, and sometimes sexual abuse by the foreman or the older fisherman. Since the use of children in "jermal" operations is considered illegal, the operators usually recruit them through illegal agents, who usually operate in plantations and agricultural sites and look for poor families with children below 15 and 16 years of age. The agents may receive Rp. 8,000 to Rp. 15,000 for each recruit from the operators.

Some parents know that their children are being recruited for "jermal" operators and realize that the employment may pose serious threats to their health, safety and morals. But in most cases they have no idea how hazardous the work is, and let their children join in "jermal" operations because of their economic difficulties and the illusions created by the agents. In some cases the parents are not even informed that their children are going to work on "jermal" operations. The hazards are so great that parents usually do not let their children return after the first experience.

Source: S. Pardoen: *Children in hazardous work in the informal sector in Indonesia* (Jakarta, ILO/IPEC, 1996), pp. 38-39.

---

ranging from US$50 to US$1,000 according to the nature and gravity of the violation, with each day that a violation continues and each child illegally employed constituting separate violations. The fines collected go to a new Child Labor Enforcement Fund. The United States Department of Labor has also instituted a penalty scheme under which employers can be assessed a fine of up to US$10,000 for each violation that causes the death or serious injury of a minor; for example, where a 15-year-old is seriously injured while operating a forklift truck at a warehouse, a US$10,000 penalty could be assessed for violating the ban on minors under the age of 18 operating a forklift truck and an additional US$10,000 for violating the ban on 14- and 15-year-olds working in a warehouse. In 1994 four companies were assessed US$242,900 in money penalties which would have been about US$75,000 under the old structure.

In Indonesia and Sri Lanka the Government reports that the legislation is being changed to impose severe penalties for the child labour violations.

A major problem faced all too often is that the labour laws relevant to child labour are unknown, not only to employers and parents but also to labour inspectors. During inspection visits to small private establishments, in Poland, for example, inspectors observed many violations of the provisions requiring medical examinations as a condition for employing a young person; when interrogated, employers said that they were not aware of the requirement. This ignorance of the law is prevalent in many countries around the world. Parents, too, are often unaware of the hazards their children face at work or of the illegal nature of the work. As a result, complaints are often never made, and so the necessary investigations are not triggered.

Some employers, particularly in small undertakings, are either unaware of the legal provisions or reluctant to observe them strictly. Parents, often themselves illiterate, attach greater economic value to child work than to schooling. And labour inspectors often hesitate to enforce the law and impose sanctions because they know that the families depend on the earnings of their children or believe that child labour makes a substantial contribution to the economy of the country. There is also a common attitude that child work helps young workers develop working skills, keeps children off the streets and is a way for young people to earn pocket money.

To increase awareness of the problem of child labour, several countries have undertaken awareness-raising campaigns. In Denmark a two-day campaign was carried out by inspectors to sensitize people to the serious health and safety problems posed by dangerous work performed by young people and the laws applicable to child labour. In Austria conferences on the observance of laws on the protection of children, juveniles and apprentices are held by the labour inspectorate at two-yearly intervals; they provide a forum for discussion between representatives of employers and employees, and other bodies concerned with the issue. Other awareness-raising initiatives have been undertaken in Brazil, Indonesia, Nepal, Pakistan, the Philippines, the United Republic of Tanzania and Venezuela. In the United Kingdom providing advice and information to farmers, farm workers, parents, teachers, schools and children themselves (free leaflets, videos aimed at children, and specially designed teachers' packs) is an important part of the strategy to prevent accidents to children in agriculture; inspectors also participate in agricultural shows across the country to get the message across and as a result of such efforts and of implementation of the code of practice mentioned above, the fatality rate is reported to have

Difficulties encountered by labour inspectorates

— lack of material resources including scarce transport;

— understaffing of inspection offices;

— overwork and low pay for inspectors;

— inspectors' perception of child labour;

— lack of appropriate training on the special vulnerability of children, child labour and hazards to which children are exposed;

— powers limited by law and lack of appropriate techniques;

— lack of motivation;

— hostile environment;

— lack of cooperation and support from other government agencies, including the education system;

— clandestine nature of child work.

been reduced from approximately 25 per year in the mid-1980s to less than ten a year in 1994.

A simple example of how creating awareness of the hazards of child labour can lead to significant change of attitudes by parents, is an initiative in Istanbul, Turkey. A group of mothers were invited to visit the workplace and observe the dangers to which their children were exposed. Following the visit, most mothers decided to withdraw them from the work.

Effective enforcement of child labour legislation suffers from inadequate labour inspection in most countries, especially those with the worst child labour problems. Child labour law violations are usually detected in the course of routine inspections, or during interventions made on the basis of complaints received. Although inspection was originally intended to deal specifically with child labour, it has over time taken on so many other functions that child labour concerns today occupy only a small portion of an inspector's duties. Numerous other factors impede the ability of inspectorates to live up to their mandate.

In most countries in Africa, Latin America and South-East Asia a common complaint by inspectors is poor working conditions. For example, the lack of sufficient staff creates overwork and frustration. A not untypical example is Indonesia, where 800 inspectors are expected to cover all of Indonesia's registered enterprises (over 4,000 enterprises for each inspector per year). Difficulties in applying the law in Sri Lanka have likewise been attributed to the shortage of labour inspectors. It is often stated that child labour infringements cannot be the inspectors' priority, as their time is also or primarily devoted to investigating compliance with labour laws in general, administrative matters, settling labour disputes and the like. In some European countries labour inspectors have been assigned the additional task of checking on illegal employment of foreigners and migrant workers. Inspectors in Austria have complained that such additional duties could interfere with the effective discharge of their primary duties. In addition, many countries do not have labour inspectors specialized in child labour matters. For example, it is reported that in Costa Rica, El Salvador, Guatemala and Panama there are few labour inspectors and none of them specialize in such issues.

Another problem is lack of transportation to reach and inspect establishments outside cities, which makes it virtually impossible to monitor agricultural areas — still the largest single sector in which children work and one in which major hazards and bonded labour are common. In Malawi, due to inadequate funds, transportation is provided only to regional offices and to inspectors in the field on a rotation basis. Inspectors are encouraged to buy their own vehicles and to seek reimbursement for their travelling and incidental expenses (food and accommodation) related to inspection visits.

Inspectors may also be restricted by the law itself. For instance, many laws do not reach the informal sector, where young people are employed mostly under verbal contracts or by subcontractors. In addition, inspection techniques that are used in the formal and industrial sector tend to be ill-suited to the informal and agricultural sectors. Some employers resort to various subterfuges to hide illegal child labour or are inaccessible to inspectors because their enterprises are not officially registered. Some of the most exploitative and hazardous conditions exist precisely in unregistered sweatshops and workplaces. Moreover, it happens that inspectors are not empowered to search certain workplaces, such as private households, or to intervene outside prescribed times or without giving previous warning to the employer; in order to do so they may need a search warrant from the police.

Lack of motivation on the part of inspectors also may result from low salaries and insufficient recognition of their work by the authorities supervising them. Inspectors are often subject to direct or indirect pressure from other authorities (administrative, judicial and political) not to carry out inspections targeting child labour, or not to pursue prosecutions. In some countries, corruption also contributes to lax enforcement.

Labour inspection for vulnerable groups

In one African country visits were carried out with the local inspector to a large goldmine employing 350 people. No children were found in the deep galleries 300 metres below the ground where excavation machinery was in operation. However, no inspector has ever visited the nearby open-cast gold-mining areas where 100,000 people live and work. Here there are excavations 80 metres deep which give access to the galleries without any safe means of access. Children are lowered down narrow shafts on ropes and bring up the ore in sacks. These children are fed by the landowner and are only paid if they actually find gold.

On another site the shafts are side by side and children have to descend 30 metres into the galleries where they are 40 or 50 metres from fresh air.

The inspectors claimed that they were unable to deal with this situation as there were no contracts of employment within these family groups. In fact, when more detailed inquiries were made, it emerged that women and children rent their services to the landowner and are paid a fixed rate. They are in fact salaried workers but in this informal sector labour inspectors have never sought to intervene. After this visit, however, they decided to spend a whole week examining the mining system on this site in order to understand better the problems.

Source: International Technical Symposium on Labour Inspection Strategies for Vulnerable Groups, Tunis, 19-20 May 1994.

While real improvements have been slow, there has been growing awareness of the problems facing inspectors in detecting illegal child labour and the beginning of some positive initiatives in enforcing the law.

In some countries, one or more inspectors have been designated to deal mainly or exclusively with monitoring child labour. In Austria, every labour inspection office must have one labour inspector for the protection of children and young persons, whose main task is to ensure the observance of the relevant child labour provisions. Recent measures have been taken to strengthen the staff of inspectors' offices and increase the number of inspectors in Bolivia, the Dominican Republic, Japan and Sri Lanka.

In Brazil a legal provision has been repealed under which enterprises with fewer than ten workers were not subject to inspection. The Government is also endeavouring to modernize labour inspection services by increasing the number of inspectors, improving working conditions and equipment, including mobile units to reach outlying areas, and raising wages. In addition, 150 labour inspectors operate under state commissions created in each federal state to carry out inspections in the areas of highest concentration of child labour. Finally, an executive group for the repression of forced labour has been established and priority is being given to the inspection of forced labour and work by children and young persons.

There have been several reported increases in the number of inspections carried out to detect child labour violations. In Pakistan, for instance, 6,803 inspections were carried out between January 1995 and March 1996, 2,531 cases of child labour were registered and 774 convictions with fines were assessed. In Spain the number of inspections involving child labour increased between 1990 and 1992, and the number of offences against minors decreased. Positive initiatives have been undertaken in Kenya with IPEC support. One hundred and eighty inspectors have had specialized training in child labour, and intensified inspections have led to 2,982 inspections; 8,074 children under 15 years of age were found working illegally in enterprises. Five cases were filed for prosecution, with two convictions. Moreover, approximately 800 complaints were received by inspectors. Community involvement in child labour issues was also enhanced, as well as collaboration and networking between the inspectorate and other agencies dealing with child labour and children's issues in general. Prior to these efforts, child labour inspections did not exist in practice.

In Pakistan, apart from the increased number of inspections mentioned above, the Ministry of Labour has taken steps to develop a systematic training programme for labour inspectors based on ILO methodology. In the Philippines, since 1993, a number of monitoring operations aimed at taking children away from exploitative work have been successful and some offenders are being prosecuted. The Government is making efforts to increase the number of inspectors and has held special training courses in line with the Government's intensified campaign against child labour. Moreover, the Department of Labour and Employment issued an administrative order in 1993 directing the inspectorate to give special priority to the inspection of establishments employing child workers.

In the United Republic of Tanzania inspections have been undertaken on a more regular basis by inspectors, especially in respect of child labour in hazardous situations; some employers have reportedly stopped employing children, while others have opted to provide them with safe work. The Government of Sri Lanka launched a large-scale campaign to combat child labour in 1992, as a result of which the Department of Protection and Child-Care Services received 1,290 complaints; 50 persons were investigated, and others were still under investigation.

The Turkish Government has been supported by ILO/IPEC for several years in its efforts to improve labour inspection in the field of child labour protection. Several training courses have taken place to sensitize inspectors about child labour problems; 60 out of 750 inspectors have been trained, and a core group of six or seven have become specialists in child labour. The Ministry of Labour in Nepal recently opened a special section to enforce provisions on minimum age for to employment in the carpet industry and on the compulsory issuing of labels stating that the product is "child labour free".

Special campaigns have also been carried out in the United States to enhance enforcement. Four nationwide sweeps, named Operation Child Watch, were carried out in 1990. The strike force of 500 investigators found more than 29,000 child labour violations.

In the majority of countries examined, the number of prosecutions for child labour law violations is low. Even lower is the number of cases actually tried in courts.

The registration of child labour complaints and prosecution of violators are sometimes so complicated that they are virtually inaccessible to children and their families, thus limiting the opportunities for enforcement. The administrative and court procedures, too, can be so intimidating that they discourage poor and uneducated victims from filing complaints. This situation tends to favour the employers over the employees, because of their economic power, the greater sophistication and their easier access to lawyers and other assistance.

Children's families are further discouraged from filing complaints by the feeling among employers and in the court itself that children benefit more by receiving a settlement than by having the employer fined. Even during the proceedings, it happens that parents or children's representatives decide to drop the charges or fail to appear in court. Sometimes, loopholes and shortcomings in the law prevent cases from being tried properly. It also happens that, because of the time and expense of litigation, cases are often settled by negotiation.

Remedial action is further hampered by the frequent uncertainty as to which public authorities are competent to assess and sanction child labour law violations, or by the split jurisdiction of the courts. In Sri Lanka, for instance, juvenile courts, labour courts and criminal courts are all competent in child labour matters. Finally, the authorities may simply not be aware of the extent of illegal child labour because they do not have

Enforcement of legislation against child bondage

Enforcement is a major problem in almost all countries of the Asian region. There are several reasons for this:

— the informality and invisibility of bonded labour and the difficulty of reaching children in bondage;

— the long delay between identification, prosecution and release;

— the inadequacy of financial resources for inspection and enforcement, and the lack of coordination among concerned agencies;

— the lack of cooperation from employers and, in some cases, the bonded child workers and parents themselves who, because the practice is illegal, may collaborate in concealing the problem;

— public apathy.

A comprehensive national programme aimed at effective enforcement will include the following components:

— establishment of a mechanism — a national authority or task force — especially mandated to promote, facilitate and ensure effective enforcement;

— strengthening the judiciary;

— imposition of penalties to deter violations of national law; adverse publicity of convicted violators;

— provision of free legal aid;

— conducting an aggressive public awareness campaign;

— extensive training and information dissemination activities such as seminars, workshops and conferences for all concerned groups, including the judiciary, religious groups and parliamentarians;

— provision of rehabilitation and counselling services.

Source: ILO: *A programme of action against child bondage* (Geneva, 1992), pp. 7-9.

the resources to investigate and pursue cases of potential illegal employment. This was demonstrated by a recent survey carried out in the United Kingdom by the Labour Research Department and covering over 100 local educational authorities. The survey found that in the whole of 1994 there were only eight prosecutions in the United Kingdom for infringement of the by-laws covering child employment. Many of the local educational authorities which responded to the survey indicated that they lacked the necessary resources for dealing with child labour. The local councils which could afford full-time child employment officers stated that a major obstacle was the vast number of children not registered for employment with the authorities.[2]

Political will is necessary to improve enforcement

The problem of accessibility is real and much more difficult to deal with than expected. Making the children who work in hazardous conditions "visible" is feasible, but there is a big difference between identifying a few cases of child labour exploitation for the purpose of exposing the problem and dealing with the problem in a systematic way.

The recent efforts with labour inspectorates in Indonesia, Philippines and Thailand, where labour inspectors have been trained on how to target the most abusive cases of child labour, have not yet yielded impressive results. Apart from the difficulties encountered in identifying the children working in exploitative and hazardous conditions there is also the problem of "real political will". Although labour inspectors may have been convinced of the usefulness of their work, they have no control over the political and social environment in which they operate. It is hard for them to single out child labour abuses in workplaces where other labour regulations are being ignored. During the training courses conducted by IPEC for labour inspectors, it transpired that labour inspectors were frustrated because, on the one hand, they were asked to enforce the rules while on the other hand the underlying message was not to disrupt the economy.

Source: ILO, Regional Office for Asia and the Pacific.

And then there is the special problem of bonded labour. While almost all countries have legal provisions against bonded labour, enforcement is particularly difficult because of its clandestine nature. This has been a concern of the ILO supervisory bodies which, in examining the application of Convention No. 29, have on many occasions raised doubts about effective enforcement measures to eliminate child bonded labour. Most cases of child bonded labour occur in very remote areas where monitoring by inspectors and law enforcement officers is difficult. As noted above, inspection units are understaffed and ill-equipped. Many smaller operations escape the scrutiny of inspection, either because they do not come under the existing regulations or because they are not registered. Public apathy and the presence of powerful vested interests are also major obstacles.

Action to eliminate child bonded labour requires renewed political commitment, effective and comprehensive national policies, legislative reform, enforcement, systems of compulsory and free education, community mobilization and information campaigns,[3] as was pointed out at the ILO Asian Regional Seminar on Children in Bondage held in Pakistan in November 1992, attended by representatives of Bangladesh,

India, Nepal, Pakistan, Sri Lanka and Thailand. An assessment of recent efforts to improve enforcement in Asia is given in the box on page 96.

For all this, we should not forget that progress is being made. Articulating the obstacles and frustration faced by labour inspectors helps governments to become more aware of the problem and to believe that remedial action is both necessary and possible.

Notes

[1] A. Bequele and W. E. Meyers: *First things first in child labour: Eliminating work detrimental to children* (Geneva, ILO, 1995); and IPEC report on Child Domestic Work in Indonesia, p. 12.

[2] "Hard labour for Britain's kids", in *Labour Research*, Nov. 1995, p. 11.

[3] IPEC: *A programme of action against child bondage* (Geneva, ILO, 1992).

Practical action

6

Introduction

A major development in the field of child labour in recent years is the reorientation of public policy along comprehensive and pragmatic lines and the search by policy-makers and practitioners in government and non-governmental organizations for new and practical ways to protect working children. The 1990s have also witnessed an increase in the number of countries adopting national policies and programmes. These have formed the basis for mobilizing broad public support as well as for developing the institutional framework and capacity to carry out research and data collection, awareness raising, training, and legislative reform, and to identify target populations and strategic action programmes. An almost unparalleled number and variety of programmes are also being carried out, especially by non-governmental organizations.

National policy and strategies: Elements and processes

A clear national policy against the exploitation of children is the fundamental basis and point of departure for governmental action to suppress hazardous child work. Several countries, for example Bangladesh, India, Indonesia, Nepal, the Philippines, the United Republic of Tanzania, Thailand and Turkey, have adopted national policies and programmes of action, most of them in the last three years. The key features of most national programmes are diagnostic analysis through data collection and research, identifying priority occupations and sectors for action, raising public awareness, developing institutional capacity, mobilizing support, and improving educational, social and health services for the benefit of poor families and their children.

International Programme on the Elimination of Child Labour

The ILO's International Programme on the Elimination of Child Labour (IPEC) has been assisting countries in elaborating and implementing comprehensive policies and targeted programmes and projects. The Programme started in 1992, thanks to the financial support of the Government of Germany. Initially it focused on six countries but it is now operational in more than 25. The number of donors has expanded to include Australia, Belgium, Canada, France, Luxembourg, Norway, Spain and the United States.

IPEC provides support to countries in developing their capacity to appraise the nature and extent of child labour, identify priority target groups, and develop and implement policies and programmes which aim at the elimination of child labour. Participating countries sign a Memorandum of Understanding (MOU) with the ILO, under which national steering committees are established. Countries which have signed MOUs include Bangladesh, Bolivia, Brazil, Chile, Costa Rica, Egypt, El Salvador, Guatemala, India, Indonesia, Kenya, Nepal, Nicaragua, Pakistan, Panama, the Philippines, the United Republic of Tanzania, Thailand and Turkey. In addition, preparatory work to the signing of MOUs is in progress in Argentina, Benin, Burkina Faso, Cameroon, Colombia, Ecuador, Ethiopia, Peru, Senegal, Sri Lanka, Uganda, Venezuela, Zambia and Zimbabwe. The types of programmes supported by IPEC vary from one country to another, depending on the national situation and the most pressing needs identified by the countries themselves. Within its overall strategy to eliminate child labour, IPEC places emphasis on children at greatest risk.

The special merit of a national policy lies in the fact that it articulates societal objectives and commitment and, if pursued faithfully, provides a coherent framework for an associated programme of action. Such a national policy and programme of action can stand on its own or comprise part of a more comprehensive policy; in either case a complete and implementable national policy and programme of action will contain at least the following elements:

— a definition of national objectives regarding child labour;
— a description of the nature and context of the problem;
— identification of the priority target groups;
— a description of the priority target groups;
— a description of the intervention approaches to be used;
— designation of the institutional actors to be involved.

Many countries have incorporated child labour concerns as part of a broad effort to promote the general welfare and rights of children, or in the framework of their obligation under the United Nations Convention on the Rights of the Child. For example, in Brazil action on child labour at the national, state and local levels has developed as part of the structures set up to defend the rights of the child and adolescents. In the Philippines the objective of eliminating child labour in hazardous work and protecting and rehabilitating abused and exploited children is included in the Philippine Plan of Action for Children adopted in 1990. Other countries have included child labour as an important element in their overall development plan because of the close links between child labour, poverty and unemployment. For example, the sixth five-year plan for 1994-99 in Indonesia clearly states that work by children under the age of 14 will gradually be prohibited so that they can enter the nine-year basic education system. It also indicates the need to set up an effective integrated protection and control system to regulate child labour.

Detailed and reliable data on the nature and magnitude of the child labour problem is essential, particularly for the setting of priorities and for the successful implementation of national programmes. The ILO has developed two instruments to assist countries to improve their information base on child labour: a statistical survey methodology and a rapid assessment technique.

The survey methodology was developed to enable countries to obtain benchmark statistics on children's work in general or to produce statistics on specific core variables. It was tested in Ghana, Indonesia, India and Senegal and has been used as part of an ongoing national survey programme in the Philippines and Turkey. In Pakistan it has been used as a free-standing survey. Bangladesh, Nepal, Indonesia and Thailand are also using the methodology.

The rapid assessment technique was designed to enable organizations to obtain qualitative and quantitative information about child labour problems quickly for the development of action programmes. It also helps locate agencies which can be mobilized in specific areas. The methodology has been tested in Bangladesh and Pakistan.

The setting up or improvement of a systematic information base can be especially useful as a launching pad for determining priorities for action to eliminate child labour. Many countries are increasingly adopting an approach which begins with particularly hazardous occupations and situations and provides for rapid and direct intervention to remove and rehabilitate working children (see box overleaf).

While the process of developing national policies to combat child labour usually begins by collecting and compiling sound information, it

---

Priority areas for action in national plans

Nepal: Children who are:
— working in hazardous and abusive work
— in prostitution
— in bonded labour
— girls

Thailand: Children who are:
— under 13 years old
— working in hazardous working conditions
— working in illegal establishments
— under confinement
— in work which is physically and/or sexually abusive

India: Children who are:
— working in hazardous employment, such as in the production of glass, brass, locks, gems, matches, fireworks, slates, tiles, carpets and bidis (cigarettes)

Philippines: Children who are:
— victims of trafficking
— working in mining and quarrying
— working in home-based industries, especially under subcontracting arrangements
— trapped in prostitution
— working on sugar-cane plantations
— working on vegetable farms
— engaged in pyrotechnics production
— engaged in deep-sea diving

Indonesia: Children who are:
— scavengers in dump sites
— working in sea-fishing
— working on jermals (offshore fishing)
— working in deep-sea pearl diving
— working as street hawkers

Kenya: Children who are:
— in domestic service
— working in the service sector
— working in commercial agriculture
— working in quarrying and mining
— working in the tourist sector
— working in the informal sector

Source: IPEC.

---

is often accompanied by an offer to the social partners of a forum to reflect on the strengths and weaknesses of existing policies and programmes. In Bangladesh, Indonesia, Kenya, the Philippines, Thailand and Turkey national seminars or conferences led to the adoption of national programmes of action, which go beyond a statement of intent and set out strategies to combat child labour. National conferences were also organized in Argentina, Ecuador, Peru, Senegal, Venezuela and Zimbabwe, all of which led to the development of guidelines for action.

The vast and complex nature of the child labour problem implies the need for country approaches. It also requires a multi-pronged strategy, encompassing not only legislation and enforcement but also action in such areas as income and employment, education, welfare and advocacy of children's rights. There is a clear evolution of public policy in many countries along these lines. It is also becoming evident that policy formulation has to go beyond the general level. It can be effective only if it is accompanied by direct practical action focused on child labour in specific industries, areas or occupations characterized by a high incidence of child workers or by extreme forms of exploitation and abusive practices. Here, again, there is now a wealth of evidence and information on different types of initiatives at the national and local level, providing vital basic services and protection to working children at low cost, involving communities, and even helping child workers themselves mount advocacy campaigns and enhance their social and economic well-being.

Action against child labour should not be taken as a technocratic or bureaucratic exercise. Child labour touches on the livelihood and survival of many millions of families and communities as well as the comfort and prosperity of others. It inspires conflicting feelings and reactions and these are best resolved if regulatory action is complemented by dialogue, education and information-sharing among all concerned. Hence the importance of public awareness-raising efforts in the prevention and elimination of child labour. Most action programmes contain an awareness-raising component to sensitize the media and society at large to the problem. Highlighting specific types of child labour and pointing to the consequences are steps in the right direction. If society as a whole recognizes that child labour is a problem, the stage has been set to stigmatize and then eradicate its most abusive manifestations. Government policy, especially the enforcement of national laws, requires public backing and the involvement of the non-governmental sector. Assistance should therefore be given to organizations and programmes which provide information on children's rights to all groups, including parliamentarians, the judiciary and the police.

Strengthening institutional capacity

Designing and implementing a programme of action against child labour requires the strengthening of institutional capacity within government to: (i) set priorities; (ii) promote and coordinate the activities of concerned ministries and other governmental institutions; (iii) encourage the participation of the private sector and ensure that measures taken by the public and private sectors complement each other; and (iv) support pilot schemes at the local level. In many countries that capacity does not exist, and its strengthening is being given increased attention. A number of countries, for example Colombia, Thailand and Turkey, have established specialized bodies within government to supervise and implement action on child labour. In Turkey, a Child Labour Unit was established in 1992 in the Ministry of Labour and Social Security to coordinate child labour activities, develop new concepts and strategies and improve national legislation. Its programme includes the strengthening of the capability of the Ministry, local government bodies, employers' and workers' organizations and other NGOs to deal effectively with child labour. High-level committees consisting of government representatives, employers' and workers' organizations, NGOs and academics have also been set up in Colombia and Thailand to assist in policy formulation and programme implementation.

Employers' and workers' organizations have established specialized units with responsibility to address child labour issues and sensitize their members. The Federation of Kenya Employers (FKE) has set up a Child Labour Unit which carries out research on hazardous conditions for child workers on sugar, coffee and rice plantations and sensitizes employers to improve working conditions and to reduce reliance on child labour. The Central Organization of Trade Unions (COTU) in Kenya has also set up a Child Labour Section which has conducted a survey on child labour practices and integrated child labour issues into COTU's regular educational programmes. COTU is expanding into fields such as the registration of child workers and the management of children's contractual arrangements and obligations, including terms and conditions of work, education and training needs. The Confederation of Turkish Trade Unions (TÜRK-IS), too, has established a Child Labour Bureau to advance the social protection of child labourers and promote awareness among its affiliates.

Improving legislation and enforcement

Assistance in the revision and development of national legislation and drafting rules or by-laws to facilitate the implementation of national legislation has been a major and traditional aspect of the ILO's work over the years. This has been reinforced in recent years with intensified assistance by IPEC to interested governments. There is considerable resistance in many countries to the application of national labour legislation and limited capacity to enforce it. This is in part related to the very small number of labour inspectors to do the job. In addition, the labour inspectorate often lacks the material infrastructure, such as transport to visit the areas or the many small enterprises where child labour is prevalent and to carry out its responsibility.

The labour inspectorate can be a powerful tool in government efforts to suppress child labour, especially its worst forms. Labour inspectors are often the only ones who can gain access to child workers in (hidden) workplaces where others such as NGOs are not allowed. In many countries where there has been joint action between labour inspectors, the media and NGOs in the detection and surveillance of child labour, such cooperation has brought intolerable situations into the open. The ILO has developed a comprehensive training package for labour inspectors, which was field-tested in Indonesia and Turkey and is now being adapted for use in other countries. This package provides guidance on how the labour inspectorate — even with a limited budget — can detect and address the most pressing child labour problems.

Education and economic support

In addition to protective labour legislation for children, affordable education of good quality and which is relevant to the needs of children and their families will ultimately be the most effective instrument for the elimination of child labour. School attendance has a major effect on eliminating child labour in hazardous work. At the very least, it should reduce excess hours of work among children and go a long way to eliminating child labour in hazardous industries where workers need to be at the worksite for a full shift. Schooling has, moreover, a number of other positive effects that help reduce child labour over the longer run. Educated persons are more aware of their rights and so less likely to accept hazardous working conditions; educated persons make more informed and active citizens; educated persons (especially women) have fewer, better educated and healthier children when they themselves become adults, and these smaller family sizes and educational expectations should reduce child labour in future generations; and educated persons are more productive workers and so help increase economic growth rates and wealth. Factors such as these are why economists and others stress the high social return to education and how it exceeds the private return to education. This divergence between social and private returns to education is especially large for poor families for whom immediate survival is such a pressing concern that they have difficulty fully taking into consideration the long-term benefits of education.

The relation between education and child work is complex, and seemingly obvious solutions may not always work. In some cases apparent solutions may have a perverse effect. Shortcomings in the public education system can and do actually encourage the flow of children into the workplace. At the very least, schools must be available, accessible and affordable (and as far as possible free).

But simply making schools available will not be sufficient to eliminate child labour for poor families. Policies and programmes that provide income replacement and economic incentives have therefore come to the fore in recent times in order to address the poverty issues and the need for poor children to earn income. This strategy of using economic incentives is in keeping with the spirit of the times to consider incentives rather than sanctions as the means for eliminating bad practices.

Since the effectiveness and problems of this approach are not well documented, the ILO recently undertook a survey of NGOs. Results of this inquiry[1] into 51 organizations, almost all NGOs, from 18 countries indicate that the use of economic incentives to eliminate child labour is a relatively recent approach; it includes various in-kind payments to encourage school attendance (such as free school lunches, books, clothes, waiving of fees, etc.); earmarked cash stipends, such as for school attendance; unearmarked cash income payments; apprenticeships and other school/work combinations; income-generating activities for parents; and community development programmes for backward areas. NGOs are generally positive about economic incentive programmes, feeling that they are necessary in situations of poverty. NGOs also feel that economic incentives are more likely to be effective when they are combined with other activities into a comprehensive approach which also includes, for example, awareness raising, improving the quality and availability of schools and community involvement.

At the same time, NGOs indicate that there are a number of practical and conceptual difficulties in effectively implementing economic incentive programmes. These include possible problems of corruption and cheating; the possibility of creating a dependency on the programme; the unattractiveness of schools because of the irrelevance of the school curriculum for poor families; the possibility that children may go to work in order to qualify for an incentive programme; the possibility that adult household members may reduce their own work efforts; and the problem of sustainability, with the risk of children simply going back to work when the incentive stops. Despite these and other problems, NGOs are positive about such programmes. None the less, because of their costliness and the fact that children go back to work when payments are withdrawn, the general feeling is that income replacement programmes are best suited to rehabilitation than to the prevention of child labour, and are best implemented as one element in a comprehensive approach. This is a significant conclusion, considering the need to remove children immediately from hazardous work and rehabilitate them.

NGOs also stress the importance of information and data collection to help in targeting, programme design, monitoring and evaluation; yet efforts in this regard have been poor to date, as indicated by the fact that none of the NGOs involved in the ILO survey knew of a systematic impact assessment study which investigates the longer- or shorter-term impact of such programmes on child labour.

In short, programmes which provide stipends face a dilemma. They can absorb a never-ending stream of funds, but they may sometimes be absolutely necessary and may well be the only way to break the vicious circle. The available evidence suggests prudence and the need to ensure that they are tailored to specific situations and needs.

Rehabilitation

A child's withdrawal from work should be accompanied by a whole range of supportive measures. This is especially important if children have been stunted in their development because they were bonded, have worked practically since they were toddlers, have been prostituted or have been living and working on the streets without their families or without any stable social environment. In addition to education, training, health services and nutrition, these children need to be provided with intensive counselling, a safe environment and often legal aid. To this end, a number of action programmes for these children have set up drop-in centres where they can stay and recuperate.

The evidence has shown that these children need a range of professional services, from social workers and family or child therapists to psychiatrists. Volunteers or community workers also play an important part, but their work is very taxing. There is a very high turnover of field workers, and therefore they need special training and guidance. Cooperation with the police is often required, too, so that "rehabilitated" children are not stigmatized or persecuted. Agencies have also tried with some success to reunite children with their families. In such cases, support has to be extended to the families as well. Comprehensive rehabilitation measures are badly needed and should be provided even if their cost is very high.

Examples of projects to assist children in forced and hazardous work

National policies and programmes of action on child labour are normally implemented through specific projects. Projects are the building blocks of programmes and are limited in scope and time (see boxes). A project may work with one target group in a particular sector using one or a limited range of interventions over a period of two or three years or may address a wide variety of concerns. The target groups may include children engaged in rural work, tanneries, automobile workshops, carpet-making and construction; sexually abused children; migrant children; children in domestic service; or bonded and trafficked children.

Projects also vary in terms of the types of activity they undertake. Some provide a range of welfare services such as nutrition and health care, while others provide skill training, carry out advocacy campaigns, and support the strengthening of organizational capacity. Projects also differ in objectives. Some are quick-action projects aimed at redressing a specific situation such as removing bonded labour from a specific employer and rehabilitating them; others have more long-term objectives such as removing child labour from a whole industry.

International cooperation

As pointed out in earlier chapters of this report, there has in recent years been increased attention to the problem of child labour in various

Child workers on the streets of Ankara

The city authorities have come to the aid of child workers on the streets of Ankara, Turkey, by creating a local centre in which they find sympathetic social support and receive nutrition, health aid, education and personal care. This is backed by a mobile unit of specialists equipped to follow the children into their working environment.

Nearly 100 children have been placed in jobs linked to formal apprenticeship schools. Some of them benefit from vocational training provided at the centre. Shoeshiners have been moved from the hazards of the open streets to work in the protected locations of public buildings, hospitals and business centres. The police are cooperating by adopting a more understanding approach with the youngsters and ensuring their security in the workplace.

For the first time in Turkey, field research has been done to assess the response of the children to the programme. In the process, many other groups of child workers on the streets — including 9-year-old girls working as car-washers and street vendors — have been identified as desperately needing protection.

The programme is ripe for replication. Other district municipalities have asked to implement a similar operation and other major cities are interested in following suit.

Source: IPEC.

international fora. The work of UNICEF and the United Nations Commission on Human Rights are well known and do not need elaboration. Regional intergovernmental organizations have also addressed aspects of the problem, such as the adoption by the Committee of Ministers of the Council of Europe of Recommendation No. R(91)11, 1991, concerning sexual exploitation, pornography and prostitution of, and trafficking in, children and young adults.

The International Confederation of Free Trade Unions (ICFTU), one of the very early campaigners against child labour, launched a global campaign for the elimination of child labour in 1994 and continues to be active in advocacy and research on behalf of working children.[2] An important development among the ILO's social partners is the emerging interest of international employers' organizations in child labour. The General Council of the International Organization of Employers (IOE) passed a resolution in June 1996 on child labour which makes a number of basic recommendations to employers and their organizations. The resolution calls, inter alia, for putting an immediate end to slave-like, bonded and dangerous forms of child labour, and for developing action plans at the international, national, industry and enterprise levels. It calls

---

Trade unions foster a new harvest: Brazil

Learning the secrets and good practice of horticulture has replaced the heavy and hazardous work of many children in a fruit-producing region between the states of Pernambuco and Bahia, in Brazil. Rescue and education came from a workers' organization, the Rural Workers' Union of Petrolina.

Constantly exposed to the most dangerous kinds of agrochemicals, the children had been working to increase the output of their families, who worked for big companies. They were unable to attend school, and those from the poorest families lacked even the most basic health care and nutrition. The trade unions conceived a scheme to provide the children with non-formal education and to train them in skills that would help them find better jobs in the future. A garden school was thus a welcome addition to the non-formal education centre which prepared the children to join the public school system. Music and drama are woven into this combination of non-formal education and skills training. As a means of expressing both their feelings and their creativity, they boost the children's self-confidence and stimulate their intellect. Handicrafts also allow them to express themselves and discover their aptitudes.

The two communities involved supported the programme by donating land for the horticultural training sessions and by building the non-formal education centre. As the scheme progressed and succeeded in withdrawing children from work and enrolling them in schools, it also attracted the interest of the media. Local television channels and radio stations featured the activities in their programmes. The local press soon joined them in publicizing the scheme.

An example of the success of the programme is the fact that 80 children, all of whom had been targeted by the programme, were all enrolled in schools. There is a need now to find out, as precisely as possible, to what extent and in what conditions child labour is expanding in the region in order to plan preventive action.

Source: IPEC.

---

on the Executive Committee to follow up the resolution with a proactive programme of work by the IOE.

There are many other less known organizations which were active in the child labour area but whose work is of fundamental significance to the campaign against child labour. For example, the main actors in the tourist trade, such as tourist agencies, hotels and air carriers, are beginning to take direct action to fight against sex tourism. The Universal Federation of Travel Agents' Associations (UFTAA) adopted in December 1994 a Child and Travel Agent Charter, committing itself to the fight against child sex tourism. Further, in August 1996, in Stockholm, the World Tourism Organization (WTO) announced that it

---

Thailand, 1992-97 — Action at the community level

Preventing the commercial sexual exploitation of children

Many countries in Asia and Latin America have projects focusing on preventive strategies against the commercial sexual exploitation of children. Prevention of prostitution requires different types of action at many levels: effective awareness-raising programmes on the risks of prostitution or trafficking; access to education and training, occupational opportunities and economic alternatives for the children and/or their families; and mobilization at the community, district, provincial and national levels. This is an area where the IPEC programme has given top priority for support in every country and the results have been promising.

IPEC has been supporting a preventive programme run by the Daughters' Education Programme (DEP) in the north of Thailand. The DEP is located in an area where there is a high incidence of trafficking of girls within the country as well as across the Thai borders. It implements a series of activities at the local level in order to prevent young village girls from being tricked into prostitution. Girls who are at extremely high risk of being sent into prostitution are given temporary shelter and are enrolled in education programmes. Such girls usually come from families of former prostitutes, drug addicts and broken homes, or from families with debts, or they may be from poorer and isolated tribal communities. The DEP has mobilized the support of teachers and local community leaders in identifying girls at risk. Together with community leaders, DEP staff visit the families and discuss with parents the effects of prostitution on their children. Then it offers alternative education, which is a combination of basic education and skills training for the children concerned. Other issues such as social values and the development of self-esteem are discussed while the girls are in the programme. In addition, leadership training is given to selected groups so that girls can play a leading role in fighting prostitution after completing the programme and returning to their community. As part of its programme, the DEP conducts a whole range of awareness-raising activities among communities prone to sending their children to prostitution to convince them that other options are available.

Source: IPEC.

---

was forming a joint public-private sector task force of tourism groups to tackle the problem of organized sex tourism and child prostitution. The task force, the Tourism and Child Prostitution Watch, aims to encourage self-regulation in the tourism industry by increasing awareness of the problems of sexual exploitation in tourism, and collecting information on sex tourism and measures that have been successful in stopping it.

The International Criminal Police Organization, Interpol, established in 1992 a Standing Working Party on Offences against

Minors to assist its member countries in combating sexual exploitation of children, including, in particular, child pornography and the activities of paedophiles. It bases its work on a resolution on offences committed against minors which was adopted by the Interpol General Assembly in 1992. This important resolution deals with the measures required to combat the sexual exploitation of children, including the setting up of an international register of paedophiles. (Updated recommendations are expected to be adopted by the Interpol General Assembly in October 1996.)

Most recently, a World Congress on Commercial Sexual Exploitation of Children was held in Stockholm, Sweden, in August 1996. The Conference adopted a Programme of Action which should contribute to the global effort to suppress this very serious problem. Other similar international events are planned. The Government of the Netherlands is planning to organize an international conference in Amsterdam in February 1997 in cooperation with the ILO on the most intolerable forms of child labour. Representatives will be invited from industrialized and developing countries that have already taken steps to eliminate abusive child labour. The purpose of the conference is to exchange views and experiences and to promote international cooperation in this area. A similar meeting will be convened by the Government of Norway in Oslo in 1997, in collaboration with the ILO.

Notes

[1] R. Anker and H. Melkas: *Economic incentives for children and families to eliminate or reduce child labour* (Geneva, ILO, 1996).

[2] During its 16th World Congress in Brussels, 25-29 June 1996, the ICFTU adopted its most recent statement on eradicating child labour.

Targeting the intolerable   7

The world situation projects two conflicting images: one conveys a positive and optimistic view of the long way we have come in our understanding and awareness of the problem of child labour and the much greater determination to bring about an end to it. The other mirrors seething anger and lingering sadness over the many millions of children who squander their future doing work totally inappropriate to their growth. This waste of valuable human potential is a continuous tragedy for them, their parents and their communities.

The great injury, even deliberate cruelty, which predatory adults inflict on many working children, and the all too frequent fact that they get away with it, is a cruel mockery of the concern for humanity and an affront to the sincerity, political will and collective undertaking of both developing and rich societies alike which profess giving a first call to children, putting people at the centre of development, and upholding respect for human rights as a unifying, though sometimes contentious, principle among all nations of the world. It is all the more cruel that the genuine deprivation of childhood for many millions is trivialized by debating doctrinal questions such as whether the child who sells newspapers before or after school should be exempted from child labour legislation. The condition of children trapped in bonded labour, toiling in heavy construction, or abused in domestic service or prostitution belongs to a world quite unlike that of a child who works intermittently to earn pocket money to buy the latest electronic gadgets or fancy sports shoes.

This said, there are reasons for optimism about the direction of change and the possibilities for action. The world we now know is quite different from that of even five or ten years ago. It offers a favourable climate and hitherto unknown opportunities and possibilities that should enable us to make a decisive assault on child labour. This, therefore, calls for a number of steps to be taken by governments and the international community. This report has identified in the individual chapters many specific measures which should be undertaken, but the following points deserve special attention.

First, the world community should manifest its commitment to act in solidarity by adopting an international Convention which forbids all extreme forms of child labour. Such a Convention would fill in the gaps in current international legal instruments dealing with children and their rights, and set clear priorities for national and international action. It would build on Convention No. 138 which remains one of the fundamental Conventions of the ILO and is a key instrument of a coherent strategy against child labour at the national level. Convention No. 138 has been ratified by 49 countries. It is the Office's experience, however, that an obstacle to greater ratification of this Convention has been that some member States view the text as too complex and too difficult to apply in its entirety, at least in the short term. The Office's proposals therefore envisage a new Convention which would complement Convention No. 138 and be consistent with it but which would focus on the most intolerable forms of child labour as described in this report. It would apply to all children under the age of 18 and would oblige member States to suppress immediately all extreme forms of child labour including: all forms of slavery or practices similar to slavery; the sale and trafficking of children; forced or compulsory labour including debt bondage and serfdom; the use of children for prostitution; the production of pornography or pornographic performances; the production of or trafficking in drugs or other illegal activities; and the engagement of children in any type of work, which by its nature or the circumstances in which it is carried out, is likely to jeopardize their health, safety or morals. It would require also the provision and strict enforcement of adequate criminal penalties. Importantly also, it would encourage member States to assist each other by means of international judicial and technical assistance or other types of cooperation to combat the intolerable.

Second, the time has come for member States which have been calling for such an international Convention over the last few years and are for the most part signatories to all the major ILO Conventions on child labour and forced labour, as well as the United Nations Convention on the Rights of the Child, to rise to their commitments and utterances by adopting a time-bound programme of action to eliminate child labour. Economic development has been accelerating at a rate of as high as 8-12 per cent a year in many Asian and Latin American countries, and is predicted to reach respectable rates in many African countries as well. Therefore, given the basis for much higher living standards achieved in many developing countries, governments can and should put a relatively quick end to child labour by adopting a time-bound programme of action in the same way that they have achieved rapid growth rates and increased per capita income and other socio-economic objectives within the compass of time-bound development plans and perspectives.

Third, because children are so important, because those in truly perilous work need assistance urgently, and because effective action is feasible, national policy should give priority in the first instance to abolishing the worst and intolerable forms of child labour such as slavery and slave-like practices, all forms of forced labour including debt bondage and child prostitution, and child work in hazardous occupations and industries.

Fourth, special attention must be devoted to those children who are subject to even greater exploitation and abuse because of their special vulnerabilities. These include the very young, and girls. Many children are put to work at a very early age, in particular in rural areas where they often begin to work as soon as they are five or six years old. The proportion of child workers under the age of ten in the total is far from negligible; it may be up to 20 per cent in some countries. The employment of very young children is an alarming problem; the younger the child, the more vulnerable he or she is to physical, chemical and other hazards at the workplace and, of course, to the economic exploitation of his or her labour. Girls, for example, are often more hidden, denied access to education, and suffer from detrimental cultural practices. Once sexually exploited, they can end up as social outcasts with little chance of reintegration into their communities. Therefore another area for action is the complete prohibition of work by young children (under 12 or 13 years of age) and the protection of girls.

Fifth, national programmes of action against forced and hazardous work should heed the well-known admonition that the best can be the enemy of the good, and ensure that action against hazardous child labour in one sector does not drive it underground or lead to its resurgence in other sectors which are just as, or even more, hazardous. Any action against hazardous child labour, therefore, should have a strong rehabilitative component.

Sixth, as with health, here too prevention is cheaper and easier than cure. The task facing the international community is the immediate suppression of all extreme forms of child labour. To this end, the provision of protection and rehabilitation schemes are absolutely

---

Targeting the intolerable: What is to be done?

1. A new Convention on child labour.
2. Time-bound programme of action to eliminate child labour.
3. Immediate suppression of extreme forms of child labour.
4. Prohibition of work for the very young (under 12 or 13 years) and special protection for girls.
5. Rehabilitation to ensure permanent removal from hazardous work.
6. Preventive measures.
7. Designation of national authority responsible for child labour.
8. Making crime against a child anywhere a crime everywhere.
9. Increased financial aid to fight against child labour.

---

essential. Nevertheless, the problem can be attacked on a lasting basis only if short-term action is conceived within the framework of a national policy that gives primacy to preventive measures, including the provision of free, universal, compulsory education, community mobilization, and other supportive measures.

Seventh, along with deciding the main approaches to be utilized in combating child labour, it is essential to indicate the most important actors who must be involved in the effort. In almost all countries, this would include a cross-section of society. But government and government alone has the capability to exert a powerful influence on national values and opinion and to mobilize the financial resources and institutional instruments to make an impact on the problem. Yet all too often this potential influence has been thwarted by the absence of a clear mechanism to promote, monitor and effect action because of the proliferation of government agencies; child labour is everybody's problem and nobody's problem. If, therefore, we are to give impetus and effective action, the laissez-faire attitude characterizing many governments should be replaced by one whereby a national authority with considerable power and influence is designated with the mandate and responsibility for the elimination of child labour.

Eighth, concerted action and international cooperation in North America, Australia and Europe, as well as in Africa, Asia and Latin America is needed to successfully suppress all extreme forms of child labour. The trafficking and commercial exploitation of children in hazardous and forced work and in prostitution and pornography cannot be stopped without it. These should be a crime in every country of the world. And a crime committed anywhere should be considered a crime everywhere.

Lastly, worldwide anger about extreme forms of child labour needs to be translated into a programme for international cooperation in the field of economic and social policy. The situation of children cannot be improved without action to combat world poverty. Laws and schools are important, and necessary. But they will fail if they are not supported by a commitment and a programme of action to deal with the poverty of nations and communities. The fight against child labour has to go hand in hand with a campaign to create full, freely chosen and productive employment and ensure that this goal is considered as an ethical, social, political and economic imperative of mankind. That is the challenge: for governments of developing countries to address the needs of the poorest of their poor, and for governments of rich countries to back up their insistence on observance of universal standards with a commensurate commitment for increased resources to attack world poverty.

Appendix. Ratifications by country of ILO conventions on minimum age and forced labour
(as at 15 August 1996)

Country	No. 5	No. 59	No. 123	No. 138	No. 29	No. 105
Total	**49**	**20**	**32**	**49**	**139**	**116**
Afghanistan						×
Albania	×	×			×	
Algeria				×	×	×
Angola					×	×
Antigua and Barbuda				×	×	×
Argentina	×				×	×
Armenia						
Australia			×		×	×
Austria	×				×	×
Azerbaijan				×	×	
Bahamas	×				×	×
Bahrain					×	
Bangladesh		×			×	×
Barbados	×				×	×
Belarus				×	×	×
Belgium				×	×	×
Belize	×				×	×
Benin	×				×	×
Bolivia	×		×			×
Bosnia and Herzegovina				×	×	
Botswana						
Brazil	×				×	×
Bulgaria				×	×	
Burkina Faso	×				×	
Burundi		×			×	×
Cambodia					×	
Cameroon	×		×		×	×
Canada						×
Cape Verde					×	×
Central African Republic	×				×	×

Country	No. 5	No. 59	No. 123	No. 138	No. 29	No. 105
Chad	×				×	×
Chile	×				×	
China		×				
Colombia	×				×	×
Comoros	×				×	×
Congo	×				×	
Costa Rica				×	×	×
Côte d'Ivoire	×				×	×
Croatia				×	×	
Cuba				×	×	×
Cyprus			×		×	×
Czech Republic	×		×		×	×
Denmark	×				×	×
Djibouti	×		×		×	×
Dominica				×	×	×
Dominican Republic	×				×	×
Ecuador			×		×	×
Egypt					×	×
El Salvador				×	×	×
Equatorial Guinea				×		
Eritrea						
Estonia	×				×	×
Ethiopia						
Fiji	×	×			×	×
Finland				×	×	×
France				×	×	×
Gabon	×		×		×	×
Gambia						
Georgia						
Germany				×	×	×
Ghana		×			×	×
Greece				×	×	×
Grenada	×				×	×
Guatemala		×		×	×	×
Guinea	×				×	×
Guinea-Bissau					×	×
Guyana	×				×	×
Haiti	×				×	×
Honduras				×	×	×
Hungary			×		×	×
Iceland					×	×
India	×		×		×	
Indonesia					×	
Iran, Islamic Republic of					×	×
Iraq				×	×	×
Ireland				×	×	×

Country	No. 5	No. 59	No. 123	No. 138	No. 29	No. 105
Israel				×	×	×
Italy				×	×	×
Jamaica					×	×
Japan	×				×	
Jordan			×		×	×
Kazakstan						
Kenya				×	×	×
Korea, Rep. of						
Kuwait					×	×
Kyrgyzstan				×	×	
Lao, People's Democratic Republic					×	
Latvia	×					×
Lebanon		×			×	×
Lesotho	×				×	
Liberia					×	×
Libyan Arab Jamahiriya				×	×	×
Lithuania					×	×
Luxembourg				×	×	×
Madagascar	×		×		×	
Malawi						
Malaysia			×		×	
Mali	×				×	×
Malta				×	×	×
Mauritania	×				×	
Mauritius				×	×	×
Mexico			×		×	×
Moldova, Republic of						×
Mongolia		×	×			
Morocco					×	×
Mozambique						×
Myanmar					×	
Namibia						
Nepal						
Netherlands				×	×	×
New Zealand		×			×	×
Nicaragua				×	×	×
Niger				×	×	×
Nigeria		×	×		×	×
Norway				×	×	×
Oman						
Pakistan		×			×	×
Panama			×		×	×
Papua New Guinea					×	×
Paraguay		×	×		×	×
Peru		×			×	×
Philippines		×				×

121

Country	No. 5	No. 59	No. 123	No. 138	No. 29	No. 105
Poland			×	×	×	×
Portugal					×	×
Qatar						
Romania			×	×		
Russian Federation			×	×		
Rwanda			×	×		×
Saint Kitts and Nevis						
Saint Lucia	×				×	×
Saint Vincent and the Grenadines						
San Marino				×	×	×
Sao Tome and Principe						
Saudi Arabia			×		×	×
Senegal	×				×	×
Seychelles	×				×	×
Sierra Leone	×	×			×	×
Singapore	×				×	
Slovakia	×		×		×	
Slovenia				×	×	
Solomon Islands					×	
Somalia					×	×
South Africa						
Spain			×	×	×	×
Sri Lanka	×				×	
Sudan					×	×
Suriname					×	×
Swaziland	×	×	×		×	×
Sweden				×		
Switzerland	×		×		×	×
Syrian Arab Republic			×		×	×
Tajikistan				×	×	
Tanzania, United Republic of	×	×			×	×
Thailand			×		×	×
The former Yugoslav Republic of Macedonia						
Togo				×	×	
Trinidad and Tobago					×	×
Tunisia			×	×	×	×
Turkey		×	×			×
Turkmenistan						
Uganda	×		×		×	×
Ukraine				×	×	
United Arab Emirates					×	
United Kingdom	×				×	×
United States						×
Uruguay				×	×	×
Uzbekistan						

Country	No. 5	No. 59	No. 123	No. 138	No. 29	No. 105
Uzbekistan						
Venezuela				×	×	×
Viet Nam	×		×			
Yemen		×			×	×
Yugoslavia				×	×	
Zaire					×	
Zambia			×	×	×	×
Zimbabwe						

Note: The title of the Conventions are as follows: Convention No. 5: Minimum Age (Industry), 1919; Convention No. 59: Minimum Age (Industry) (Revised), 1937; Convention No. 123: Minimum Age (Underground Work), 1965; Convention No. 138: Minimum Age, 1973; Convention No. 29; Forced Labour, 1930; Convention No. 105: Abolition of Forced Labour, 1957.

Labour Rights as Human Rights

Edited by

PHILIP ALSTON

Academy of European Law
European University Institute
in collaboration with the Center for
Human Rights and Global Justice,
New York University School of Law

OXFORD

UNIVERSITY PRESS

OXFORD
UNIVERSITY PRESS

Great Clarendon Street, Oxford OX2 6DP

Oxford University Press is a department of the University of Oxford.
It furthers the University's objective of excellence in research, scholarship,
and education by publishing worldwide in

Oxford New York

Auckland Cape Town Dar es Salaam Hong Kong Karachi
Kuala Lumpur Madrid Melbourne Mexico City Nairobi
New Delhi Shanghai Taipei Toronto

With offices in

Argentina Austria Brazil Chile Czech Republic France Greece
Guatemala Hungary Italy Japan South Korea Poland Portugal
Singapore Switzerland Thailand Turkey Ukraine Vietnam

Published in the United States
by Oxford University Press Inc., New York

British Library Cataloguing in Publication Data
Data available

Library of Congress Cataloging-in-Publication Data

Labour rights as human rights / edited by Philip Alston ; Academy of European Law,
European University Institute in collaboration with the Center for Human Rights and
Global Justice, New York University School of Law.
    p. cm.
Includes bibliographical references and index.
ISBN 0–19–928105–X
1. Labor laws and legislation. 2. Labor laws and legislation, International. 3.
Human rights. I. Alston, Philip. II. Academy of European Law. III. New York
University. Center for Human Rights and Global Justice.
K1705. L334 2005
344. 01—dc22   2004028757
        ISBN 0–19–928105–X (Hbk.) EAN 9780199281053
        ISBN 0–19–928106–8 (Pbk.) EAN 9780199281060

1 3 5 7 9 10 8 6 4 2

Typeset by Newgen Imaging Systems (P) Ltd., Chennai, India
Printed in Great Britain
on acid-free paper by
Biddles Ltd., King's Lynn

Contents

Notes on Contributors

Philip Alston is Professor of Law at New York University School of Law and Faculty Director of the Center for Human Rights and Global Justice. He is currently United Nations Special Rapporteur on Extrajudicial, Summary and Arbitrary Executions and Special Adviser to the High Commissioner for Human Rights on the Millennium Development Goals. He chaired the UN Committee on Economic, Social, and Cultural Rights for eight years (1991–8). He is also Editor-in-Chief of the *European Journal of International Law*.

Steve Charnovitz is an Associate Professor of Law at the George Washington University Law School in Washington, DC. He was an international relations officer at the US Department of Labor for many years where, among other projects, he had responsibility for the labor component of the first US trade preference negotiations (in 1983–4) featuring labor conditionality. From 1992 to 1995, he was Policy Director of the US Competitiveness Policy Council. A collection of his essays, *Trade Law and Global Governance*, was published in 2002 by Cameron May. A full listing of his publications on international labor law and international trade law can be found on his website at http://www.geocities.com/charnovitz.

Anne C. L. Davies has been Fellow and Tutor in Law at Brasenose College, Oxford University since 2001. She is the author of *Perspectives on Labour Law*, published in 2004 by Cambridge University Press in the Law in Context series. This book uses human rights arguments and economic analysis in order to explore a selection of topics in English employment/labour law. She also works on public law, with particular interests in the regulation of health care, and government contracts. She has written several articles on these topics and a critically acclaimed book entitled *Accountability: A Public Law Analysis of Government by Contract*, published by Oxford University Press in 2001.

Simon Deakin is the Robert Monks Professor of Corporate Governance at the University of Cambridge. He teaches courses on labour law and private law in the Faculty of Law at Cambridge and courses on corporate governance in the university's business school, the Judge Institute of Management. For the past decade he has been a member of an interdisciplinary research group based in Cambridge, the Centre for Business Research, which has carried out a series of empirical studies of the social and economic effects of legal change. He is the co-author of treatises on UK *Tort Law* (with Angus Johnston and Basil Markesinis) and *Labour Law* (with Gillian Morris) and has published extensively in law, management, and economics journals.

Patrick Macklem is a Professor of Law at the University of Toronto. He is a co-editor of *Labour & Employment Law* (Queen's University, 2004), *Canadian Constitutional Law* (Emond Montgomery Publications, 2003); *The Security of Freedom: Essays on Canada's Anti-terrorism Bill* (University of Toronto Press, 2001), and the author of *Indigenous Difference and the Constitution of Canada* (University of Toronto Press, 2001). He has also published numerous articles on constitutional law, labour law, indigenous peoples and the law, and international human rights law. Professor Macklem's teaching interests include labour law and policy, constitutional law, international human rights law, indigenous peoples, and ethnic and cultural minorities. He is a Fellow of the Royal Society of Canada.

Francis Maupain graduated in Law and Political Science at the University of Bordeaux in 1964, at the College of Europe in 1965, at Harvard (LL.M and MPA) in 1967–8, and completed his doctorate at the Sorbonne. In 1969 he joined the International Labour Office as a member of the Director-General's Office, and was subsequently appointed as the ILO Legal Adviser. He is currently a Special Adviser to the ILO Director-General. He has written various articles and contributions on administrative, international, and labour law. He has participated in various conferences and has taught at the Hague Academy of International Law and at the Toronto University Law School.

Tonia Novitz is a senior lecturer in law at the University of Bristol. She first qualified as a Barrister and Solicitor in New Zealand and then studied at Balliol College, Oxford, where she received the BCL degree and completed her doctorate. She has been a visiting fellow at the International Institute for Labour Studies, attached to the International Labour Organisation in Geneva, as well as a Jean Monnet Fellow and a Marie Curie Fellow at the European University Institute in Florence. She has written extensively on UK labour law, including a book with Paul Skidmore on *Fairness at Work: A Critical Analysis of the Employment Relations Act 1999 and its Treatment of Collective Rights* (Hart Publishing, 2001). She also has written on international labour standards, EU social policy, and mechanisms for the protection of human rights. She was the co-editor of *The Future of Remedies in Europe* (Hart Publishing, 2000) and, most recently, author of *International and European Protection of the Right to Strike* (Oxford University Press, 2003).

1

Labour Rights as Human Rights: The Not So Happy State of the Art

PHILIP ALSTON

The role of workers' rights in the globalizing economy of the early part of the twenty-first century is much contested, both in theory and in practice. In contrast, the place of human rights seems significantly more secure, at least in theory, even if the tributes regularly paid to their central importance smack of hypocrisy. What does it mean then to ask, as the contributors to the present volume do—each in a different context and from varying perspectives—whether it is helpful or appropriate to approach labour rights as human rights? Why not transcend the arguments about the nature of rights, about their universalist pretensions, and about their cultural applicability to all peoples, by using a different language? We could choose instead to talk of labour 'principles', 'standards', or 'guidelines', or even workers' 'rights' but as an unspecified and separate category of rights that does not necessarily import all of the baggage of the human rights debates into efforts to promote and secure decent working conditions for all.

In part the choice of terminology will depend on context and on the role(s) that labour rights are perceived to have in addressing current challenges within the global order. Inter-governmental assessments of the nature of those challenges are often bland and uninformative and thus unlikely to shed much light on the debate over whether labour rights should be seen as human rights. A classic example is the diagnosis offered in the 'Sao Paolo Consensus', adopted by the eleventh conference of the United Nations Conference on Trade and Development (UNCTAD) in June 2004. Globalization itself is presented as a positive force that is capable of improving 'the overall performance of developing countries' economies by opening up market opportunities for their exports, by promoting the transfer of information, skills and technology, and by increasing the financial resources available for investment'. But the statement then goes on to present the other side of the balance sheet, albeit in rather muted terms. Thus, '[s]ome countries have successfully adapted to the changes and benefited from globalization, but many others, especially the least developed countries, have remained marginalized in the globalizing world economy. As stated in the Millennium Declaration, the benefits and costs of globalization are very unevenly distributed.'[1]

---

[1] See UN doc. TD/410, 25 June 2004, para. 1.

In fact, such carefully negotiated, lowest common denominator, statements tell us all too little about the real nature of the challenges faced. They also stand in marked contrast to the widely accepted starting point for the debate among labour rights specialists, which is the perception that labour rights have fared poorly as a result of globalization. This conventional wisdom is well captured by Sabel, O'Rourke, and Fung:

the present wave of globalization has given rise to widespread abuses, including child labor, punishingly long work days, harsh discipline, hazardous work conditions, sexual predation, and suppression of the freedom to associate and organize. These forms of servitude recall outright slavery in some instances, and provoke moral outrage the world over whenever they come to light. There is broad agreement among the world's publics that labor markets must be reregulated to curb these abuses.[2]

But even if those concerned with labour rights can agree on the diagnosis, they are much more divided when it comes to specifying the prescriptions that follow. In particular, from the perspective of the present volume, the key question remains whether the response is optimally, or even usefully, formulated in terms of labour rights. At one level this could be argued to be a non-question, since a bevy of labour rights were reflected in the Universal Declaration of Human Rights (UDHR) of 1948 and have subsequently been translated into a wide range of treaty provisions in both universal and regional contexts. They include: the right to be free from slavery, broadly defined to encompass the modern forms thereof (Art. 5 of the UDHR); the right to non-discrimination and equal protection of the law (Art. 7); the right to freedom of association (Art. 20); the right to social security (Art. 22); the right to work, to free choice of employment, to just and favourable conditions of work, and to protection against unemployment (Art. 23); the right to equal pay for equal work (Art. 23); the right to form and to join trade unions (Art. 23); and the right to reasonable limitation of working hours (Art. 24).

But this formal recognition is only part of the overall picture. We must also look at what states and international organizations, not to mention employers in general and major transnational employers in particular, are doing and saying in relation to those rights.

One starting point is the increasing popularity of the term 'labour principles', which is used in both the North American Agreement on Labor Cooperation (NAALC) annexed to the North American Free Trade Agreement (NAFTA),[3] and the International Labour Organization's (ILO) 1998 Declaration on Fundamental Principles and Rights at Work.[4] In the case of the NAALC the explanation for the choice of terminology ('guiding principles') is that the drafters specifically wished to

---

[2] Charles Sabel, Dara O'Rourke, and Archon Fung, 'Ratcheting Labor Standards: Regulation for Continuous Improvement in the Global Workplace' (2000), available at: http://web.mit.edu/dorourke/www/PDF/RLS21.pdf, p. 4.

[3] For the text of NAALC, see http://www.naalc.org/english/agreement.shtml.

[4] ILO Declaration on Fundamental Principles and Rights at Work, International Labour Conference, 86th Session, Geneva, June 1998 [hereinafter ILO Declaration], available at: http://www.ilo.org/public/english/standards/decl/declaration/index.htm.

avoid references to international standards and needed a term that would embrace the principles underlying the disparate national law of the three contracting states (Canada, the United States, and Mexico). The explanation is different in the case of the 1998 ILO Declaration. It asserts that all member states of the ILO, regardless of which specific labour conventions they have ratified, are bound by a set of four 'core labour standards', consisting of freedom of association, freedom from forced labour and from child labour, and non-discrimination in employment. Several competing explanations for its emphasis on principles have been offered.[5] The most plausible is that the drafters felt they could not refer to the relevant principles as rights in relation to states that had not ratified the specific International Labour Conventions that correspond to each of the four issues identified. This explanation overlooks the fact that each of the relevant principles is recognized as a human right in the Universal Declaration of Human Rights, in the International Covenant on Economic, Social and Cultural Rights, which is binding upon 149 states, and in a very large body of other international legal standards.

But rather than focus on questions of terminology, the main concern of the contributors to this volume is with the institutional arrangements by which effect can be given to labour rights, whether at the national or international level. The contributors thus pay considerable attention to the implementation arrangements contained in some of the key international agreements, such as the NAFTA and the Free Trade Agreement of the Americas (FTAA), and to the approaches adopted within the context of the main institutional settings, such as those of the ILO and the European Union (EU). It is for the readers of this collection to decide for themselves, based on the overall picture that emerges, as to whether labour rights really are best promoted under the rubric, or within the framework, of human rights.

While the perspectives of the various contributors to the volume vary significantly, it must be acknowledged that they are united by an acceptance of the view that labour rights warrant certain forms of protection within the framework of the emerging global economic system. They also agree that the institutions that are the focus of their analyses have important roles to play in that regard. As a result of these shared assumptions, the range of views expressed in the volume does not reflect the extent to which labour rights are not only strongly under siege in various settings, but also of very limited relevance in some national contexts.

The latter phenomena are perhaps best illustrated by taking note of some of the attitudes that prevail towards internationally recognized labour rights in the United States. While the US example is not necessarily a good indicator of the attitudes of a great many other countries, including in particular those of the European Union, there are several reasons why it is highly instructive for present purposes: (1) because of the extent to which US policies have succeeded in influencing the approaches adopted in international organizations, such as the ILO; (2) because the labour

---

[5] For a detailed analysis, see Philip Alston, ' "Core Labour Standards" and the Transformation of the International Labour Rights Regime', 15 *European J. Int'l L.* (2004) 457.

policies promulgated by US-based corporations are highly influential; and (3) because the bilateral and regional trade policies of the United States have been of major importance in shaping the international debate over the relationship between trade liberalization and respect for core labour standards.

Representatives of the United States sometimes present themselves as strong supporters of the labour rights approach of the ILO,[6] but the reality is rather more complex. The United States has indeed sought to encourage other countries to accept various obligations designed to ensure that those countries will respect core labour standards. The rationale is that competitiveness in international trade will thereby be ensured through the establishment of a level playing field in terms of labour conditions.[7] But within the United States itself the situation is not so straightforward. A leading US labour lawyer has succinctly summed up the current position:

International human rights, including labor rights, have made almost no discernible mark upon American domestic law. That is not because the United States rejects the existence of international human rights in the labor context.... But the United States does not embrace the full scope of the obligations that international law imposes on states with respect to those rights. If it did, or if there were more effective mechanisms for the enforcement of international norms, then international law would provide critical traction for efforts to expand and invigorate the protection of workers' associational activity.[8]

But even this rather sobering assessment does not reflect the extent to which there are continuing challenges stemming from US labour lawyers, policy-makers, and academics to the very notion of labour rights as understood internationally. In the name of flexibility and competition, strong arguments have been put forward for treating labour standards as impediments to market freedom and thus to the promotion of economic development. For present purposes it is perhaps best illustrated by revisionist analyses of US constitutional law that seek to show that the overturning of the so-called Lochner era was a mistake. *Lochner v. New York*[9] was the high point in a series of cases in which the Supreme Court held that common law rights to property and to contractual autonomy could not be overridden by legislative attempts to regulate working hours and conditions, such as minimum wages. Although the US Constitution did not explicitly recognize any right to 'liberty of contract', the Court effectively read it into the Due Process Clause of the Fourteenth Amendment. In later years this approach was definitively overturned and the Court looked benignly upon efforts to ensure workers' rights, an approach which continues to prevail today.[10]

---

[6] Thus, the long-time representative of the US employers to the International Labour Conference, Edward Potter, has noted that '[o]ver the last 20 years, the U.S. business community has been at the forefront of being a positive, proactive participant in the promotion of ILO human rights in the United States and in other countries'. Potter, 'Swimming Upstream: Ratification of ILO Conventions' (2003), available at: http://images.ctsg.com/pdfs/ilo/speeches/04edwardpotter.pdf, at 3.

[7] See generally Charnovitz, Chapter 5 below.

[8] Cynthia L. Estlund, 'The Ossification of American Labor Law', 102 *Columbia L. Rev.* (2002) 1527, at 1587–8.　　　　　　　　　　　　　　　　　　　　[9] 198 US 45 (1905).

[10] See generally David E. Bernstein, 'Lochner's Legacy's Legacy', 82 *Texas L. Rev.* 1 (2003).

In a recent analysis, and one which is not atypical of a significant stream of US labour law analysis, it has been argued that the Lochner approach represented far better economic theory than the regulatory assumptions that came to replace it:

> [Lochner] allowed greater room for workers and their employers to create hours of work that suited their concrete situations. Long and painful hours would decline when advances in productivity made them unnecessary, but it does not follow that good things would come from forcing those hours to fall before any such advance took place.[11]

Although the historical analysis deals with the situation in the nineteenth and early twentieth centuries, the author argues that the lessons for today have yet to be learned:

> In the twenty first century, those laws still stand as an obstacle to getting the package of hours and wages that suits workers, in terms of work during the daytime, with flexible hours, and benefits determined by demand rather than by their relative ability to circumvent hours rules.[12]

In other words, the sort of protections for workers that were upheld by the Court in Lochner actually constitute counter-productive interferences in the free choice of workers, who should be able to decide for themselves whether to work very long hours, to do so at weekends or overnight, to be entitled to certain minimum benefits in terms of vacation, health insurance, or maternity leave, and so on.

But the situation in the United States is less atypical than labour rights proponents might wish. At the international level there is no shortage of voices playing down the utility of labour rights and advocating instead the need to promote labour market flexibility and overall economic growth as not only the best, but the only realistic, way to move towards the realization of the adequate standard of living to which workers, and indeed all individuals, are entitled. The current state of international thinking and of the political consensus on these issues can be gauged from two recent events, which at first glance yielded quite different results, but on closer inspection suggest an equally pessimistic prospect in terms of the promotion of labour rights as human rights. They are the outcome of the eleventh United Nations Conference on Trade and Development (UNCTAD XI) and the report of the Global Commission on the Social Dimensions of Globalization. Each of these will now be examined with a view to drawing conclusions as to the current status of international support for the promotion of labour rights.

1. UNCTAD XI (2004)

The United Nations Conference on Trade and Development, which is in fact an organization, despite its misleading title, is in some respects the international

---

[11] Christopher T. Wonnell, *Lochner v. New York* as Economic Theory (unpublished manuscript), available at: http://papers.ssrn.com/sol3/papers.cfm?abstract<uscore>id=259857, p. 97.

[12] *Ibid.*

institutional incarnation of George Bernard Shaw's youthful communist. Shaw is reputed to have said that '[a]ny man who is not a communist at the age of twenty is a fool. Any man who is still a communist at the age of thirty is an even bigger fool.'[13] UNCTAD was founded in 1964 by Raúl Prebisch and strongly reflected the views of Latin American dependency theorists and other radical development economists.[14] By the age of 20, it had become the *bête noire* of the Reagan Administration, which unsuccessfully put forward a good many proposals for its disbandment. But by the age of 30, and even more so 40 (in 2004), it had followed Shaw's advice and become a reputable member of the trade establishment. So much so that the most prominent opponent of any linkage between labour rights and the World Trade Organization, Jagdish Bhagwati, has often suggested that the best way to break the stalemate in this area is for the ILO and UNCTAD to collaborate with a view to promoting respect for international labour standards in the context of international trade.[15]

The international trade union movement took this prospect seriously and submitted a lengthy and detailed statement of objectives[16] to UNCTAD XI, which took place in June 2004. The statement argued that the 'evidence of the past few years shows that without effective protection for basic workers' rights in the international trading system, those developing countries which genuinely seek to protect workers' human rights and raise basic living standards are vulnerable'. Unusually in such a context, the statement singled out the problems caused by 'competition from authoritarian governments like China which are ready to violate their own workers' basic rights in order to achieve export maximisation'.[17] Seeking to respond to the fear that labour standards would disadvantage the poorer countries whose competitive advantage lies partly in low wages, the trade unions argued that the least developed countries would be the primary beneficiaries of measures to achieve the more effective protection of fundamental workers' rights, because they are in direct competition with one another rather than with the workers in industrialized countries.[18] The statement then presented an instrumentalist appeal to the UNCTAD conferees:

Besides the fact that core labour standards are fundamental human rights for all workers irrespective of countries' level of development, they provide numerous benefits which

---

[13] http://www.elise.com/quotes/quotes/shawquotes.htm.

[14] See Rubens Ricupero, 'The Globalization of Raúl Prebisch' (11 October 2001), available at: http://www.southcentre.org/info/southbulletin/bulletin22/bulletin22-03.htm#P125_23382.

[15] Bhagwati, 'Let the Millennium Round Begin in New Delhi', article cited in Panagariya, 'Trade–Labor Link: A Post-Seattle Analysis' (2000), available at: http://www1.worldbank.org/wbiep/trade/videoconf/panagariya.pdf, at 18.

[16] ICFTU [International Confederation of Free Trade Unions] and TUAC [Trade Union Advisory Committee—affiliated with the Organization of Economic Co-operation and Development] Statement to UNCTAD XI, available at: http://www.icftu.org/displaydocument.asp?Index=991219322&Language=EN.   [17] *Ibid.*, para. 11.

[18] *Ibid.*, para. 12.

outweigh their superficial cost, such as higher productivity, more social and political stability, fewer accidents and a lower level of absences due to illness.[19]

It concluded by arguing that 'respect for core labour standards needs to become a sine qua non for development strategies in all countries world-wide'.[20] Given the importance attached to UNCTAD by commentators like Bhagwati, the response of the conference to these arguments was little short of stunning. In the 27 single-spaced pages of the 'Sao Paolo Consensus',[21] which reflected the carefully negotiated outcome of UNCTAD XI, there is not a single reference to labour standards, labour rights, workers' rights, or core standards.

2. THE WORLD COMMISSION

In their statement to the UNCTAD conference, the trade union movement had attached great importance to the recommendations contained in the report of the World Commission on the Social Dimensions of Globalization, which was issued in February 2004. The International Labour Conference, meeting at the same time as UNCTAD XI, also strongly welcomed the approach reflected in that report.[22]

The Commission was appointed by the Governing Body of the ILO in 2001 with the mandate of preparing a 'major authoritative report' with a particular emphasis on 'the interaction between the global economy and the world of work'.[23] Even by the standards of most of its predecessors in the genre of world commission reports, this one boasted a large and influential group of Commissioners and was launched with significant fanfare. It was chaired by two Heads of State (from Finland and Tanzania), and included 19 Commissioners 'of recognized eminence and authority'.[24] The group also included a former President of Uruguay, a former Prime Minister of Italy, Nobel Prize-winning economist Joseph Stiglitz, the President of the American Federation of Labor and Congress of Industrial Organizations (AFL-CIO), and the President of the International Organization of Employers. One of the central challenges for the World Commission was to identify the best means by which the global trade agenda could best be reconciled with the ILO's long-standing emphasis on the protection of workers' rights.

The importance of the work of the Commission in terms has been noted by Virginia Leary, who characterized it as an encouraging sign that labour rights would

---

[19] *Ibid.*, para. 16.　　[20] *Ibid.*　　[21] UN doc. TD/410, 25 June 2004.

[22] For responses to the report, see International Labour Conference, Ninety-second Session, Geneva, 2004, *Provisional Record* 10.

[23] *A Fair Globalization: Creating Opportunities for all: Report of the World Commission on the Social Dimensions of Globalization* (2004) 148, Annex 2. Part of the analysis that follows draws upon Philip Alston and James Heenan, 'Shrinking the International Labor Code: An Unintended Consequence of the 1998 ILO Declaration on Fundamental Principles and Rights at Work', 36 *New York University Journal of International Law and Politics* (2004).　　[24] *A Fair Globalization*, note 23 above, p. 148.

be given their due in the emerging international response to globalization.[25] Unsurprisingly, the Commission concluded that 'core labour standards' must be a key part of the 'broader international agenda for development' which the report identified and called for a reinforcement of 'the capacity of the ILO to promote' such standards.[26] But the real question that it was called upon to answer in this respect is how such broad but worthy goals can be effectively promoted and how an agenda of both growth and social equity can be combined. The Commission answered this part of its mandate by proposing a four-part agenda. In identifying the most important steps that it considers should be taken in terms of the global debate over the appropriate relationship between the world's trade and labour agendas, it has made a major contribution to the ongoing dialogue.

The Commission's agenda in relation to labour standards consists of: (1) mainstreaming; (2) technical assistance; (3) increased resources for the ILO; and (4) possible sanctions in response to persistent violations of labour rights. We need to examine each of these options in turn.

The first element is to adopt a strategy of mainstreaming. While the World Commission does not use that term, it is an expression that is well known in the human rights domain and that perfectly describes the proposed strategy. Thus, the Commission addresses itself to 'all relevant international institutions' and calls upon them to 'assume their part in promoting the core international labour standards and the Declaration'. More specifically, those institutions are called upon to 'ensure that no aspect of their policies or programmes impedes realization' of the core standards.[27] The strategy of mainstreaming is one that is usually premissed upon a recognition (even if it remains unacknowledged), that the human rights actor on its own lacks much of the clout necessary to achieve the goals in question and that it therefore needs to invoke the assistance of other more powerful actors. While the Commission does not identify those actors specifically, it is clear that at least the World Trade Organization and the World Bank would be among those to which the invocation is directed. In so far as the recommendation is addressed to the WTO, it is, in most respects, a convenient fudge, since that Organization has made it clear in the Declaration adopted at its Singapore Ministerial Meeting in 1996 that it saw no role for itself in relation to labour standards and that the ILO 'is the competent body to set and deal with these [internationally recognized core labour] standards', and reaffirmed the Ministers' support for the ILO in 'its work promoting them'.[28]

---

[25] Virginia A. Leary, 'Form Follows Function: Formulations of International Labor Standards: Treaties, Codes, Soft Law, Trade Agreements', in Robert J. Flanagan and William B. Gould IV (eds.), *International Labor Standards: Globalization, Trade, and Public Policy* (Stanford: Stanford University Press, 2003) 179.   [26] *A Fair Globalization*, note 23 above, p. 94, para. 426.

[27] *Ibid.*, p. 94, para. 426.

[28] WTO, Singapore Ministerial Declaration, WTO doc. WT/MIN(96)/DEC/W, 13 Dec. 1996, para. 4. Available at: http://www.wto.org/english/thewto_e/minist_e/min96_e/wtodec_e.htm. See generally Virginia A. Leary, 'The WTO and the Social Clause: Post-Singapore', 8 *European J. Int'l L.* (1997) 118.

Two other dimensions of this first element are also worthy of attention. One is that the focus of the recommendation is explicitly upon core labour standards, and not on either labour rights in general or on the Conventions that have been specifically ratified by individual states. The other is that the standard of responsibility specified is a very vague and potentially undemanding one. They are asked to ensure that their work does not 'impede' realization of those standards, rather than being asked to facilitate realization, or actively to promote it.

The second element is less problematic. The World Commission first draws a distinction between situations in which the Declaration standards have not been implemented due to a lack of political will and those where a lack of capacity is the problem. In practice, of course, such a distinction is very hard to draw, mainly because many states will be lacking in both in almost equal measure. But where capacity is the obstacle, the Commission recommends that:

Existing technical assistance programmes for the implementation of standards should be stepped up, including the strengthening of labour administrations, training, and assistance to the organization of workers and enterprises. This should include reinforcement of existing action to eliminate child labour.[29]

This is a very traditional ILO approach, but it is noteworthy that the recommendation again refers not to labour rights in general but only to the core standards (the 'fundamental principles and rights at work'), and that no new programs or innovations are called for, thus assuming that a lack of ILO resources is one of the major problems. And it is that specific issue to which the third element of the agenda is directed.

The third component is that the ILO should be strengthened by increasing the resources available to it for the following specific purposes: 'fair and appropriate supervision and monitoring, for promotional assistance, and for the Follow-up to the Declaration . . . and other procedures established in the ILO's Constitution.'[30] Once again, the emphasis is upon the Declaration but it must also be said that this particular recommendation might be seen to leave the door open for strengthening some of the more traditional ILO labour standards mechanisms. But the addition of the phrase 'fair and appropriate' to describe the supervisory and monitoring activities that should be supported can only be interpreted as implying that not all of the ILO's procedures could or should be thus characterized. It is clearly a qualification inserted in response to criticisms of some of the supervisory work being undertaken. The reference to 'other procedures established in the ILO's Constitution' also needs to be read in a technical manner as excluding, for example, the work of the Committee on Freedom of Association, which although based on principles contained in the Constitution is not established by it. Overall then, this third element, especially when combined with the first two, exhibits a marked reluctance to endorse the mainstream of the ILO supervisory activities in relation to labour rights. It also places an emphasis on the Declaration procedures, which are only ones specifically referred to, and reinforces this by an additional reference to promotional assistance.

---

[29] *A Fair Globalization*, note 23 above, p. 94, para. 426.   [30] *Ibid.*

The fourth and final element consists of a recommendation that, in response to situations 'where persistent violations of rights continue despite recommendations of the ILO's supervisory mechanisms', use be made of a procedure provided for in Article 33 of the ILO Constitution[31] in order to secure what the World Commission terms 'enforcement'.[32] This procedure has only ever been invoked once in the history of the ILO and that is in relation to Myanmar. That case study is explored in depth by Francis Maupain in Chapter 4 below. By June 2004 the International Labour Conference was compelled to conclude that none of the steps that Myanmar had been urged to take in the course of the preceding four years had been taken.[33]

Nevertheless, despite the ILO's reluctance to proceed down the Article 33 path, even in relation to Myanmar, the fact remains that this provision lies very much at the hard end of the spectrum of measures open to an international organization in such cases. Its invocation is thus not a matter to be taken lightly and the World Commission's suggestion that such a last resort measure could be used more frequently in the future is therefore significant. What is odd, however, is that the resort to sanctions seems rather far away on the spectrum from each of the other three elements identified. The Commission might reasonably have been expected to devote at least some attention to the strengthening of other aspects of the existing supervisory machinery before moving to that final level.

On the basis of this review of the recommendations adopted by the World Commission several conclusions seem appropriate. The first is that despite expectations that the trade and labour linkage would occupy a significant part of the report, relatively little space is devoted to the issue of enhancing respect for labour rights. The second is that the report focuses very heavily on the 1998 Declaration and the concept of core labour standards and by implication at least seems to diminish the importance of other means by which labour rights in general are being protected. The third is that, despite the reference to Article 33, the report is essentially concerned with promotional measures of the type associated with the Declaration rather than any of the more formal supervisory mechanisms of the ILO.

The report of the World Commission, which had been the brainchild of the ILO's Director-General Juan Somavia, was, perhaps unsurprisingly, welcomed unreservedly by the ILO. In his response to the Commission's report, the Director-General characterized it as charting 'a new way forward', being 'the first systematic

---

[31] Article 33 provides that: 'In the event of any Member failing to carry out within the time specified the recommendations, if any, contained in the report of the Commission of Inquiry, or in the decision of the International Court of Justice, as the case may be, the Governing Body may recommend to the Conference such action as it may deem wise and expedient to secure compliance therewith.' ILO Constitution, available at: http://www.ilo.org/public/english/about/iloconst.htm.

[32] *A Fair Globalization*, note 23 above, p. 95, para. 426.

[33] See International Labour Conference, Ninety-second Session, Geneva, 2004, *Provisional Record* 24, Part 3, 'Special sitting to examine developments concerning the question of the observance by the Government of Myanmar of the Forced Labour Convention, 1930 (No. 29)'; and also 'Developments concerning the question of the observance by the Government of Myanmar of the Forced Labour Convention, 1930 (No. 29)', ILO doc. GB.289/8, March 2004.

international effort to find consensus' on globalization, and succeeding in being at once 'critical', 'positive', and 'realistic'.[34] But in the space of his 62 single-spaced page report the term 'labour rights' appeared only twice. The first time was to observe that the core labour standards are 'the stepping-stones to the realization of other human and labour rights',[35] and the second was to assert that the ILO is an organization 'based on the promotion of human and labour rights as a foundation for development'.[36] 'Core labour standards', on the other hand, are referred to almost twenty times in the report.

In contrast to this enthusiastic in-house reception, the external response has been rather more critical. While some commentators welcomed the report, the comments of others have served to underscore the lack of enthusiasm for labour rights that permeates much of the business community. Thus, the report was said by one commentator to be 'long on pious aspirations and short on rigorous analysis'. In his view 'Democracy, sovereignty and higher labour standards do not always, or even necessarily, go together with faster economic growth and more widely spread prosperity. Sometimes, we have to choose.'[37] The clear implication was that countries might opt for prosperity rather than labour standards, assuming that the two do not go together. Another commentator characterized much of the Report as 'starry-eyed and pie-in-the-sky'. He made a similar argument, albeit on a scale going beyond a focus on mere labour standards:

Democracy and civil society are no doubt fine things—social equity and the rule of law are certainly more likely in societies where they are present—but the embarrassing truth is that they are neither necessary nor sufficient to achieve economic growth.[38]

It is against the background of the relative neglect of labour rights by many participants in the international debates over appropriate responses to globalization that we now turn to consider the approach adopted by the different contributors to this volume.

3. OUTLINE OF THE BOOK

A. The Historical and Recent Evolution of International Labour Rights

In the cottage industry of academic production that has emerged around the meaning of 'globalization', two points are almost invariably made: (1) that globalization strengthens the hand of social, economic, and political forces that erode the social protections that once characterized welfare capitalism; and (2) that

---

[34] *A Fair Globalization*, note 23 above, pp. 4–5.   [35] *Ibid.*, p. 34.   [36] *Ibid.*, p. 47.

[37] Martin Wolf, 'Growth requires painful choices, not platitudes', *Financial Times*, 3 March 2004, p. 19.

[38] Janadas Devan, 'Bigger markets, faster pace...but who's in charge?', *Straits Times*, 12 March 2004, p. 11.

globalization generates a degree of functional integration between national and transnational institutions that is conducive to a harmonization of the practices, principles, and rules of governance (whether through 'networks', supranational adjudicative bodies, or treaty-based international organizations). Simon Deakin's chapter helps us move beyond these stock-standard understandings by providing both a historical context to the emergence of social protections (and their latest incarnation as 'social rights'), and an analytical framework for differentiating the different processes of harmonization that globalization can engender.[39]

Deakin begins by revisiting the emergence of welfare in England during the Industrial Revolution, noting that more recent historical work reveals a cycle in the provision and retrenchment of social protection that coincides with particular phases in the development of industrial capitalism. Feudal forms of settlement-based support survived and facilitated the emergence of capitalism by cushioning the social impact of the shift towards wage labour by an increasingly itinerant workforce. While they smoothed the transition to industrialization, quasi-feudal forms of protection became untenably expensive as the transformation of agricultural society accelerated and rural wages fell. In Deakin's account,[40] the 1834 Poor Laws marked a trough in the cycle of social protection, spurred by the cost of providing for a destitute rural workforce and justified by the new political economy of free labour and free markets in which the old poor laws were condemned as impeding the 'natural' laws of supply and demand.

The growing strength of the labour movement and the critique of capitalist political economy advanced by pro-labour intellectuals, such as Beveridge and the Webbs, were part of the response to the shortcomings of the punitive Poor Law regime. In competition with the view that unemployment was a consequence of the moral failing of working-class men and women and their unwillingness to work (a reprise not unfamiliar to workers in modern capitalist economies), the argument that unemployment, poverty, and destitution were inevitable products of the normal functioning of the capitalist organization of production, gained strength. On this argument, non-punitive and universalist social protections were essential to insulate citizens from the vicissitudes of capitalist business cycles. Contemporary ideas about social rights are informed by this history, and like the forms of social protection that preceded them, must be understood as the concrete products of material and ideal struggles over the organization of economy and society. What explains the emergence of a particular framework of social protection at a given time is not only which groups and forces are objectively dominant, but the subjective possibilities of shared interests and solidarities in relation to the organization of economic risks.[41] Deakin's historical review suggests that these possibilities are always present and that 'social rights' have 'been part of the process now described in terms of "globalization" right from the start'.[42]

---

[39] Simon Deakin, 'Social Rights in a Globalized Economy', Chapter 2 below.
[40] *Ibid.*, pp. 27–31.   [41] *Ibid.*, p. 35.   [42] *Ibid.*, p. 38.

This historical context puts into question any simple models of 'state vs. market' as adequate to understanding globalization. Consistent with this attention to specific dynamics, Deakin argues that processes of regulatory 'harmonization' under globalization can take several forms and need not be understood as either 'a race to the bottom' or an inevitable upward trend. Noting that regulatory competition has some historical antecedents, he defines it as a process whereby 'legal rules are selected and de-selected through competition between decentralized, rule-making entities, which could be nation-states or other units such as regions or localities'.[43] Regulatory competition takes two forms: 'competitive federalism' and 'reflexive harmonization'. In competitive federalism, a central authority guarantees the free movement of capital and or labour while law-making competence is devolved to a lower level. The lower-level entities compete by selecting legal rules that are likely to attract resource flows, effectively equilibrating the supply and demand for certain kinds of rules. Deakin suggests that competitive federalism is more likely to result in a 'race to the bottom'. By contrast, 'reflexive harmonization' values competition not for its equilibrating effects, but as a means of selecting solutions from a range of potential answers to regulatory problems.[44] The aim of reflexive harmonization is to preserve the diversity and autonomy of national or local rule-making systems, while seeking to steer rule-making through the promotion of adaptation to changing conditions. Deakin contends that the United States has developed towards competitive federalism, while the European Union's approach to labour laws is a version of reflexive harmonization.

In the final section of his chapter, Deakin returns to the issue of social rights, and considers how they may be formulated in a manner that can be a response to the prevailing neo-liberal understanding of economy and society. Using Hayek's arguments as a foil, he deploys Amartya Sen's well-known 'capability approach' to contend that 'social rights' should be understood as the institutionalization of the process of formation of capabilities and that capabilities are in turn the precondition for effective participation in markets. The promotion of market participation through support for the equal formation of capabilities is welfare maximizing and thus consistent with neo-liberal economic criteria for social policy. However, caution must be used in appropriating the language of 'rights' so as not to falsely individualize what is in fact a collective social process of capability formation and mobilization. Again, the history of the notion of 'social right' should be recalled in order to recognize that social protection was not only a claim on resources, but also an institutionalization of collective action that permitted the dominant to fight the dominated with their own vision of a just society.

Workers' entitlement to collective action (through unionization, collective bargaining, strikes, and boycotts) gained (a fragile and always somewhat provisional) recognition in capitalist democracies through labour–capital confrontations, which occurred in different ways in different national contexts. 'Labour rights' were encoded in forms that varied greatly between national jurisdictions, reflecting these different

---

[43] *Ibid.*, p. 40.   [44] *Ibid.*, p. 41.

histories. Patrick Macklem's chapter describes the two different ways in which workers' rights to collective action have been conceived at the international level.[45] The first form was through conventions promulgated by the International Labour Organization (ILO), which were aimed principally at protecting domestic labour rights in capitalist welfare states against competition from states that did not abide by these standards.[46] The 'second wave' of international recognition came through the inclusion of labour-related rights (such as freedom of association) in international human rights instruments, such as the Universal Declaration on Human Rights, the International Covenant on Civil and Political Rights and the International Covenant on Economic, Social and Cultural Rights. In these international legal instruments, labour rights became a subset of universal human rights (although as Macklem shows, the collective nature of labour rights did not always sit easily with the individualist interpretations dominant in the human rights field).

The ILO's treaty-by-treaty approach to the harmonization of labour standards has to some extent yielded to a mode of declaring universal principles more characteristic of human rights instruments, as evidenced by the ILO's 1998 Declaration on Fundamental Principles and Rights at Work. This transition perhaps reflects the organization's response to employers' regulatory arbitrage,[47] but Macklem also argues that labour rights are now regarded as part of the means by which the international legal order can 'mitigate some of the adverse distributional consequences of globalization and transnational flexible production'—and thereby buttress its own legitimacy.[48] Rather than being seen as a form of protection of a domestic social order, the idea of international labour rights is being invoked by international institutions from the World Bank to the World Trade Organization as a way of demonstrating the justness of the international legal order. In this view international labour law is realigning its relationship to international human rights law around a shared task of mitigating the distributional consequences of globalization and transnational flexible production—a task in which the right to bargain collectively performs a critical function.[49]

B. The Role of the ILO

But what has become of the mission and practices of the ILO in the new international context? Francis Maupain seeks to answer this question through the concrete example of the ILO's approach to forced labour in Myanmar (Burma).[50] A former Legal Adviser to the International Labour Office and subsequent Senior Adviser to the ILO Director-General, Maupain himself has played a central role in the ILO's

---

[45] Patrick Macklem, 'The Right to Bargain Collectively in International Law: Workers' Right, Human Right, International Right?', Chapter 3 below. [46] *Ibid.*, p. 62.

[47] *Ibid.*, p. 68. [48] *Ibid.*, p. 82.

[49] A very different perspective on the implications of the 1998 Declaration is reflected in Alston, note 5 above.

[50] Francis Maupain, 'Is the ILO Effective in Upholding Labour Rights?: Reflections on the Myanmar Case', Chapter 4 below.

endeavours in this case. Myanmar's military dictatorship has, since 1988, been recognized as among the world's worst human rights violators. Among the many allegations of human rights violations that have been made is that the military dictatorship has systematically used forced labour in pursuit of its campaign to crush separatist insurgencies on Myanmar's northern borders. The ILO's lengthy engagement with Myanmar on the issue of forced labour is examined by Maupain as an instance where the combination of institutional legitimacy and diplomatic intelligence enabled the organization to have a positive impact on a recalcitrant government.

The inherent difficulties in pursuing labour rights through an intergovernmental organization are highlighted in Maupain's first section, where he notes that the ILO's impact rests on a combination of 'will' and 'goodwill'. The ILO remains tied to state-centric models of the international legal order, in which social progress requires voluntary action by the state. The organization's ability to promote labour standards depends upon the voluntary assumption of these standards by states, and on the willingness of member states to implement the obligations they accept at the international level. Faced with Myanmar's refusal to remedy violations of the prohibition on forced labour, the ILO needed to find the right balance of threats and incentives to promote positive action, while at the same time not disturbing other states' commitment to the standards in question, or alienating their willingness to cooperate by appearing to be too heavy-handed as an organization.

Maupain's fascinating account reveals the uses to which the sometimes arcane procedures of international organizations can be put in order to nudge a state down the path towards cooperation. After receiving consistent reports of the widespread use of forced labour in Myanmar, and after the continued non-cooperation by Myanmar's government with ILO requests, the ILO's Governing Body authorized an investigation by a Commission of Inquiry into the use of forced labour in Myanmar.[51] The Commission produced a damning report in 1998, concluding that the widespread use of forced labour in Myanmar amounted to a crime against humanity. The report was not formally contested by the Government of Myanmar, but it reacted negatively and maintained an attitude of non-cooperation. Unable under its Constitution to suspend a member, the ILO's plenary organ took the next best step: it condemned Myanmar under the little-used Article 33 of the Constitution. Article 33 allows the Governing Body of the ILO to recommend to the plenary organ such 'action as it may deem wise and expedient to secure compliance' with the recommendations of a Commission of Inquiry. The effect of such a recommendation is unclear, and Maupain observes that the very vagueness of this provision both accentuated the sense of threat and restrained the ILO from using it too widely, for fear that it would prove hollow. At its strongest, the article may be read as an authorization for ILO member states to individually impose sanctions or

---

[51] *Ibid.*, p. 96.

other measures upon the defaulting member; at its weakest, the recommendation may be no more than a hortatory statement, the effect of which is countermanded by multilateral trade treaties.[52]

Nevertheless, the indeterminate nature of the threat provided an incentive to Myanmar to alter its posture, in the hope that member states would adopt a 'wait and see' attitude and refrain from following through on the Article 33 resolution. Maupain describes the dialectic between the threat of reactivating the Article 33 measures, and the hope of the Myanmar authorities that cooperation might lead to the suspension of Article 33 measures.[53] The other dynamic in play was the tension between condemnations and threats made by ILO organs, and the maintenance of avenues of dialogue and negotiation by the ILO Director-General and his representatives. Both the defaulting state and the organization have an interest in ensuring that the scope of powers under Article 33 are not actually tested, because of the uncertainty of consequences for each. In the end, Maupain demonstrates that this uncertainty was effective in producing a more cooperative attitude from the Myanmar authorities—cooperation that enmeshed the government in a pro-cedural gambit that led it towards steps that it may not have contemplated at the beginning.

The other major aspect of Maupain's contribution concerns the impact of the new global economy on the ILO's efficacy in promoting global labour standards. He notes that the mobility of capital and disintegration of production appear to have affected states' willingness to commit to new international commitments because of 'fear of their consequences on their competitive position or on foreign investment'.[54] The ILO needed to find a way to link the respect for a 'floor' of workers' rights to the economic benefits expected from further economic liberalization. One response was the ILO's Declaration on Fundamental Principles and Rights at Work, as an effort to delimit which workers' rights deserve universal recognition. Maupain reprises the history of the formulation of this document[55] and contends that it has 'managed to overcome the dilemma between voluntarism and the universal protection of workers' rights' by establishing a reporting mechanism for the implementation of the Fun-damental Principles and Rights for all member states.[56] Maupain is distinctly sceptical that 'trade–labour rights linkages' incorporated into trade treaties will be effective in the global promotion of labour standards because of the potential that the standards will be diluted in the process of negotiating them into trade treaties and because trade conditionalities would unfairly penalize all workers in the defaulting country even if only a small percentage of traded goods were not com-pliant.[57] More importantly, social progress must be a product of the active involve-ment of all those concerned and cannot be imposed from outside or granted internally by the actions of a benevolent employer. Thus, in Maupain's view,

---

[52] Francis Maupain, 'Is the ILO Effective in Upholding Labour Rights?: Reflections on the Myanmar Case', Chapter 4 below.   [53] *Ibid.*, p. 106.
[54] *Ibid.*, p. 124.   [55] *Ibid.*, p. 126.   [56] *Ibid.*, p. 131.   [57] *Ibid.*, p. 134.

apparent 'quick fixes', such as trade treaty linkages and corporate social responsibility platforms, may only generate benefits for certain internationally oriented sectors of the economy, without the society-wide effects brought about through widespread exercise of rights of collective action.[58]

C. Labour Rights in the Americas

While the chapter by Steve Charnovitz focuses specifically on the proposed Free Trade Area of the Americas, his analysis also provides a comprehensive overview of the various policies being pursued by the United States in its bilateral and regional trade relations, and includes some additional comparative information by examining the practice of the European Community and Canada in terms of their agreements with Chile.[59] He undertakes a very succinct and enlightening comparison of the key features of the NAFTA Labor Side Agreement, the Canada–Chile Labour Side Agreement, the Canada–Costa Rica Labour Side Agreement, the Association Agreement between the European Community and Chile, and the US–Chile Trade Agreement. These agreements are of major importance, not only because of the size of the US economy but because of the number of such agreements under negotiation or discussion and the important impact of these agreements on overall US trade policy. Charnovitz begins by situating the current negotiations within the framework of almost two centuries of diplomatic and legal efforts to forge closer ties among the various American republics. His starting point, however, is to point out that as of mid-2004 no specific proposals have been made for the inclusion of labour provisions in the FTAA.[60] As a result the principal focus of his chapter is on the question of whether the FTAA should contain such provisions and, if so, what approach ought to be taken. He thus seeks to draw lessons from the other agreements that have already been negotiated.

One of the most important of these, and a pioneering agreement in linking trade and labour rights, is the NAFTA Side Agreement. But Charnovitz points to the ineffectiveness of the relevant provisions to date. Although twenty-eight complaints have been lodged with the relevant authorities, the only tangible outcome so far has been some joint statements and a series of seminars designed to shed light on the problems. His conclusion is that the enforcement provisions 'have proved a nullity'.[61]

He points out, however, that while the other free trade agreements signed or under negotiation in the Americas tend to have very weak provisions designed to promote the harmonization of laws governing labour rights, their approach to other issues is far more aggressive and focused. Thus, when it comes to ensuring market access, opening up opportunities for foreign investment, and protecting intellectual

---

[58] *Ibid.*, pp. 136–9.

[59] Steve Charnovitz, 'The Labor Dimension of the Emerging Free Trade Area of the Americas', Chapter 5 below. [60] *Ibid.*, p. 143.

[61] *Ibid.*, p. 156.

property rights, the agreements are all much stronger and more compelling than they are in relation to labour issues.

He then turns to the challenge of constructing a normative basis or underpinning for any labour provisions that might eventually be included in the FTAA. He starts by making the case in favour of national labour law, an analysis that might strike many lawyers as somewhat superfluous but the need for which is underscored by the number of economists who have indeed questioned whether there is such a need. From there he moves to survey the arguments that have been used historically to justify the need for international labour law and puts current efforts into a long-term historical context. He examines arguments based on a fear of generating an international race to the bottom, on the need for fairness, and the need to protect the dignity of workers. Returning to the theme of labour rights as human rights, he recalls that the fairness and dignity arguments in favour of labour standards have long pre-dated modern notions of human rights.[62]

In looking to the future Charnovitz examines the merits of the traditional approaches to linking trade and labour issues. He argues that, for various reasons, considerable weight should be given to the view that the mixing of these two issues in a single regime might be harmful to each of the two areas. In other words, trade agreements might be discombobulated by efforts to include labour rights provisions, and the labour regime might suffer from being tethered to trading rules. He thus advocates the adoption, in the FTAA context, of a very different and much more innovative set of arrangements designed to protect labour rights.

The first element would be to strengthen what he terms the role of consumers through measures such as social labelling, industry partnerships, and voluntary codes of conduct provided that the latter are subject to careful monitoring.[63] Second, the agreement should contain enhanced measures to promote 'worker adjustment' or to assist those workers whose jobs are displaced as a result of the agreement. In this respect he picks up on a proposal made by Robert Howse in 1993 in relation to NAFTA but never pursued.[64] Third, existing bans on the activities of trade unions in export processing zones (EPZs) should be disallowed. This should be achieved through the creation of a complaints procedure, enabling aggrieved individuals or affected groups to bring an action against the government concerned, with the possibility of financial sanctions being imposed where violations are found. The fourth and final element in Charnovitz's proposed FTAA package would be greater protection for migrant workers.

D. Labour Rights in the Internal and External Policies of the EU

The last two contributions to the book concern the possibilities and limitations of realizing labour rights through the European Union (EU). The EU is the most

---

[62] Steve Charnovitz, 'The Labor Dimension of the Emerging Free Trade Area of the Americas', p. 165.   [63] *Ibid.*, p. 171.
[64] *Ibid.*, p. 173.

extensive experiment with transnational federal structures of governance in the contemporary world, but as the contributions by Anne Davies and Tonia Novitz illustrate, the competence of the EU to set and enforce labour standards is constrained. As Davies outlines, the EU's power to set labour standards for all members relies upon the use of directives to implement agreements reached by dialogue between 'social partners'.[65] The legitimacy of such directives depends upon the representativeness of the social partners striking the underlying agreement, and as Davies argues, this representativeness is not always assured. It requires that member states have active, independent trade unions and membership-based associations that are able to participate fully as part of the EU's consecrated 'social partner' organizations. Further, these directives may be implemented or derogated from as part of the collective bargaining process within member states. While this raises the possibility that collective agreements within states will exceed the standards contained in the directives, it also entails the risk that basic standards will be bargained away. It relies upon the strength and efficacy of collective bargaining arrangements within member states, which may be lacking.

The EU has been more insistent in its promotion of labour rights in its external relations, through the inclusion of human rights clauses in bilateral and multilateral trading agreements and through its Generalized System of Preferences (GSP). The compatibility of the human rights clauses and the GSP with the non-discrimination requirements of the General Agreement on Tariffs and Trade is open to question, as illustrated by the decision of the WTO Appellate Body in a 2004 ruling that any preferences granted must be based on objective and transparent criteria for the selection of the beneficiary countries.[66] But of greater concern to Davies is that the EU's own lack of internal regulation of labour rights may expose it to charges of hypocrisy that undermine its laudable external policies.

Tonia Novitz's review of the EU's regulation of member states' compliance with ILO conventions highlights further concerns.[67] While the EU's competence to set social policy was expanded by the incorporation into the EU treaty of the Agreement on Social Policy, Novitz observes that few regulatory measures have been taken to ensure EU implementation of ILO standards. For example, no specific EC legislation has been adopted relating to forced labour, even though there appears to be competence to adopt a directive on this subject matter. While the EU has adopted ILO standards as a benchmark for the application of the GSP, ILO supervisory body findings in respect of EU member states are not regarded as sufficient grounds for action by the European Commission. Echoing some of Davies's concerns about the legitimacy of the social dialogue, Novitz notes that there is no regulation of the

---

[65] Anne Davies, 'Should the EU Have the Power to Set Minimum Standards for Collective Labour Rights in the Member States?', Chapter 6 below.

[66] European Communities—Conditions for the Granting of Tariff Preferences to Developing Countries, AB-2004-1, WTO doc. WT/DS246/AB/R, 7 April 2004.

[67] Tonia Novitz, 'The European Union and International Labour Standards: The Dynamics of Dialogue between the EU and the ILO', Chapter 7 below.

process by which decisions are reached in social dialogue. Unlike the ILO tripartite consultation procedures, there exist no official records of debates or engagement of management and labour with government representatives in EU social dialogues.

Both Novitz and Davies note that some scope for the protection of labour rights exists through the European Convention on Human Rights (ECHR), which protects freedom of association. The jurisprudence of the European Court for Human Rights on freedom of association has tended to be narrow and individualistic, but in the *Albany* case the European Court of Justice expanded the content of freedom of association to include a right to collective representation and bargaining. Nevertheless, the ECHR is primarily devoted to the protection of civil and political rights, and it remains to be seen whether the inclusion of economic and social rights, including labour rights, in the European Charter of Fundamental Rights will make a major difference or not. Much will, of course, depend on the approval of the EU Constitution by the member states.

Both authors find that the EU's approach to collective labour rights enforcement within member states is piecemeal, a product of limited competences and of an apparent lack of political will to enable labour rights to play the same role as civil and political rights in the internal regulation of EU states. With the expansion of the EU to twenty-five in May 2004 entailing the admission of ten new states enjoying very different levels of economic development, the potential for regulatory competition between EU member states on the basis of labour standards will be heightened by the continued absence of minimum standards for collective bargaining and collective defence of workers' interests. It may well be that the access of capital to the common market remains a more important priority than common minimum labour standards.

4. CONCLUSION

One of the key questions that emerges from these essays concerns the future of international institution-based efforts to promote labour rights. Most of the contributions have focused on the actual or potential role of organizations, such as the ILO, the EU, the WTO, NAFTA, UNCTAD, and the FTAA, in promoting a concept of labour rights as human rights and then providing the institutional support to make such a vision effective. But looking to such institutions to play those roles is not unproblematic if we take account of the trends towards deregulation, de-institutionalization, and voluntarization of labour rights, which many commentators have observed. Karl Klare, for example, has noted that 'investment protections, fiscal discipline, and exit ramps for capital are setting the substantive [global] agenda, rather than, say, establishment of a transnational floor of social and economic rights'.[68] The fact that international efforts are focused overwhelmingly on the

---

[68] Karl Klare, 'The Horizons of Transformative Labour and Employment Law', in J. Conaghan, R. M. Fischl, and K. Klare (eds.), *Labour Law in an Era of Globalization: Transformative Practices and Possibilities* (Oxford: Oxford University Press, 2002) at 27–8.

liberalization of financial and investment markets and of global trade rules means that efforts to promote labour rights will have to involve a stronger focus on holding transnational corporations and other private actors accountable for their impact upon the enjoyment of human rights in general and labour rights in particular. That in turn raises new questions about the role of international organizations such as the ILO in the light of their own increasing marginalization as a result of the accelerating decentralization of efforts to uphold and protect workers' rights.

At the international level, voluntary codes of conduct are much favoured by many actors. Similarly, at the national level, it has been suggested that in recent years domestic labour law enforcement systems have increasingly taken on many of the characteristics of such codes. Thus, using Canada as a model, Harry Arthurs has argued that the setting of domestic labour standards has become more and more a matter of negotiation, their form is more likely to be hortatory rather than obligatory, labour inspection has been abandoned or downgraded in favour of self-reporting schemes by employers, alternative dispute resolution mechanisms have replaced formal adjudication and sanctions, and 'enforcement' is increasingly the result of bad publicity and/or consumer activism.[69] He explains the attraction of voluntary codes, at both the national and international levels, on the basis that they 'appear to be a promising strategy for enhancing compliance: they are written by employers, administered by employers, and, hopefully, internalized in the operating procedures of employers'.[70]

The challenge of voluntary codes is thus a very important one in terms of the future of labour rights as human rights. The central issues raised have been addressed in detail elsewhere[71] and in the present volume only one aspect of the question needs to be highlighted. It is the need to anchor codes of conduct within the international normative framework of labour rights and to ensure that appropriate standards of accountability are upheld. It is for that reason that in his chapter above, Charnovitz emphasizes the potential of these codes while qualifying his support by insisting that they be effectively monitored. But the challenge of monitoring codes of conduct is one which the ILO has not yet taken up. And the omens do not look good to judge by the fact that the World Commission on the Social Dimensions of Globalization was apparently unable to agree on any constructive moves in this direction. Its report refers to the UN's Global Compact as a 'particularly influential initiative' that has made progress in a number of important respects, such as 'facilitating compliance with relevant national legislation, promoting dialogue and addressing the obstacles to realizing universal principles in global supply chains'.[72] But based on the available evidence this is a curiously optimistic assessment and one which takes no account of the detailed critiques of the Compact made by a great many commentators and human rights

---

[69] Harry Arthurs, 'Private Ordering and Workers' Rights in the Global Economy: Corporate Codes of Conduct as a Regime of Labour Market Regulation', in *ibid.*, 471 at 480.   [70] *Ibid.*, p. 483.

[71] See Philip Alston (ed.), *Non-State Actors and Human Rights* (Oxford: Oxford University Press, forthcoming 2005).   [72] *A Fair Globalization*, note 23 above, p. 122, para. 553.

groups.[73] The Commission goes on to note that some actors have been sceptical about the real impact of voluntary initiatives and reports that 'the view was expressed, in Commission dialogues and elsewhere, that for voluntary initiatives to be credible, there is a need for transparency and accountability'.[74] It almost ostentatiously fails to support that view, however. Indeed, far from following up on such concerns, the Commission proceeds instead to emphasize the important role to be played by business groups and singles out one particular organization. It suggests that 'the International Organization of Employers (IOE) could expand its current efforts in this field'.[75] Curiously, it omits to mention that the IOE has taken the lead among international business groups in opposing efforts to move beyond purely voluntary codes or to ensure some form of independent monitoring or accountability.[76]

But even those who see a major role for the development and application of voluntary corporate and multi-stakeholder codes generally accept that the ILO has a vital role to play in the years ahead. Francis Maupain, who looks in depth in the present volume at certain aspects of the ILO's role, has argued elsewhere that its 'golden age of normative action' lies not in the past but in the future.[77]

Yet the ILO system has been subject to increasing criticism in recent years. Some of the critiques focus on relatively long-standing defects, such as the disproportionate Western representation on the Organization's Governing Body because of the guaranteed presence of the states of 'chief industrial importance'[78] and the only recently abandoned assumption that the Director-General should come from a Western state, such as France, the United States, Belgium, or the United Kingdom.[79] Perhaps more problematic in the twenty-first century is the extent to which the ILO system is geared to a model of employment that is fast disappearing in most states. The late twentieth-century model of a workforce that is highly unionized, working full-time, based in fixed enterprises, and largely male is being displaced by a model that collapses many of the old distinctions between the formal and informal

---

[73] See Philip Alston, 'Creating Space for Non-State Actors in the International Human Rights Regime: An Agenda', in *Non-State Actors and Human Rights*, note 71 above, Chapter 9.

[74] *A Fair Globalization*, note 23 above, p. 122, para. 554.   [75] *Ibid.*, p. 123, para. 556.

[76] In a 'Joint written statement submitted by the International Chamber of Commerce and the International Organization of Employers' commenting on the draft UN Norms on the Responsibilities of Transnational Corporations and Other Business Enterprises with regard to Human Rights the IOE observed that '[t]he binding and legalistic approach of the draft norms will not meet the diverse needs and circumstances of companies and will limit the innovation and creativity shown by companies'. UN doc. E/CN.4/Sub.2/2003/NGO/44, p. 1. For details of the IOE's campaign against any non-voluntary initiatives in this area, see Corporate Europe Observatory, 'Shell Leads International Business Campaign Against UN Human Rights Norms: CEO Info Brief, March 2004', available at: http://www.corporateeurope. org/norms.pdf ('the most vocal opposition has come from the' ICC and the IOE). *Ibid.*, p. 1.

[77] Maupain, 'Le Renouveau du débat normative à l'OIT de la fin guerre froide à la mondialisation', paper presented to ILO, International Labour Standards Department, First Seminar, Geneva, May 2002, at 24.   [78] See ILO Constitution, Art. 7(2).

[79] For a strong statement of these criticisms, see Cooney, 'Testing Times for the ILO: Institutional Reform for the New International Political Economy', 20 *Comp. Lab. L.& Pol'y J.* (1999) 365, at 368.

sectors. It involves a workforce that is less homogeneous, less likely to be unionized, frequently physically decentralized, often part-time, and whose workers harbour few realistic aspirations to obtain the type of benefits and protections inherent in the traditional model.[80] The 'Decent Work' initiative of the ILO Director-General[81] is of course designed to address many of these problems, but it is by no means clear that the supervisory and standard-setting arrangements will be adapted accordingly. Similarly, the famous tripartite system looks less and less like an accurate reflection of the actual model of industrial relations. In relation to workers its emphasis upon established trade unions, which represent an ever-diminishing proportion of most workforces and are ill-equipped to pick up the slack in relation to informal sector and self-employed (home-based) workers, is increasingly anachronistic. In relation to governments, its assumption that governments will represent the national interest and provide a counter-balance to employers and workers is more and more fraught as governments seek to shrink the public sector, unleash the private sector, and are ever more likely to be preoccupied by the need to attract private foreign investment at almost any cost. The third pillar, the employers, have also been transformed by the growth of giant transnational corporations whose importance is poorly recognized in the traditional ILO system and by the rise of outsourcing, which makes it ever more difficult to locate the real employer in any given situation.

If labour rights are to be taken seriously as human rights in the years ahead, much will depend on the approach adopted by the ILO and on the extent to which it opts to pursue a rights-based approach or moves to a much more subtle and flexible approach based, partly on rights, but mainly on principles, guidelines, codes, and the like. While considerable flexibility and ingenuity will be needed, there is a significant risk that attempts will be made to achieve these goals at the expense of a human rights approach. If that happens, then labour rights will become just one more consideration to be taken into account in shaping the values underpinning a liberalized global economy. Given the way in which the power and resources have been distributed amongst the key players in that endeavour there is little reason to expect that labour rights will be accorded anything near the sort of priority which is inherent in the very notion of a human right.

If the ILO is to perform its labour rights mission effectively, it could start by heeding one of the recommendations made by the World Commission, which is that multilateral agencies need to do more in the way of making themselves publicly accountable. While the Commission's recommendations are directed primarily at the World Bank and the International Monetary Fund, it also recommends 'that all UN agencies strengthen their evaluation units, adopt clear disclosure policies with regard to the results of internal and external evaluations of their programmes, policies and projects, and publish these findings accordingly'.[82] The irony is that the

---

[80] *Ibid.*

[81] See *Reducing the Decent Work Deficit—A Global Challenge*, Report by the Director-General for the International Labour Conference, 89th Session, 2001, available at: http://www.ilo.org/public/english/ standards/relm/ilc/ilc89/rep-i-a.htm#1.   [82] *Ibid.*, p. 117, para. 529.

ILO itself is a prime example of an agency that undertakes only the most carefully circumscribed self-evaluations, facilitates virtually no external evaluations worthy of the name, and has no equivalent of the Independent Evaluation Office of the IMF or the Inspection Panel of the World Bank to undertake either genuinely probing evaluations of the effectiveness of its programmes or to respond to complaints lodged by those affected by its programmes. If the future of labour rights as human rights is to rely so heavily upon the ILO in the years ahead, it is essential that such mechanisms be established.

2

Social Rights in a Globalized Economy

SIMON DEAKIN

1. INTRODUCTION

One of the side effects of globalization is a growing interest in the field of fundamental social rights. A number of attempts have been made to restate social rights in the context of transnational legal instruments, most notably through the ILO Declaration on Fundamental Rights and Principles of 1998 and Chapters 3 and 4 of the EU Charter of Fundamental Rights of 2000. Many of the issues surrounding social rights nevertheless remain controversial. The relationship of systems of social protection to processes of economic development is a matter of intense dispute, with claims and counterclaims continually being made concerning their impact on economic growth. Nor is it clear, from a different perspective, how the project of asserting claims to social protection in the form of fundamental rights relates to the existing institutions of welfare state regimes. Since most national welfare state systems are currently undergoing some form of crisis, whether financial, structural, or both, this question has a particular contemporary relevance. Depending on one's point of view, social rights could be a bulwark against neo-liberalism and a mechanism for equipping the welfare state to survive in a globalized world; or, alternatively, a corrosive force, which by individualizing legal claims to access to resources undermines those solidaristic forms of social cohesion around which the twentieth century welfare state was constructed.

The aim of the present chapter is to explore more deeply the nature of these controversies and to see if they can be resolved in a way that lends greater coherence to the notion of social rights. It is possible to address this question in a number of different ways, some of which will involve the empirical analysis of the effects of labour laws and social security laws. Although reference will be made to such studies where appropriate, the main focus of the analysis presented here will be on the institutional form and function of social rights, and in particular on their juridical or legal nature. The approach taken will be, in turn, historical, doctrinal, and conceptual. Thus, Part 2 looks at the complex genealogy of social rights with a view to clarifying their relationship, first, to the growth of industrial capitalism and, secondly, to the advent of the welfare state, drawing principally on the British experience. In Part 3 the focus shifts to the present-day conflict between social rights and transnational economic law in the context of the free movement jurisprudence of the ECJ. Part 4 discusses the potential for renewing the institutions of the welfare state by linking social rights to the concept of 'capability'.

2. SOCIAL RIGHTS, INDUSTRIAL CAPITALISM, AND THE WELFARE STATE IN BRITAIN

A. Social Rights and Industrialization

Our understanding of the evolution of social rights and their relationship to industrialization owes much to T. H. Marshall's classic account in his 1949 Cambridge Lectures, *Citizenship and Social Class*.[1] For Marshall, the concept of citizenship consisted of three parts: the civil, the political, and the social. The civil element 'is composed of the rights necessary for individual freedom—liberty of the person, freedom of speech, thought and faith, the right to own property and to conclude valid contracts, and the right to justice',[2] and was associated above all with the courts. Political rights were 'the right to participate in the exercise of political power, as a member of a body invested with political authority or as an elector of the members of such a body';[3] these rights were the province of the national legislature and local government. Finally, the social element 'covered the whole range from the right to a modicum of economic welfare and security to the right to share in the full in the social heritage and to live the life of a civilized being according to the standards prevailing in society', rights that were expressed through 'the educational system and the social services'.[4]

In Marshall's account, these three components of citizenship were not only conceptually discrete; they were subject to distinct processes of evolution. Thus, 'it is possible, without doing too much violence to historical accuracy, to assign the formative period in the life of each to a different century—civil rights to the eighteenth, political to the nineteenth and social to the twentieth'.[5] In Marshall's view, there had been a time when 'these three strands were woven into a single thread'. Although, in feudal society, 'status was the hallmark of class and the measure of inequality', institutions had nevertheless existed to give expression to 'social rights which had been rooted in membership of the village community, the town and the guild'.[6] It was the process of economic development, beginning in the late Middle Ages and accelerating during the seventeenth and eighteenth centuries, which eroded these institutions and led to the eclipse of social rights during the period of industrialization.

---

[1] T. H. Marshall, 'Citizenship and Social Class', reprinted in T. H. Marshall and T. Bottomore, *Citizenship and Social Class* (1992) (originally published 1949).   [2] *Ibid.*, at p. 8.
[3] *Ibid.*, at p. 8.   [4] *Ibid.*, at p. 8.   [5] *Ibid.*, at p. 10.   [6] *Ibid.*, at p. 9.

This type of interpretation of the British 'Industrial Revolution' has a long history. According to Arnold Toynbee, the first historian to use the phrase, the essence of the Industrial Revolution was 'the substitution of competition for the medieval regulations which had previously controlled the production and distribution of wealth'.[7] Toynbee was writing in the 1880s; the process he was referring to was going on as late as the second decade of the nineteenth century, when the wage-fixing and guild-protection provisions of the mid-sixteenth century Statute of Artificers were repealed. Adam Smith, writing in the mid-eighteenth century, had deemed these laws responsible for 'obstructing the free circulation of labour and stock'.[8] The idea that economic development is a function of liberalization is as old as industrialization itself.

An important institution to consider in this context is the English poor law, the precursor, in many ways, not just of the welfare state, but of employment policy. In the sixteenth and seventeenth centuries, the 'poor' were not simply those with a low income, but all who were dependent on wages from employment as their principal means of subsistence: 'those who labour to live, and such as are old and decrepit, unable to work, poor widows, and fatherless children, and tenants driven to poverty; not by riot, expense and carelessness, but by mischance.'[9] The poor law was, in one sense, a survivor of feudalism; as Marshall put it, 'as the pattern of the old order dissolved under the blows of a competitive economy . . . the Poor Law was left high and dry as an isolated survival from which the idea of social rights was gradually drained away'.[10] Yet there was another sense in which the poor law was a response to the emergence of a labour market. The enactment of legislation dealing with wage rates, poor relief, and labour mobility (or, as it was put, 'vagrancy') from the fourteenth century onwards is evidence how far traditional feudal ties had already declined by that point.

Under the poor law, relief was delivered locally, through parishes (small administrative units covering only a few square miles), but organized nationally, in the sense that within the framework set by the Elizabethan legislation, every parish was required to set a local tax to be paid by householders (a 'poor rate'), to suppress indiscriminate giving, and to organize in its place a regular system of welfare support.[11] Legislation called for the unemployed to be set to work, but the cost of implementing this provision was found to be excessive, and only a minority of parishes constructed workhouses for the purpose; for the most part, those suffering destitution for lack of work received cash doles ('outdoor relief') in the same way as the

---

[7] A. Toynbee, *Lectures on the Industrial Revolution in England*, ed. with an Introduction by T. S. Ashton (1969) (originally published 1884), at p. 78.

[8] A. Smith, *An Inquiry into the Nature and Causes of the Wealth of Nations* ed. J. Nicholson (1886) (originally published 1776), Vol. I, at p. 57.

[9] M. Dalton, *The Country Justice: Containing the Practice, Duty and Power of the Justices of the Peace, as well In as Out of Their Sessions* (1746), at 164.

[10] *Citizenship and Social Class, supra* note 1, at p. 14.

[11] Poor Relief Act 1601 (43 Elizabeth I c. 2), s. 1.

sick and the aged. Local poor law officers were required to provide relief to all those with a *settlement* in the parish in question. Thus, relief became, in a customary sense if not necessarily in the modern legal sense of a justiciable entitlement, the 'peculiar privilege' of the rural poor.[12]

One of the principal means of acquiring a settlement, from the late seventeenth century, was through a yearly hiring, which was the normal form of employment for young, unmarried workers in agriculture. The young thereby had an incentive to leave their home parish to search for employment elsewhere, acquiring a settlement in return for annual service as they moved from one employer to another, thereby ensuring that they would not be subject to removal to their parish of origin. In this way, the poor law, along with the emerging notion of the contract of service, encouraged and supported labour mobility.[13]

The importance of the early modern poor law for economic growth has been highlighted by a revisionist historiography that, contrary to Toynbee's account, stresses how far the English economy had already advanced towards industrialization by the mid-eighteenth century. At that point, within Western Europe, England had the smallest proportion of male adult workers employed in agriculture, the highest rate of urbanization, the fastest growing population, and the most rapidly increasing per capita income.[14] It also had the highest rate of expenditure on poor relief, about seven times per head of population than that of France, for example.[15] Although the major technological advances in the harnessing of coal and steam power to industrial ends were yet to occur, wage labour was already the norm for the majority of both the urban and rural populations. If, as E. A. Wrigley suggests, the essence of the Industrial Revolution was an increase in productivity that made it possible for economic growth to outstrip the rate of growth of the population, the poor law is cast in a new light:

the creation and elaboration of the poor law system from the reign of Elizabeth onwards was an important reason for the development of a capitalist system in England, affording the kind of provision for those in need which gave individuals a degree of protection against the hazards of life that in typical peasant cultures was provided by kin . . . . [I]t facilitated the growth of an economy where mobility was high, where contract could supplant custom, where the individual could risk losing intimate contact with kin.[16]

In Wrigley's account, the British Industrial Revolution consisted of two distinct but overlapping processes: the growth of an 'advanced organic economy' dependent largely upon the more effective use of agricultural resources and techniques, together with the emergence of a 'mineral-based energy economy', which exploited reserves of

---

[12] K. D. M. Snell, *Annals of the Labouring Poor: Social Change and Agrarian England 1660–1900* (1985), at p. 73.   [13] P. Slack, *The English Poor Law 1531–1782* (1990), at 37–8.

[14] E. A. Wrigley, *Continuity, Chance and Change: The Character of the Industrial Revolution in England* (1988), at 12–17.

[15] P. Solar, 'Poor Relief and English Economic Development before the Industrial Revolution', 48 *Economic History Review* (1995), 1, at 7.   [16] *Continuity, Chance and Change, supra* note 14, at 120.

mineral raw materials to advance the mechanization of industry and transport. The positive feedback effects that stemmed from mechanization ensured, over time, that real incomes continued to rise and that the economy could support the growth in population, which Malthus and his followers had predicted would result in a return to poverty and immiseration. But this process of improvement in the living stand-ards of the large majority of the population only unfolded gradually in the course of the nineteenth century. The second half of the eighteenth century saw falling real wages in agriculture at the same time as access to the land was restricted by enclos-ure.[17] The social upheaval that accompanied the depopulation of rural areas was matched, during this time, by a similarly far-reaching process of transformation in the poor law and labour legislation.

The response of those charged with the administration of the poor law to falling real incomes in agriculture in the 1790s was the institution of a practice of wage supplementation, known as the Speenhamland system after the rural district in which it was first adopted. It began as an ad hoc addition of poor relief to wages, designed to bring incomes up to subsistence level. At the same time, attempts to deal with the problem through the implementation of a minimum wage (through the revival of the wage-fixing powers of the Elizabethan Statute of Artificers) were rejected both locally and in the national parliament.[18] The combined effect was to relieve employers of the obligation to pay the customary level of wages; during the same period, yearly hirings were becoming increasingly uncommon,[19] and changes to the law of settlement made it more difficult for wage earners and their dependants to acquire the right to relief.[20] Thus, as employment grew less stable and access to relief by the traditional route of the settlement by hiring, under which the employer absorbed the costs of short-term interruptions to earnings, became increasingly restricted, expenditure on poor relief grew to the point where a national debate was launched on the feasibility of maintaining the poor law system. This continued, at intervals, over several decades in the early nineteenth century, during which time the administration of poor relief became steadily more disciplinary. This process culminated in the 1834 Poor Law Report[21] and the Poor Law (Amendment) Act[22] of the same year.

The new poor law that was put in place after 1834 was founded on the principle of 'less eligibility', meaning that relief should not provide a standard of living superior to that enjoyed by the least-well-off 'independent' household. The

---

[17] *Ibid.*, at 66.

[18] The classic account of Speenhamland remains J. L. Hammond and B. Hammond, *The Village Labourer 1760–1832* (1920).

[19] E. Hobsbawm and G. Rudé, *Captain Swing* (1973) ch 2; Snell, *Annals of the Labouring Poor, supra* note 12, ch 2.

[20] S. Deakin, 'The Contract of Employment: A Study in Legal Evolution', 11 *Historical Studies in Industrial Relations* (2001) 1, at 12–17.

[21] Reproduced in S. G. and E. O. A. Checkland (eds.), *The Poor Law Report of 1834* (1973).

[22] 4 & 5 George IV c. 76.

assumption was that once the 'distortion' of wage supplementation was removed, wages would rise to the point where the subsistence needs could be met. On this basis, the unwillingness of individuals to accept wages set by the market could only be evidence of poor 'character', which it was the role of the law to address by disciplinary means. Thus, a wilful refusal to accept an offer of employment at the going rate of wages became a criminal offence punishable by imprisonment.[23] At this point, in the absence of a minimum wage and before the development of collective bargaining, the relevant wage was whatever an employer was willing to offer, and not the customary rate for that trade. In addition, the simple fact of destitution as a result of unemployment or sickness would normally lead to the confinement in the workhouse of the wage earner and other family members.[24] Beginning in the 1840s, a series of regulatory orders spelled out the implications of this policy for the administration of poor relief: outdoor relief was to be limited as far as possible to the aged and infirm, denied to the adult 'able bodied', and under no circumstances combined with wages; if it were to be paid, exceptionally, to those who were able to work, it had to be combined with a 'labour test' designed to deter the work shy; and in order to ensure that conditions inside the workhouse were, as far as possible, below those of the worst-off household outside, a consciously degrading and punitive regime for workhouse inmates was put in place.[25]

The shift from the old poor law to the new was a pivotal moment in the history of British social and economic policy; controversial at the time, it has proved ever since to be a focal point for rival interpretations of the role of social welfare and labour market regulation in a capitalist economy. The assumption that the practice of wage supplementation was a principal cause of low pay and growing poverty in the rural labour force was the central premiss not just of the 1834 report but of several earlier parliamentary inquiries, some going back to the 1810s. The accuracy of that belief has been questioned by modern economic historians, who have sought to show that the causes of rural poverty in the early nineteenth century were independent of the administration of the poor law.[26] The historical record here is hard to reconstruct because of the paucity of data and the question remains open. More to the point, this

---

[23] Under the Vagrancy Act 1824 (5 George IV c. 83), it was an offence punishable by one month's hard labour to become chargeable to poor relief in the case of 'every person being able wholly or in part to maintain himself, or his or her family, by work or other means, and wilfully refusing or neglecting to do so'. In earlier vagrancy legislation, dating from 1744, a crime was committed only where there was 'a refusal to work for the usual and common wages given to other labourers in the like work'. In the 1824 Act, the reference to 'usual and common wages' was removed.

[24] Workhouses existed in certain parishes prior to 1834, but after that point their use increased substantially thanks to the restriction of outdoor relief.

[25] The principal orders were the Outdoor Relief Prohibitory Order of 21 December 1844, the Outdoor Relief Regulation Order of 14 December 1852, and General Consolidated Order of 24 July 1847 (dealing with workhouse conditions). They are reproduced, with amendments and consolidations, in H. R. Jenner-Fust, *Poor Law Orders* (1907).

[26] In particular, M. Blaug, 'The Poor Law Report Re-examined', 24 *Journal of Economic History* (1964) 229.

line of analysis tells us little about why the system should have changed as radically as it did. The issue is not so much whether the belief in the detrimental effects of poor relief can be seen, with the benefit of hindsight, to have been justified, but why it should have been so prevalent among administrators, commentators, and policy-makers at the time.

The significance of the 1834 reform becomes clearer when it is placed in the context of contemporary debates concerning the nature of emerging market order. For the nineteenth-century utilitarian philosophers and political economists, the demise of the old poor law was necessary if the forces of the supply and demand in the market for labour were to be allowed to operate. Bentham complained that the old poor law had ceased to draw the appropriate distinction between 'natural' poverty, which the law could not hope to relieve, and the 'evil' of indigence. By enabling 'the condition of persons maintained without property by the labour of others [to be] rendered more eligible than that of persons maintained by their own labour', the old poor law removed the incentive to work upon which the market depended for its effectiveness: 'individuals destitute of property would be con-tinually withdrawing themselves from the class of persons maintained by their own labour, to the class of persons maintained by the labour of others; and the sort of idleness, which at present is more or less confined to persons of independent fortune, would thus extend itself sooner or later to every individual . . . till at last there would be nobody left to labour at all for anybody.'[27] In similar terms, J. S. Mill maintained that 'taxation for the support of the poor would engross the whole income of the country; the payers and the receivers would be melted down into one mass'. This could only be avoided if 'a change can be wrought in the ideas and requirements of the labouring class; an alteration in the relative values which they set upon the gratification of their instincts, and upon the increase of their comforts and of the comforts of those connected with them'.[28] In this way, belief in the 'natural' properties of the labour market led to a legal regime designed to punish the workless and destitute.

B. Social Rights and the Welfare State

Just as the new poor law was a response to the perceived failings of Speenhamland, so the welfare state of the twentieth century was constructed by way of reaction against what were seen as the shortcomings of the system put in place after 1834. By the end of the nineteenth century, there was a general consensus that the new poor law had failed in its own terms. Wages had risen following the restriction of outdoor relief, but not to the extent that had been anticipated. Destitution was an ever-present phenomenon in Britain's major urban areas and in many rural districts. When numbers of the unemployed increased, as they did in particular during the long

---

[27] Cited in J. R. Poynter, *Society and Pauperism: English Ideas on Poor Relief 1795–1834* (1969), at 125–6.

[28] J. S. Mill, *Principles of Political Economy* (1909) (originally published 1848), at 368.

recession which lasted from the 1870s to the 1890s, the response of the poor law administrators was to tighten the disciplinary operation of the system; outdoor relief was made more selective, the labour test more severe, and workhouse conditions made more demeaning. Thus, throughout the 1880s and 1890s, a number of urban poor law unions were constructing special 'test workhouses' with the aim of subjecting the adult able-bodied to a particularly stringent regime of discipline.[29]

The sheer expense of this effort was one factor that helped to turn the tide of opinion; also important was the work of the 'social science' movement, which set out to measure the extent of destitution outside the poor law system. In this respect, the empirical work carried out by Charles Booth, Seebohm Rowntree, and William Beveridge demonstrated that the assumptions on which the poor law operated were not borne out in practice. 'Independent' households could not subsist on the wages offered for low-paid work, and were reliant in practice on ad-hoc charitable giving; the casualization of urban occupations undermined efforts to establish a living wage and imposed unnecessary search costs on employers and workers alike.[30]

A key text in laying bare the deficiencies of the new poor law was the Minority Report of the Poor Law Commission of 1909, which was drafted by Sidney and Beatrice Webb. For the Webbs, the new poor law was constructed on a false premiss, namely that destitution was always and everywhere the result of personal irresponsibility. This, in turn, was the result of the undue attention placed in 1834 on 'one plague spot—the demoralization of character and waste of wealth produced in the agricultural districts by an hypertrophied Poor Law'.[31] The Webbs did not believe that the 'personal character' of those in poverty was completely irrelevant; it was 'of vital importance to the method of treatment to be adopted with regard to the individuals in distress'. However, it was not 'of significance with regard to the existence of or the amount of Unemployment'.[32]

As Beveridge had put it, unemployment was 'a problem of industry', that is, a feature of economic organization, rather than the result of personal irresponsibility. His research on casualization[33] was called in aid to show that 'chronic over supply of casual labour in relation to the local demand was produced and continued, irrespective of any excess of population or depression of trade, *by the method by which employers engaged their casual workers*' (emphasis in original). This 'inevitably creates and perpetuates what have been called "stagnant pools" of labour in which there is nearly always some reserve of labour left, however great may be the employer's demand'.[34] It was continued exposure to the effects of underemployment that

---

[29] S. Webb and B. Webb, *The Public Organisation of the Labour Market: Being Part Two of the Minority Report of the Poor Law Commission* (1909), chs 1 and 2.

[30] On the significance of the surveys of urban poverty carried out by Booth and Rowntree, see the account of Rowntree's work in A. Briggs, *Social Thought and Social Action: A Study of the Work of Seebohm Rowntree* (1974); on Beveridge, see J. Harris, *William Beveridge: A Biography* (2nd edn) (1997).

[31] *The Public Organisation of the Labour Market, supra* note 29, at 4.   [32] *Ibid.*, at 233.

[33] *Unemployment: A Problem of Industry* (1909).

[34] *The Public Organisation of the Labour Market, supra* note 29, at 200.

precipitated decline into the final and fourth group, a body which, leaving aside 'the rare figure of the ruined baronet or clergyman' consisted of 'those Unemployables who represent the wastage from the manual, wage earning class'.[35]

To this, the Webbs added a crucial rider: the effects of casualization were exacerbated by the poor law itself. The outdoor labour test, by providing intermittent work for the unemployed, 'facilitates and encourages the worst kind of Underemployment, namely, the unorganized, intermittent jobs of the casual labourer'. Likewise, the workhouse test for the able-bodied, by 'establishing a worse state of things for its inmates than is provided by the least eligible employment outside', not only engendered 'deliberate cruelty and degradation, thereby manufacturing and hardening the very class it seeks to exterminate'; it also 'protects and, so to speak, standardizes the worst conditions of commercial employment'.[36] Thus, the 'fatal ambiguity'[37] of 'less eligibility' was that standards inside and outside the workhouse, since they were mutually reinforcing, would drive each other down, until 'the premises, the sleeping accommodation, the food and the amount of work exacted, taken together, constitute a treatment more penal and more brutalizing than that of any gaol in England'.[38]

The solutions advanced by the Minority Report reflected its diagnosis of the problem. Their principal aim was to remove the 'able-bodied' from the reach of the poor law. The key mechanisms for achieving this end were labour exchanges that, in addition to reducing search costs, would break the power that employers had to maintain 'pools of labour' in reserve, waiting for work:

What a National Labour Exchange could remedy would be the habit of each employer of keeping around him his own reserve of labour. By substituting one common reservoir, at any rate for the unspecialised labourers, we could drain the Stagnant Pools of Labour which this habit produces and perpetuates.[39]

The Minority Report also addressed the issue of unemployment compensation as an alternative to poor law relief. It argued in favour of a hybrid public–private system, under which government would have the power to subsidize the private insurance schemes already run, at that point, by certain trade unions. In the event, the Part II of the National Insurance Act 1911 went further by instituting a fully state-administered system. However, the form of unemployment compensation that initially emerged was similar to that discussed by the Minority Report, namely a system of compulsory insurance 'applied only to particular sections of workers or to certain specified industries, under carefully considered conditions'.[40] This was gradually extended during the inter-war period to cover the vast majority of the workforce; a key feature of the system, and a significant departure from the poor law, was that workers were entitled for the most part to refuse work at wages below those which they had received in their previous employment, or which were out of line

---

[35] *Ibid.*, at 200. [36] *Ibid.*, at 67. [37] *Ibid.*, at 72. [38] *Ibid.*, at 79.
[39] *Ibid.*, at 261. [40] *Ibid.*, at 291.

with standards set by collective agreements between employers' associations and trade unions in the relevant district.

In this respect, social insurance dovetailed with state support for labour standards. The case for general legislative standards in the labour market was put by the Webbs in *Industrial Democracy*, the first edition of which appeared in 1896. Their 'National Minimum' of living and working conditions would 'extend the conception of the Common Rule from the trade to whole community'. Low-paying and casualized trades were 'parasitic' as by paying wages below subsistence they received a subsidy from the rest of the community; thus 'the enforcement of a common minimum standard throughout the trade not only stops the degradation, but in every way conduces to efficiency'. In this respect, the deficiencies of the selective model of regulation contained in nineteenth-century factory legislation were clearly recognized:

this policy of prescribing minimum conditions, below which no employer is allowed to drive even his most necessitous operatives, has yet been only imperfectly carried out. Factory legislation applies, usually, only to sanitary conditions and, as regards particular classes, to the hours of labour. Even within this limited sphere it is everywhere unsystematic and lop-sided. When any European statesman makes up his mind to grapple seriously with the problem of the 'sweated trades' he will have to expand the Factory Acts of his country into a systematic and comprehensive Labour Code, prescribing the minimum conditions under which the community can afford to allow industry to be carried on; and including not merely definite precautions of sanitation and safety, and maximum hours of toil, but also a minimum of weekly earnings.[41]

A third component in the re-regulation of the labour market was provided by full employment policy. In Beveridge's view, an effective social insurance scheme could not work unless 'employment is maintained, and mass unemployment prevented'.[42] The responsibility for providing the conditions for full employment lay with the state: '[i]t must be the function of the State to defend the citizens against mass unemployment, as definitely as it is now the function of the State to defend the citizens against attack from abroad and against robbery and violence at home.'[43] Full employment, in turn, had a specific sense. It did not just refer to the absence of unemployment, but to the availability of employment of a particular kind: 'at fair wages, of such a kind, and so located that the unemployed men can reasonably be expected to take them; it means, by consequence, that the normal lag between losing one job and finding another will be very short.'[44] Beveridge's combined scheme for social security and full employment therefore sought to complete the work of the Minority Report of 1909 in reversing the effect of the poor law. As he put it, 'the labour market should always be a seller's market rather than a buyer's market'.[45]

The welfare state of the mid-twentieth century therefore gave rise to a specific conception of social rights; this was a model of social citizenship based on

[41] S. Webb and B. Webb, *Industrial Democracy* (1920) (originally published 1896), at 767.
[42] W. Beveridge, *Full Employment in a Free Society* (1967) (originally published 1944) at 29.
[43] *Ibid.*, at 29.   [44] *Ibid.*, at 18.   [45] *Ibid.*, at 18.

employment. The duty to work was not completely neutralized. On the contrary, access to economic security depended on labour market participation. However, this was conditional upon the capacity of the state, through a combination of regulation and macroeconomic management, to guarantee access to stable and well-remunerated employment, and to provide for collective provision against the principal hazards for wage earners in a market economy, in particular unemployment, illness, and old age. Encoded in the complex mass of detail of national insurance legislation was a commitment to social integration and solidarity across different occupational groups: '[w]orkers of every grade in every town and village in the country are now banded together in mutual State-aided insurance.... They are harnessed together to carry the industrial population through every vicissitude.'[46]

There were qualifications to this idea, the most important of which was the differential treatment of male and female workers. Beveridge's social insurance scheme treated married women as dependent on a male breadwinner, and allowed them to opt out of most aspects of the scheme; in return they were able to claim the long-term benefits of retirement and widows' pensions on the basis of their husbands' contributions. As a result of decisions taken in the 1940s, a high proportion of married women either stayed outside the national insurance scheme altogether or opted to pay a lower rate, up to the late 1970s.[47] Nevertheless, the reforms of the mid-1970s recognized the need for married women to have access, in their own right, to social insurance benefits, and attempted to make provision for their need to greater flexibility in contribution conditions.[48] Although many of these reforms were rolled back in the deregulatory changes of the 1980s, they suggest that Beveridge's scheme was not structurally incompatible with equal participation by male and female earners.

C. The Genealogy of Social Rights

The social rights that emerged from the mid-twentieth-century welfare state embodied a notion of citizenship centred on labour market participation. Social security legislation—social insurance and social assistance—addressed a specific set of economic risks, those arising from the fact that the vast majority of the population were directly or indirectly dependent on wages for subsistence. The aim of stabilizing employment through collective bargaining and employment policy was to avoid a situation in which the costs of dealing with insecurity fell entirely on the social welfare system. Speenhamland was now reinterpreted as the inevitable consequence of the de-institutionalization of the labour market that occurred at the turn of the nineteenth century. Karl Polanyi's *The Great Transformation*, the first version of which appeared in 1944, saw the old poor law as having 'sheltered' the rural poor 'from the full force of the market mechanism'. However, a policy 'which proclaimed

---

[46] P. Cohen, *Unemployment Insurance and Assistance in Britain* (1938), at 10.
[47] D. W. Williams, *Social Security Taxation* (1982), at para. 10.04.
[48] See A. I. Ogus and E. M. Barendt, *The Law of Social Security* (2nd edn) (1982), at 210.

the "right to live" whether a man earned a living wage or not' was bound to fail, in the process discrediting the traditional objectives of the poor relief system.[49] The solution, for Polanyi and others, lay in the institutional re-regulation of the labour market that accompanied the construction of the welfare state. As a result, social rights were instituted as part of a wider effort to regulate the market mechanism.

Yet a striking feature of British social legislation of this period was how few legal rights it conferred upon individuals, either as workers or as recipients of social security benefits. Social insurance was a partial exception here; it had earlier been conceived as a form of property right, through which benefits were claimed as of right in return for contributions, and a national insurance fund was set up on a quasi-actuarial basis, separate from the revenues raised by general taxation. However, frequent revisions to the contribution conditions, in particular during the 1980s, undermined the notion of entitlement, and changes to the financial structure of the fund rendered meaningless the actuarial calculations of future liabilities that had been made.[50] There was no return to the workhouse and the remnants of the poor law were formally abolished in 1948. However, social assistance benefits, because they were means-tested, contained a significant discretionary element, notwithstanding efforts to put them on a firmer legal footing in the mid-1960s.[51] From the mid-1980s there was a tightening of benefit conditions for both insurance-based and means-tested benefits, and a widening of the range of circumstances under which claimants could be denied support on the grounds of a refusal to take up an offer of employment.[52]

Writing in the late 1940s, Marshall had identified the absence of a clear legal framework for many of the social welfare provisions created at that time. The legal form of social rights differed, he argued, from that of civil and political rights: in relation to the receipt of welfare services, 'the rights of the citizen cannot be precisely defined. . . . A modicum of legally enforceable rights may be granted, but what matters to the citizen is the superstructure of legitimate expectations.'[53] In particular the principle of universal access to health and education services took the concrete form of state provision funded by general taxation and delivered through public employment—so-called 'collective consumption'. This was in contrast to individual civil rights, which Marshall saw as 'an eighteenth century achievement . . . in large measure the work of the courts'. Civil rights, Marshall thought, were 'intensely individual, and that is why they harmonized with the individualistic phase of capitalism'.[54] The social rights of the twentieth century, by contrast, displaced market relations: the process of 'incorporating social rights in the status of citizenship' involved 'creating a universal right to real income which is not proportionate to

---

[49] K. Polanyi, *The Great Transformation: The Political and Economic Origins of our Time* (1957), at 80.

[50] S. Deakin and F. Wilkinson, 'Labour Law, Social Security and Economic Inequality', 15 *Cambridge Journal of Economics* (1991) 125, at 126–32.   [51] Supplementary Benefits Act 1966.

[52] Deakin and Wilkinson, 'Labour Law, Social Security and Economic Inequality', *supra* note 50.

[53] *Citizenship and Social Class, supra* note 1, at 34.   [54] *Ibid.*, at 26.

the market value of the claimant'.[55] As a result, the welfare state was characterized by 'a basic conflict between social rights and market value'.[56]

At the same time, Marshall was also aware that social rights could be seen as embedded within the market order:

Social rights in their modern form imply an invasion of contract by status, the subordination of market price to social justice, the replacement of the free bargain by the declaration of rights. But are these principles quite foreign to the practice of the market today, or are they there already, entrenched within the contract system itself? I think it is clear that they are.[57]

This was particularly true of collective bargaining, which had a dual nature as 'a normal peaceful market operation' that gives expression to 'the right of the citizen to a minimum standard of civilized living'.[58]

Marshall's own work reflects the fundamental tension that he saw as characterizing the welfare state: as he wrote, 'the basic conflict between social rights and market value has not been resolved'.[59] Fifty years on from Marshall's Cambridge lectures, that conflict is posed more sharply than ever. As Alain Supiot reminds us, globalization is 'the latest stage of a process that has unfolded over several centuries'.[60] One part of this is the ascendancy of the Western conception of the market economy, which Supiot argues is 'closely bound up with' Western science and technology. We can observe today many of the transformative features that characterized earlier phases of economic development. In particular, the Industrial Revolution marked a period during which an extension of the market into new areas of social and economic life coincided with rapid technological change. According to E. A. Wrigley, 'the industrial revolution is the centrepiece of world history over recent centuries, and *a fortiori* of the country in which it began'.[61] What lessons then can we draw for the present phase of globalization from a consideration of the British experience?

A long historical tradition associates economic growth with the displacement of regulations governing trade and commerce; for those who take this view, it is appropriate that the British Industrial Revolution should have been a time of what might now be called deregulation, when the last vestiges of pre-modern controls over the economy were swept away. But a closer look at the period in question suggests that this characterization of the Industrial Revolution does not fit the facts. Many of the features of the old poor law were not simply compatible with a market order; they actively promoted labour mobility and the loosening of the ties of kinship and custom that characterized the pre-modern economy. A narrow focus on the period between 1780 and 1830, when social unrest accompanied the final phases of land enclosure and the depopulation of rural areas, masks the significance of the prior period of rapid economic growth, in particular in the first half of the eighteenth

---

[55] *Ibid.*, at 28.   [56] *Ibid.*, at 42.   [57] *Ibid.*, at 40.   [58] *Ibid.*, at 40.

[59] *Ibid.*, at 42.

[60] A. Supiot, 'The Labyrinth of Human Rights: Credo or Common Resource?' 21 *New Left Review* (2003) 118, at 118.   [61] *Continuity, Chance and Change, supra* note 14, at 7.

century, when the system of poor law settlements provided access to a form of economic security for the rural population.

What replaced Speenhamland was a system in which the poor law, rather than being abolished, remained to fulfil a new, disciplinary role. The new poor law, in its turn, came to an end not simply as a consequence of the extension of the franchise and the mobilization of progressive political forces, but because it was seen to have failed in its own terms. The resulting welfare state was constructed on the premiss of solidarity between occupational groups and across generations in relation to the organization of economic risks. The continuation of the new poor law was inconceivable once it was realized, in the Webbs' memorable expression, that 'a hundred different threads of communication connect the slum and the square'.[62]

Thus, far from social rights being inherently antithetical to a market order, it can be argued that they have been part of the process now described in terms of 'globalization' right from the start. Their status may have been severely contested, and the means chosen to articulate them may have changed over time, but their presence, far from being contingent, has been structural and deep-rooted. It remains to explore, in the remaining sections, some of the manifestations of that presence in contemporary doctrinal and conceptual disputes.

3. SOCIAL RIGHTS AND REGULATORY COMPETITION

A. Regulatory Competition and Transnational Economic Law

Transnational flows of goods and services would not be possible without a certain legal and institutional architecture, consisting of the rules of contract and commercial law, which facilitate international trade and protect property rights. Increasingly, in particular over the past two decades, a further type of transnational regulation has emerged, which aims to ensure the free flow of economic resources across borders and the removal of regulatory barriers to trade. This type of regulation has as its aim the integration of national markets, based on the free circulation of goods, capital, and (to a much lesser degree, in practice) labour. At the same time, it creates an additional market mechanism, a market for legal rules in which different regulatory systems are thrown into competition with one another. As states compete to attract and retain scarce resources, the quality and substance of the regulation that they provide becomes an aspect of comparative economic advantage. This process particularly affects social welfare systems, since they are, quintessentially, creations of nation states, dependent upon the regulatory space of country-specific regimes and the tax-raising powers of governments.

Transnational regulatory competition is not an entirely new phenomenon; at other times of liberalization in inter-state trade, states have copied institutional

---

[62] *The Public Organisation of the Labour Market, supra* note 29, at xi.

innovations from one another,[63] and have also taken steps to limit what were seen as the negative consequences of capital movement, in terms of what would now be called 'social dumping'. The last few decades of the nineteenth century and first decade and a half of the twentieth were one such period. The advent of social insurance in Germany in the 1880s spurred on similar developments (although with significant national variations) in Britain and France; while the danger that the standards set by national-level factories legislation would be undercut through competition was one of the motivations for the first international labour treaties in the 1890s.[64] What is new about the more recent appearance of regulatory competition is the exploitation of new possibilities for entry to and exit from jurisdictions, in particular by corporate entities. There is evidence of competition between jurisdictions to attract incorporations in the 1850s, which encouraged the adoption of statutory limited liability in Britain.[65] However, in all these cases, states retained the option to use national legislation to restrict the access of producers or investors to what were seen as lax foreign legal regimes. What gives this phenomenon its current high degree of importance is the degree to which courts exercising the powers granted to them under transnational economic law have sought to prevent states from doing this by ruling against national-level provisions that are either aimed at, or have the effect of, restricting economic movement.

The outcome of this process is not pre-ordained: it is not inevitable that welfare states offering a low-tax, low-regulation regime will win out over alternatives. The quality of public infrastructure and the level of training and education of the workforce are among factors that can induce beneficial capital movements. However, in common with any other competitive process, the market for legal rules operates according to the 'rules of the game', which set the basic conditions for the participation of the relevant actors. For transnational economic law, the issue is one of institutional design; depending on how the rules of the game are set out, different outcomes can be expected. Different rule systems, in turn, can be understood in terms of different theoretical starting-points for regulatory competition.

B. Theories of Regulatory Competition

Regulatory competition can be defined as a process whereby legal rules are selected and de-selected through competition between decentralized, rule-making entities,

---

[63] Thus, the British social insurance model of the early twentieth century drew, in part, on the German model first established in the 1880s (see E. P. Hennock, *British Social Reform and German Precedents: The Case of Social Insurance 1880–1914* (1987)), while the Beveridge blueprint for the reform of the British welfare state influenced developments on the continent of Europe in the 1940s and 1950s, although, again, with significant variations (see R. Kuisel, *Capitalism and the State in Modern France: Renovation and Economic Management in the Twentieth Century* (1981)).

[64] See H. Feis, 'International Labour Legislation in the Light of Economic Theory', *International Labour Review* (1927) 425.

[65] See J. Saville, 'Sleeping Partnership and Limited Liability, 1850–1856', 8 *Economic History Review* (1956) 418, at 429.

which could be nation states or other units, such as regions or localities. Three beneficial effects are expected to flow from this process: (1) it allows the content of rules to be matched more effectively to the preferences or *wants* of the consumers of laws (citizens and others affected); (2) it promotes diversity and experimentation in the search for effective legal solutions; and (3) by providing mechanisms for preferences to be expressed and alternative solutions compared, it enhances the flow of information on effective law making.

The idea was first applied to the production of local public goods.[66] Here, competition operates on the basis of mobility of persons and resources across jurisdictional boundaries. Local authorities compete to attract residents by offering packages of services in return for levying taxes at differential rates. Consumers with homogenous wants then 'cluster' in particular localities. The effect is to match local preferences to particular levels of service provision, thereby maximizing the satisfaction of wants while maintaining diversity and promoting information flows between jurisdictions. Laws, similarly, can be seen as products that jurisdictions *supply* through their law-making activities, in response to the *demands* of consumers of the laws, that is, individuals, companies, and other affected parties.

Regulatory competition, in its various forms, requires a particular division of labour between different levels of rule-making. It cannot work unless effective regulatory authority is exercised by entities operating at a devolved or local level. Law-making powers should be conferred on lower-level units, subject only to the principle that there must be some level below which further decentralization becomes infeasible because of diseconomies of scale. But there is also a role for a federal or transnational body, which involves superintending the process of competition between the lower-level units. Individual units could shut down competition unilaterally, either by placing barriers to the movement of the factors of production beyond their own territory or by denying access to incoming capital, labour, and services, or both. Hence, the central or federal authority has the task of guaranteeing effective freedom of movement. But this task, in and of itself, may well require active interventions of various kinds.

In Tiebout's pure theory, freedom of movement is *assumed* for the purpose of setting up the formal economic model. The model does not aim to explain the institutional underpinnings of mobility (such as the mechanics of the principle of non-discrimination, and the (federal) legislation to facilitate free movement). Instead, the model is aimed at showing that, *given* an effective threat of exit, spontaneous forces would operate in such a way as to discipline states against enacting laws that set an inappropriately high (or low) level of regulation. The model can, however, be used as a benchmark against which to judge institutional measures aimed at instituting regulatory competition. Since, in the 'real' world, mobility of persons and of non-human economic resources is self-evidently more limited than it is in the world of pure theory, two prerequisites for making exit effective may be

---

[66] C. Tiebout, 'A Pure Theory of Local Expenditure', 64 *Journal of Political Economy* (1956) 416.

identified: legal guarantees of freedom of movement for persons and resources, and application of the principle of mutual recognition. In addition, it is accepted that some unwanted side effects of competition ('externalities' or spill-over effects of various kinds) may arise, thereby giving rise to an efficiency-related argument for some harmonization, although there is in general a presumption against federal intervention and in favour of allowing rules to emerge through the competitive process. Thus, the task of analysis, in this approach, becomes that of identifying how far the 'real world' departs from the pure theory and using legal mechanisms to realign the two.[67] This is the approach to regulatory competition that is generally characterized as *competitive federalism*. Competitive federalism is therefore based on the idea that selected institutional interventions can be deployed in such a way as to bring supply and demand for laws into equilibrium.

By contrast, the second model, that of *reflexive harmonization*,[68] begins from the presumption that competition is a process of discovery through which knowledge and resources are mobilized. From this point of view, which is associated with the 'Austrian' economics of Schumpeter and Hayek, competition is valued not for the end state or equilibrium which it brings about, but for the process which it engenders, namely a process whereby information is generated and put into circulation. Hence 'hidden in the historical experience of economic integration, there is . . . a very important aspect of "system dynamics": international competition in the field of the welfare state serves as a kind of process of discovery to identify which welfare state package—for whatever reason—turns out to be economically viable in practice'.[69] The wealth or well-being of society is increased according to how far information (including knowledge or 'applied information') that is privately held can be mobilized through the market process. In the case of regulatory competition, the information in question is that which relates to the variety of different approaches to regulation that are possible in a decentralized system. Moreover, the aim of intervention is not the correction of so-called imperfections, which prevent the market from arriving at an optimal allocation. These 'imperfections', which in another sense are simply *differences* between systems, are the very basis on which learning can take place. In this sense, diversity of national systems is a good in its own right. It is only on the basis of diversity that a wide range of potential solutions to common regulatory problems can emerge. The wider the 'pool' of solutions from which lawmakers can choose, the more likely that the system as a whole will achieve *dynamic efficiency*, in the sense of its capacity to adapt and survive under rapidly changing environmental conditions.

[67] R. Van den Bergh, 'The Subsidiarity Principle in European Community Law: Some Insights from Law and Economics', 1 *Maastricht Journal of European and Comparative Law* (1994) 337.

[68] S. Deakin, 'Two Types of Regulatory Competition: Competitive Federalism versus Reflexive Harmonisation. A Law and Economics Perspective on *Centros*', 2 *Cambridge Yearbook of European Legal Studies* (1999) 231.

[69] K. H. Paqué, 'Does Europe's Common Market Need a Social Dimension? Some Academic Thoughts on a Popular Theme', in J. Addison and W. S. Siebert (eds.), *Labour Markets in Europe: Issues of Harmonisation and Regulation* (1997), at 109.

Even though uniformity is not being achieved, it remains appropriate to speak of 'harmonization' in this context, since the dynamic model presupposes a particular role for the federal or central authority beyond simply ensuring freedom of movement. The aim of reflexive harmonization is to protect the autonomy and diversity of national or local rule-making systems, while at the same time seeking to 'steer' or channel the process of evolutionary adaptation of rules at state level. In this model, the process by which states may observe and emulate practices in jurisdictions to which they are closely related by trade and by institutional connections is more akin to the concept of 'co-evolution' than to convergence around an 'evolutionary peak'. Co-evolution assumes that a variety of diverse systems can co-exist within an environment, each one retaining its viability.[70]

This idea is adapted from theories of reflexive law, which represent an attempt to move beyond a straightforward dichotomy between, on the one hand, 'instrumentalist' theories of regulation and, on the other, 'deregulatory' theories that argue for the removal of all external regulatory controls.[71] The essence of reflexive law is the acknowledgement that regulatory interventions are most likely to be successful when they seek to achieve their ends not by direct prescription, but by inducing 'second-order effects' on the part of social actors. In other words, this approach aims to 'couple' external regulation with self-regulatory processes. The preferred mode of intervention is for the law to underpin and encourage autonomous processes of adjustment, in particular by supporting mechanisms of group representation and participation, rather than to intervene by imposing particular distributive outcomes. This type of approach is illustrated by legislation that seeks, in various ways, to devolve or confer rule-making powers to self-regulatory processes. This occurs where, for example, laws which permit collective bargaining by trade unions and employers to make qualified exceptions to limits on working time or similar labour standards,[72] or confer statutory authority on the rules drawn up by professional associations for the conduct of financial transactions.[73] 'Reflexive harmonization' is the equivalent of this process at the level of transnational or federal economic law.

C. Negative Harmonization: The Role of the Courts

The power of courts to require the elimination of national-level rules that are thought to constitute a de facto barrier to trade can lead to what may be characterized as 'negative harmonization', that is, to the reduction of state-level regulations to a low common standard. Courts have a power to order the removal of laws that fall foul of the principle of free movement, but do not normally have the

---

[70] G. Teubner, *Law as an Autopoietic System* (1992), at 52.

[71] *Ibid.*; see also R. Rogowski and T. Wilthagen (eds.), *Reflexive Labour Law* (1994).

[72] S. Deakin and F. Wilkinson, 'Rights v. Efficiency? The Economic Case for Transnational Labour Standards', 23 *Industrial Law Journal* (1994) 289.   [73] J. Black, *Rules and Regulators* (1998).

capacity to insist on the raising of standards through national legislation; hence the 'negative' aspect of this form of harmonization. In practice, this is a familiar technique in systems based on the model of competitive federalism.

The so-called Delaware effect in US corporate law is an example of this process. The state of Delaware is the principal site for the incorporation of larger US companies: over 40 per cent of companies listed on the New York Stock Exchange and over 50 per cent of the top Fortune 500 companies are incorporated in that state. At the two extremes of the debate over the Delaware effect are two views: one holds that the Delaware legislature and courts attracted incorporations by diluting standards of shareholder protection, thereby engineering a 'race to the bottom';[74] the other maintains that Delaware has won out because its laws offer the best available set of solutions to the problem of agency costs arising between shareholders and managers.[75] Adherents of the race to the bottom hypothesis claim that, although the process of law-making in Delaware is susceptible to the threat of disincorporation by companies, it is managers rather than shareholders who typically take decisions relating to the company's legal domicile. In the event of potential conflicts of interests between shareholders and managers, it is the interests of the latter that will tend to prevail. This can be seen in the willingness in the 1990s of the Delaware legislature, and to a certain extent of the courts, to adopt rules that can be construed as pro-management in the sense of allowing potential takeover targets to put defensive mechanisms in place against the threat of hostile takeover,[76] and in the passage in the 1990s of a law allowing companies to opt out of stringent standards of care in respect of directors' liability for negligence.[77]

The idea that Delaware law represents a lowest common denominator has, however, been challenged by accounts which insist that any attempt by managers to downgrade shareholder interests would, over time, have led to a hostile response by the capital markets. Managers would have an incentive to incorporate under the law of a state that favoured shareholder interests and to shun states that harmed investors, thereby driving up the cost of capital.[78]

It is not possible to resolve here the debate over the optimality or otherwise of Delaware corporate law. Of more interest is the process by which Delaware achieved its pre-eminence. Regulatory competition rested upon the existence of a set of prior conditions, which provided the basis for freedom of companies to incorporate in the state of their choice. A nineteenth-century US Supreme Court decision,

---

[74] W. Cary, 'Federalism and Corporate Law: Reflections on Delaware', 83 *Yale Law Journal* (1974) 663.

[75] F. Easterbrook and D. Fischel, *The Economic Structure of Corporate Law* (1992).

[76] L. Bebchuk and A. Ferrell, 'Federalism and Takeover Law: The Race to Protect Managers from Takeovers', 99 *Columbia Law Review* (1999) 1168.

[77] D. Charny, 'Competition among Jurisdictions in Formulating Corporate Law Rules: An American Perspective on the "Race to the Bottom" in the European Communities', in S. Wheeler (ed.), *A Reader on the Law of the Business Enterprise* (1994), at 368.

[78] Easterbrook and Fischel, *The Economic Structure of Corporate Law, supra* note 75.

Paul v. *Virginia* (1869),[79] established that states were not able to attach special requirements to corporations that had been chartered in other jurisdictions as a condition of allowing them to do business on their territory. This was interpreted as meaning that states had to operate a rule of mutual recognition, according to which an incorporation that was effective in one state was acknowledged by the others. In the final quarter of the nineteenth century, New York based corporations began to reincorporate in New Jersey to take advantage of a looser regulatory regime, designed by members of the New York corporate bar. In the 1890s and 1900s Delaware displaced New Jersey when the latter, under the influence of the Progressive political movement, introduced a number of regulatory constraints on large corporations including controls over the holding of shares in one company by another. The Delaware corporate regime had been initially designed to facilitate the operations of the Du Pont corporation, which, at that stage, was the only significant company that was registered in the state. The Delaware law had been 'drafted under the auspices of the Du Pont family to protect their managerial and shareholder interests' and 'appeared relatively favourable to manager-shareholders of other corporations as well'.[80] Since it obtained its initial advantage, a number of factors have served to consolidate Delaware's position. Specialization means that Delaware enjoys an advantage over other states in terms of the large body of case law that it has built up, the expertise of its courts, and the speed with which they can deal with complex corporate litigation.[81]

One of the reasons for the absence of a market for incorporations in the EU, by contrast to the United States, is the absence of a similar principle of mutual recognition for the decisions of companies to incorporate in a particular jurisdiction. As a result the EU member states do not have a common approach to the issue of the applicable law of corporate constitutions. The United Kingdom, along with Ireland, the Netherlands, and Denmark, operates a 'state of incorporation' rule, according to which the applicable law is that of the state in which the company is incorporated or registered. The effect of the incorporation approach is that, as in the United States, the applicable law is a matter of choice for managers of the company or, in the final analysis, for its shareholders; a company can carry on business in one member state while being incorporated in another. The company laws of the state of incorporation will prevail.

This is in contrast to the position in member states that operate the so-called 'real seat' or *siège réel* doctrine. The effects of the *siège réel* doctrine are complex and differ from one state to another, and according to the context which is being considered. Essentially, however, it means that courts will regard the applicable law as that of the member state in which the company has its main centre of operations—its head office or principal place of business. If the company in question has incorporated elsewhere, a number of consequences may then follow. In some instances, the effect

---

[79] 75 US 168.   [80] Charny, 'Competition among Jurisdictions', *supra* note 77, at 368.
[81] M. Roe, 'Takeover Politics', in M. Blair (ed.), *The Deal Decade* (1993).

will be to deny certain advantages of corporate form to the shareholders; in others, the law of the state in which the company has its head office will be applied over that of the state of incorporation. In either event, the effect of the *siège réel* doctrine is to limit freedom of incorporation; in that sense, it obstructs the emergence of a 'Delaware effect', since a key aspect of that is the principle that entities can be incorporated in a state where they have no physical or other business presence.

The legality of the *siège réel* doctrine under EU law has often been called into question under the EC Treaty, most importantly as a result of the *Centros* decision of the European Court of Justice of 9 March 1999 and two later decisions confirming (and to some degree extending) *Centros*,[82] *Überseering*[83] and *Inspire Art*.[84] In *Centros* two Danish citizens, Mr and Mrs Bryde, incorporated a private company of which they were the sole shareholders, named Centros Ltd, in the United Kingdom. One of the two shareholders then applied to have a 'branch' of the company registered in Denmark for the purposes of carrying on business there. A 'branch', for this purpose, refers not to a subsidiary company, but simply to a business or trading presence, in one country, of a company that is registered in another country.

At the time of the registration request, Centros Ltd had never traded in the United Kingdom. The Danish Registrar of companies refused to register the branch as requested, on the grounds that what the company was trying to do was to register not a branch but, rather, its principal business establishment. The Registrar took the view by incorporating in the United Kingdom, which has no minimum capital requirement for private companies, and subsequently seeking to carry on business in Denmark through a branch, the company's owners were seeking to evade the Danish minimum capital requirements, which are designed to protect third-party creditors and minimize the risk of fraud.

The Court ruled that the refusal to accede to the registration request was contrary to the right of freedom of establishment under Article 43 (ex. Art. 52) of the Treaty, read with Articles 46 (ex. 56), and 48 (ex. 58). It held, first, that there was a potential infringement of freedom of establishment in any case where 'it is the practice of a Member State, in certain circumstances, to refuse to register a branch of a company having its registered office in another Member State'. The Court then went on to conclude that the Danish government had failed to show that the refusal to register was justifiable in the circumstances.[85]

A full consideration of the doctrinal implications of *Centros* and its progeny lies beyond the scope of the present discussion, which will focus instead on its likely implications for regulatory competition in the EU. *Centros* needs to be seen in the context of a wider range of decisions in which the Court has developed a principle of

---

[82] Case C-212/97, *Centros Ltd. v. Erhvervs-og Selskabsstryrelsen*, [1999] ECR-I 1459.

[83] Case C-208/100, *Überseering BV v. Nordic Construction Co. Baumanagement GmbH*, [2002] ECR I-9919.

[84] Case C-167/01, *Kamer van Koophandel en Fabrieken voor Amsterdam v. Inspire Art Ltd.*, [2003] ECR I-10155.

[85] For further details, see Deakin, 'Two Types of Regulatory Competition', *supra* note 68.

free access to national markets for the economic resources of goods, persons, services, and capital. Different concepts have been applied in the case law, which has been generated by the respective Treaty provisions governing these 'economic freedoms' and different results have followed in each case. Over time, however, the Court has moved away from requiring the complainant to show that the national law which is being attacked has a discriminatory effect, based on the nationality of the goods, services, or persons in question. Nor is it necessary in all cases to demonstrate a *formal* barrier to movement, blocking market access; it is enough to show a *substantive* barrier in the sense of a measure that appreciably increases the *costs* of movement.[86] *Centros* was just such a case, and lies, indeed, at the extreme end of the decisions that the Court has decided. This is because the true issue of access in this case was not the access of Centros Ltd to Danish markets but the access of Mr and Mrs Bryde to English company law. And from this perspective, it is abundantly clear that not only was there no discrimination on the grounds of nationality in the decision of the Danish company registrar, but that the decision to deny the Brydes the right to use Centros Ltd to trade in Denmark did not so much bar their access to English law as simply decrease the benefit to them of using it, in the sense that they could no longer take advantage of the less stringent UK rules on minimum capital.

Centros does not necessarily imply that principles of company law that could be seen as raising the costs of market access, such as German-style co-determination laws granting employees seats on the board, will be struck down in future; all depends on the application of the proportionality test. Nor does the principle in *Centros* yet operate in the context of labour legislation, where a principle of territoriality applies: member states are entitled to apply employment laws to all employers operating on their territory regardless of the state of their incorporation or seat, and to place strict limits on attempts to stipulate an alternative applicable law in the contract of employment.[87] But it is not difficult to see what the consequences for welfare state regimes would be if these existing limits on the logic of free movement were to be removed. The wide ruling on the meaning of the market access principle in *Centros* would have the effect of placing a burden on member states to justify national-level regulations across a broad range of areas affecting economic activity, according to criteria to be set in the final analysis by the Court itself, using the proportionality test. In that sense, *Centros* is characteristic of the legal techniques used to promote globalization: in empowering corporations, it disempowers nation states, and in subjecting state laws to a test of proportionality, it transfers the decision on the content of legislation from elected representatives to judges applying a quasi-federal law.

[86] This point is discussed in greater detail in C. Barnard and S. Deakin, 'Market Access and Regulatory Competition', in C. Barnard and J. Scott (eds.), *The Law of the Single Market: Unpacking the Premises* (2002) 197.

[87] See generally S. Deakin, 'Labour Law as Market Regulation', in P. Davies *et al.* (eds.), *European Community Labour Law: Principles and Perspectives. Liber Amicorum Lord Wedderburn* (1997), and the case law cited there.

The inherently deregulatory tendency of the Court's approach to free movement and mutual recognition can be seen by contrasting *Centros* with a case on free movement of labour, *Graf*.[88] Mr Graf was a German national who, after working in Austria for four years, returned to take up an employment in Germany. Under Germany employment law he would have been entitled to severance pay, but in Austria this was not available in his case because he terminated the employment on his own initiative. Mr Graf complained that the absence in Austrian law of a similarly generous principle of severance pay to that found in Germany constituted a barrier to his freedom of movement. Unsurprisingly, perhaps, the Court threw out this argument, citing two grounds: in the first place, there was no discrimination on the grounds of nationality in this case; and secondly, the interference with Mr Graf's rights of free movement was 'trivial and uncertain'. As Advocate General Fennelly put it, 'neutral national rules could only be deemed to constitute material barriers to market access, if it were established that they had actual effects on market actors akin to exclusion from the market'; he criticized the use of the freedom of movement principle as a 'means of challenging any national rules whose effect is simply to limit commercial freedom'.[89]

In respect of the use of a discrimination test and of an insistence on the need to show a formal bar on access, *Graf* stands at the opposite end of the scale to *Centros*, demonstrating how widely varying the effects of the Court's jurisprudence can be depending on context. In this regard it is surely not accidental that what Mr Graf was asking the Court to do was to impose a higher standard of employment protection upon Austrian law, requiring it to level up to the German norm. It seems that it is when the Court is asked to *raise* regulatory standards, that resort to a formal and restrictive test of market access once again becomes appropriate.

D. Positive Harmonization: The Form and Function of Transnational Labour Standards

The power to raise standards to a common norm is generally the province of transnational regulatory bodies (such as the ILO) or federal legislatures (such as the US Congress or, to extend somewhat the qualification 'federal', the law-making bodies of the European Union). This power is, however, only incompletely exercised, even in the European context where there is now a substantial body of Treaty provisions, directives, and other forms of legal instruments setting labour standards. The incomplete coverage of EU provisions in the labour and social field is not simply the result of the difficulty in arriving at a political consensus between the member states; it originates in the structure of the Treaty of Rome, which relegated social policy to a marginal position from which it has never effectively recovered. This was the consequence, in turn, of a conscious decision not to seek to harmonize

---

[88] Case C-190/98, *Graf v. Filzmozer Maschinenbau GmbH* [2000] ECR I-493.
[89] Case C-190/98, *Graf v. Filzmozer Maschinenbau GmbH* [2000] ECR I-493, Opinion, at para. 32.

basic labour standards across the original six member states. There were a number of reasons for this stance. The Community's founders accepted the economic argument that free trade, in itself, should lead to a levelling up of standards, at least in the context of a relatively homogeneous set of national economies; they also believed that a broad, cross-party commitment to the maintenance and, indeed, extension of national welfare state regimes was sufficient protection against the threat of social dumping. In those few areas of regulation where they accepted the principle of harmonization, such as equal pay between men and women, they were only prepared to insert a reference to social rights in the Treaty by a rather complex economic argument that sought to show that a distortion of competition could be assumed to exist as a result of social discrimination; social policy arguments on their own would not suffice.[90]

Notwithstanding this slow start, the range of social and labour policy matters subjected to Community-level regulation has gradually increased over the years,[91] and the influence of European social policy on member states otherwise committed to a neo-liberal policy stance, in particular the United Kingdom, has been highly significant.[92] For present purposes the most noteworthy feature of the labour law and social policy directives is their form. They do not seek to impose a single level of provision in the member states, either in the sense of uniform laws or by reference to the idea of a 'level playing field'.[93] On the contrary, more or less without exception, these directives set a floor of rights upon which, it is supposed, the member states will build. A uniform cost structure is not, and cannot be, the intended result; scope for experimentation and diversity is built into the system. This is an illustration of one of the more puzzling and paradoxical, and yet fundamental, features of harmonization European-style, namely that it is a force for *averting uniformity* and *preserving diversity* between member states.

Thus, the level of diversity within the system as a whole is what truly distinguishes the European Union from the United States. Delaware represents, curiously, a race to converge; by comparison to the great degree of variety in the corporate laws of the European Union, the state laws of the United States, *in relative terms*, cluster around the Delaware model. There is no such cluster in Europe, where significant differences remain not simply between civil law and common law countries but within these legal families in respect of some of the most basic features of corporate law, in particular concerning the respective positions of shareholders, employees, and creditors. This is, in part, the result of the continuing influence of the real seat principle. But it is also related to the different regulatory styles in the area of harmonization.

---

[90] See Deakin, 'Labour Law as Market Regulation', *supra* note 86, for a more extended analysis of these points.

[91] For a full account, see J. Kenner, *EU Employment Law: From Rome to Amsterdam and Beyond* (2003).

[92] See W. Brown, S. Deakin, and P. Ryan, 'The Effects of British Industrial Relations Legislation 1979–1997', 161 *National Institute Economic Review* (1997) 69.

[93] See the examples discussed in Deakin and Wilkinson, 'Rights v. Efficiency?', *supra* note 72, and Deakin, 'Labour Law as Market Regulation', *supra* note 87.

US accounts of the Delaware effect neglect to take full account of the tendency for central regulation to be imposed in situations where inter-state competition has been seen to fail, or is too slow or haphazard in its effect. In these situations, harmonization tends to take a particular form, namely that of *federal pre-emption*. US federal regulation in such areas as company law, labour law, and environmental law frequently acts as a 'monopoly regulator', excluding all scope for state initiative.[94] This is the case, for example, with regard to securities regulation and the law governing collective bargaining. In both these areas, the federal legislature intervened in the 1930s to cure what were seen as fundamental failings of state-level regulation. The courts subsequently applied the pre-emption doctrine to hold that these federal regulations 'occupied the field' in such a way as to prevent the states from legislating in the area. This form of pre-emption contains a very strong version of centrally imposed uniformity: where it applies, states are not simply prevented from derogating from the standards set by the federal legislature; it is very often the case that they cannot improve on them either. The Securities and Exchange Act 1934 and the National Labor Relations Act 1935 are still (partially) in force today, notwithstanding long-standing criticisms from commentators on all sides of the policy debate who argue that a return to state autonomy would better serve the policy goals of intervention in these areas.

US-style competitive federalism, therefore, is distinguished not simply by its stress on a particular form of inter-state competition, but also its use of a certain type of centralized regulation as a way of achieving policy goals when inter-state competition breaks down. The description of a 'monopoly regulator' which US critics use to attack federal intervention is appropriate in a system that tends to react to extreme failures in the market for regulation by shutting down competition entirely. The criticisms may be justified, but the critics should also recognize that the counterpoint of unbridled competition versus monopoly regulation has a certain logic to it: it is precisely because the system of decentralized law-making so often led to extreme coordination failures, as in the case of the capital markets and labour markets of the 1930s, that the federal legislature, in its turn, came to intervene with the goal of shutting down inter-competition entirely in contexts where it was perceived to have failed.

A different logic underpins the transnational harmonization of laws in the European Community. Here, the purpose of harmonization is not to substitute for state-level regulation; hence, the transnational standard only rarely operates to 'occupy the field' in the manner of a 'monopoly regulator'. Rather, transnational standards in effect seek to promote diverse, local-level approaches to regulatory problems by creating a space for autonomous solutions to emerge when, because of market failures, they would not otherwise do so. Because directives in the areas of labour law, consumer protection, and environmental law are mostly interpreted as setting basic standards in the form of a 'floor of rights', prohibiting 'downwards' derogation, member states are allowed, and implicitly encouraged, to improve on the standards set centrally.[95]

---

[94] R. Romano, 'Empowering Investors: A Market Approach to Securities Regulation', 107 *Yale Law Journal* (1998) 2359, at 2394.   [95] Deakin and Wilkinson, 'Rights v. Efficiency', *supra* note 72.

Further features of EC labour and corporate law suggest that the model of reflexive harmonization offers an innovative and distinctive solution to some of the issues arising from the growth in transnational regulatory competition. The Social Dialogue process involves non-state entities, the social partners, directly in the law-making process. At EC level, the inter-professional social partners, UNICE, CEEP, and TUC, have the right to be consulted on proposals put forward by the organs of the Community in the social policy sphere; they may also negotiate collective agreements that can be given legal effect by a decision of the EU Council, a process that has led to the adoption of a number of directives.[96]

The involvement of the social partners also operates at the level of supplementing and implementing these directives, since many of the norms they contain can be varied or modified by agreement between employers and employee representatives at national or sub-national level. Thus, the Parental Leave Directive lays down two main rights: the right of both male and female workers to parental leave for at least three months on the birth or adoption of a child, and time off work in situations of urgent family need. The framework agreement made between the social partners at the EU level provides that 'the conditions of access and detailed rules of application' concerning these rights are to be agreed by the member state and/or by agreement between management and labour.[97] In the United Kingdom, legislation implementing the directive has incorporated a role for self-regulation, by allowing the relevant standards to be given effect, in part, through a collective agreement or workplace agreement. It is only if no such agreement is made that a set of 'default rules', specifying minimum fallback standards, comes into play.[98] Thus, the involvement of the social partners at all levels—in negotiating the content of the framework agreements at the pre-legislative stage and in implementing the resulting standards—illustrates the possibilities inherent in reflexive harmonization.[99]

---

[96] The most important of these are Council Directive 96/34/EC on the framework agreement on parental leave concluded by UNICE, CEEP, and the ETUC, OJ 1996 L145, 19.6.96; Council Directive 97/81/EC concerning the framework agreement on part-time work concluded by UNICE, CEEP, and the ETUC, OJ 1998 L14, 20.1.98; and Council Directive 99/70/EC concerning the framework agreement on fixed-term work concluded by UNICE, CEEP, and the ETUC, OJ 1999 L175, 10.7.99.

[97] Directive 96/34/EC, Annex: Framework Agreement on Parental Leave, cls 2(3), 3(2).

[98] See the Maternity and Parental Leave etc. Regulations, SI 1999/3312, Part III and Scheds. 1–2 (stipulating, respectively, the conditions for workforce agreements, and the default conditions which apply if collective or workplace agreement is made).

[99] This is not to say that solutions which depend upon the encouragement by law of self-regulation will always work smoothly. The implementation in the United Kingdom of the Working Time Directive (Council Directive 93/104/EC concerning certain aspects of the organization of working time, OJ 1993 L307, 12.12.93) offers a case study in the ineffectiveness of 'reflexive law' in a context where local-level mechanisms for transposing and implementing labour standards, at the same time as making their application more flexible, are lacking. See C. Barnard, S. Deakin, and R. Hobbs, 'Opting Out of the 48 Hour Week: Employer Necessity or Individual Choice? An Empirical Study of the Operation of Article 18(1)(b) of the Working Time Directive in the UK', 32 *Industrial Law Journal* (2003) 223.

E. Regulatory Competition and the Welfare State

The conclusion to draw from the discussion in this section is that there is no one best model of regulatory competition. Rather, the nature of regulatory competition is dependent on the institutional environment or 'framework' that defines the relationship between the different levels of government. Systems that approximate to the model described above in terms of 'competitive federalism' tend to give rise to a race to converge, which could be either a race to the top or to the bottom; an optimal outcome is not guaranteed. The solution to extreme market failures, which would otherwise lock in inefficient rules, is pre-emption, that is, federal intervention that occupies the field to the complete exclusion of local initiative. By contrast, in the model referred to as 'reflexive harmonization', intervention has the goal of preserving diversity in order to make it possible for regulatory competition to operate as a process of discovery, based on a form of mutual learning between states. We see here the beginnings of a 'human and social hermeneutics of economic law'[100] to set against the deregulatory effects of globalization.

It follows that it would be a mistake to conclude that regulatory competition is necessarily harmful to welfare state systems. There is scope for a 'race to the top' and for systems to learn from each other's innovations, just as they did in the formative years of the welfare state at the end of the nineteenth century. It is equally important, though, not to neglect or somehow to overlook the role played by the framework conditions that set the rules of the game for transnational economic law. In the European context, this requires a close focus on case law in the area of freedom of movement and on the technical form in which directives are drafted, since it is at this level of micro-juridical analysis that large issues of principle are currently being fought out.

4. SOCIAL RIGHTS, CAPABILITIES, AND THE RENEWAL OF THE WELFARE STATE

A. Social Rights as a Response to Neo-liberalism

As we have seen,[101] idea of social rights was on the margins of the mid-twentieth-century welfare state, which was focused instead on collective provision of social goods. In the case of health, housing and education, form mirrored functions. The state intervened through 'collective consumption'—the direct provision of services, financed through general taxation—with the aim of overcoming inequalities resulting from market forces. In the labour market, collective bargaining and employment protection legislation provided countervailing power to set against the superior bargaining strength of the employer. With direct state provision of social

---

[100] Supiot, 'The Labyrinth of Human Rights', *supra* note 60, at 135.
[101] See section 2, above.

goods and collective bargaining now in decline, legal and constitutional mechanisms are increasingly being used to assert social claims. As these social claims are framed in the language of civil and political rights, they become accommodated to certain aspects of a neo-liberal economic logic. This is a process with unsettling and unpredictable effects. On the one hand, market discourses, based on notions of contract, competitiveness, and efficiency, enter the field of labour and social law; on the other, market relations are infused by notions of equality of access to economic resources drawn from the jurisprudence of social rights. In both respects, the familiar division between the 'social' and the 'economic' is blurred.

The key question posed by these developments is whether social *rights*, so conceived, offer a way out of an impasse created by the neo-liberal critique of the traditional welfare state. That critique gained much of its force precisely by highlighting the tension or, as the critique would have it, contradiction, between the social and economic spheres that characterized the post-1945 settlement. F. A. Hayek's critique of social legislation is particularly important in this respect. Unlike many neo-liberal opponents of social rights, Hayek does not make the mistake of identifying the free market with the absence of regulation or law. On the contrary, he accepts that a market order rests upon norms of a certain kind, in particular those that derive from the private law of contract, property, and tort. Hayek also engages in a discussion about the conditions under which social legislation, while qualifying private law in many respects, may nevertheless play a legitimate role in a market-orientated system. For these reasons, Hayek's work deserves close study. The following subsections will look at his argument in closer detail and contrast it with Amartya Sen's 'capability approach', which, without endorsing a particular substantive conception of social rights, has come to be seen as offering a potential foundation for alternatives to deregulatory policies.

B. Hayek's Critique of Social Legislation

Hayek's mature legal-philosophical writings are contained in his three-volume work *Law, Legislation and Liberty*, published in the 1970s.[102] Hayek believed that economic behaviour presupposes the existence of a body of social and legal norms, which serve to coordinate the expectations of individual agents. The 'market order' he describes rests on rules of a particular kind, the 'abstract rules of just conduct', which Hayek associated with private law. Private law and the market are mutually supportive elements of a 'spontaneous order' that is both the foundation of a society's well-being and also the necessary condition for the freedom of its individual members. Social legislation, by contrast, interferes with the abstract rules of just conduct in a way that undermines personal autonomy and the well-being of society.

---

[102] The three volumes were initially published separately: *Rules and Order* (1973); *The Mirage of Social Justice* (1976); and *The Political Order of a Free People* (1979). They were then published in a consolidated volume: *Law, Legislation and Liberty: A New Statement of the Liberal Principles of Justice and Political Economy* (1980).

The market is a type of system or 'order' in the sense of being 'a state of affairs in which a multiplicity of elements of various kinds are so related to each other that we may learn from our acquaintance with some spatial or temporal part of the whole to form correct expectations concerning the rest, or at least expectations which have a good chance of proving correct'.[103] For this purpose, an essential distinction is drawn between 'spontaneous order' or (in Hayek's terminology) *cosmos*, on the one hand, and a made or imposed order, *taxis*, on the other. A *taxis* is an order which is purpose-orientated and is the result of conscious planning or organization; as such, there is a limit to the degree of complexity that it can achieve. By contrast, 'very complex orders, comprising more particular facts than any brain could ascertain or manipulate, can be brought about only through forces inducing the formation of spontaneous orders'.[104]

The distinction between *cosmos* and *taxis* corresponds to a distinction between types of norms, that is, between the abstract rules of just conduct (*nomos*) and the rules of organization (*thesis*). Although a spontaneous order cannot be consciously planned, it nevertheless depends on the abstract rules of just conduct in the sense that 'the formation of spontaneous orders is the result of their elements following certain rules in their responses to their immediate environment'.[105] The principal features of the rules of just conduct are first, that they are purpose-independent; secondly, that they apply generally across a large range of cases and situations whose nature cannot be known in advance; and thirdly, that 'by defining a protected domain of each, [they] enable an order of actions to form itself wherein the individuals can make feasible plans'.[106] By contrast, the rules of organization are concerned with the internal ordering of governmental and similar bodies; they are 'designed to achieve particular ends, to supplement positive orders that something should be done or that particular results should be achieved, and to set up for these purposes the various agencies through which government operates'.[107] Here 'the distinction between the rules of just conduct and the rules of organisation is closely related to, and sometimes explicitly equated with, the distinction between private and public law'.[108]

This distinction is important because in Hayek's view, public law cannot substitute for private law as the basis for a spontaneous order; nor can the two forms be combined. This is because private law respects, whereas public law does not, the autonomy and capacity for action of individuals:

It would . . . seem that wherever a Great Society has arisen, it has been made possible by a system of rules of just conduct which included what David Hume called 'the three fundamental laws of nature', *that of stability of possession, of its transference by consent*, and *of the performance of promises*, or . . . the essential content of all contemporary systems of private law.[109]

---

[103] *Rules and Order, supra* note 102, at 36.   [104] *Ibid.*, at 38.   [105] *Ibid.*, at 33.
[106] *Ibid.*, at 85–6.   [107] *Ibid.*, at 125.   [108] *Ibid.*, at 132.
[109] *The Mirage of Social Justice, supra* note 102, at 140.

Although he does not undertake a detailed examination of juridical structures, Hayek implies that the relationship between contract, property, and tort is determined by their respective roles in defining and protecting the autonomy of individual agents. Private law is the precondition of the market order in the sense that without it, individuals would not be free to use their own information and knowledge for their own purposes. Although market transactions may be supported by conventions or social norms that are the consequence of interaction between individuals, these norms are not sufficient for the preservation of the spontaneous order of the market 'in most circumstances the organisation which we call government becomes indispensable to assure that those rules are obeyed'.[110] Hence, the exercise of 'coercion' or legal enforcement of norms is justified within a spontaneous order 'where this is necessary to secure the private domain of the individual against interference by others'.[111] While a given rule of just conduct almost certainly has a spontaneous origin, in the sense that 'individuals followed rules which had not been deliberately made but had arisen spontaneously',[112] such rules do not lose their essential character merely by virtue of being systematized: '[t]he spontaneous character of the resulting order must therefore be distinguished from the spontaneous origin of the rules on which it rests, and it is possible that an order which would still have to be described as spontaneous rests on rules which are entirely the result of deliberate design.'[113]

Public or regulatory law, by contrast, is understood to consist of specific commands and directions that, in aiming at certain substantive redistributions of resources, undermine the autonomy of economic agents. What is illegitimate and counter-productive, in Hayek's view, is not legal ordering of the market as such—this is essential at the level of the rules of private law—but rather the application of public law to the regulation to the market, understood as a spontaneous order. The law can most appropriately support economic progress by protecting private property rights and by ensuring that returns accrue to those who make investments in the process of discovery. This is so even though certain gains may accrue by chance, leaving some agents with 'undeserved disappointments'.[114] Ex-post redistribution of resources blunts incentives for individuals to invest in their own skills and efforts.

Thus, Hayek did not suggest that legal intervention, for example, for the enforcement of property and contract rights, is unnecessary and illegitimate. On the contrary, he accepted the occasionally 'coercive' character of private law. Nor did he claim that the techniques of public law could never be legitimately deployed. Nor, even, were forms of legislative intervention in market activity deemed to be inappropriate. Hayek excluded from condemnation legislation that involved 'the removal of discriminations by law which had crept in as a result of the greater influence that certain groups like landlords, employers, creditors, etc., had had on

---

[110] *Rules and Order, supra* note 102, at 47.   [111] *Ibid.*, at 57.   [112] *Ibid.*, at 45.
[113] *Ibid.*, at 45–6.   [114] *The Mirage of Social Justice, supra* note 102, at 127.

the law';[115] he also accepted a role for 'the provision by government of certain services which are of special importance to some unfortunate minorities, the weak or those unable to provide for themselves'.[116] But he drew the line at a 'third kind of "social" legislation', whose aim is 'to direct private activity towards particular ends and to the benefit of particular groups', and referred in this context to the UK Trade Disputes Act 1906 and to legislation of the US New Deal. Here, it was precisely the 'progressive replacement of private law by public law' that was the source of difficulty.[117]

C. Sen's Capability Approach[118]

In Hayek's account of the role of law in market ordering, it is the institutions of private law—in particular, property and contract—which guarantee to individuals the conditions for their effective participation in the market. However, this conception is plainly inadequate to the task of explaining the persistence of inequalities whose effects on markets, and the labour market in particular, cannot simply be dismissed as 'undeserved disappointments'. It is possible to argue from *within* the theory of spontaneous order, as Robert Sugden has done, that for the market to generate social well-being it is necessary not simply to have a system of property rights, but for individuals to have *endowments* in the sense of items of value which are tradable—'the market has a strong tendency to supply each person with those things he wants, *provided that he owns things that other people want, and provided that the things he wants are things that other people own*' (emphasis added).[119] Another way of putting this is to say that the market has no inbuilt tendency to satisfy the wants of those who do not have things that other people want.

Extremes of inequality have the effect of excluding certain groups from the market altogether. The result is not just that these individuals no longer have access to the goods that the market can supply; the rest of society also suffers a loss from their inability to take part in the system of exchange. Resources that could have been mobilized for the benefit of society as a whole will, instead, remain unutilized. The logic of this position, as Sugden makes clear,[120] is that redistribution is needed not to reverse the unpleasant results of the market, but rather to provide the preconditions for the market working in the first place. Although Sugden does not put it in such terms, one implication of his approach is that many of the redistributive and protective rules of labour law and the welfare state have a market-creating function. The tension between social rights and the market cannot be abolished by simply reducing the scope of the former in favour of the latter.

---

[115] *Rules and Order, supra* note 102, at 141.   [116] *Ibid.*, at 141–2.   [117] *Ibid.*, at 142–3.

[118] The interpretation of Sen's work offered in this subsection draws on ideas developed through joint work with Jude Browne and Frank Wilkinson, to whom I am most grateful for permission to present them here. See J. Browne, S. Deakin, and F. Wilkinson, 'Capabilities, Social Rights, and European Market Integration', in R. Salais and R. Villeneuve (eds.), *Towards a European Politics of Capabilities* (2004).

[119] R. Sugden, 'Spontaneous Order', in P. Newman (ed.), *The Palgrave Dictionary of Economics and the Law*, Vol. III (1998), at 492.   [120] *Ibid.*, at 493.

A market-creating role for social rights is one possible implication of the 'capability approach' developed by Amartya Sen.[121] Sen describes individual well-being in terms of a person's ability to achieve a given set of functionings. In this context,

the concept of 'functionings' . . . reflects the various things a person may value doing or being. The valued functionings may vary from elementary ones, such as being adequately nourished and being free from avoidable disease, to very complex activities or personal states, such as being able to take part in the life of the community and having self-respect. . . . A 'capability' [is] a kind of freedom: the substantive freedom to achieve alternative functioning combinations.[122]

An individual's capability is to some degree a consequence of their entitlements, that is, their ability to possess, control, and extract benefits from a particular commodity. An individual's feasible set of utilization functions is therefore constrained by the limits upon the resources that he or she has available. However, there are additional non-choice factors affecting functioning, for example, an individual's metabolic rate, which is a consequence of his or her physical state. The state of an individual's knowledge may also be a non-choice factor, although this can be improved by education. Here the element of choice may lie elsewhere, at the collective or societal level, that is to say, with policy-makers, government officials, and judges. The same questions arise in the choice of commodities. Apart from the resources available to an individual, his or her capability to make use of a commodity may depend at a fundamental level not just upon access to a legal system that recognizes and guarantees protection of contract and property rights (although this is important), but also upon access to health care, education, and other resources that equip them to enter into relations of exchange with others.

Sen's 'capability approach' therefore envisages a central role for what he calls *conversion factors*. A person's capability to achieve a particular range of functionings is determined by characteristics of their *person* (such as their metabolism or bio-logical sex), their *society* (such as social norms, legal rules and legal-political insti-tutions), and their *environment* (which could include climate, physical surroundings, and technological infrastructure). In this context, the suggestion has been made that a key role for social rights is to act as conversion factors that extend the range of alternative functionings available to individuals.[123] In particular, social rights may serve to *institutionalize* the process of formation of capabilities. By re-orientating social rights in this way, we may go some way to resolving the tension between social rights and the market order, which, as we have seen, is apparent, albeit in different ways, in the works of both F. A. Hayek and T. H. Marshall.

---

[121] See in particular A. Sen, *Commodities and Capabilities* (1985) and *Development as Freedom* (1999).

[122] *Development as Freedom, supra* note 121, at 75.

[123] Browne, Deakin, and Wilkinson, 'Capabilities, Social Rights, and European Market Integration', *supra* note 118.

D. Social Rights as Institutionalized Capabilities

If capabilities are a consequence not simply of the endowments and motivations of individuals but also of the access they have to the processes of socialization, education, and training that enable them to exploit their resource endowments, then by providing the conditions under which access to these processes is made generally available, mechanisms of redistribution may be not just compatible with, but become a precondition to, the operation of the labour market. In this way, social rights may play a pivotal role in providing an institutional foundation for individual capabilities.

This point may be illustrated by considering laws against sex discrimination.[124] A conventional economic view of laws that protect women against dismissal on the grounds of pregnancy would be as follows. From the viewpoint of enterprises that would otherwise dismiss pregnant employees once they become unable to carry on working as normally, such laws impose a private cost. These enterprises may respond by declining to hire women of child-bearing age who will, as a result, find it more difficult to get jobs. If this happens, there may be an overall loss to society in terms of efficiency, because resources are misallocated and under-utilized, as well as a disadvantage to the women who are unemployed as a result.

An alternative way of thinking about discrimination against pregnant workers is as follows. In the absence of legal protection against this type of discrimination, women of child-bearing age will not expect to continue in employment once (or shortly after) they become pregnant. It is not necessary for all market participants to make a precise calculation along these lines; rather, a norm or convention will emerge, according to which pregnant women expect to lose their jobs and their employers expect to be able to dismiss them without any harm attaching to their reputation. The overall effect is that investments in skills and training are not undertaken, making society worse off as a result. Women workers will have an incentive not to make relation-specific investments in the jobs that they undertake. In an extreme situation, they may withdraw from active participation from the labour market altogether, and norms may encourage this too—as in the case of the 'marriage bar' norm, according to which any woman who married was expected thereupon to resign her position. This norm was widely observed, for example, in the British public sector up to the 1950s and, in the case of some parts of the public sector, was enshrined in regulations.[125]

What is the effect of the introduction of a prohibition on the dismissal of pregnant women under these circumstances? In addition to remedying the injustice that would otherwise affect individuals who are dismissed for this reason, a law of this kind has the potential to alter incentive structures in such a way as to encourage women employees to seek out, and employer to provide training for, jobs involving

---

[124] The discussion in the text builds on an earlier analysis of pregnancy law in S. Deakin and F. Wilkinson, ' "Capabilities", ordineo spontaneo del mercato e diritti sociali' 2 *Il diritto del mercato del lavoro* (2000) 317.

[125] For discussion of the marriage bar, see S. Walby, *Patriarchy at Work* (1986).

relation-specific skills. The demonstration effect of damages awards against employers may over time lead to a situation in which the norm of automatic dismissal is replaced by its opposite. Stigma attaches to those employers who flout the law. As more employers observe the new norm as a matter of course, it will tend to become self-enforcing, in a way that is independent of the law itself. Conversely, more women will expect, as a matter of course, to carry on working while raising families, in a way that may have a wider destabilizing effect on the set of conventions that together make up the 'traditional' household division of labour between men and women.

Recent empirical research casts light on this theoretical conjecture. In the United Kingdom, pregnancy protection laws were significantly strengthened in the mid-1990s, as a result of the combined effect of a number of rulings of the European Court of Justice,[126] extending the scope of the (then) Equal Treatment Directive to pregnancy cases, and the implementation of the Pregnant Workers' Directive of 1992.[127] These changes meant that both protection against dismissal and the right to return to work after pregnancy were more effectively guaranteed. The result has been a lengthening of the average job tenure of full-time women workers that has contributed to a more general rise in labour market participation by women of working age.[128]

E. The Uses and Limits of the Capability Approach

Much of the significance currently attached to Sen's capability approach in the context of the political and economic project of European integration is due to its use in the Supiot Report on the *Transformation of Work and the Future of Labour Law in Europe.*[129] The Supiot Report used the notion of 'capability' to structure its discussion of labour market measures that, as it put it, could transform the notion of 'passive protection' into one of 'active security' in relation to social and economic risks. The usefulness of the capability approach, in this context, is that it aims to provide individuals with more than purely formal guarantees of market access of the kind provided by contract and property rights. For access to be meaningful, a number of additional, institutional preconditions have to be met.

However, this is not the same thing as saying that the capability approach, in itself, can provide a blueprint for labour market reform, in Europe or elsewhere.

---

[126] In particular Case C-177/88 *Dekker v. VJV Centrum* [1991] IRLR 27 and Case C-32/93, *Webb v. EMO Air Cargo (UK) Ltd.* [1994] IRLR 482.

[127] Council Directive 92/85/EEC on the introduction of measures to encourage improvements in the safety and health of pregnant workers and workers who have recently given birth or are breastfeeding, OJ 1992 L348, 28.11.92. The relevant domestic legislation is now to be found in various provisions of the Employment Rights Act 1996 (as amended) and in the Maternity and Parental Leave etc. Regulations, SI 1999/3312. See S. Deakin and G. Morris, *Labour Law* (3rd edn) (2001), at 645–55.

[128] See H. Robinson, 'Gender and Labour Market Performance in the Recovery', in R. Dickens, P. Gregg, and J. Wadsworth (eds.), *The Labour Market under New Labour: The State of Working Britain 2003* (2003) 232, at 237.

[129] A. Supiot (ed.), *Au-delà de l'emploi: Transformations du travail et devenir du droit du travail en Europe* (1999).

As Sen himself has remarked, '[i]t is not clear that there is any royal road to eva-luation of economic or social policies'.[130] In other words, there is no universally-applicable, prescriptive list of functionings and capabilities; attention should instead be focused instead on social choice procedures by which the content of capability sets can be collectively determined in particular contexts. A social choice procedure that aims to bring about greater equality of capability is one that focuses on those mechanisms or conversion factors by which endowments in the form of human and physical capital are translated into capabilities and functionings. From this per-spective, while the capability approach need not in itself offer a definitive account of the content of policy initiatives, it may nevertheless provide us with a normative framework of point of reference from which to compare different proposals.

In particular, a capability-orientated perspective helps us to see that social rights are not different in their essence from the civil and political rights that Hayek identified as underpinning market activity. There is nothing inherently natural about claims in the form of contract and property rights; as with social rights, they are institutional creations that depend upon a complex machinery of interpretation, adjudication, and enforcement. Thus, social, civil, and political rights, far from being in fundamental opposition to each other, are to be found at different points along a single continuum.

A capability-orientated analysis also focuses our attention on how, more precisely, social rights can be used to shape the institutional environment in such a way as to enable all (or more) individuals to convert endowments in the form of human and physical assets into positive outcomes. They can do this in one of two ways: either as claims to resources, such as social security benefits, or access to health and education services; or as rights to take part in forms of procedural or institutionalized inter-actions, such as those arising out of collective bargaining or corporate governance. When social rights take the form of claims on resources, they are the equivalent of commodities that individuals can convert into potential or actual functionings. When they take the form of proceduralized rights, they come close to what Sen calls 'social conversion factors', that is, social or institutional settings that shape the set of possibilities open to individuals in terms of achieving their goals.

At the same time, there are potential difficulties, even dangers, inherent in the capability approach. Sen's account of the capability approach focuses on the position of the individual and the real or effective choices that are available to each person. Alain Supiot, on the other hand, reminds us why social rights cannot be conceived exclusively in individualized terms: 'the most innovative aspect of the welfare state was not its social provisions—typically less generous than those of fascist or communist states—but its guarantee of right to collective action, which allowed the dominated to fight the dominant classes with their own vision of a just society.'[131] Little will be gained if individualized claims to access to resources are used to undermine still further the principal institutions of the welfare state—collective bargaining, social insurance,

---

[130] *Development as Freedom, supra* note 121, at 84.
[131] 'The Labyrinth of Human Rights', *supra* note 60, at 135.

and progressive taxation. Yet the right to equal treatment between men and women, to take perhaps the most prominent example, has been used on numerous occasions to level down the standard of social protection enjoyed workers. There is undoubtedly a dimension to the law of human rights that is quite at home with the idea that, in a globalized economy, collective institutions should continually have to justify their existence in the face of market imperatives. From this perspective, a capability-based analysis *needs* the idea of social rights if it is not to become a pretext for weakening collective provision. It will therefore be important, in any discussion about social rights and capabilities, to insist on a distinction between the empowerment of persons that results from an extension of their *individual* capability sets, and the *collective* mechanisms through which this empowerment is achieved.

5. CONCLUSION

If claims to social resources are increasingly phrased in terms of juridical rights, this reflects, in part, the loss of organic solidarity that has accompanied the decline of collective bargaining as a mechanism of redistribution, and to a weakening in the state's role of direct service provider in health, education, and related public services. As social rights in this juridical sense of the term have grown in importance, the issue of their reconciliation with civil and political rights, and with market-orientated guarantees of economic participation, has become more pressing. In the practice and philosophy of the mid-twentieth-century welfare state, the tension between social and economic values was recognized, but was not resolved. It took the advent of neo-liberalism to offer one kind of solution, namely the restriction of social rights in the name of freeing up the market; but there is now a growing perception that an account of the market order based exclusively on the mechanisms of private law cannot be sustained.

As the limits of the neo-liberal project become clear, the question of what will replace it acquires new urgency. It has been suggested that the capability approach offers one possible way forward. It is apparent that a capability-based conception of social rights contains within it the potential for tension and contradiction, just as its predecessors did. The purpose of the argument that has been presented in the present chapter is to identify the emergence of this conception of social rights at the micro-level of institutional change and to study some of its implications, rather than to subject it to a comprehensive critique. What is striking about this development is the particular institutional solution that it offers to the apparent conflict between markets and social rights. In this conception, the primary *function* of social rights is to provide the conditions for substantive market access on the part of individuals, thereby promoting individual freedom but also enhancing the benefits to society of the mobilization, through the market, of economic resources. In terms of *form*, social rights are constructed around a particular combination of substantive and procedural norms. The work of further articulating and developing this approach is likely to be a central task in the renewal of welfare state systems.

3

The Right to Bargain Collectively in International Law: Workers' Right, Human Right, International Right?

PATRICK MACKLEM

1.

In an influential essay, 'The Paradox of Workers' Rights as Human Rights', Virginia Leary identified 'a regrettable paradox: the human rights movement and the labor movement run on tracks that are sometimes parallel and rarely meet'.[1] Yet, as Leary notes, international human rights law and international labour law—two legal fields in which these political movements operate and help to define—relate to each other in complex ways. Each field seeks to promote a set of norms through international and regional instruments, institutions and processes shared by the other. Each is also comprised of specialized instruments and unique institutions that lend an artificial air of relative autonomy to their relationship. Scholars and practitioners certainly are not unaware of these significant normative and regulatory intersections. But scholarship and practice in international human rights law and international labour law are relatively specialized, manifesting relatively distinct intellectual preoccupations and professional norms. The two fields are akin to distant cousins who share a common heritage but rarely explore the extent to which they share similar values and aspirations.

International human rights law is often understood in terms of a normative aspiration—or mission—to protect universal elements of what it means to be a human being from the exercise of sovereign power. For reasons that aspire to transcend 'specific historical institutions and traditions, legal systems, governments, or national and even regional communities',[2] the field regards protection of freedom of expression, religion, association, and assembly, as well as a host of other rights and freedoms, as inherent in this task. International labour law also manifests a

---

[1] Virginia A. Leary, 'The Paradox of Workers' Rights as Human Rights', in L. Compa and S. Diamond (eds.), *Human Rights, Labor Rights and International Trade* (1996) 22–47, at 22.

[2] Eugene Kamenka, 'Human Rights, Peoples' Rights', in J. Crawford (ed.), *The Rights of Peoples* (1998), at 127.

normative mission. It seeks to promote the exercise of sovereign power in ways that foster just relationships between employers and employees. It requires states to enable employees, individually or collectively, to negotiate freely the terms and conditions of employment, and to guarantee a basic set of entitlements to employees, such as a minimum wage and a safe and healthy working environment, regardless of the relative bargaining power between employers and employees.

These two missions share much in common, including a commitment to protect and promote a right to bargain collectively as a matter of international law. International labour law is committed to the right because domestic social justice requires that employees be entitled to participate in establishing the terms and conditions of work. On this first account, labour rights are workers' rights; their international entrenchment is designed to protect domestic rights of workers from international competition. International human rights law is committed to the right to bargain collectively as an element of freedom of association, which it regards as part of what it means to be a human being. On this second account, labour rights are human rights; their international entrenchment aims to protect universal features of human beings from state or state-authorized forms of coercion.

Although their details vary from jurisdiction to jurisdiction, collective bargaining regimes exist in many states that protect and regulate the capacity of workers to form a union, bargain collectively, and strike. This model of industrial relations typically operates most successfully in nationally bounded economies dedicated to mass production. Yet it is now commonplace to note that national economic boundaries are increasingly becoming porous as a result of processes associated with economic globalization. Firms are enjoying heightened capital mobility, putting pressure on states to engage in regulatory reform to reduce labour costs and attract and retain capital investment. Technological and managerial innovation is ushering in flexible forms of transnational production that rely on teamwork, participatory production, and atypical employment. Transnational flexible production is increasingly supplementing if not supplanting mass production in many sectors and economies, and producing employment relations not easily amenable to traditional methods of labour market regulation.[3]

Many scholars have argued that these changes pose grave threats to the traditional labour law model of industrial relations.[4] Some have argued that labour law risks

---

[3] I address these two developments in greater detail in 'Labour Law Beyond Borders', 5 *Journal of International Economic Law* (2002) 605–45.

[4] See, e.g., Richard Hyman, 'Industrial Relations in Europe: Crisis or Reconstruction', in T. Wilthagen (ed.), *Advancing Theory in Labour Law and Industrial Relations in a Global Context* (1998) 181–94, at 185–6 (the rise of multinational corporations and 'the increasingly coercive hand of finance capital' operate to 'threaten established institutions of social regulation of labour markets'). Hyman urges students of industrial relations to turn their attention to the possibility of a European industrial relations system. See also Harry Arthurs, 'Landscape and Memory: Labour Law, Legal Pluralism and Globalization', in Wilthagen, *ibid.*, 21–34, at 22, 23 ('changes in the social organization of production threaten to destabilize the concept of the bargaining unit, and the whole edifice of employment-based rights constructed on that fundament', and 'unless and until globalization is somehow constrained or domesticated, . . . regimes

losing its normative moorings by failing to adapt to new economic realities and continuing to assume a capacity to regulate a world of work that no longer exists.[5] Much of this scholarship focuses on the influence of these changes on domestic labour law. This essay explores instead their influence on international law. It focuses specifically on the international right to bargain collectively and details the role that the right plays in international labour law, identifying relevant developments in the International Labour Organization. It also identifies recent developments concerning the right in various international and regional human rights instruments, concentrating on UN and European developments. In contrast to what many claim is occurring at a domestic level, there appears not to be a weakening of protection of the right to bargain collectively in either international legal field. Instead, contemporary developments in both fields suggest a trend towards greater protection of the right.

Although they may have not weakened the international legal commitment to collective bargaining, economic globalization and transnational flexible production are changing the normative relationship between international labour law and international human rights law. They have sparked a third conception of labour rights as international rights—as instruments that possess the potential to vest the international legal order with a measure of normative legitimacy by attending to state and non-state action that international law otherwise authorizes in the name of economic globalization or transnational flexible production. Armed with this new conception, international labour law is realigning its relationship to international human rights law around a shared task of mitigating the distributional consequences of globalization and transnational flexible production—a task in which the right to bargain collectively performs a critical function.

2.

Contributing to the paradox of workers' rights as labour rights is the fact that, in Leary's words, 'the international human rights movement may be said to have begun with the founding of the ILO in 1919 and the adoption thereafter of the first international labour conventions'.[6] International regulation of terms and conditions of work initially rested on a vision of labour rights as workers' rights.

---

of state regulation and state-mandated collective bargaining will continue to erode'). Arthurs predicts that local informal norms, institutions, and processes will assume greater significance in the regulation of relations between employers and employees.

[5] See, e.g., Massimo D'Antona, 'Labour Law at the Century's End: An Identity Crisis', in Joanne Conaghan, Richard Fischl, and Karl Klare (eds.), *Labour Law in an Era of Globalization: Transformative Practices & Possibilities* (2002) 31–49, at 32 (writing of 'the identity crisis of labour law' provoked by globalization and new forms of production). See also Hugh Collins, 'A Third Way in Labour Law?', in Conaghan et al., *ibid.*, 449–69, at 451 (identifying a new normative mission for labour law, one that secures worker protection not primarily to secure social justice in the world of work but to promote the competitiveness of business). [6] Leary, *supra* note 1, at 25.

The establishment of the ILO was primarily a response to concerns by states that domestic labour market regulation would increase the price of production and create competitive disadvantages as against states that chose not to legislate to protect the interests of workers. Having accepted—in some if not all cases, grudgingly—the social justice of domestic labour standards and collective bargaining law, states looked to international labour law to ensure that domestic protection of workers did not produce international competitive disadvantage.[7] International labour law would operate to prevent this form of competition by constituting, 'between employers and between countries, a form of code of fair competition'.[8] The normative significance of international labour rights, originally conceived, lay in their capacity to protect domestic rights of workers from international competition.

Since 1919, the ILO has been the pre-eminent international body concerned with the promotion and enforcement of international labour rights and standards. More than 175 member states send government, employer, and employee representatives to the ILO's yearly International Labour Conference. ILO membership obliges states to submit treaties to the proper domestic authority for ratification and to report on non-ratified treaties when requested. In addition, employers and workers groups can lodge complaints that a government is not fulfilling its obligations under a ratified convention.

The ILO's Constitution, adopted immediately after the First World War and enshrined in the Treaty of Versailles, proclaims freedom of association to be 'of special and urgent importance'. The 1944 ILO Declaration of Philadelphia reaffirms the ILO's commitment to freedom of association and calls for 'the effective recognition of the right of collective bargaining, the cooperation of management and labour in the continuous improvement of productive efficiency, and the collaboration of workers and measures in the preparation and application of social and economic measures'. Four years later, just before the adoption of the Universal Declaration of Human Rights in 1948, the ILO adopted the Freedom of Association and Protection of the Right to Organize Convention (No. 87).[9]

Article 2 of Convention No. 87 provides that 'workers and employers . . . shall have the right to establish and, subject only to the rules of the organisation

---

[7] Ernest B. Haas, *Beyond the Nation-State: Functionalism and International Organization* (1964), at 142. See also Paul O'Higgins, citing John W. Follows, *Antecedents of the ILO* (1951), who points to 'fear of social disorder and revolution' as another reason for the adoption of international labour standards: P. O'Higgins, 'The Interaction of the ILO, the Council of Europe and European Union Labour Standards', in B. Hepple (ed.), *Social and Labour Rights in a Global Context* (2002) 55–69, at 56. See also Louis Henkin, 'International Law: Politics, Values and Functions', 216 *Collected Courses of Hague Academy of International Law* 13 (Vol. IV, 1989), at 208 (stating international labour rights initially stood as 'capitalism's defence against the spectre of spreading socialism' and protected the interests of states 'in the conditions of labour in countries with which they competed in a common international market').

[8] N. Valticos and G. von Potobsky, *International Labour Law* (2nd rev. edn 1995), at para. 10.

[9] As of writing, 142 states have ratified Convention No. 87. Forty-six—32%—of these ratifications occurred in the last 15 years. Convention No. 87 was foreshadowed by two sector-specific Conventions on freedom of association: the Right of Association (Agriculture) Convention (No. 11), 1921; and the Right of Association (Non-Metropolitan Territories) Convention (No. 84), 1947.

concerned, to joint organisations of their own choosing without any previous authorisation'.[10] Article 2 protects the rights of workers to organize 'without distinction whatsoever'. Although Article 9 creates a potential exception for members of the armed forces and the police, Convention No. 87 applies to all other public, as well as private, sector employees.[11]

In 1949, a year after it adopted Convention No. 87, the ILO adopted the Right to Organise and Bargain Collectively Convention (No. 98).[12] Article 4 of Convention No. 98 provides that 'measures appropriate to national conditions shall be taken, where necessary, to encourage and promote the full development and utilisation of machinery for voluntary negotiation between employers or employers' organisations and workers' organisations, with a view to the regulation of terms and conditions of employment by means of collective agreements'. Article 5 creates a possible exception for the armed forces and the police, and Article 6 stipulates that the 'Convention does not deal with the position of public servants engaged in the administration of the State, nor shall it be construed as prejudicing their rights or status in any way.'

The voluntary negotiation of collective agreements—enshrined as a right implicitly in the ILO Constitution and Convention No. 87 and explicitly in the 1944 Declaration of Philadelphia and Convention No. 98—is considered by the ILO to be 'a fundamental aspect of the principles of freedom of association'.[13] The ILO's Committee on Freedom of Association ('CFA'), a body ultimately charged with monitoring compliance with the Constitution, requires member states to ensure that collective bargaining 'assume a voluntary character and not entail recourse to measures of compulsion which would alter the voluntary nature of such bargaining'.[14]

The CFA has also stated that 'it is essential that the introduction of draft legislation affecting collective bargaining or conditions of employment should be preceded by full and detailed consultations with the appropriate organizations of workers and employers'.[15] A state cannot impose a compulsory arbitration procedure in cases where negotiations break down 'except in the context of essential services in the strict sense of the term', namely, 'services the interruption of which would endanger the life, personal safety or health of the whole or part of the population'. Nor can a state authorize an employer to modify unilaterally the content of signed collective agreements, or require that they be renegotiated.[16] The CFA has also held that 'the suspension or derogation by decree—without the agreement of the parties—of collective agreements freely entered into by the parties violates the principle of free and voluntary collective bargaining'.[17] The CFA

---

[10] Art. 2, Convention No. 87.

[11] Committee on Freedom of Association Digest of Decisions 1996 (hereafter 'CFA Digest'), paras. 205–206, 212.

[12] As of writing, 154 states have ratified Convention No. 98. Forty-four of these ratifications—28.5%—occurred in the last 15 years.   [13] CFA Digest, para. 844.

[14] *Ibid.*, para. 845.   [15] *Ibid.*, para. 931.   [16] *Ibid.*, para. 848.

[17] Committee on Freedom of Association Cases (hereafter 'CFA Cases'), 1900 Vol. LXXX, 1997, Series B, No. 3 at para. 189.

criticized Canada, for example, for the province of Ontario's decision to annul existing collective agreements pertaining to agricultural workers and professional employees.[18]

Generally speaking, the CFA regards these principles as equally applicable to public sector employment. The CFA has repeatedly criticized governments for not sufficiently respecting collective bargaining as an instrument for determining the terms and conditions of employment of their own employees. Emphasizing the need for consultation before legislating changes to public sector employment, the CFA has stated that 'broad consultation of this kind is especially important when the Government is also the employer and may resort to legislation to alter the negotiating balance with the unions'.[19]

Even if a government seeks only to alter the bargaining structure in which it acts as an employer, it is important to follow an adequate consultation process.[20] For example, in 1999 the CFA 'deplored' Saskatchewan's decision to order hydro employees back to work without consultation and extend their collective agreement for three years. Noting the 'special nature' of public sector collective bargaining, the CFA stated:

168 . . . . [T]he Committee has emphasized that collective bargaining in the public sector 'calls for verification of the available resources in the various public bodies or undertakings, that such resources are dependent on state budgets and that the period of duration of collective agreements in the public sector does not always coincide with the duration of the budgetary laws—a situation which can give rise to difficulties'. Thus, in the view of the Committee and of the Committee of Experts on the Application of Conventions and Recommendations, legislative provisions which allow Parliament or the competent budgetary authority to set upper and lower limits for wage negotiations or to establish an overall 'budgetary package' within which the parties may negotiate terms and conditions of employment clauses are compatible with the principles of freedom of association (see Digest, op. cit., para. 899). However, the Committee stresses that, in this process, workers and their organizations must be fully consulted in designing this overall bargaining framework, which implies in particular that they must have access to all the financial, budgetary and other data enabling them to assess the situation on the basis of the facts.

169. The Committee considers that if such conditions had been observed in the present case, i.e. that upper and lower limits or a 'budgetary package' had been established in consultation with the workers concerned and their organizations, the hesitation of the Government with regard to arbitration would have been reduced, even to naught. Compliance with such a procedure guaranteeing transparency and prior consultation of the workers concerned and their organizations would have enabled the Government to avoid resorting to hasty legislation which can only prove to be an obstacle in the establishment of sound industrial relations. Thus, the Committee requests the Government to explore this possibility in future, in consultation with the parties concerned, and to keep it informed in this respect.[21]

---

[18] CFA Cases, 1900 Vol. LXXX, 1997, Series B, No. 3, at paras. 145–6 and 187.
[19] CFA Cases, 1616 Vol. LXXV, 1992, Series B, No. 3, para. 639.
[20] CFA Digest, para. 856.   [21] CFA Cases, 318 Vol. LXXXII, 1999, Series B, No. 3.

The CFA has also held states to have infringed the freedom of association of public sector employees by imposing unilateral pay freezes,[22] extensions of legislated conditions of employment beyond a reasonable time limit,[23] and restrictions on the scope of issues open to collective bargaining beyond those which 'appertain primarily or essentially to the management and operation of government business'.[24] The CFA has noted that 'repeated recourse to such statutory restrictions on collective bargaining can, in the long term, only prove harmful and destabilize labour relations, as it deprives workers of a fundamental right and means of defending and promoting their economic and social interests'.[25]

The CFA's approach to freedom of association and the right to bargain collectively in the context of public sector flexibility initiatives is illustrated in several recent, combined cases against Canada, which is party to Convention No. 87 but not party to Convention No. 98.[26] The cases concerned draft legislation introduced by British Columbia, with little or no consultation with affected parties, proposing to restructure the education and health care sectors in the province in ways that would affect dramatically the working environment of approximately 100,000 workers. In the name of flexibility, the legislation sought to impose collective agreements containing pay and working conditions reflecting the employer's position on workers whose collective agreements had expired. In addition, it sought to override terms and conditions of additional existing collective agreements respecting job security and to contract out work to non-union employees. It also sought to restrict and in some cases eliminate existing rights to strike in the sectors. The government defended its restructuring initiatives on the basis that changes in the global economy and public sector expenditure commitments led to unsustainable pressures on its capacity to service its debt and deficit.

In strongly worded remarks, the CFA stated that the government was proposing to intervene legislatively in collective bargaining processes, either to put an end to a legal strike, impose wages and working conditions, circumscribe the scope of collective bargaining, or restructure bargaining processes themselves. It acknowledged that public sector collective bargaining requires verification of available resources and that such resources are dependent on the timing and duration of budgets,

---

[22] CFA Cases, 1758 Vol. LXXVII, 1995, Series B, No. 1, para. 230.

[23] CFA Cases, 1800 Vol. LXXVIII, 1995, Series B, No. 2, para. 182.

[24] CFA Cases, 1859 Vol. LXXX, 1997, Series B, No. 1, para. 242. In the same paragraph, the Committee stated that staffing levels or departments to be affected as a result of financial difficulties may be considered to be matters relating primarily or essentially to the management and operation of government business and therefore reasonably regarded as outside the scope of negotiation, but questions which speak primarily or essentially to conditions of employment, such as pre-dismissal rights and indemnities, should not be excluded. With respect to teachers, matters such as the broad lines of educational policy are reasonably excluded from negotiation. However, issues such as teaching time overlap with conditions of employment and policy so the government must at least fully consult unions when formulating such educational policy. CFA Cases, 2119 Vol. LXXXV, 2002, Series B, No. 1, para. 253.

[25] CFA Cases, 1758 Vol. LXXVII, 1995, Series B, No. 1, para. 227.

[26] CFA Cases, 2166, 2173, 2180 Vol. LXXXVI, 2003, Series B, No. 1.

which do not always correspond to collective agreements in the sector. It also acknowledged that it would be not objectionable in certain circumstances for a government to legislate wage ceilings in the face of debt and deficit pressures. It stated that 'the bargaining parties should, however, be free to reach an agreement; if this is not possible, any exercise by the public authorities of their prerogatives in financial matters which hampers the free negotiation of collective agreements is incompatible with the principle of freedom of collective bargaining'.[27]

In such circumstances, the CFA concluded, the government should provide a mechanism to ensure that trade unions and employers are adequately consulted. Any legislated changes 'should be limited in time and protect the standard of living of the most affected workers'.[28] The CFA recommended that the government repeal certain measures and amend others to enable employees to exercise their rights to bargain collectively and strike, provide appropriate and meaningful consultations in the present and any future dispute, and refrain from resorting to legislatively imposed settlements in the future.[29]

Perhaps the most significant evidence of a trend towards greater protection of the right to bargain collectively in international labour law is the 1998 ILO Declaration on Fundamental Principles and Rights at Work. The 1998 Declaration is the culmination of intense efforts on the part of the ILO and member states to speak to the international legal significance of increased calls for employer flexibility and regulatory experimentation in the light of economic globalization and technological innovation. Engaging these developments, the ILO, together with several international and regional international institutions, has distilled international labour law down to a core set of labour rights that are to operate as universal constraints on employer flexibility and regulatory experimentation. Enshrined in the 1998 Declaration, the ILO is of the view that core labour rights constitute baseline entitlements or a floor set of rights that, as a matter of international law, all states must comply regardless of their level of development or location in the international economy.

Specifically, the 1998 Declaration states that:

The International Labour Conference,
1. Recalls:
    (a) that if freely joining the ILO, all Members have endorsed the principles and rights
    set out in its Constitution and the Declaration of Philadelphia, and have undertaken to
    work towards attaining the overall objectives of the Organization to the best of their
    resources and fully in line with their specific circumstances;
    (b) that these principles and rights have been expressed and developed in the form of
    specific rights and obligations in Conventions recognized as fundamental both inside and
    outside the Organization.[30]

---

[27] CFA Cases, 2166, 2173, 2180 Vol. LXXXVI, 2003, Series B, No. 1. para. 209.   [28] *Ibid.*
[29] *Ibid.*, para. 305.
[30] ILO, 'Declaration on Fundamental Principles and Rights at Work and its Followup' (1998) International Labour Conference, 86th Session (hereafter '1998 Declaration').

The seven 'fundamental' Conventions to which Article 1(b) refers govern freedom of association and collective bargaining (Nos. 87 and 98); forced labour (Nos. 29 and 105); non-discrimination (Nos. 100 and 111); and minimum age (No. 138). These Conventions define and elaborate four basic principles: freedom of association and the effective right of collective bargaining; the prohibition of forced or compulsory labour; the effective abolition of child labour; and the elimination of discrimination in respect of employment or occupation. The principles together constitute what has been referred to as a set of core labour rights.[31]

The significance of the 1998 Declaration lies in the fact that it identifies an international conception of what constitutes the core of international labour law to be respected by all states. More importantly, the 1998 Declaration was drafted in such a way as to draw directly from the ILO Constitution, meaning that all ILO member states are automatically committed to the Declaration simply by virtue of membership. Article 2 of the 1998 Declaration states that

all Members, even if they have not ratified the Conventions in question, have an obligation arising from the very fact of membership in the Organization, to respect, to promote and to realize, in good faith and in accordance with the Constitution, the principles concerning the fundamental rights which are the subject of those conventions, including 'freedom of association and the effective recognition of the right to collective bargaining'.[32]

The strategy embraced by the 1998 Declaration of promoting core labour rights has drawn criticism from several quarters. Some scholars raise concerns that its promotional character and its underinclusive and ambiguous scope and content will do little to alter the international and domestic legal environments in which processes of economic globalization and transnational flexible production operate and reinforce.[33] Others fear that the ILO's relatively successful traditional approach towards the protection of labour standards, one that includes an open legislative process, clearly defined standards, and a respected system of oversight and compliance, is being eclipsed by a diffuse political strategy of uncertain legal effect.[34]

---

[31] For an earlier articulation, see OECD, *Trade, Employment and Labour Standards: A Study of Core Workers' Rights and International Trade* (1996) (articulating five core labour standards, separating freedom of association from the right to organize and bargain collectively).

[32] 1998 Declaration, *supra* note 30, para. A.2(a).

[33] For extended assessments of this strategy, see Guy Mundlak, 'The Transformative Weakness of Core Labour Rights in Changing Welfare Regimes', in E. Benevisti and G. Nolte (eds.), *The Welfare State, Globalization, and International Law* (2004) 231–69; Kerry Rittich, 'Core Labor Rights and Labor Market Flexibility: Two Paths Entwined?', in International Bureau of the Permanent Court of Arbitration (eds.), *Labor Law Beyond Borders: ADR and the Internationalization of Labor Dispute Settlement* (2003), 157–208.

[34] Philip Alston and James Heenan, 'The Role of International Labor Standards within the Trade Debate: The Need to Return to Fundamentals' (European University Institute Discussion Paper) (23 May 2002). For the view that 'the Declaration does not seek to impose any new obligations on member states', see H. Kellerson, 'The ILO Declaration of 1998 on Fundamental Principles and Rights: A Challenge for the Future', 137 *International Labour Review* (1998) 223, 225. For the view that the Declaration imposes obligations on the ILO itself, see Brian Langille, 'The ILO and the New Economy: Recent Developments', 15 *Int. J. Comp. Lab. L. & Ind. Rel.* (1999) 229, 255.

For present purposes, the significance of the 1998 Declaration lies in the fact that it is part of a recent trend whereby international law, unlike its domestic counterparts, is attaching greater significance to the right to bargain collectively.

3.

The 1944 ILO Declaration of Philadelphia did more than reaffirm international labour law's commitment to the right to bargain collectively. It announced that 'all human beings, irrespective of race, creed or sex, have the right to pursue both their material well-being and their spiritual development in conditions of freedom and dignity, of economic security and equal opportunity'. It declared that 'the attainment of the conditions in which this shall be possible must constitute the central aim of national and international policy', and concluded that 'the principles set forth in this Declaration are fully applicable to all peoples everywhere'. One of these principles is 'the effective recognition of the right of collective bargaining'. The Declaration was 'subsequently incorporated as the central article of faith in the amended ILO Constitution'.[35]

The conception of labour rights at the heart of the 1944 Declaration, labour rights as human rights, set the stage for their inclusion in a broader register of civil, political, social, and economic rights protected and promoted by international and regional human rights institutions. From its post-war formal inception as a field of law, international human rights law has regarded freedom of association and, by extension, a right to bargain collectively as human rights that merit international legal protection.[36] The architects of the field regarded labour rights, including the right to bargain collectively, as protecting universal elements of what it means to be a human being in the face of sovereign authority. This vision of labour rights differs from the conception of labour rights as workers' rights that initially launched their international protection through the auspices of the ILO. While labour rights as workers' rights operate primarily to protect the domestic rights of workers from international competition, the normative significance of labour rights in international human rights law lies in the universality of the interests they seek to protect.

At the heart of international human rights law is the Universal Declaration of Human Rights of 1948, a unanimous resolution of the UN General Assembly in

---

[35] Haas, *Beyond the Nation-State, supra* note 7, at 155.

[36] The ILO's Committee of Experts now regards Convention No. 87 and Convention No. 98 in similar terms, as instruments that elaborate and translate into binding terms the nature and scope of freedom of association as guaranteed by the Universal Declaration of Human Rights. See ILO: *Report of the Committee of Experts on the Application of Conventions and Recommendations: General report and observations concerning particular countries*, Report III (Part 1A), International Labour Conference, 86th Session, 1998, Geneva, at 17, para. 18 ('the ILO's standards on human rights along with the instruments adopted in the UN and in other international organizations give practical application to the general expression of human aspirations made in the Universal Declaration, and have translated into binding terms the principles of that noble document').

December of the same year. Article 20(1) of the Universal Declaration affirms that '[e]veryone has the right to . . . freedom of association', and Article 23(4) affirms that '[e]veryone has the right to form and join trade unions for the protection of his interests'. Although Article 20(1) does not expressly refer to a right to bargain collectively, many if not all of the rights enshrined in the Universal Declaration are rendered binding in conventional international law through and by several treaties overseen and monitored by UN institutions. Each of these treaties establishes a specialized body charged with the oversight of treaty performance, and imposes regular reporting obligations on state parties to promote a dialogue between each state and the relevant treaty body, in the expectation that such measures will lead to progressive improvements in compliance. Some of these treaties allow for individual complaints to be heard by a treaty monitoring body that possesses the authority to express its views on whether a state is in breach of its treaty obligations.[37]

Of these UN treaties, two are relevant to the status of the right to bargain collectively. The first, the International Covenant on Economic, Social and Cultural Rights ('ICESCR'), came into force in 1976. Article 8(1)(a) of the ICESCR protects the right to form and join trade unions for the promotion and protection of their economic and social interests. Article 8(1)(b) provides that trade unions have the right to form national or international federations. Article 8(1)(c) enshrines the right of trade unions to function freely. Article 8(1)(d) guarantees the right to strike. Article 8(3) of the ICESCR provides that

Nothing in this Article shall authorise States Parties to the International Labour Organisation Convention of 1948 concerning Freedom of Association and Protection of the Right to Organise to take legislative measures which would prejudice, or apply the law in such a manner as would prejudice, the guarantees provided for in that Convention.

By preventing states from relying on Article 8 to prejudice rights enshrined in ILO Convention No. 87, Article 8(3) comes close to effectively incorporating Convention No. 87 rights into the guarantee of freedom of association in the ICESCR, at least as it relates to states party to Convention No. 87. As noted, the International Labour Organization's Committee on Freedom of Association has held that freedom of association as guaranteed by Convention No. 87 protects a right to bargain collectively.

In recent years, the Committee on Economic, Social and Cultural Rights ('CESCR') has consistently held that the right of a trade union to function freely, as guaranteed by Article 8(1)(c), includes a right to bargain collectively. In its 2001 Concluding Comment on Korea, for example, the CESCR reminded Korea that 'the provisions of article 8 guarantee for all persons the right to freely form and join trade unions, the right to engage in collective bargaining through trade unions for the promotion and protection of their economic and social interests, as well as the right to strike'.[38] Similarly, in its 2001 Concluding Comment on France, the CESCR called on France to ensure that its requirement that trade unions demonstrate

---

[37] See generally P. Alston and J. Crawford (eds.), *The Future of UN Human Rights Treaty Monitoring* (2000).   [38] E/C.12/1/Add.59 (09-05-2001), para. 39.

'representativity' does 'not impede the right of trade unions to participate freely in processes such as collective bargaining, irrespective of their size, in accordance with article 8(c) of the Covenant'.[39]

The second UN treaty of relevance is the International Covenant on Civil and Political Rights ('ICCPR').[40] The ICCPR is accompanied by a Protocol that authorizes the UN Human Rights Committee ('HRC') to hear complaints from individuals or governments regarding the failure of signatory states to effectively protect the rights enshrined in the Covenant. Article 22(1) of the ICCPR provides that '[e]veryone shall have the right to freedom of association with others, including the right to form and join trade unions for the protection of his interests'. The armed forces and police are not protected by this provision. Restrictions of freedom of association may be imposed for reasons of 'national security or public safety, public order, the protection of public health or morals or the protection of the rights and freedoms of others'. The ICCPR, like the ICESCR, contains a provision, Article 22(4), preventing states from relying on the guarantee of freedom of association to prejudice rights enshrined in ILO Convention No. 87.[41]

Whether due to reluctance or a lack of opportunity, the HRC initially had little to say about freedom of association in the context of work. In 1986, in *JB v. Canada*, the HRC assessed whether a legislative prohibition on striking public employees constitutes a breach of Article 22 of the ICCPR. In its decision, the HRC expressed no view on whether Article 22 protects the right to bargain collectively but it stated that Article 22 does not protect a right to strike.[42] Its reasons were sparse. Leary argues that 'the opinion of the committee is unpersuasive and its credibility is lessened' by a forceful dissent.[43] The HRC has since reversed itself and concluded that Article 22 does protect a right to strike. In its 1999 Concluding Comment on Chile's periodic report on compliance with the ICCPR, for example, the HRC

---

[39] E/C.12/1/Add.72, para. 29. See also Concluding Comment on Ireland, E/C.12/1/Add.77 (10-05-2002), para. 29 ('The Committee recommends that the State party adequately protect in law and practice trade unions' rights to conduct collective bargaining'); Concluding Comment on Zimbabwe, E/C.12/1/Add.12 (15-05-1997), para. 20 ('The Committee recommends that a constitutional reform be undertaken to allow public servants, teachers and nurses to organize in unions, in keeping with article 8 of the Covenant, and to enable them to bargain collectively and to strike'); Concluding Comment on Libyan Arab Jamahiriya, E/C.12/1/Add.15 (16-05-1997), para. 22 (recommending the protection of 'the right to strike and the right to free collective bargaining'); Concluding Comment on Portugal, Macau, E/C.12/1/Add.9, (06-12-1996) para. 20 ('The Committee urges the Portuguese Administration to promote appropriate policies which would facilitate the right to form labour unions, the right to engage in collective bargaining and the right to strike').

[40] There are currently 148 state parties to the ICCPR.

[41] For commentary, see Lee Swepston, 'Human Rights Law and Freedom of Association: Development through ILO supervision', *Int. Lab. Rev.* (1998) 169, at 172 ('entire legislative conformity is guaranteed with Convention No. 87 in this remarkable provision').

[42] *J.B. et al. v. Canada*, CCPR/C/D/R.26/118. Decision of 18 July 1986, Communication No. 118/1982.

[43] Leary, *supra* note 1, at 34. The dissenting opinion was authored by Rosalyn Higgins, Rajsoomer Lallh, Andreas Mavrommatis, Torkel Opsahl, and Amos Wako.

expressed 'serious concerns' over a Chilean law that imposed a general prohibition on 'the right of civil servants to organize a trade union and bargain collectively, as well as their right to strike, . . . under article 22 of the Covenant'.[44]

The HRC has also recently made it clear that Article 22 protects the right to bargain collectively. In its 1999 Concluding Comment on Canada, the HRC stated that Canada 'has not secured throughout its territory freedom of association', noting in particular that Ontario's 'workfare' program, which prohibits participants 'from joining unions and bargaining collectively, affects implementation of Article 22'.[45] In its 1999 Concluding Comment on Chile, the HRC advised Chile to 'review the relevant provisions of laws and decrees in order to guarantee to civil servants the rights to join trade unions and to bargain collectively, guaranteed under article 22 of the Covenant'.[46] In its 1999 Concluding Comment on Costa Rica, the HRC noted 'with concern that freedom of association, including the right to collective bargaining, is not adequately respected in conformity with article 22 of the Covenant'.[47]

In summary, each of the two relevant UN human rights instruments guarantees explicitly freedom of association and implicitly a right to bargain collectively in the context of work. In recent years, the monitoring body of each Covenant has interpreted freedom of association to include a right to bargain collectively. In the face of economic globalization and the introduction of transnational flexible production, amid fears that states have begun to or will abandon their commitment to collective bargaining, recent developments in international human rights law suggest an enhanced willingness to provide international legal protection to collective

---

[44] CCPR/C/79/Add.104 (30-03-1999), para. 25. See also CCPR/CO/80/LTU (01-04-2004) (Lithuania), para. 18 (expressing concern that Lithuania's new collective bargaining regime 'is too restrictive in providing, inter alia, for the prohibition of strikes in services which cannot be considered as essential, and the requirement of a two thirds majority to call a strike, which may amount to a violation of article 22'); CCPR/C/79/Add.73 (07-11-1996) (Germany) ('The Committee is concerned that there is an absolute ban on strikes by public servants who are not exercising authority in the name of the State and are not engaged in essential services, which may violate article 22 of the Covenant').

Article 22(4), preventing states from relying on the guarantee of freedom of association to prejudice rights enshrined in ILO Convention No. 87, also suggests that *JB v. Canada* no longer is a valid interpretation of Art. 22. Before 1986, the ILO had intimated that Convention No. 87 protects a right to strike as an incident of freedom of association: see ILO, *General Survey*, 1994 (a 'general prohibition of strikes constitutes a considerable restriction of the opportunities open to trade unions for furthering and defending the interests of its members (Article 10 of Convention No. 87) and of the right of trade unions to organize their activities'). After 1986, its position became clearer: see, e.g., *General Survey*, 1994, para. 179 ('the right to strike is an intrinsic corollary of the right of association protected by Convention No. 87'). For a detailed account of the ILO's approach to the right to strike, see Swepston, *supra* note 41, at 186–90.   [45] CCPR/C/79/Add.105 (06-04-1999), para. 17.

[46] CCPR/C/79/Add.104 (30-03-1999), para. 25.

[47] CCPR/C/79/Add.107, para. 17. Although it has not been noted expressly by the HRC, Article 22(4), to the extent that it supports an interpretation of Article 22 that is not inconsistent with rights guaranteed by ILO Convention No. 87, also supports the conclusion that Article 22 protects collective bargaining. As noted, the ILO Committee of Freedom of Association has held that freedom of association as guaranteed by Convention No. 87 protects a right to bargain collectively.

bargaining. As the next Part reveals, a similar phenomenon appears to be occurring in European human rights law.

4.

Founded in 1949 to promote democracy, the rule of law and greater European integration, the Council of Europe is composed of more than forty states. It has been responsible for the adoption of the European Convention on Human Rights, the European Social Charter, the European Convention for the Prevention of Torture, the Framework Convention for the Protection of National Minorities, and the European Charter for Regional or Minority Languages. Of these instruments, the European Convention on Human Rights and the European Social Charter are relevant to the status of the right to bargain collectively in European human rights law.

Article 11 of the European Convention on Human Rights provides that 'everyone has the right to freedom of peaceful assembly and to freedom of association with others, including the right to form and to join trade unions for the protection of his interests'. Until recently, the European Court of Human Rights had interpreted Article 11 restrictively, at least with respect to its reference to 'the right to form and join trade unions'. Freedom of association within the meaning of Article 11 protected a right to be represented by a union but did not protect a right to bargain collectively or strike to secure the interests of workers.[48] At the same time, the Court had been actively promoting an interpretation of freedom of association that protected an individual's right not to belong to a union.[49]

In *Wilson v. United Kingdom*,[50] however, the Court delivered what one scholar has referred to as 'probably the most important labour law decision for at least a generation'.[51] In *Wilson*, an employer announced that it would provide a backdated wage increase to employees who signed an individual contract before the expiry of their collective agreement. In the name of flexibility, the United Kingdom had recently amended its labour law regime to excuse such an action in cases where an employer was seeking to introduce a change in its formal relationship with its unionized workers. The Court held that the state's failure to prevent employers from engaging in this kind of activity violates Article 11.

---

[48] *Schmidt and Dahlstrom v. Sweden* (1975) 1 EHRR 637; *Swedish Engine Drivers' Union v. Sweden* (1975) 1 EHRR 617.

[49] See *Young, James and Webster v. UK* (1981) 4 EHRR 38; *Sigurjonsson v. Iceland* (1993) 16 EHRR 462; *Gustafsson v. Sweden* (1996) 22 EHRR 409.

[50] *Wilson v. United Kingdom* (2002) 35 EHRR 523.

[51] Keith Ewing, 'The Implications of Wilson and Palmer', 32 ILJ (2003) 1, at 20. Compare Bernard Ryan, 'The Charter and Collective Labour Law', in T. K. Hervey and J. Kenner (eds.), *Economic and Social Rights under the EU Charter of Fundamental Rights* (2003) 67–90, at 71 ('It remains to be seen whether the judgment in *Wilson* was simply a response to an extreme example of failure to support trade unionism, or instead reflects a greater willingness on the part of the European Court of Human Rights to use Article 11 ECHR to the advantage of trade unions').

According to the Court,

the words 'for the protection of his interests' in Article 11 § 1 are not redundant, and the Convention safeguards freedom to protect the occupational interests of trade union members by trade union action, the conduct and development of which the Contracting States must both permit and make possible. A trade union must thus be free to strive for the protection of its members' interests, and the individual members have a right, in order to protect their interests, that the trade union should be heard.[52]

The Court held that a state must enable trade unions to engage in action to protect the interests of workers, and that workers have a right to be heard collectively in order to protect their interests.

Complicating this holding was the Court's statement that 'although collective bargaining may be one of the ways by which trade unions may be enabled to protect their members' interests, it is not indispensable for the effective enjoyment of trade union freedom'.[53] Although this suggests that Article 11 does not protect a right to bargain collectively, the Court's reasons were more nuanced. It held that Article 11 does not necessarily protect a collective bargaining process that imposes an obligation on an employer to negotiate the terms and conditions of employment in good faith. According to the Court, 'compulsory collective bargaining would impose on employers an obligation to conduct negotiations with trade unions'.[54] Instead, Article 11 requires the state to ensure that trade union members are not prevented or restrained from using their union to represent them in attempts to regulate their relations with their employers. Given that British labour law apparently confers on the union a right to strike as a means of securing its members' interests and inducing the employer to bargain collectively with the union, the Court concluded that Article 11 does not require the state to impose an additional duty on employers to negotiate in good faith.

Wilson stands for the proposition that Article 11 protects a right of collective representation—a right that is somewhat less robust than a full-blown right to bargain collectively, which, according to the Court, contemplates a corresponding duty to negotiate in good faith. The Court refers to this right as a right to represent employee interests in a collective manner and a right to be heard, which, in the British context, yields a corresponding employer duty to listen to the collective representations of employee interests when determining the terms and conditions of employment. That this is the case is revealed by the following passage:

46. The Court agrees with the Government that the essence of a voluntary system of collective bargaining is that it must be possible for a trade union which is not recognised by an employer to take steps including, if necessary, organising industrial action, with a view to persuading the employer to enter into collective bargaining with it on those issues which the union believes are important for its members' interests. *Furthermore, it is of the essence of the right to join a trade union for the protection of their interests that employees should be free to instruct or permit the union to make representations to their employer or to take action in support of their interests on their behalf. If workers are prevented from so doing, their freedom to belong to a trade union, for*

[52] *Wilson, supra* note 50, para. 42.   [53] *Ibid.*, at para. 44.   [54] *Ibid.*

the protection of their interests, becomes illusory. It is the role of the State to ensure that trade union members are not prevented or restrained from using their union to represent them in attempts to regulate their relations with their employers.[55]

As a result of *Wilson*, Article 11 protects more than a right to form a union, and extends to core incidents of collective bargaining, such as the freedom 'to instruct or permit the union to make representations to their employer or to take action in support of their interests on their behalf'. Article 11 does not necessarily protect all the features of a statutory collective bargaining regime, including a duty on employers to negotiate in good faith. But Article 11 imposes on an employer other duties contemplated by a right to bargain collectively, such as a duty to listen to collective representations, which in turn implies an obligation to establish a forum or process in which such representations can be made,[56] and a duty not to interfere with a union's capacity to make representations on behalf of its members. *Wilson* thus is consistent with the more general trend in international human rights law toward enhanced protection of collective bargaining.

Also consistent with this trend are developments surrounding the European Social Charter. Adopted in 1961 within the framework of the Council of Europe, the European Social Charter is a regional treaty creating legally binding obligations on contracting parties. Article 5 of the European Social Charter establishes the right to organize. Under Article 5, contracting parties undertake to ensure that national law not impair or be applied to impair the 'freedom of workers and employers to form local, national or international organizations for the protection of their economic and social interests and to join these organizations'. Excepted groups are police and armed forces, whose freedoms are left solely to national laws or regulations. The European Social Charter applies to all other public employees.

Article 6 of the European Social Charter establishes the right to bargain collectively. Contracting parties undertake:

(1) to promote joint consultation between workers and employers; (2) to promote, where necessary and appropriate, machinery for voluntary negotiations between employers

---

[55] *Wilson, supra* note 50 (emphasis added). The Court's discussion of the right to strike in *Wilson* referred to *Unison v. UK* [2002] IRLR 497, where the Court, in language similar to *Wilson*, held that the 'ability to strike represents one of the most important of the means by which trade unions can fulfil this function' and the strike in question concerned 'the occupational interests of the applicant's members in the sense covered by Article 11 of the Convention'. The Court went on to hold that the prohibition in question was a proportionate measure and necessary in a democratic society for the protection of the rights of others. That Art. 11 protects striking in certain circumstances is in marked contrast to at least the tone of earlier jurisprudence. See *Schmidt and Dahlstrom v. Sweden* (1975) 1 EHRR 637; *Swedish Engine Drivers' Union v. Sweden* (1975) 1 EHRR 617. For extended analysis of the right to strike in international and European law, see Tonia Novitz, *International and European Protection of the Right to Strike: A Comparative Study of Standards Set by the International Labour Organization, the Council of Europe and the European Union* (2003).

[56] Compare *Sanchez Navajas v. Spain* (Decision of 21 June 2001), where the Court held that, in principle, workers' representatives should be entitled to appropriate facilities to enable them to carry out their functions quickly and effectively.

or employers' organizations, with a view to the regulation of terms and conditions of employment by means of collective agreements; (3) to promote the establishment and use of appropriate machinery for conciliation and voluntary arbitration for the settlement of labour disputes.

The European Court of Human Rights has found that the requirement of joint consultation in Article 6(1) obligates a state to promote joint consultation with respect to the terms and conditions of work. Article 6(1) applies to government employees employed through employment contracts in the same way it applies to private employees.[57] In the case of public employees whose employment is governed by law rather than contract, Article 6(1) 'requires that machinery exist for consultation between them and the government, as employer, in the drafting of the relevant legislation or regulations'.[58]

The European Committee on Social Rights, the Social Charter's monitoring body, has interpreted Article 6(2) to mean that employers and workers must, 'in accordance with legislation or industrial practice . . . [be] at liberty to conclude collective agreements'.[59] Echoing the European Court of Human Rights in *Wilson*, the Committee criticized the United Kingdom for generally permitting employers to induce employees to relinquish union representation and collective bargaining, stating such authorization was incompatible with Article 6(2).[60]

Article 6(2) requires states to actively promote the conclusion of such agreements if their spontaneous development is unsatisfactory. The United Kingdom was found in breach of Article 6(2) with respect to teachers' pay, for example, for authorizing the Secretary of State for Education to exercise discretionary power to determine pay without considering the views of the teaching unions.[61] The Committee also called on Spain to provide procedural safeguards before authorizing the suspension of wage rates that pose a threat to the financial health of a firm and employment stability.[62]

Article 6(2) also requires machinery to ensure that employers bound by collective agreements apply their provisions to all persons employed in their enterprise even if they are not members of a trade union party to the agreement.[63] As with Article 6(1), Article 6(2) applies to public and private employees. According to the Committee, although the right to collective bargaining can be limited for public employees, Article 6(2) requires the state to afford public employees a measure of participation in determining terms and conditions of work.[64]

---

[57] See *National Union of Belgium v. Belgium*, Series A, No. 19 (1975) 1 EHRR 578.

[58] David Harris, *The European Social Charter* (2nd edn) (2001), at 100. See C III 34–35 (Germany).

[59] C I 35, cited in Harris, *The European Social Charter, ibid.*, at 101.   [60] C XIII 3 (UK).

[61] C XII-1 125 (UK), cited in Harris, *The European Social Charter, supra* note 58, at 101.

[62] C XIV-1 (Spain).   [63] C XIV-1 (Luxembourg).

[64] See, e.g., C XV-1 add. (Poland); C XIV-1 (Germany). See generally Harris, *supra* note 58, at 102–3 ('whereas the ordinary procedures of collective bargaining cannot apply in the case of public employees whose employment is subject in some degree to regulation by law instead of by contract of employment, public employees can and must be consulted in the preparation of the laws and regulations that govern their employment').

State intervention in the right to bargain collectively, such as unilateral changes to an existing collective agreement[65] or limits on the scope of a future agreement,[66] is permissible under the Social Charter only insofar as it can be justified under Article 31, which requires limitations to be 'prescribed by law and are necessary in a democratic society for the protection of the rights and freedoms of others or for the protection of public interest, national security, public health, or morals'. As is well established in respect of the same wording in the European Convention on Human Rights, the concept of 'necessity' invites a proportionality analysis, which in turn requires the limitation to respond to a 'pressing social need', and permits limitations only in 'exceptional cases'.[67] The Committee has stated that direct state intervention in the collective bargaining process is 'a very serious measure which . . . should be taken only for the time needed to return to a normal situation in which the exercise of the right to collective bargaining would again be fully ensured'.[68]

5.

Much smaller and more economically and politically integrated than the Council of Europe, the European Union initially possessed little if any competence over human rights in general and freedom of association in particular and thus could not issue directives or regulations requiring their protection by member states.[69] The Treaty of Rome, establishing the European Economic Union, contained a few references to labour market regulation, including a reference to the need to improve working conditions and specific provisions on equal pay and holidays.[70] But the primary thrust of the Treaty of Rome was in the direction of regional economic liberalization. It established institutions devoted to the establishment and protection of a common market on the assumption that other international and regional institutions would provide for the protection of fundamental rights and freedoms. This assumption extended to the protection of social and economic rights, leaving—at least initially—its members' domestic systems of social protection and industrial relations relatively intact.[71]

Despite this institutional division of regional responsibilities, it became clear that the European Court of Justice would be called on to address workers' interests in the application of EU law. In *Albany*, a case involving the anti-competitive effects of

---

[65] C XV-1, Vol. 2 (Spain).   [66] C XII-1 (Denmark).   [67] C XIII-1 (Netherlands).

[68] See, e.g., C XII-1 (Netherlands); C X-1 (Denmark).

[69] Art. 137(6)EC. *Albany International BV and Stichting Bedrijfspensioenfonds Textielindustrie*, Case C-67/96, 1999 ECR 5751 (hereafter '*Albany*').

[70] Arts. 117–20, now Treaty of Amsterdam, Arts. 140–3. See Catherine Barnard and Simon Deakin, ' "Negative" and "Positive" Harmonization of Labor Law in the European Union', 8 *Colum. J. Eur. L.* (2003) 389, at 389.

[71] See Gráinne de Búrca, 'The Language of Rights and European Integration', in J. Shaw and G. More (eds.), *New Legal Dynamics of European Integration* (1995) 29–54, at 29.

a Dutch law requiring employers in the textile industry to be governed by a sector-level collective agreement, the Court addressed the relationship between domestic initiatives promoting collective bargaining and EU competition policy enshrined in Article 85(1) of the Treaty. The ECJ stated that 'social policy objectives pursued by [collective] agreements would be seriously undermined if management and labour were subject to Article 85(1) of the Treaty when seeking jointly to adopt measures to improve conditions of work and employment'.[72] As a result, *Albany* immunizes potentially anti-competitive effects of collective agreements from EU competition policy.[73]

The ECJ has also required EU institutions, as employers, to respect the freedom of association of its employees. In *Maurissen v. Court of Auditors*, it held that

13. . . . The freedom of trade union activity . . . means not only that officials and servants have the right without hindrance to form associations of their own choosing but also that such associations are free to do anything lawful to protect the interests of their members as employees.

14. It thus follows, in the first place, that the Community institutions and bodies may not prohibit their officials and servants from joining a trade union or staff association or from participating in trade union activities, or impose any penalty whatsoever on them by reason of such membership or activities.

15. It also follows that the Community institutions and bodies must allow trade unions and staff associations to fulfil their proper role, *inter alia* by keeping officials and servants informed, representing them *vis-à-vis* the institutions and other bodies on all matters affecting staff, and may not treat them differently without justification.[74]

More generally, the European Union has also begun to actively engage international and regional human rights norms, including freedom of association and the right to bargain collectively. In the 1997 Treaty of Amsterdam, reiterated in 2002, EU member states confirmed 'their attachment to fundamental social rights as

---

[72] *Albany, supra* note 69, para. 59.

[73] Catharine Barnard and Simon Deakin characterize the decision as placing 'great emphasis on provisions of the EC Treaty which, while not going so far as to confer a right to collective bargaining, nevertheless can be read as strongly encouraging the institutions and practice of collective bargaining'. Barnard and Deakin, *supra* note 70, at 393. They temper enthusiasm by noting the ECJ's jurisprudence on freedom of establishment, which has the potential to repudiate state autonomy over labour standards. They also note that the Court in *Albany* held the specific subject matter at issue in the sectoral agreement—a pension scheme—was 'commercial' because of the way it linked individual contributions and benefits and actuarially calculated risks; as a result, it fell within the scope of EU competition law.

[74] *Maurissen and European Public Service Union v. Court of Auditors*, joined cases C–193 and 194/87 [1990] ECR I-95. The EU's approach to union recognition of its employees is to be contrasted with that of the UN. See O'Higgins, 'The Interaction of the ILO, the Council of Europe and European Union Labour Standards', *supra* note 7, at 68 ('no UN body, with the single exception of the ILO, recognizes a trade union to which its employees belong and with which it engages in collective bargaining').

contained in the European Social Charter...and in the 1989 Community
Charter of the Fundamental Social Rights of Workers'.[75] The Community Charter
of Fundamental Social Rights for Workers was a 1989 political declaration of
intent by heads of state of EU member states that created no legally binding
obligations for the European Community or for the member states themselves.
Instead, it was 'meant to discover how far the Member States have recognized
common values and to illustrate such commitments in the form of rights'.[76]
Although the Community Charter differs significantly from the rights identified in
the European Social Charter, it includes similar provisions addressing freedom of
association and the right to bargain collectively. Despite the fact that it is not
legally binding, the Community Charter has provided interpretive guidance to the
European Court on Human Rights, served as a 'platform' for Treaty amendments,
and provided enhanced legitimacy to the European Social Charter in EU law.[77]

The Charter of Fundamental Rights of the European Union, to date a non-
binding instrument of the European Parliament, succeeded the Community Charter
of Fundamental Social Rights for Workers in 2000. An impressive combination of
studied ambiguity and high principle, the Charter of Fundamental Rights declares
that the European Union, 'conscious of its spiritual and moral heritage,...is
founded on the indivisible, universal values of human dignity, freedom, equality
and solidarity'. It affirms and, formally at least, appears to place on an equal footing
civil, political, economic, and social rights previously covered by a variety of
national, European, and international instruments.[78]

Three provisions of the Charter of Fundamental Rights speak directly to freedom
of association in the context of work.[79] Article 12 addresses freedom of assembly and
of association, including 'the right of everyone to form and to join trade unions for
the protection of his or her interests'. Article 27 stipulates that 'workers or their
representatives must, at the appropriate levels, be guaranteed information and
consultation in good time in the cases and under the conditions provided for by
Community law and national laws and practices'. Article 28 addresses rights of
collective bargaining and collective action:

Workers and employers, or their respective organizations, have, in accordance with Community law and national laws and practices, the right to negotiate and conclude collective

---

[75] Preamble, Treaty of Amsterdam; preamble, Treaty on European Union.

[76] Lammy Betten and Nicholas Grief, *EU Law and Human Rights* (1998), at 72.

[77] Jeff Kenner, 'Economic and Social Rights in the EU Legal Order: The Mirage of Indivisibility', in
T. K. Hervey and J. Kenner (eds.), *Economic and Social Rights under the EU Charter of Fundamental Rights*,
1–25, at 10–13.

[78] For a history of the drafting of the Charter, see Gráinne de Búrca, 'The Drafting of the European
Union Charter of Fundamental Rights', 26 *European Law Review* (2001) 126.

[79] For a thorough account of the origins of these provisions, see Ryan, 'The Charter and Collective
Labour Law', in Hervey and Kenner (eds.), *Economic and Social Rights under the EU Charter of Fundamental Rights, supra* note 51, 67–90.

agreements at the appropriate levels and, in cases of conflicts of interest, to take collective action to defend their interests, including strike action.

Many questions remain as to the text and legal effect of the Charter of Fundamental Rights.[80] Unlike its predecessor, the 1989 Community Charter, it does not protect a right of fair remuneration.[81] Nor does it offer a programme of action that, by imposing positive obligations on authorities, explicitly gives effect to its provisions.[82] It obliquely draws a distinction between 'rights' and 'principles',[83] leading commentators to fear that its social and economic guarantees it likely will 'be downgraded to "principles"' and be regarded as less significant or weighty than their civil and political counterparts.[84] And it defines justifiable restrictions on fundamental rights in vague and general language.[85]

Despite these potential drawbacks, the Charter's explicit reference to the right to negotiate and conclude collective agreements, in the words of Bernard Ryan, 'goes well beyond the rights which previously have been recognised in Community law'. According to Ryan, 'if the Charter is taken as an authoritarian guide to the fundamental rights in the EU order', it likely will affect the interpretation of EU directives affecting workers, perhaps induce Community courts to rely more explicitly on the 1989 Community Charter in cases involving the interests of workers, broaden and deepen the immunity that collective agreements enjoy from EU competition policy, and strengthen the legislative authority of EU institutions in the labour law field.[86] Together with the other Articles pertaining to freedom of

---

[80] For discussion that locates issues surrounding the future status and legal effect of the Charter in the light of competing historical narratives of the relationship between the EU and the Council of Europe, see Christopher McCrudden, 'The Future of the EU Charter of Fundamental Rights' (Jean Monnet Working Paper, No. 10/01, 2001). See also A. Menéndez, 'Chartering Europe: Legal Status and Policy Implications of the Charter of Fundamental Rights of the European Union', 40 *Journal of Common Market Studies* (2002) 471.

[81] Keith Ewing, *The EU Charter of Fundamental Rights: Waste of Time or Wasted Opportunity?* (2002).

[82] Aileen McColgan, 'The EU Charter of Fundamental Rights', 1 EHRLR (2004) 2, 2–3.

[83] Art. 52(5) provides:

> 'The provisions of this Charter which contain principles may be implemented by legislative and executive acts taken by Institutions and bodies of the Union, and by acts of Member States when they are implementing Union law, in the exercise of their respective powers. They shall be judicially cognizable only in the interpretation of such acts and in the ruling on their legality.'

[84] McColgan, *supra* note 82, at 3–4; Diamond Ashiagbor, 'Economic and Social Rights in the European Charter of Fundamental Freedoms', 1 EHRLR (2004) 62, at 71; Sionaidh Douglas-Scott, 'The Charter of Fundamental Rights as a Constitutional Document', 1 EHRLR (2004) 37, 45.

[85] Art. 52(1) provides that 'any limitation on the exercise of the rights and freedoms recognised by this Charter must be provided for by law and respect the essence of those rights and freedoms. Subject to the principle of proportionality, limitations may be made only if they are necessary and genuinely meet objectives of general interest recognised by the Union or the need to protect the rights and freedoms of others.' For commentary, see Miguel Poiares Maduro, 'The Double Constitutional Life of the Charter', in T. K. Hervey and J. Kenner (eds.), *Economic and Social Rights Under the EU Charter*, 269–99, at 278–81, esp. 279 ('the reference to general interests, in particular, can continue to raise some concerns due to its potentially broad and undetermined character').   [86] Ryan, 'The Charter and Collective Labour Law', *supra* note 51.

association, Article 28 is further evidence that collective bargaining is assuming greater prominence in European law.

6.

Recent developments in international labour law and international—and regional—human rights law thus reveal a trend towards enhanced protection of the right to bargain collectively. It would be a mistake to infer from this trend that economic globalization and transnational flexible production have not altered domestic commitments to collective bargaining. Whether and the extent to which these developments have affected the nature and structure of labour markets and in turn domestic labour market regulation are complex empirical questions that no doubt vary from sector to sector and jurisdiction to jurisdiction. It would also be a mistake to assume that the formality of this trend has improved the capacity of either field to achieve substantive compliance with the norms they seek to promote. Both fields tend to be long on promise and short on delivery. And even if states have been legislatively receptive to this trend—an unlikely possibility given the extent of scholarship asserting and in some cases demonstrating the steady erosion of domestic commitments to collective bargaining regimes—the international and domestic recognition of a right to bargain collectively is no guarantee that workers effectively enjoy such a right. A collective bargaining regime, in Harry Arthurs's words, 'need not be repealed or even amended; rather, as in the United States, it can be left to wilt and wither'.[87]

But it would also be a mistake to underestimate the substantive implications of this trend. Economic globalization and transnational flexible production have sparked a new conception of labour rights as international rights. Labour rights have become instruments by which the international legal order can mitigate some of the adverse distributional consequences of globalization and transnational flexible production. Their normative significance transcends the fact that they are workers' rights or human rights and extends to the justice of the international legal order itself. To the extent they protect the interests of workers from state or non-state action that international law—private or public—otherwise authorizes in the name of economic globalization or flexibility, international labour rights vest the international legal order with a measure of normative legitimacy.

Work done under the auspices of the ILO supports this new conception of labour rights as international rights The 1998 Declaration itself links core labour rights, including the right to bargain collectively, to economic globalization, noting that it is 'urgent, in a situation of growing economic interdependence, to reaffirm the immutable nature of the Organization and to promote their universal application'. The World Commission on the Social Dimension of Globalization, established by the ILO, reports that 'increasing globalization has generated a need for better global

---

[87] Harry Arthurs, 'Labour Law Without the State?, 46 *University of Toronto Law Journal* (1996) 1, 27.

governance' and that core labour standards, including the right to bargain collectively, must be a component of the reform of global governance.[88]

Other international institutions have also called on states to promote core labour rights in the face of economic globalization. The CESCR, for example, recently stated that 'the right to form and join trade unions may be threatened by restrictions upon freedom of association, restrictions claimed to be "necessary" in a global economy, or by the effective exclusion of possibilities for collective bargaining, or by the closing off of the right to strike for various occupational and other groups'.[89] The OECD, the World Bank, the WTO, the United Nations, the Council of Europe, and the European Union have also accepted the idea—if not the reality—of core labour rights as appropriate international legal aspirations in the face of economic globalization.[90]

This new understanding of labour rights as international rights is similar to the ILO's original view of labour rights as workers' rights. Labour rights as workers' rights receive international legal protection to prevent states that are seeking to attract foreign direct investment from abandoning their domestic commitments to just relations at work. Comprehending labour rights as international rights also treats them as mechanisms that possess the capacity to regulate international competition. But these accounts differ in one critical respect. On the traditional account, labour rights received international legal protection because of the normative importance of their domestic legal counterparts. Domestic collective bargaining regimes, regarded as essential to a just domestic legal order, required protection from international competition. On the field's newer account, labour rights merit international legal protection because they mitigate adverse outcomes produced or authorized by the international legal order itself.

This understanding of the nature and purpose of labour rights and particularly the right to bargain collectively has important normative consequences for international human rights law. As Virginia Leary notes, despite its enshrinement in major international human rights instruments, international human rights scholarship and practice historically regarded the right to bargain collectively and labour rights more generally as peripheral to the field. Civil and political rights have long been regarded by many state and non-state actors as the cornerstones of international human rights law, notwithstanding pious assertions of a principle of interdependence that holds all human rights to be of equal value.

Several factors account for the marginal status historically accorded to labour rights in international human rights law. Labour rights and specifically a right to bargain collectively differ significantly from civil and political rights in several

---

[88] World Commission on the Social Dimension of Globalization, *A Fair Globalization: Creating Opportunities for All* (2004), at paras. 336, 414–42.

[89] CESCR, Statement on Globalization and Economic, Social and Cultural Rights (1998).

[90] See OECD, *Trade, Employment and Labour Standards, supra* note 31; World Bank, *Workers in a Changing World (in World Development Report, 1995)*; WTO, *Singapore Ministerial Declaration* (1996); UN, *Global Compact* (2000).

respects. Like social rights, such as a right to housing or a right to education, labour rights create a different set of legal obligations and tend to invite a different form of adjudication than are contemplated by civil and political rights. A right to bargain collectively typically conjures up a complex legal code regulating the relationship between labour and capital, the contours of which vary dramatically from jurisdiction to jurisdiction and which may require constant monitoring and adjustment. The complexity and specificity of state action required to secure the right invite questions about whether it is truly appropriate to comprehend collective bargaining as an essential feature of what it means to be human.

Despite extensive scholarship detailing why these concerns do not justify the marginalization of labour rights in international human rights law, this has been their effect. But the significance of these concerns pales in the face of a conception of labour rights as instruments that promote a just international legal order. Given the gravity of this task, this conception has the potential of placing labour rights—and social and economic rights more generally—at the centre of international human rights law. It suggests that the mission of contemporary international human rights law involves much more than protecting what it means to be human in the face of sovereign power. It extends to monitoring the justice of the international legal order itself. The paradox of labour rights as international rights is that, for the task they assign to both international labour law and international human rights law, we have economic globalization and flexible production to thank.

4

Is the ILO Effective in Upholding Workers' Rights?: Reflections on the Myanmar Experience

FRANCIS MAUPAIN

1. INTRODUCTION

This topic is a particularly challenging one, for three reasons.

First, I am not an academic by profession but write as someone who has had, and to some extent still has, responsibilities within the ILO. I should make it clear, however, that I am not seeking to express or defend an official view. I am writing in a personal capacity, with the conviction that the case for the ILO is best made by letting history and facts speak for themselves.

Second, my topic is the 'efficacy' of the ILO. A few decades ago, in the years following the Second World War ('WWII') and the beginning of the Cold War, this topic would have smacked of complacency. The ILO was considered, at least in the small circle of specialists who knew about its existence, as quite distinct from what General de Gaulle called the 'machin' of the United Nations and its related agencies. It enjoyed the prestige of having survived the League of Nations thanks to its attitude during WWII and its tripartite support across countries. More significantly, it had developed unique procedures, which ensured an independent and impartial review of the observance by member states of the obligations they had freely accepted.

In the context of the post-Cold War era and of the globalization of the economy, the theme may now rather strike of masochism. Paradoxically, globalization may have helped to draw the attention of a wider public to the existence of the ILO. At the same time, globalization may have contributed to arouse some doubts about its efficacy. Thus, not so long ago, a distinguished participant at a meeting of the American Society of International Law commented that 'The ILO has been around forever, but it has done nothing forever, so it is not terribly interesting'.[1]

---

[1] Steve Charnovitz indignantly reported the comment by Jessica Mathews in S. Charnovitz, 'The ILO in its Second Century', 4 *Max Planck Yearbook of United Nations Law* (2000) 148–84. This article is also available at: http://www.netamericas.net/Researchpapers/Documents/Charnovitz/Charnovitz6.doc.

The root cause for such scepticism is the perception that, as the Singapore Prime Minister once observed, 'The ILO has no teeth'.[2] In a way, this comment is perfectly consistent with the fact that the ILO also used to be known as the 'old lady' of the UN system! More importantly, this remark reflects the fact that the efficacy of an organization tends to be examined through the lenses of the model offered by the World Trade Organization ('WTO'). WTO is considered the harbinger of a new generation of international organizations having the capacity to enforce obligations, through measures that hurt.[3]

Interestingly, however, the WTO's image of efficacy declined quickly as a result of the failure of recent ministerial conferences in Seattle[4] and Cancun,[5] which revealed severe limitations in its decision-making process. Furthermore, as Steve Charnovitz and others have reminded us, the possibility of using trade measures is a 'mixed blessing' for the WTO itself.[6] Not only are such measures not necessarily effective, but they may also be inconsistent with the WTO's primary objective of trade liberalization.[7]

Practically at the same time, a reverse phenomenon occurred with respect to the ILO: the 'old lady' that appeared to have been born without teeth seemed to be growing them exactly as she passed her 80th year with respect to Myanmar!

The third challenge I have to face is precisely that the chapter is about the problem of efficacy 'in the light of the ILO's experience in Myanmar'. However, not only is this experience still in progress and perhaps gravely jeopardized by recent events,[8] but it may be considered largely atypical and of limited scope as it relates to the implementation of a ratified convention in a very unusual political context.

All these challenges, as well as the cyclical perception of the respective efficacy of the ILO and WTO, strongly suggest that the issue cannot be limited to the efficiency of supervisory mechanisms or even the capacity to enforce obligations whether they derive from the Constitutive charter of the organization or from ratified conventions. The issue has to be placed in a wider perspective. Charnovitz's observation about the possible inconsistencies between WTO's fundamental objectives and the

---

[2] Quoted in M. Hansenne, *Un garde-fou pour la mondialisation: Le BIT dans l'après-guerre froide* (Gerpinnes: Editions Quorum; Carange-Genève: Editions Zoé 1999) 152.

[3] This perception is illustrated by a striking fact: there are theses written about the ILO, but nobody has ever marched down the street for or against it.

[4] The Third WTO Ministerial Conference was held in Seattle between 30 November and 3 December 1999. See http://www.wto.org/english/thewto_e/minist_e/min99_e/min99_e.htm.

[5] The Fifth WTO Ministerial Conference was held in Cancún from 10 to 14 September 2003. See http://www.wto.org/english/thewto_e/minist_e/min03_e/min03_e.htm.

[6] S. Charnovitz, 'Rethinking WTO Trade Sanctions', 95/4 *American Journal of International Law* (October 2001).

[7] 'In approving trade sanctions for commercial purposes, the WTO subverts the goal of open trade by allowing Governments to ban trade in response to violations by others. International agencies do not generally sponsor actions that contradict the agency's purpose. For example, the World Health Organization does not authorize spreading viruses to countries that do not cooperate in international health efforts' (Charnovitz, 'Rethinking WTO Trade Sanctions', *ibid.*).

[8] On the events of 30 May 2003, see below, Part 3.

use of trade sanctions to remedy violations is a useful reminder that the efficacy of the means can hardly be assessed without reference to their congruence with the organization's objectives. This reminder suggests a broader and more adequate definition of efficacy as '*the capacity of any given organization to make a verifiable impact towards the attainment of its specific Constitutional objectives*'.

In the light of this definition, in the second part of the chapter, I shall try to identify the parameters of the ILO's capacity to make an impact towards the achievement of its objectives. In the third part, I shall treat the Myanmar experience as a test of the ILO's capacity to ensure compliance with accepted obligations. Finally, in the fourth part, I shall examine, in the context of the global economy, what the ILO has to say about its capacity to make an impact towards the achievement of its objectives in countries that are not bound by obligations other than those inherent in their membership in the organization.[9]

2. PARAMETERS OF THE ILO'S CAPACITY TO MAKE A VERIFIABLE IMPACT ON THE ACHIEVEMENT OF ITS CONSTITUTIONAL OBJECTIVES

The shift in emphasis from the efficacy of procedural means available (including supervisory mechanisms and sanctions) to the capacity of different organizations to achieve their objectives highlights some fundamental differences between the situations of the WTO and the ILO.

The first difference is that contrary to WTO, the ILO's objectives have been defined a long time ago, in a context that was radically different from that of the post-Cold War and global economy in which WTO was born. Therefore, a first test of efficacy consists in assessing whether the relevance of the objectives of the organization has been maintained throughout these changing circumstances.

The second difference that springs to the eyes is that, contrary to the WTO, the ILO's objectives are not 'self-contained' in the form of a comprehensive 'single undertaking'.[10] The Constitution's preamble[11] contains a general statement of the values on which the ILO is based and the objectives it is expected to pursue, but these values and objectives have to be made 'operational' through specific standards. A second test of efficacy is thus to appraise the institutional capacity of the ILO to develop meaningful standards.

---

[9] For an explanation of the concept, see below, Part 4.

[10] To use the words of Gabrielle Marceau. G. Marceau, 'The WTO Dispute Settlement and Human Rights', in International Labour Standards: Future Challenges and Opportunities to Enhance the Relevance of International Labour Standards, First Seminar, International Labour Standards Department, Geneva, 23 and 24 May 2002, p. 16. A revised version of this article has been published in the 13/4 *European Journal of International Law* (2002) 753–814.

[11] The ILO Constitution is available at: http://www.ilo.org/public/english/about/iloconst.htm.

The third difference is that contrary to the various principles and obligations under the WTO's charter and related or 'covered' agreements which form part of the 'single undertaking', ILO standards, which are the translation of its Constitutional objectives into concrete provisions, are not automatically binding (i.e. self-executing on all members, but subject to their voluntary acceptance). In other words, a member becomes bound only after it has, by ratification, exercised its will to be bound; it is in this sense that I shall be using the word 'voluntary' here.[12]

I shall briefly examine how these important differences impact on the capacity of the ILO to achieve its objectives.

A. Efficacy as the Capacity of the ILO to Keep its Objectives Relevant

When one considers the fact that indeed the ILO was born in a radically different context, Jessica Mathews's comment referred to above that the ILO 'has been around forever', while certainly not meant as a compliment, may be seen as the involuntary recognition of a rather remarkable accomplishment.

After surviving the great depression—which represented a serious blow to the credibility of achieving social progress through voluntary state action, the ILO had to face WWII. Unlike the League of Nations, it had survived thanks to its decision to join the camp of the allies materialized by its move from Geneva to Montreal, and the tripartite support it has enjoyed across countries after the war. Afterwards, the ILO had to endure the process of decolonization and the Cold War. From an initial membership that was largely limited to European industrialized countries, the ILO became a truly universal organization. The ILO is now facing the new challenges of globalization. This phenomenon represents to many observers, a qualitative change in the system even more significant than the change between the pre-WWII and the post-WWII international system. What makes it more remarkable is that this longevity is not a form of passive survival, or the manifestation of the 'capacity of the being to persevere in being'. It has been a dialectical process of active adaptation to changing circumstances.

The first manifestation of this adaptation process was the Declaration of Philadelphia immediately after WWII. The main contribution of this document was to make the humanist and democratic values on which the organization rests much more explicit than in the Preamble which, in some respects, strikes of 'utilitarianism'. The second has been the effort at re-mobilizing the support of its members to the organization's objectives and values as well as to recast them in the new context of the global economy. This was achieved without any formal amendment to the Constitution[13] through the discussion of landmark Director-General's reports at successive International Labour Conferences, most recently in 1994 and 1999.

---

[12] See Art. 19 of the ILO Constitution.

[13] Formally, the ILO's Constitutional framework was updated and completed only once (through the Declaration of Philadelphia).

The introduction of the concept and strategy of 'decent work' proposed by the new Director-General, J. Somavia, after his election in 1999 offers a good illustration of this process. What may look, at first sight, like a 'semantic' lifting of the old constitutional concept of 'humane conditions of work', represents potentially a much more significant move from a compartmentalized to an integrated vision of the ILO's constitutional objectives. The Preamble to the Constitution contains only a non-exhaustive and somewhat random list of these objectives. This fragmented vision has been accentuated by normative action, which for obvious considerations of efficacy (making ratification easier) also tends to adopt the 'building blocks' tactics in developing instruments that relate to each one of these objectives and indeed very often to one aspect of these various objectives. In this context one of the essential aspects of the 'added value' of the concept of 'decent work' is to recast the vision of these objectives into a coherent whole, the four components of which—fundamental rights at work, employment, social protection, and social dialogue—are both complementary and interdependent.

B. Efficacy as the Capacity to Translate the Objectives into Meaningful Legal Instruments: Congruence between the Nature of the Objectives and the Tripartite Philosophy/Structure

If the ILO's Constitution contains a rather sketchy and somewhat random presentation of the organization's objectives, it is probably because in the view of its founders, the method whereby they would be given a specific content, in particular, in the form of international labour standards, was more important than their actual formulation. This raises the question of the validity and relevance of the method used to translate the organization's objectives into legal instruments.

As you all know, the method chosen by the founders was revolutionary and remains unique among international governmental organizations: it was the method of 'social dialogue', which is reflected in its tripartite structure; this method is based on a reformist vision of social justice as a process of reconciling the divergent interests concerned rather than as a pre-determined product. The ILO is thus the only international organization whose structure is determined by axiological assumptions about the nature and specificity of its objectives.

Obviously this reformist vision can be, and has—sometimes violently—been challenged. The ILO had to face the implacable hostility of the Bolsheviks, who claimed to possess a 'definite solution' of their own to the achievement of social justice;[14] but it can also be questioned from a rationalist or constructivist perspective. Although the latter shares with reformism the vision of justice as a process,

---

[14] The ILO's reformist vision of social justice is diametrically opposed to the revolutionary option: the Marxist vision of social progress claims that the alienation of the proletariat could only be eliminated through the overthrow of the regime of private ownership of the means of production. Therefore, reformism was merely the expression of class cooperation and the ILO was described as the rallying point of the international bourgeoisie.

constructivists, for the most eminent of them, have a radically different perception of the nature of that process, which should be conducted behind the 'veil of ignorance'.[15]

However, from an efficacy viewpoint, the question is not so much one of the validity of the philosophical or axiological assumptions of the reformist option in the Constitution. It is whether the 'device' whereby it is translated into realities through the rules of the 'tripartite game' is really consistent with that assumption. The answer is by no means as evident as the present virtual monopoly position enjoyed by the reformist vision of social justice may suggest.

It should not be forgotten that the ILO at its creation was literally torn between two opposite 'consistency' requirements. On the one hand, the logic of its reformist assumption implied that the reconciliation of the interests of workers and employers, to be meaningful, should take place between persons who genuinely (or freely) represent these interests in all member states; but industrial democracy—implying organizations free from outside interferences from governments and others—existed only in a handful of countries. On the other hand, the logic of the ILO's social justice objectives would be completely frustrated if it was not universal. As clearly reflected in Article 3, paragraph 5 of the Constitution,[16] the founders chose to be consistent with these universal values and objectives and to open up the organization to countries where industrial democracy was not a reality in the expectation that industrial democracy would progressively gain ground.

This most honourable concern for consistency with its universal values and objectives made the ILO vulnerable to the risk of having the decision-making process of its political organs contaminated by the participation of 'pseudo-delegates' of both workers and employers. Thus, the whole fabric of its standards was in a way falsified by the participation of elements, which did not reflect the true interests of workers and employers. This period started with the participation of the so-called fascist corporate workers before WWII and continued with the participation of employers from the Socialist countries after the war.[17]

When the United States withdrew from the organization in 1977, it seemed as if the ILO had definitely lost its risky gamble of reconciling tripartism and universalism. But, a few years later, the Solidarnocsz episode evidenced a reverse contamination of the 'democratic centralism' model by the ILO membership and

---

[15] John Rawls, *A Theory of Justice* (Oxford: Oxford University Press, 1999) 538.

[16] According to Art. 3.5 of the Constitution, 'the Members undertake to nominate non-Government delegates and advisers chosen in agreement with the industrial organizations, *if such organizations exist*, which are most representative of employers or workpeople, as the case may be, in their respective countries' [emphasis added].

[17] On this issue, see B. Beguin, 'The ILO and the Tripartite System', 523 *International Conciliation* (May 1959) 401–48. W. Jenks, 'The Significance for International Law of the Tripartite Character of the International Labour Organization', read before the Grotius Society on 28 May 1936. F. Maupain, 'L'OIT, la justice sociale et la mondialisation', 278 *Collected Courses*, Hague Academy of International Law (1999) 201–396.

procedures. After years of apparent impasse and 'dialogue of the deaf' between the ILO supervisory bodies and the Soviet bloc, this episode showed that ILO mechanisms can have a real impact provided that the beneficiaries have the determination and courage to use them. The ILO then offers a sort of 'green house' in which the fragile plant of freedom and pluralism can develop. Even though it would be going too far to say that the fall of the Berlin Wall was due to the ILO, there seems to be no doubt that the ILO contributed in no small measure to changing the international environment in which such a remarkable event became possible.[18]

While this contribution represents one of the most impressive pieces of evidence of the ILO's efficacy, it would be hasty to conclude that the virtual universality reached by the 'social dialogue' model puts an end to the chapter of the 'consistency challenge' for tripartism. To be fully effective in translating the objectives into normative action, the ILO tripartite structure must not only be able to ensure the free and genuine representation of the interest concerned; it must also be able to *reflect all* these interests concerned *fully*. The difficulty is that the almost indefinite expansion of the ILO's objectives resulting from the pre-war jurisprudence of the Permanent Court of International Justice[19] and subsequent practice, have by way of consequence expanded the categories and range of those interested by these objectives from industrial workers to all types of workers and even to 'persons' in need of protection and solidarity.[20] The ILO is thus confronted with what may be called the dilemma of the Procrustean bed and the frog's syndrome. According to some critics, the claim of the ILO to cover all workers is frustrated by the composition of its organs, which is distorted in favour of organized industrial workers and employers and consequently induces a 'neo-corporatist' bias in its actions and decisions.[21] This is a major challenge, which again could be the object of a separate discussion. I shall limit myself to point out that ultimately this challenge is more a challenge to the capacity of national unions to represent all types of workers rather than a challenge to the ILO as such.

It is important to recall that the ILO Constitution requires that workers' and employers' delegates be appointed by the most representative organizations at the national level. Taking into account the very first 'quantitative' interpretation given to

---

[18] For an analysis of this episode, see the book by Francis Blanchard (the Director-General at the time), *Tois clés en mains*, to be published in 2004.

[19] In the early 1920s the French government took the position that the ILO was not competent to deal with agricultural matters and the Permanent Court of International Justice was requested to give an advisory opinion on the question. The Court found that, despite the accidental use of the word 'industrial' in certain provisions of the Constitution, the competence of the ILO did extend to international regulation of the conditions of labour of persons employed in agriculture. *Advisory Opinion No. 2, Competence of the ILO to Regulate Agricultural Labor* (1922), PCIJ, Ser. B, Nos 2 and 3.

[20] See, for instance, in the Declaration of Philadelphia, developments regarding the extension of social security measures 'to all . . . in need of such protection' (III(d)).

[21] See, for example, S. Cooney, 'Testing Times for the ILO: Institutional Reform for the New International Political Economy', 20 *Comparative Labor Law and Policy Journal* (1999) 365–99.

that provision by the PCIJ,[22] and the Court's subsequent recognition of the extent of the ILO's mandate, nothing would seem to prevent an organization of workers in the informal sector—if they were capable of organizing—to be considered as the most representative for the purpose of appointing the workers' delegate to the International Labour Conference.

C. Efficacy and Voluntary Standards in the Context of Globalization

It is accepted—as maintained above—that the ILO has the capacity to develop its objectives into meaningful and relevant standards. The next question is, the extent to which it is capable of having these standards impacting on the realities of its members.

The ILO normative action rests on a 'voluntary approach'[23] which in fact covers two different meanings: 'will' and 'good will'. The 'will' dimension of the voluntary approach directly derives from the reformist approach of the ILO. It means that social progress is not expected to take place spontaneously—a fairly reasonable assumption in the light of the nineteenth-century experience; it requires voluntary action *by the state*. This 'stato-centric' assumption obviously raises some fundamental problems of efficacy in the present context of globalization where additional layers of decision-making develop at non-state, infra-state, and supra-state levels. And even within the national environment of the most advanced and powerful industrialized countries, the development of the 'informal sector' has clearly established the limits of states' 'will' to regulate the conditions of all those who work.

The 'good will' dimension means that, contrary to the WTO's approach, which makes all the obligations covered by the 'single undertaking' *ipso jure* binding on all its members, ILO standards rest on the 'voluntary' acceptance of the traditionally privileged form of standards—international labour conventions—which are treaties creating obligations when they are ratified and requiring incorporation into national legislation. This is, indeed, the general situation in international law still based on the consent of states. It is also the case for recommendations, which have to be submitted to the competent national authority and may have an impact on national legislation to the extent that their guidance is freely taken into account by the said authorities.

This second dimension raises two very different problems from the viewpoint of efficacy.

---

[22] According to the concept of representativity, as interpreted by the PCIJ in its first Advisory Opinion, the objective of the appointment of the workers' delegate through the most representative organization is 'to ensure the representation of the workers of the country'. Nothing in this definition would seem to exclude persons who work, have worked, or want to work and thus are concerned with the ILO's objectives, irrespective of their specific status. Advisory Opinion No. 1, Designation of the Workers' Delegate for the Netherlands at ILC (1922), reproduced in Official Bulletin, ILO, Vol. VI, No. 7, 16.08.1922.

[23] The word 'voluntary' has been placed inside quotation marks as a reminder that it is being used in its etymological sense related to the exercise of a state's will to accept an international labour standard as binding on it.

The first aspect is whether the ILO has the capacity to ensure that this voluntary acceptance is made effective in the realities of its members. At first sight it does not seem to represent a great challenge to the extent that members are supposed to have the will to implement these standards. However, the Myanmar case, which I shall examine in the third part of this chapter, shows that it is not necessarily so easy, and that the issue represents indeed a very significant test of efficacy.

The second possible limitation inherent in the good will was in a way clearly anticipated by the Constitution. According to its last preambular paragraph, 'Failure of any nation to adopt humane conditions of labour is an obstacle in the way of other nations which desire to improve the conditions in their own countries.'

This paragraph encapsulates the essence of the problem: the 'will' and 'good will' of the members to pay the price of social progress in an open economy depends on the 'good will' of the others, and this interdependence (or negative solidarity) obviously applies also to the 'good will' necessary to ratify ILO conventions. This 'prisoner's dilemma' was the very reason why some of the ILO founders had initially envisaged a much more ambitious, 'supranational' scheme whereby the International Labour Conference would be empowered to adopt a genuine 'international' labour legislation that would become directly applicable subject to a right of 'opting out' to be exercised within a specified time limit. They quickly realized, however, that such a scheme would deter countries from joining or, if they did join, would induce them to adopt the lowest common denominator.

Under these circumstances, the 'voluntary' option seemed the only realistic one, and the founders made the bet that peer pressure as well as the benefits expected from ratification from the view point of social stability would make it effective. It was also expected that countries voting in favour of a draft convention would feel morally bound to ratify it.[24] As previously noted, despite strenuous efforts of the first ILO Director, Albert Thomas, and his constant travels to persuade countries to ratify, this hope quickly proved unrealistic and the great economic depression of the 1930s gave it the 'coup de grâce'. The beginning of the post-war period, however, seemed much more promising. Indeed, several factors combined to create the hope of a 'virtuous circle'[25] of simultaneous economic growth and social progress.

This virtuous circle—some may say mirage—quickly vanished with the emergence of the so-called globalization phenomenon. This phenomenon has far-reaching implications for our purpose as it has led to put into question the very principle of

---

[24] Hence the efforts to make conventions acceptable to a vast majority of countries going as far as introducing 'country specific' provisions (see, for instance, the references to India, Siam, or Persia in early conventions).

[25] The first factor was the 'thirty glorious' years of economic prosperity in advanced industrialized countries, which encouraged governments and enterprises to show generosity within the framework and limits of the Fordist model.

The second and perhaps much less-known factor in favour of this virtuous circle was the success of the International Labour Office—notwithstanding the then prevailing orthodoxy of the *tabula rasa*—to persuade former colonial countries to succeed more or less automatically to the ratifications of their former rulers, which provoked a rising tide of ratifications from non-industrialized countries.

both the will and good will dimension of the 'voluntary' option itself as an efficient tool for achieving the ILO's objectives of social progress in an interdependent economy. I will return to these implications in the fourth part of this chapter.

3. EFFICACY AS THE ILO'S CAPACITY TO ENSURE THE IMPLEMENTATION OF OBLIGATIONS INCURRED TO ACHIEVE ITS OBJECTIVES: THE CASE OF MYANMAR[25a]

The ILO has always taken pride in the unique character of its supervisory system for the implementation of conventions. This system is indeed unique for its richness and diversity.

In addition to the two formal contentious procedures specifically provided for in the Constitution,[26] another 'regular' mechanism has developed and has become a key part of the system—although this mechanism is based on the regular reports that governments must submit under Article 22 of the Constitution, regarding their implementation of ratified conventions—to systematically review possible inconsistencies between ratified conventions and national law and practice. This 'regular' mechanism is entrusted to an independent body, the Committee of Experts on the Application of Conventions and Recommendations.

Mention should also be made of the freedom of association procedure, which is completely *sui generis* and goes beyond all of the previous mechanisms in that it applies even to countries that have not ratified the relevant conventions.

Two features are especially relevant to explain the potential and impact of the system: first, the synergies that exist between the legal analysis objectively carried out by legal experts (either the Committee of Experts under Article 22, or in the case of complaints, an independent Commission of Inquiry) and the pressure from tripartite political organs (either at the International Labour Conference or in the Governing Body). The second distinctive feature is the unique role granted to non-state actors to reveal possible inconsistencies between the requirements of conventions or recommendations and the domestic situation of states.[27] This means that those who are in a better position to know the realities within a country are also in a position to bring them to the notice of the competent ILO bodies.

The richness and uniqueness of the ILO's mechanisms are, however, not in themselves sufficient evidence of their efficacy. Two types of problems may be identified in this respect.

[25a] For important developments since the completion of this chapter see: http://www.ilo.org/public/english/standards/relm/gb/docs/gb291/pdf/gb-5-1.pdf, and also gb-5-1-ad.pdf, gb-5-2.pdf, and gb-5-conc.pdf.

[26] Representations under Art. 24, and Complaints under Art. 26.

[27] N. Valitcos, *International Labour Law* (Deventer: Kluwer Law International, 1979) 268. See also F. Maupain, 'L'OIT, la justice sociale et la mondialisation', *supra* note 17, 331 *et seq.*, and B. Beguin, 'The ILO and the Tripartite System', *supra* note 17.

The first relates to the capacity of the organization to force an unwilling country into compliance. The ILO's record is somewhat inconclusive in this respect. The most serious cases of violations brought under the complaint procedure of Article 26 have been solved either because the countries concerned were reluctantly led to accept the ILO recommendations and progressively managed to implement them, or very significantly, because the collapse of the regime guilty of the violations solved the problem.[28] This is why the case of Myanmar has a special significance: it had become clear at an early stage that the military regime had no real intention to implement the recommendations of the Commission of Inquiry, but there was also no sign that it would collapse any time soon.

It is also evident, however, that the addition of successes achieved by the ILO's procedures in obtaining compliance or even progress in specific cases of violations, however remarkable and perhaps insufficiently publicized, does not suffice to form a valid and balanced picture of the overall efficacy of the system. I shall thus devote some brief remarks to the extent to which the system is successful in ensuring a balanced implementation of its conventions beyond specific cases of compliance or progress.

A. Efficacy as the Capacity to Enforce Obligations: The Lessons of the Myanmar Experience

As I have just noted, the Myanmar case was very unusual. On the one hand, the Commission of Inquiry, which was appointed to examine the complaint filed against the country, reached devastating conclusions about the gravity of the violations of Convention No. 29;[29] on the other hand, the ILO was faced with a very unco-operative and even highly critical attitude of the authorities, and no sign that a change would occur.[30]

---

[28] This was the case with the Greek Colonels in the 1970s, the Pinochet regime, and the Jaruzelski regime in Poland.

[29] See Part V of the Report of the Commission of Inquiry appointed under Art. 26 of the Constitution of the ILO to examine the observance by Myanmar of the Forced Labour Convention 1930 (No. 29). Governing Body, 273rd Session, Geneva, November 1998. Document GB.273/5 available online at: http://www.ilo.org/public/english/standards/relm/gb/docs/gb273/myanmar5.htm.

[30] After violently criticizing the Commission of Inquiry, the government authorities said they would have little difficulty in implementing its recommendations, which implied that forced labour in fact did not exist in the country. In its reply to the report of the Commission of Inquiry, the Government of Myanmar stated that some of the information contained in the report was 'politically motivated, highly biased, lacked objectivity, and without any good will'. Letter sent by the Government of Myanmar on 23 September 1998, appended to Document GB.273/5, *supra* note 29.

A new Order was adopted according to which relevant government authorities were banned to exercise powers conferred upon them by the Towns and Village Acts ('TVA'). It is important to point out that the TVA gives the authorities a legal basis to use forced labour in the country. Government authorities virulently rejected the Office's statement that this order did not meet the Commission's recommendations.

First, the new Order made an exception for types of forced labour only authorized by the convention during the transitional period. Second, this move could be reversed at any time. Finally, it referred to

These circumstances left the ILO little alternative but to react. After thirty years of dialogue of the deaf between the Committee of Experts and successive authorities of Myanmar, after the filing of an Article 24 representation (which was seen as a step in the escalation of the pressure), the refusal to implement the recommendations of the Commission of Inquiry could have been a fatal blow to the ILO's machinery.

The problem was: How should the ILO react? The ILO does not have the power to expel or suspend a member from membership. At the beginning of the 1960s the organization faced the problem of South Africa and apartheid. In this case, the pressure exercised by the ILO led the country to voluntarily withdraw from the organization. Under Article 1(5) of the Constitution, however, such withdrawal does not affect the continued obligations of the country under ratified conventions.[31]

This option was indirectly considered in the case of Myanmar. Indeed, the first Technical Cooperation Mission,[32] which went to Myanmar in May 2000, pointed out to the authorities that the only attitude consistent with their refusal to implement the recommendations of the Commission of Inquiry and thus to eradicate forced labour would be to withdraw from the organization, as the 1998 Declaration on Fundamental Principles and Rights at Work[33] makes it clear that the elimination of forced labour is an obligation inherent in ILO membership.

It is clear, however, that this option would be a dead end for both sides. As far as Myanmar was concerned, the withdrawal could have placed the country in a

---

authority exercised under the Towns and Village Acts, although the practice of forced labour had developed without reference to these texts.

See Order No. 1-99, Yangon, the 15th Waning of Kason 1361 (14 May 1999). The Order is reproduced in Appendix III of the Report of the Director-General to the members of the Governing Body on Measures taken by the Government of Myanmar following the recommendations of the Commission of Inquiry established to examine its observance of the Forced Labour Convention 1930 (No. 29), 21 May 1999. Available online at: http://www.ilo.org/public/english/standards/relm/gb/docs/gb274/dg-myanm.htm.

The government described the comments that the new order did not meet the Commission's recommendations as unfounded, biased, and politically motivated, consisting of 'false accusations concocted with evil intent to bring about the destruction of Myanmar by Myanmar expatriates and renegade groups'.

See the Memorandum of the Government of Myanmar on the Report of the Director-General to the members of the Governing Body dated 21 May 1999. This document was appended to the Governing Body document GB.276/6: measures, including action under Art. 33 of the Constitution of the International Labour Organization, to secure compliance by the Government of Myanmar with the recommendations of the Commission of Inquiry established to examine the observance of the Forced Labour Convention 1930 (No. 29), Governing Body, 276th Session Geneva, November 1999. Available online at: http://www.ilo.org/public/english/standards/relm/gb/docs/gb276/gb-6-a2.htm.

[31] Art. 1.5 of the Constitution of the ILO reads as follows: 'When a Member has ratified any international labour Convention, such withdrawal shall not affect the continued validity for the period provided for in the Convention of all obligations arising thereunder or relating thereto.'

[32] Technical Cooperation Mission, hereinafter TCM.

[33] Report of the Technical Cooperation Mission to Myanmar, ILC Provisional Record, 88th Session, Geneva, 2000. Similarly, the Resolution adopted by the ILC in 1999 at its 87th Session stated that 'the attitude and behaviour of the Government of Myanmar are grossly incompatible with the conditions and principles governing membership of the Organization'.

situation of complete isolation, even towards its most willing neighbours, and would not have made it less vulnerable to economic sanctions quite on the contrary.[34] As far as the ILO was concerned, it would have meant throwing out the baby of forced workers in need of protection, with the water of the regime in place.

The only remaining course, unexplored up to then, was the one offered by Article 33 according to which, '[i]n the event of any Member failing to carry out within the time specified the recommendations, if any, contained in the report of the Commission of Inquiry, or in the decision of the International Court of Justice, as the case may be, the Governing Body may recommend to the Conference such action as it may deem wise and expedient to secure compliance therewith'.

This course was first envisaged in 1999[35] and effectively taken in 2000. This move in itself did have a measurable impact, as it triggered a series of significant steps to remedy the situation, which I shall examine in a first section. However, this process was brought to a brutal halt as a result of the events of 30 May 2003,[36] whose implications go far beyond the forced labour issue. The situation nevertheless raises more sharply the issue—which I will examine in a second section—of moving from the threat to the actual application of measures by members under Article 33. Finally, I shall try to draw some tentative conclusions as regards the question as to whether this first experience may be a unique one.

Historical background of the implementation of Article 33 and the evidence of the impact on the situation

Until 1948 Myanmar was part of the British Empire, except for the brief period of occupation by Japan during WWII. Myanmar became independent on 4 January 1948. Shortly thereafter, Myanmar's first Constitution was adopted. The new Constitution provided that 'forced labour in any form and involuntary servitude, except as punishment for a crime . . . shall be prohibited'.[37]

From its independence onwards, the country was plagued by ethnic and Communist insurgency. The military assumed full legislative and judicial power following the March 1962 coup. After a new Constitution was adopted in 1974, the country followed the 'Burmese way to socialism' (sometimes described as the 'Burmese way to economic decay') until the military took over again in a different guise in 1988.

To a large extent, British legislation remained on the books, including the Penal Code and the Town and Village Acts. Section 374 of the Penal Code prohibits the unlawful compulsion of forced labour. The TVA provides a framework for the administration of villages and cities, and in particular defines the powers of Village Heads. Pursuant to the TVA, those Village Heads have the power 'to furnish guides,

---

[34] And this is one of the reasons why, confronted with the threat, the authorities started to be more cooperative.　　　　　　　　　　[35] See Governing Body document GB.276/6, *supra* note 30.

[36] On the Tabyin 'massacre', see: http://www.burmanet.org/bnn_archives/2003/20030602.txt.

[37] Art. 19(ii) of the Myanmar Constitution.

messengers, porters, supplies of food for any troops and police posted in or near or marching through their village-tract or for any servant on duty'.[38] Thus, the requisition of forced labour, for the purposes covered in these Acts, is not 'unlawful'.[39] This is presumably why the United Kingdom had not ratified Convention No. 29 on forced labour with respect to Burma.

Under Convention No. 29 of 1930, which has received the greatest number of ratifications, forced labour is defined as 'all work or service, which is exacted from any person under the menace of any penalty and for which the said person has not offered himself voluntarily'.[40] Convention No. 29 provides for the progressive suppression of forced labour that is used for public purposes and as an exceptional measure, subject to the conditions and guarantees detailed in the convention. Forced labour exacted as a tax or for the execution of public works falls into this category.

During a short period of civilian rule, Burma ratified Convention No. 29 in 1955—but it did not modify its legislation. Consequently, from 1964 onwards, the Committee of Experts on the Application of Conventions and Recommendations consistently pointed out that the provisions of the TVA were inconsistent with the convention. The Government of Myanmar essentially insisted that the colonial legislation, although still on the books, was obsolete. The dialogue did not seem to lead anywhere in view of the prevailing political situation. The military junta that took over in 1988 refused to recognize the overwhelming victory of the National League for Democracy[41] on the occasion of free elections in 1990. The situation quickly worsened, as the military junta used forced labour on an unprecedented scale, both quantitatively and qualitatively.

It is in these circumstances that, during the 83rd session of the International Labour Conference, twenty-five worker delegates filed a complaint against the Government of Myanmar for non-observance of Convention No. 29. The decision to establish a Commission of Inquiry was taken in 1997 and was followed by the refusal of the Government of Myanmar to accept its visit.

This was not the first time that a government had refused to cooperate with a Commission of Inquiry. In any case, such a refusal has never prevented the examination of the complaint.[42] The Commission of Inquiry held a hearing in Geneva and travelled in countries bordering Myanmar to hear victims who had fled the country. Its conclusions were couched in unusually damning terms:

This report reveals a saga of untold misery and suffering, oppression and exploitation of large sections of the population inhabiting Myanmar by the Government, military and other public

---

[38] TVA, sections 7 and 8.

[39] It should perhaps be noted, however, that those requisitioning labour in Myanmar never invoked these Acts and did not limit themselves to practices sanctioned by these Acts.

[40] Forced Labour Convention 1930 (No. 29), Art. 2(1).   [41] Hereinafter, NLD.

[42] Greece in 1970 and Poland in 1983 chose not to cooperate with the Commission of Inquiry. These reluctant attitudes did not prevent the Commission from issuing its report. See N. Valticos, 'Les Commissions d'enquête de l'Organisation Internationale du Travail', 3 *Revue Générale de Droit International Public* (1987) 866–7.

officers. It is a story of gross denial of human rights to which the people of Myanmar have been subjected particularly since 1988 and from which they find no escape except fleeing from the country.[43]

It is important to keep in mind that the complaint procedure under Article 26 and the report of the Commission of Inquiry appointed to examine it is the only way whereby a legally binding determination can be made that a member has breached its obligations under a convention.[44] However, the Recommendations of a Commission of Inquiry do not as such constitute a 'ruling' or adjudication. Under the Constitution, the findings of the Commission become binding when the member state concerned chooses to acquiesce, either by its explicit acceptance of the findings or by not referring the matter to the International Court of Justice (as provided for under Article 29 of the ILO Constitution).[45] In the Myanmar case (as in all previous Article 26 complaints), the government abstained from appealing to the ICJ against the Recommendations of the Commission of Inquiry.

The impact of the decision to implement Article 33

While Myanmar did not choose to challenge the report of the Commission before the ICJ, it reacted very negatively. Thus, following a resolution adopted by the International Labour Conference in 1999, which already introduced some forms of 'internal sanctions',[46] the Governing Body decided in March 2000 to place on the agenda of the ILC the question of implementing Article 33 of the Constitution of the ILO. What is really striking is that this decision immediately triggered a significant change in the attitude of the authorities, which then accepted the visit of the first Technical Cooperation Mission to discuss the implementation of the Commission of Inquiry's recommendations in May 2000 just before the ILC was

---

[43] Document GB.273/5, *supra* note 30.

[44] No such binding legal effect arises in the case of observations from the Committee of Experts or reports resulting from a representation under Art. 24 of the Constitution of the ILO.

[45] Art. 29 reads as follows: '(1) The Director-General of the International Labour Office shall communicate the report of the Commission of Inquiry to the Governing Body and to each of the Governments concerned in the complaint, and shall cause it to be published. (2) Each of these Governments shall within three months inform the Director-General of the International Labour Office whether or not it accepts the recommendations contained in the report of the Commission; and if not, whether it proposes to refer the complaint to the International Court of Justice.' One may have doubts as to the scope of the Constitution and its compatibility in connection with the Statute of the ICJ. However it may be, one thing is certain: it proved very useful in resisting attempts from the authorities to reopen the assessment of the Commission of Inquiry on the occasion of the visit of the first Technical Cooperation Mission in May 2000. The authorities were told that the recommendations being *res judicata*, the only question open for discussion was how to implement them (see Report of the Technical Cooperation Mission to Myanmar, ILC, Provisional Record, 88th Session, 8th item on the agenda, Geneva, 2000. Available online at: http://www.ilo.org/public/english/standards/relm/ilc/ilc88/pr-8.htm.

[46] In particular a ban on technical cooperation with Myanmar. ILC Resolution of 1999, *supra* note 33.

due to consider acting under Article 33. The ILC nevertheless decided to go ahead with the adoption of a Resolution addressed to ILO Members and international governmental organizations requesting that they review their relations with Myanmar to avoid abetting the practice of forced labour and 'to contribute as far as possible to the implementation of the Recommendations of the Commission of Inquiry'.[47]

This was followed by a regular succession practically of new requests at monthly intervals, corresponding to the successive sessions of the Governing Body (in March and November) and the ILC (in June) each year.

Rather than simply engaging in a chronological summary, it seems convenient to distinguish three main phases in the successive steps taken by the ILO and to assess their results up to this point in time.

From the recognition of the existence of the problem to the change in legislation under the threat of Article 33

The recognition of the problem and the adoption of the resolution (May 2000)
As I have just noted, the attitude of Myanmar changed as soon as the Governing Body decided to discuss the implementation of the Commission of Inquiry's recommendations. As a result, Myanmar accepted the visit of a Technical Cooperation Mission to Yangon, as a result of which the government finally recognized for the first time, even though in veiled terms, that forced labour had occurred in Myanmar and announced that it would take 'appropriate measures including administrative, executive and legislative measures to ensure prevention of such occurrences (of forced labour) in the future'.[48]

The International Labour Conference acknowledged this vague commitment as a 'welcome intention', but did not consider it sufficient for the Conference to postpone the consideration and adoption of a Resolution to implement measures pursuant to Article 33.[49] However, the International Labour Conference empowered the Governing Body at its November 2000 session, to freeze the implementation of the Resolution if the Government of Myanmar took 'measures that [were] sufficiently concrete and detailed'.[50]

The adoption of new regulations prohibiting forced labour (November 2000)
This threat, together with the pressure of a second Technical Cooperation Mission

---

[47] Resolution concerning the measures recommended by the Governing Body under Art. 33 of the ILO Constitution on the Subject of Myanmar, ILC, Provisional Record, 88th Session, Geneva, 2000. http://www.ilo.org/public/english/standards/relm/ilc/ilc88/resolutions.htm#I.

[48] Letter dated 27 May 2000, written by the Minister of Labour, Major General Tin Ngwe, and delivered to the members of the Technical Cooperation Mission. See ILO Press Release, 14 June 2000. http://www.ilo.org/public/english/bureau/inf/pr/2000/27.htm.

[49] ILC, Provisional Record, 88th Session, *supra* note 47.

[50] Governing Body, 279th Session, Geneva, November 2000, Document GB.279/6/2. Available at: http://www.ilo.org/public/english/standards/relm/gb/docs/gb279/pdf/gb-6-2.pdf.

visit in the second part of October 2000, finally resulted in the government adopting a supplementary order in October 2000 by which, the government agreed to remove the exceptions left in the initial Order.[51] Additionally the government accepted to threaten penal sanctions against those who failed to comply with the order.[52]

The Committee of Experts, which was due to meet shortly thereafter, acknowledged that these orders 'could provide the statutory basis for compliance with the Convention if given *bona fide* effect', but called for 'further measures'.[53]

However, when the Governing Body met in November 2000, just a few days after the adoption by Myanmar of the supplementary order, the question was whether the measures before it were 'sufficiently concrete and detailed' to meet the condition established by the ILC. The Governing Body considered that the action taken was 'too little too late' (terms of the Employers' spokesman[54]) and that, therefore, it was impossible to assess its effective impact on forced labour. Accordingly, the Governing Body decided to let the Resolution take effect as foreseen by the ILC on 30 November 2000.[55] It was nevertheless understood that the Director-General should continue to extend cooperation to Myanmar to promote full compliance.

The Director-General was thus requested to communicate the Resolution to tripartite constituents and international governmental organizations, which were both to review their relations with Myanmar (to ensure that they were not abetting forced labour), and then to report on their findings.

From the threat to stop cooperation to the acceptance of an independent inspection
At first, the authorities in Myanmar reacted angrily to the decision of the Governing Body to 'activate' the Resolution, which they described as 'arbitrary'. They went as far as saying that, while they would continue their efforts to implement the orders, they would cease all cooperation with the ILO.[56]

The Director-General quickly reacted by pointing out that, if the Government of Myanmar were sincere with its determination to implement the new legislation, it had nothing to gain from such an attitude of non-cooperation at a time when ILO

---

[51] Order of October the 27th 2000. See Governing Body, 279th Session, Geneva, November 2000. The Order is appended to Document GB.279/6/1(Add.2). Available online at: http://www.ilo.org/ public/english/standards/relm/gb/docs/gb279/pdf/gb-6-1-ad2.pdf.   [52] *Ibid.*

[53] Committee of Experts on the Application of Conventions and Recommendations (CEACR), Individual Observation concerning Convention No. 29, Forced Labour 1930 Myanmar (ratification: 1955) Published: 2001. Available online at: http://ilolex.ilo.ch:1567/english/iloquery.htm.

[54] Governing Body, 282nd Session, Geneva, November 2001. Document 282/4/Appendices available at: http://www.ilo.org/public/english/standards/relm/gb/docs/gb282/pdf/gb-4-ax.pdf.

[55] Governing Body, 279th Session, Geneva, November 2000. Document GB.279/6/2, *supra* note 50.

[56] Communication dated 11 February 2001 from the Government of Myanmar to the Director-General forwarded by the Permanent Mission of Myanmar. Governing Body, 280th Session, Geneva, March 2001. Document GB.280/6, Appendix 4. Available online at: http://www.ilo.org/public/english/ standards/relm/gb/docs/gb280/pdf/gb-6.pdf.

members were considering the effect that the government's stated determination to implement the new legislation would have on the measures that members would take pursuant to the Resolution. If Myanmar wanted to get any credit for progress, it should rather accept an independent assessment of the 'practical implementation and actual impact' of the orders it had taken.[57] It was pointed out that the prospect of such an inspection could—and actually did as we will see—induce a 'wait and see' attitude from even the most determined members of the ILO.[58]

This strategy proved effective. After difficult negotiations, the authorities accepted a very far-reaching understanding whereby an international High Level Team (HLT)[59] would carry out a completely free and independent evaluation of the implementation and impact of the new legislation throughout the country. The HLT was quickly constituted after the International Labour Conference in July–August 2001. It included eminent persons and Supreme Court judges of unimpeachable credentials under the chairmanship of a former Governor General of Australia, Sir Ninian Stephen.

This exercise constituted a form of international inspection, which is in fact *sui generis*. It is tempting to see it as a sort of substitute for the Commission of Inquiry, which, Myanmar could have requested under Article 34 of the Constitution in order to verify its contention that it had fulfilled the recommendations of the first Commission of Inquiry.

During a three-week visit to Myanmar (from September to October 2000) and subsequent interviews in bordering countries, the HLT covered a large spectrum of ethnic and regional situations. The findings of the HLT were generally positive regarding the dissemination of the Orders[60] not, however, without noting indices such as freshly posted copies of the Orders, which pointed to a 'Potemkine' type of preparation of the Mission by the authorities.

The assessment was greatly more critical as regards the realities of enforcement. The HLT findings underlined that, although the situation had improved in the central part of Myanmar, this was not the case in all other areas. Improvements appeared to be particularly weak in places where—due to insurgency or other factors—the presence of the army remained strong.[61]

---

[57] Communication dated 1 March 2001 from the Director-General to the Minister for Labour of the Government of Myanmar. Governing Body, 280th Session, Geneva, March 2001. Document GB.280/6, Appendix 5.

[58] Even those who actively pushed for an immediate implementation of the Conference Resolution in November 2000, and are generally known to be in favour of the principle of trade sanctions for the violation of workers' rights, seemed relieved (around March 2001) to wait for the assessment of the High Level Team (HLT).

[59] See the 'Understanding on an ILO Objective Assessment', Governing Body, 282nd Session, Geneva, November 2001. Document GB.282/4/Appendices, *supra* note 54.

[60] See Part IV of the Report of the HLT, Governing Body, 282nd Session, Geneva, November 2001. Document GB.282/4. Available online at: http://www.ilo.org/public/english/standards/relm/gb/docs/gb282/pdf/gb-4.pdf. [61] *Ibid.*

The HLT firmly underlined the absence of an independent judiciary as the reason why only few isolated administrative proceedings, and no criminal prosecutions whatsoever, had been initiated.

Most originally, the HLT's analysis suggested that the disproportionate size of the military and its attitude of 'self-reliance' contributed significantly to the practice of forced labour. The HLT further suggested that economic modernization was central to eradicating the problem. However, in order to escape the 'vicious circle' created by the fact that forced labour increased international economic pressures, which in turn continued to maintain the backwardness of the country and of its (virtual) fiscal system and as a consequence recourse to forced labour for 'community work', Myanmar's authorities would have to display an unequivocal commitment to eliminate forced labour. Consequently, the HLT suggested: (i) a long-term representation of the ILO in the country;[62] and (ii) some sort of independent 'ombudsperson'.

The implementation of the HLT's recommendation

The acceptance of a continued ILO presence as a result of the HLT The HLT report was unanimously well received among the tripartite constituents of the Governing Body in November 2000. Once again, the Government of Myanmar was at first reported to be very angered by the HLT's frank assessment of the situation, but they had eventually to admit that it had occurred in conditions of full impartiality, transparency, and objectivity. Myanmar also quickly realized that the only hope for the measures of Article 33 to be removed—even if they were provisionally dormant—would be to engage in a discussion on the implementation of the Recommendations.

Months of negotiations ultimately led to an Understanding on the assignment of an ILO Liaison Officer to the country in March 2002.[63] However, the Governing Body and the ILC insisted that all the steps taken until then were merely a means towards the eradication of forced labour, and not an end in itself. Despite recognizing the importance of these steps—including the HLT and the appointment of the Liaison Officer—many governments and the Workers' group in the Governing Body and in the International Labour Conference were of the opinion that there was no sufficient evidence that the realities of forced labour had substantially changed, even though improvements in the central part of the country—thanks to ILO efforts and presence—had been acknowledged by Aung San Suu Kyi herself.

The acceptance of a mechanism to assist victims and the establishment of a Plan of Action The acceptance of a mechanism to assist the potential victims

---

[62] *Ibid.*

[63] For the text of the Understanding on the Appointment of an ILO Liaison Officer in Myanmar, see Governing Body, 283rd Session, Geneva, March 2002. Document GB.283/5/2 available online at: http://www.ilo.org/public/english/standards/relm/gb/docs/gb283/pdf/gb-5-2.pdf.

was to be the most significant step, and understandably the most difficult one to negotiate.

As already indicated, the HLT had pointed to the fact that the absence of complaints was not an evidence of the effective eradication of forced labour following the adoption of the supplementary Order, as was claimed by the authorities. To the contrary, it was a confirmation of the fact that, in view of the judiciary's total lack of independence, the victims had no complaint mechanism to rely upon, hence the introduction of the idea of an independent 'ombudsperson' that could receive complaints.

The idea was obviously far-reaching as it struck at the core of a dictatorial and secretive regime. Not surprisingly, in March 2002, the authorities turned down this part of the recommendations. They probably felt that their acceptance of the Liaison Officer should be enough to gain the good will of the majority in the Governing Body and the International Labour Conference. This was, however, not the case. The Conference, in June,[64] and the Governing Body, in November 2002,[65] insisted that procedural progress was no substitute for substantive progress towards the effective diminution of forced labour. In March 2003 the question raised was whether the Director-General should ask the members to reactivate measures under the 2000 Resolution.

Parallel to this threat, the idea of the 'ombudsperson' was, in July 2002, made more palatable to the authorities through its inclusion by the Director-General in a 'Plan of Action'. This plan would focus on the complete elimination of forced labour in one 'pilot' region and would offer technical cooperation projects in order to experiment with alternatives.[66] A semantic change from 'ombudsperson' to 'Facilitator' was agreed upon, although the essential features of the institutions remained the same as had been previously proposed.

The 'Facilitator' is supposed to operate in the whole country (even though he will at the beginning concentrate his efforts on the pilot region) and will be a completely independent person. His or her mandate is to confidentially receive complaints and make a determination as to whether they represent a *prima facie* case of forced labour. Depending on this assessment, the case may be settled to the satisfaction of the victims or referred to the judiciary for prosecution. The protection of the victims as well as the credibility of the judicial outcome is ensured by the fact that the Facilitator can keep in touch with the victim at all stages of the procedure, and report developments to the Governing Body. It was also understood that, in the light of these reports, an evaluation would be made at an early stage. Should the authorities fail to implement the system in good faith, the organization could quickly decide on the consequences of such a failure.

[64] ILC, Provisional Record, Part III, 90th Session, Geneva, June 2002. Available at: http://www.ilo.org/public/english/standards/relm/ilc/ilc90/records.htm.

[65] Governing Body, 285th Session, Geneva, November 2002. Document GB.285/4. Available at: http://www.ilo.org/public/english/standards/relm/gb/docs/gb285/pdf/gb-4.pdf.

[66] See Governing Body, 286th Session, Geneva, March 2003. Document GB.286/6/1. Available at: http://www.ilo.org/public/english/standards/relm/gb/docs/gb286/pdf/gb-6-1.pdf.

A remarkable feature of the agreement, from the viewpoint of the Facilitator's status and independence, is that he would not be a national of Myanmar, but a Swiss national.[67]

The whole scheme cannot but be considered as a rather far-reaching 'internationalization' of the solution of a national problem. It was also clear that such a step was the turning point from 'procedural' to 'substantive' progress.

Unfortunately, the May 2003 events above-mentioned have raised serious doubts regarding the implementation of the Plan of Action. It was clear to the International Labour Conference's Committee on the Application of Conventions and Recommendations ('Application Committee'), at its meeting on 8 June 2003 that the credibility of the scheme assumed a minimum of commitment from the authorities and a certain level of normalcy within the country.[68] At the same time, the Applications Committee was unanimous in recognizing the importance of the progress, which the scheme could represent. It thus left it to the Director-General to go ahead with implementation of the Plan as soon as the circumstances would make it possible.[69]

From application of Article 33 to the actual implementation of measures under Article 33 (the dialectics between the threat of sanctions and their actual use)

What is remarkable in the process that I have just described is that until the last session of the Conference all the steps taken towards the objective were accomplished as a result of the adoption of the 2000 Resolution, but without any of the measures contemplated by the said resolution actually being implemented, at least by governments.[70]

---

[67] The person chosen to assume the function of facilitator is Mr Riedmatten. Mr de Riedmatten had formerly served as Chief of Mission of the International Committee of the Red Cross. He had been closely involved in the reconciliation process and in Aung San Suu Kyi's release.

[68] See Developments concerning the question of the observance by the Government of Myanmar of the Forced Labour Convention 1930 (No. 29), Section 1, 'Discussion in the Committee on the Application of Standards', Governing Body, 288th Session, Geneva, November 2003. Document GB.288/5. Available at: http://www.ilo.org/public/english/standards/relm/gb/docs/gb288/pdf/gb-5.pdf.

Despite the insistence of Myanmar's Ambassador in the International Labour Conference's Applications Committee that the debate would not be politicized and his reiterated assurances of the authorities' commitment, the Committee was unconvinced that the Facilitator could discharge his responsibilities in a climate of 'uncertainty and intimidation'.

[69] *Ibid.* Aung San Suu Kyi's liberation was, of course, understood to be one of the parameters in assessing the return to normalcy.

[70] It has indeed to be kept in mind that the workers were also 'party' to the implementation of the resolution and showed much less restraint. Although it is arguable whether their pressure, threat of boycotts, and on some occasions actual boycotts, could by themselves have been decisive, their combination with strictly economic considerations such as uncertainty and low returns on investment may have, in a few cases, resulted in 'disinvestment decisions'. It is also important to note that the special sittings of the Applications Committee devoted to Myanmar at each session of the ILC under the 2000 Resolution is an occasion for the workers to publicly vilify the countries and firms that are most active in Myanmar. It is clear more generally that the attitude of the international community is, as pointed out by the High Level Team, critical for the business community. It is critical also for the financial institutions that had initially broken off relations with Myanmar for reasons that were also related to the authorities' financial and economic policy, but could hardly resume cooperation unless that issue was also resolved.

The analysis shows that the result was achieved through a combination of dialectical considerations, which I shall only briefly recapitulate as they already transpire from the above analysis.

1. The first is the dialectic between, on the one hand, the threat of 'reactivating' the measures under Article 33, i.e. asking the Director-General to write to the governments to put an end to their 'wait and see' attitude in the light of the lack of progress (the Workers' group introduced a motion to that effect on two occasions); and on the other, the hope of the authorities that their cooperation might lead the Governing Body to reconsider or freeze the application of Article 33. The extraordinary step, which the acceptance of the HLT represents, has to be seen in that perspective and may indeed be interpreted at least from a political and practical point of view as an informal alternative to the application of Article 34,[71] which must be requested by the defaulting government—a very implausible hypothesis in the circumstances.

2. The second is the dialectic between 'unilateral action' by the competent organs of the ILO (either the International Labour Conference or the Governing Body) and dialogue between the authorities and the Director-General or his representatives. Through all the successive phases of the saga, a clear division of labour emerged between the ILO's political organs and the Office which, even when the authorities claimed they would stop cooperation with the ILO following the 'punitive' action taken by representative organs, managed to maintain the channels of communication and dialogue open and thereby made the dialectic between the stick of activating the measures and the carrot of a possible removal or suspension of Article 33 much more effective.[72]

---

[71] Art. 34 of the Constitution states, 'The defaulting government may at any time inform the Governing Body that it has taken the steps necessary to comply with the recommendations of the Commission of Inquiry or with those in the decision of the International Court of Justice, as the case may be and may request it to constitute a Commission of Inquiry to verify its contention. (I)f the report of the Commission of Inquiry or the decision of the International Court of Justice is in favour of the defaulting government, the Governing Body shall forthwith recommend the discontinuance of any action taken in pursuance of article 33.'

[72] The Director-General and his representatives maintained the dialogue by explaining what the requests of the ILO's competent organs implied in terms of the changes in Myanmar's legislation and practice. The Director-General and his representatives also always made a point to be clear about possible reactions for Myanmar's failure to meet these expectations. In most cases, these warnings proved correct. Indeed, when it was clear that the legislative changes undertaken by Myanmar came too late and showed no willingness to accept an ILO presence, the majority of the Governing Body's opinion swayed towards those who did not believe in Myanmar's sincerity. Conversely, and as already noted, when the Governing Body decided to let sanctions apply, it was careful at the same time to mandate the Director-General to continue the dialogue, which he was ultimately able to do. The development and impact of this dialogue rested first, and to a large extent, on its transparency since all substantive discussions between the TCM and the authorities were reported in detail to the competent organs; and second, on the fact that the Office's warnings about the Governing Body and Conference's reactions to insufficient progress always proved to be correct.

3. The third and last factor pertains to the dialectic between the legal uncertainty of trade measures that members might be ready to apply to Myanmar on the basis of the 2000 Resolution, and the certainty that such measures could not be found illegal short of a WTO ruling on the matter, a step that nobody was really keen to take until June 2003, for reasons that I will further elaborate below.

As previously pointed out, the combination of these dialectics has been sufficiently effective to ensure a meaningful process towards the eradication of forced labour. Although this progress had initially been of a 'legislative' and procedural nature, in May 2003, it was about to spill over into the realities of the situation through the Plan of Action and the Facilitator. In June 2003 the question was whether the combined effect of these dialectics had not exhausted its potential. The situation resulting from the events of May 2003 and Aung San Suu Kyi's new incarceration (although they had nothing to do with the forced labour situation) seem to have radically changed the picture. Not only because they led to freezing the implementation of the joint Plan of Action, but also because following these events, the US Government decided to move ahead with the application of trade and economic measures against Myanmar (based at least in part on the ILO Resolution) through the 'Burmese Freedom and Democracy Act' ('BFDA'). The Act was adopted on 28 July 2003.[73]

The new situation thus raised two questions from the viewpoint of efficacy: from a legal point of view such 'measures' can be effective in the long term only to the extent that they would be recognized as compatible with the legal obligations of the members under international law; from a practical point of view, the question is the extent to which the actual application of these measures has—or may prove to have—a more concrete impact than their threat.

The legal uncertainty of possible trade measures pursuant to the 2000 ILC Resolution and its impact

It is clear that one of the main issues looming behind the debate around the first application of Article 33, was whether member states could use the authority to be given by the Conference Resolution to take any action that might 'contribute as far as possible to the implementation of the recommendations of the Commission of Inquiry'. The hostility shown by many countries to the enforcement of Article 33, especially among Asian countries, suggests that the issue of possible trade sanctions was indeed in the back of many minds.

While the issue of the relationship between trade sanctions and human rights is certainly politically contentious, the legal assessment of the possibility of taking trade action depends on the evaluation of how such trade action by an ILO

---

[73] For further developments on the BFDA, see 'The possible impact of the recent Burmese Freedom and Democracy Act on the situation of legal uncertainty' below.

member state could be reconciled with its concurrent obligations as a member of the WTO.

It is important to recall that the original version of Article 33 of the Constitution specifically referred to the possibility of adopting 'measures of an economic character' to secure the implementation of the recommendations of the Commission of Inquiry.[74] The implications of the removal of this phrase in 1946 (in the new context created by the entry into force of the UN Charter), have been the subject of some speculation.[75] It does not necessarily mean that 'measures of an economic character' are henceforth ruled out. The 2000 Resolution has carefully left this option open and leaves to the members a wide discretion as regards the type of measures they may be led to take as a result of the review of their relations with Myanmar. As we shall see, this means that the issue of 'compatibility' arises with respect to each member's WTO commitments and its obligations under the ILO Constitution.

There are several critical aspects to this problem that seem interesting to at least briefly sketch out: (1) the 2000 Resolution of the ILC as a possible legal basis to invoke a moral exception under Article XX of the GATT or Article XIV of the GATS; (2) from the legitimacy of possible actions based on such international authority to its necessity from the viewpoint of achieving the objective; (3) the possible impact of the recent BFDA on the situation of legal uncertainty.

(1) *The ILO Resolution as a possible source of authority/legitimacy to invoke a 'moral' exception* The starting point of the debate is that the GATT does not contain any provision regarding the relation between the obligations it imposes on its members and their obligations under the charters of other international governmental organizations, except for Article XXI, paragraph (c), which bows to the UN, implicitly to Article 103 of its Charter.[76] Short of appropriate action from the competent UN body, there is no explicit provision in the WTO Charter that would make it legal to infringe the National Treatment principle or the most-favoured Nation principle on account of the ILO Resolution. And it can be argued that the issue of whether obligations under the ILO Constitution might take 'precedence' over obligations under those of the GATT (component of the WTO) does not really

---

[74] Art. 419 of the Versailles Peace Treaty reads as follows: 'In the event of any Member failing to carry out within the time specified the recommendations, if any, contained in the report of the Commission of Enquiry, or in the decision of the Permanent Court of International Justice, as the case may be, any other Member may take against that Member the measures of an economic character indicated in the report of the Commission or in the decision of the Court as appropriate to the case.' This is why the procedure of Art. 26 of the ILO Constitution, in contrast to the one of Art. 24, is only open to other Governments that have ratified the relevant Convention: it is designed to re-establish the balance of burden between countries.   [75] See, in general, Document GB.276/6, *supra* note 30.

[76] According to Art. XXI 'Security Exceptions' of the GATT, 'Nothing in this Agreement shall be construed, (c) to prevent any contracting party from taking any action in pursuance of its obligations under the United Nations Charter for the maintenance of international peace and security.'

arise to the extent that the ILO Resolution does not actually *request* members to take action.

Leaving aside the complexities of the relation between the GATT, the ILO Constitution, and the UN Charter, I would like to consider briefly the key questions of whether or not the ILO Resolution could be relevant to the legality of trade measures that some members might take at their own initiative. More specifically, the question whether the ILO Resolution could serve as one of a justification to invoke the exceptions provided for in the GATT under Article XX.[77]

The list of 'general principles' includes a reference to 'prison labour' in Article XX (e), itself an exception to forced labour under Convention No. 29, but it also contains three grounds that may appear especially relevant here: '(a) [measures] necessary to protect public morals'; '(b) [measures] necessary to protect human, animal or plant life'; and '(d) [measures] necessary to secure compliance with laws or regulations which are not inconsistent with the provisions of this Agreement, including those relating to customs enforcement, the enforcement of monopolies operated under paragraph 4 of Article II and Article XVII, the protection of patents, trade marks and copyrights, and the prevention of deceptive practices'.

Some of the developments of the report of the Commission of Inquiry might well suggest that forced labour, as practised in Myanmar, was indeed a question of 'life and death', in particular for the many porters requisitioned by the army and who died of sickness, starvation, or walking on mines. But taking into account the 'necessity' requirement, which will be examined further down, the need to protect public morals appears more appropriate. This does not mean, however, that its application to the situation is straightforward.

Charnovitz's distinction about whether this exception is 'inwardly' or 'outwardly' directed[78] helps understand one aspect of the complexities involved. 'Inwardly directed' exceptions aim at morality within the jurisdiction of members, subject to their non-discriminatory application. Prohibitions on the importation of pornographic material or non-kosher food are obvious illustrations. More difficult is the question of whether this exception could be 'outwardly directed' at offences to public morals occurring outside of members' jurisdiction, which was precisely the case with Myanmar. In other words, whether the exception can be seen as having an 'extraterritorial' reach.[79] The obvious risk inherent in the 'outward' interpretation is the possibility that subsection (b) could be used to 'export' one country's own conception of morality. If the offence to public morals were to be

---

[77] A similar analysis could be done under Art. XIV of the GATT, where the exception of public morals is extended to include public order. Trade with Myanmar may include trade in services.

[78] S. Charnovitz, 'The Moral Exception in Trade Policy', 38 *Virginia Journal of International Law* (Summer 1998) 4. Article available online at: http://www.worldtradelaw.net/articles/charnovitzmoral.pdf.

[79] Clearly some exception such as the one on prison labour in Art. XX(e) had an extraterritorial reach but seems to have been introduced on the basis of strictly economic (unfair competition) rather than moral consideration.

determined by a competent and credible international authority, this concern would dissolve.

In the case of forced labour in Myanmar, the report of the Commission of Inquiry, which went as far as describing the practices of forced labour in that country as a crime against humanity,[80] did indeed suggest that, irrespective of its legal qualifications, there was an objective internationally recognized moral dimension to the problem.[81] The report of the Commission of Inquiry was, however, not as such a sufficient basis for all members to draw consequences of their own of this moral situation as it contains only 'recommendations' addressed to Myanmar and the ILO's competent organs. What appears more relevant from that perspective is that the decision of the Governing Body to place the question of possible action under Article 33 on the Conference agenda from 1999 establishes a link between the moral dimension of the situation and the need for the ILO to react, as it referred to the 'disapproval that the gravity of the government's failure to act must inspire in everyone's conscience'[82] among the considerations relevant to the proposal to place action under Article 33 on the agenda of the ILC.

(2) *From the legitimacy of possible trade action to their necessity or 'appropriateness'* The two relevant sub-paragraphs (a) and (b) of Article XX of GATT provide that the national measures it authorizes as an exception must be 'necessary' for the purpose.[83]

Broadly speaking, in the context of sub-paragraph (b), the concept of necessity had initially been interpreted as meaning that there are no other means available to reach the objectives, which would be less harmful to international trade. The 'necessity' test has been further developed and refined in the *Korea—Various Measures on Beef* and in *EC—Asbestos* cases in the (admittedly quite different) context of Article XX sub-paragraph (d). On paragraph 161 of the *Korea—Various Measures on Beef* Appellate Body report[84] the emphasis is placed on the fact that a 'necessary measure' is located significantly closer to the pole of 'indispensable' than to the opposite pole of simply 'making a contribution to'. In paragraph 172 of the Appellate Body report in the *EC—Asbestos* case, the

---

[80] See Part IV (paragraph 204) of the Report of the Commission of Inquiry, *supra* note 29.

[81] What is however important, from a legal perspective, is not the intensity of the moral outrage; it is the fact that the moral dimension is clearly identified as relevant for action.

[82] Governing Body, 277th Session, Geneva, March 2000. Document GB.277/6Add.1. Available online at: http://www.ilo.org/public/english/standards/relm/gb/docs/gb277/pdf/gb-6-add1.pdf. It is to be noted that the language was not reproduced in the ILC Resolution adopted as a result of that decision.

[83] The meaning of this adjective in the context of sub-paragraph (a) has not been the subject of case law from the panels and one thus has to refer to the meaning as it has been clarified in the context of sub-paragraph (b).

[84] Appellate Body Report, *Korea—Measures Affecting Imports of Fresh, Chilled and Frozen Beef* (*Korea—Various Measures on Beef*), WT/DS161/AB/R, WT/DS169/AB/R, adopted on 10 January 2001.

Appellate Body stressed the relevance of the values and common interests inherent in the objective pursued when accepting as 'necessary' the measures designed to achieve these ends.[85]

> '172. We indicated in *Korea—Beef* that one aspect of the 'weighing and balancing process . . . comprehended in the determination of whether a WTO-consistent alternative measure' is reasonably available is the extent to which the alternative measure 'contributes to the realization of the end pursued'.[86] In addition, we observed, in that case, that '[t]he more vital or important [the] common interests or values' pursued, the easier it would be to accept as 'necessary' measures designed to achieve those ends. [87] In this case, the objective pursued by the measure is the preservation of human life and health through the elimination, or reduction, of the well-known, and life-threatening, health risks posed by asbestos fibers. The value pursued is both vital and important in the highest degree. The remaining question, then, is whether there is an alternative measure that would achieve the same end and that is less restrictive of trade than a prohibition.'

Great caution must, however, be exercised in extrapolating these indications into the different context of sub-paragraph (a). What may be necessary for making a national regulation effective is not the same thing as what is necessary to protect public morals. Among possible questions, one may wonder if the objective of 'protection' is to eradicate the moral harm at its source or to appease the moral conscience of consumers and clients in the hope that it may ultimately 'tackle up' to the source of the problem.[88] In the case of a good made in contravention with fundamental rights, prohibiting its access, depending on its scope of application, may not remedy the harm that has already been done with respect to the good excluded from the market or it may not reach the harm resulting from the continuation of such practices with respect to non-traded goods.

To the extent however that, in the Myanmar case, the moral dimension of the massive practice of forced labour was instrumental in the decision to take action under Article 33, it may seem redundant to engage into all these subtleties and complexities. Is not the answer to what is necessary to eradicate the moral harm inherent in these practices to be found in the nature of the action taken or requested under Article 33 'to secure compliance' with the recommendations of the Commission of Inquiry designed to eliminate this massive practice.

It is striking in this respect to note that the concept that seems to characterize the said action is the word 'appropriate'. First, in the document submitted to the Governing Body when it considered first in November 1999 the issue of whether to activate Article 33 and what action could be taken to secure compliance.

First the Office pointed out that the range of such measures could be extremely broad provided that all the measures must correspond to the objectives of the

---

[85] Appellate Body Report, *European Communities—Measures Affecting Asbestos and Asbestos Containing Products* (*EC—Asbestos*), WT/DS135/AB/R, adopted on 5 April 2001.

[86] Appellate Body Report, *Korea—Various Measures on Beef, supra* note 84, paras. 166 and 163.

[87] *Ibid.*, para. 162.   [88] S. Charnovitz, 'The Moral Exception in Trade Policy', *supra* note 78.

Commission's Recommendations, and second, that they must be deemed 'appropriate' by the Governing Body to secure compliance.[89]

Second, in the Resolution adopted by the ILC in the framework of the question placed by the Governing Body on its agenda, the word 'appropriate' is also used to qualify the 'measures' that each member is invited to consider to ensure that Myanmar cannot take advantage of its possible relation with the said member to 'perpetuate or extend the system of forced or compulsory labour referred to by the Commission of Inquiry'.

It is difficult not to establish the parallel between the conditions of 'appropriateness' in the ILO Resolution and of 'necessity' in Article XX of the WTO. One possible question raised by these two criteria is whether it would be consistent with the 'necessity' criteria that some members, having trade relations with Myanmar, would find it 'appropriate' to take trade sanctions while some others do not. It would be risky to propose an answer at this stage. It seems safe to assume, however, that the question of what is 'appropriate' is prejudicial to the question of what is 'necessary' even though it does not exhaust it. As a consequence, in case of doubt, the ILO's competent organs would have to assess whether the measures taken by a member are 'appropriate' for the purpose of implementing the Commission of Inquiry's recommendations before assessing the question as to whether other measures, less harmful to trade, could be considered to meet the 'necessity' test. From a more practical point of view, it would also seem relevant to consider the extent to which the countries that had adopted a 'wait and see' attitude could argue that, in the view of the failure to obtain substantive results (as opposed to procedural progress) there was no alternative left at least to make a try towards the result sought. But especially in view of the fact that the issue may be considered by the Appellate Body long after the adoption of the measures the next question may then be: Has the trial been a success?

(3) *The possible impact of the recent Burmese Freedom and Democracy Act on the situation of legal uncertainty* It seems clear from the above considerations, that while there are enough legal elements to make a possible use of trade measures worth testing, there are also enough doubts to make the outcome of the test hard to predict. Besides the strictly legal elements that have been mentioned, account must be taken of the psycho-political dimension of making a ruling that would inevitably be interpreted

---

[89] In underlying the wide discretion left to the Governing Body, which could go as far as 'measures that can be considered as penalties', be subject to three criteria. The Office however pointed out that its proposals must come within the terms of reference of the Conference. Second, they must derive from the recommendations of the Commission of Inquiry; and third, they must be conducive to the implementation of these recommendations. See 'Measures, including action under article 33 of the Constitution of the International Labour Organization, to secure compliance by the Government of Myanmar with the recommendations of the Commission of Inquiry established to examine the observance of the Forced Labour Convention, 1930 (No. 29)', Governing Body, 276th Session, Geneva, November 1999. Document GB.276/6, *supra* note 30, para. 19.

as bringing the WTO dispute settlement jurisprudence (whose environment record has already been subject to criticisms) to the rescue of gross human rights abuses.

The paradox is that this state of legal uncertainty is not incompatible with the efficacy of the threat, quite to the contrary. The reason is fairly simple to understand. For countries that oppose the use of trade measures, the possibility that a challenge by Myanmar of trade measures, taken pursuant to the ILO Resolution, might be rejected in the WTO, would really mean that a social clause[90] or trade linkage already existed for ratified conventions.[91] Those countries have an interest in avoiding such a ruling and, therefore, have an incentive to put some pressure on Myanmar to improve the situation so that the temptation for a developed country to reactivate the consideration of its trade relations with Myanmar under the pressure of workers' organizations does not become too great.

As far as developed countries are concerned, the risk of acting is exactly symmetrical, yet reversed: if trade measures were found contrary to WTO disciplines, and were not caught by the exceptions, the possibility of introducing a 'social clause' through the back door of Article XX of GATT would definitely be lost. This is an incentive to avoid pressing the issue and to use other pressure tactics. In short, the actual use of trade measures under the resolution is like a match: it can set fire to the hidden trade powder in the gun of Article 33; or, it can show that the powder is wet. But, in both cases it can be used only once for the same purpose.

However, this applies only to the extent that the country, which is the subject of the measures, decides to bring the matter before the Dispute Settlement Body in WTO. If it does not, there may be a practical precedent of some significance, but once again from a strictly legal point of view, the uncertainty remains.

In that respect, it is interesting to note that the United States, which under the Clinton administration apparently had already considered taking trade sanctions on the basis of the ILC Resolution, finally decided to act after the events of May 2003 by enacting the BFDA.[92] This 'move' taken by the US government supplemented non-governmental boycotts, such as the one launched by the American Apparel and Footwear Association.

In its Preamble, the Act refers to the misdeeds of the Burmese military junta, such as appalling human rights violations and drug trafficking. It also directly refers to the resolution of the ILC, which, 'for the first time in its 82-year history [recommended that] Governments, employers and workers' organizations take appropriate measures . . .'.[93] On the basis of the ILC Resolution, the BFDA prohibits the import of articles 'produced, mined, manufactured, grown, or assembled in

---

[90] The term 'social clause' refers to the creation of a rule, within WTO law, which would link access to the market to the guarantee of workers' rights. The background to the concept is dealt with in Part 4 below.

[91] Without the complications, controversies, package deals, and consensus required in the WTO framework.

[92] HR 2330, Burmese Freedom and Democracy Act of 2003, available at: http://www.cbo.gov/showdoc.cfm?index=4483&sequence=0. The Act was adopted by the US Congress on 10 July and signed into law by the President on 28 July.   [93] *Ibid.*

Burma', while identifying several entities or even individuals related to the Junta.[94] In a separate section, the BFDA enumerates the conditions under which these trade sanctions may be lifted.

These conditions pertain broadly to 'substantial and measurable progress' as regards each of the misdeeds enumerated in the Preamble to the Act, including the 'conclusion of an agreement between the SPDC and the democratic forces led by the NLD . . . on the transfer of power to a civilian government accountable to the Burmese people through democratic elections'.[95] More specifically, human rights violations must end and 'the Secretary of State, after consultation with the ILO Secretary General and relevant nongovernmental organizations, reports to the appropriate congressional committees that the SPDC no longer systematically violates workers' rights, including the use of forced and child labor, and conscription of child-soldiers.'[96]

The adoption of the BFDA defies Myanmar to challenge the consistency of the US legislation with WTO law. Indeed, the BFDA is said to deprive Myanmar from about 30 per cent of its export resources (especially in the garment sector).[97]

The continued uncertainty as regards the practical impact of the BFDA A few months only have elapsed since the adoption of the BFDA by the United States. It would thus be premature and risky to venture any evaluation of the experience, which is already fuelling the continuing debate over efficacy of 'blind' sanctions which in the end can hurt the civilian population more than the authorities. In the wake of the adoption of the law some eminent personalities like Professor J. Sachs have advocated the use of 'smart' sanctions. According to their proponents, smart sanctions would target more specifically the members of the political elite and their assets abroad and would arguably have a lighter impact on the population (conversely, they would be more likely to pass the veto of China at the UN Security Council).

For some specialists, the risk that sanctions will in the end hurt the civilian population rather than the authorities, which they are targeting, appears to be quite important in the case of Myanmar. The country indeed boasts large natural

---

[94] HR 2330, Burmese Freedom and Democracy Act of 2003, available at: http://www.cbo.gov/ showdoc.cfm?index=4483&sequence=0. The Act was adopted by the US Congress on 10 July and signed into law by the President on 28 July.   [95] *Ibid.*

[96] *Ibid.*

[97] In this respect it must be noted that an article published in the *Asia Times* soon after the adoption of the Act underlines that 'the US could face legal sanctions of its own after endorsing an economic embargo . . . that technically violates global free-trade commitments'. This article rightly suggests that the circumstances surrounding the adoption of trade sanctions by the United States were, in this case, quite favourable: 'Washington is evidently gambling that the weight of international opinion, bolstered by parallel sanctions imposed in Western Europe, Japan and Canada will dissuade Yangon from pursuing the issue through the WTO's disputes panel' (A. Boyd, 'A WTO trick up Yangon's sleeve', *Asia Times*, 18 July 2003).

resources and a favourable geopolitical situation as well as a long tradition of isolation as illustrated by the not-so-far-away period of Ne Win. In so far as it can be described as a subsistence-oriented economy, it does not seem likely to collapse anytime soon.

Some evidence has already been presented to suggest that the sanctions may hurt the most vulnerable segment of Burmese society: Matthew Daley, Deputy Assistant Secretary of State for East Asia and Pacific Affairs, who testified in a 'hearing' before subcommittees of the US House of Representatives, thus said that 'reports from international groups in Myanmar show young women driven out of the country's hard-hit garment sector are being forced into prostitution'.[98] It is, however, difficult to draw general conclusions from this rather scattered evidence. The presence of the ILO liaison Office in Yangon may in this respect help to make a more systematic assessment.[99]

This being said, we should not lose sight of the fact that the real question is not whether the measures have a negative impact on other workers but whether they have had any *positive* impact on the forced labour situation (not to mention other human rights situations). This question draws attention to the fundamental ambivalence of the object of the 'sanctions'.

Ambivalence of the objective The efficacy and impact of the measures cannot be assessed without a clear vision of the objective sought. Is the objective the immediate improvement of the situation of the victims or is it the removal of its cause? What is 'efficacy' when the breach of the obligation seems inherent in the nature of the regime? In the case of Myanmar, forced labour has very deep historical roots, but as suggested very explicitly by the Commission of Inquiry in its conclusions, it is also linked to the nature of the regime and thus cannot really improve unless there is a fundamental change.

'The experience of the past decade tends to prove that the establishment of a government freely chosen by the people and the submission of all public authorities to the rule of law are in practice, indispensable prerequisites for the suppression of forced labour in Myanmar.'[100]

In that perspective, it may seem quite logical to accentuate international pressure in all forms in the hope that the regime collapses. But, on the one hand, as already noted, experience shows that such military regimes, especially in a country with a tradition of isolation, have a great capacity to survive and in the meantime, those concerned are left helpless with authorities who refuse to cooperate. And on the other, it may be argued that it is hardly for an international organization like the

---

[98] 'US sanctions on Myanmar forcing young women into prostitution', *Agence France Presse*, 3 October 2003.

[99] It has in fact commissioned a study to review the impact on employment and other aspects of the conditions of work in the country.

[100] Report of the Commission of Inquiry, *supra* note 29, para. 542.

ILO, which does not have the power to expel, to choose the type of government best suited to implement the legal obligations of members. In the circumstances a reasonable middle course is, as the report of the HLT suggests, to take the authorities at their word, and to exercise maximum pressure with all the means at disposal to make them behave accordingly.[101] This was indeed the sense of the Plan of Action and the establishment of the Facilitator referred above.

A first and a unique experience? All the above comments show that the Myanmar chapter is far from closed. It is clear that the legal ramifications and uncertainty may affect the possibility of its repetition in future cases; but at the time of writing it is not clear whether the stalemate on the implementation of the Plan of Action will continue.

These uncertainties as regards the final outcome of a case make it difficult to draw general conclusions as to its impact on future practice. Yet, it seems possible to identify at least some factors, which had a special significance in the ability of the ILO to move away from a very dangerous impasse and in the process to 'reinvent' in some respects Article 33 in a way that may influence possible future practice. Three of these factors seem particularly relevant in that respect: (i) the capacity to take a majority decision; (ii) the application of a 'subsidiarity' formula ('re-delegation' of the ultimate responsibility as regards the nature of the measures to ILO constituents); (iii) the shift from a logic of reciprocity to a logic of safeguarding public morals.

(i) The capacity to take a majority decision on measures

From a political point of view some may say that, it was because Myanmar was considered by some, already a sort of pariah state and not because of the unique gravity of the violations of a fundamental right, that it could be an easy target for exceptional measures and that there was little risk—and little glory—for the organization and its members in taking action against it.[102]

The reactions—especially outside of the ILO—clearly suggest that this cynical assessment is not necessarily shared by other more influential potential targets of

---

[101] Report of the Commission of Inquiry, *supra* note 29, at paras. 72 and 73. In sketching the dilemma, the HLT suggested that history would ultimately decide which of the two approaches was right but also pointed to the 'generation of young talented people' lost as a result of the verdict of history coming too late.

[102] As Bernard Kouchner, a former French minister said in a controversial report, 'why is it easier for militants to focus on Myanmar than on China, which uses child labor on a wide scale? For one thing, the Burmese generals seem more pathetic than others and their communication skills are non-existent. There's little risk in pressuring Myanmar, compared with the difficulties involved in challenging China over Tibet or standing up to Vietnam's residual Communist Party or North Korea's odious regime. What's more, the Burmese opposition holds enormous moral authority. It would be hard for anyone to confront the opinion of the very beautiful, brave, dignified and charismatic Aung San Suu Kyi. As a result, a single corporation is denounced and attacked more than any other, with criticism combining excellent reasons and the most fantastic allegations. That corporation is TotalFinaElf, now renamed Total', in *Report on a Trip to Myanmar and the Discovery of a Silent Industry* (following the arrest of Aung San Suu Kyi), B. Kouchner, 29 September 2003.

Article 33 measures. The strong tension surrounding the debates that took place at the ECOSOC in July 2000 and 2001 as a result of the request made in the 2000 ILC Resolution suggests an awareness from certain states that the Myanmar precedent might be dangerously contagious for reasons that have to do with the ILO's institutional structure and decision-making. Within the ILO, the competent organs, both the Governing Body and the Conference, are not bound by consensus. Unlike other bodies such as the ones of the WTO, they can take a decision by simple majority. Thus, the 2000 ILC Resolution was adopted by a simple vote. The Governing Body decision in November 2002 to implement that resolution was also adopted by 'virtual majority vote'.[103]

The tripartite structure of the ILO considerably reduces the weight of political considerations inherent in purely intergovernmental bodies. In the particular case of Myanmar, the feeling of moral outrage was certainly instrumental in the emergence of a wide measure of consensus between workers and employers at the International Labour Conference, which despite some great divergences among governments continued to facilitate the decision.

This capacity of the ILO's representative organs to take a difficult decision does not however mean that the experience can easily be repeated unless the other two conditions which were present in that case are also met: First, the application of the 'subsidiarity' to the determination of 'appropriate' measures and second the 'fundamental' character of the rights that were violated.

(ii) The application of a 'subsidiarity' principle to the determination of the specific 'action' to be taken pursuant to Article 33

As opposed to the original Constitution, where the responsibility as regards the nature of the action to be taken was essentially vested with the Commission of Inquiry and the Permanent Court of International Justice,[104] the present text vests the responsibility for such decisions—and the discretion to take action—with the political body.

Pursuant to Article 33, '[i]n the event of any member failing to carry out ... recommendations ... of the Commission of Inquiry, or ... the ICJ ... the Governing body may recommend to the Conference such action as it may deem wise and expedient to secure compliance therewith'.[105] The vesting of the responsibility and discretion in the political bodies is however again a mixed blessing, as it may prove to be extremely divisive.

---

[103] In *EC—Trade Description of Sardines* (*EC—Sardines*), WT/DS231/AB/R, adopted on 23 October 2002, the Appellate Body stated that standards from international bodies where decisions are NOT adopted by consensus could be 'relevant standards' for the purpose of the Agreement on Technical Barriers to Trade (TBT Agreement). Such an approach may be expanded into the interpretation of Art. XX of GATT.

[104] Paradoxically, this may have had the unintended consequence of making the Commission bolder in its recommendations. Although final authority is now in the hands of the Conference, the Constitution does not explicitly provide that the measures adopted could be directly binding or enforceable. This is not a problem when such measures are addressed to the organization itself, but if they were to be addressed to members, it is unclear how compliance would be ensured.

[105] Art. 33 of the Constitution.

A decisive factor to explain why such a decision was possible in the case of Myanmar is that the draft Resolution prepared by the International Labour Office for submission to the 2000 ILC essentially passed the main responsibility back to the members. It requested that the member states—as well as relevant international organizations—review their relations with Myanmar to ensure that they were not in any way abetting the practice of forced labour in that country. As far as ILO constituents were concerned, the ILC Resolution required them: (i) to review, in the light of the conclusions of the Commission of Inquiry, the relations that they may have with the member state concerned, (ii) to take appropriate measures to ensure that the said member cannot take advantage of such relations to perpetuate or extend the system of forced or compulsory labour referred to by the Commission of Inquiry, (iii) to contribute as far as possible to the implementation of its recommendations; and (iv) to report back in due course to the Governing Body.[106]

Thus, the discretion granted to the ILO's constituents could be exercised as far as the measures are 'appropriate' to reach the objective of the implementation of the recommendations. But it represents a significant innovation, which was not challenged by anybody and will certainly influence future practice—if any.

(iii) The shift from reciprocity to the defence of the international public (moral) order

Although Article 33 had never been used before, it is important to realize that it was not simply because there was no case sufficiently serious to warrant its application. There are also some limitations inherent in its logic. Indeed, the application of Article 33 may appear in some respects, not only as a paradox, but as an aberration as it is tantamount to a form of double jeopardy: the country which is showing good will in accepting the burden of ratifying *vis-à-vis* its competitors is penalized a second time through the application of sanctions for possible failures in that good will! This apparent aberration however is perfectly consistent with the original vision of the founders, which was a logic of reciprocity in a context where it was (optimistically) assumed that most countries that accepted to vote for a draft convention would subsequently feel morally bound to ratify it.

It should not be forgotten that, in the first draft of the text, the possibility to lodge a complaint under Article 26 of the ILO Constitution against one member for its alleged violation of a ratified convention—which is supposedly the first step before applying Article 33—was initially to be limited to other members of the organization having ratified the same convention. While the possibility to lodge a complaint was, at a subsequent stage of the 'travaux préparatoires', extended to all Delegates to the ILC, the initial logic of the provision was based on the notion of 'reciprocity' of obligations, that is to say on the vision that the violation by one member of the provisions of a convention constitutes a distortion of competition for other ratifying members of the organization.

---

[106] ILC, Provisional Record, 8th item on the agenda, 88th Session, Geneva, 2000.

History has shown that the hypothesis on which this reciprocity vision was based was over-optimistic and that ratification was the exception rather than the rule. And in practice, the complaint procedure has been used only in relation to violations of fundamental rights.

The Myanmar experience may help to extricate the ILO from this paradox. It clearly points to the fact that the rationale for the application of Article 33 is not so much a rationale of economic reciprocity as a rationale of safeguarding moral considerations, and more broadly a form of international public order; this is however likely to happen only with respect to a grave and persistent violation of a fundamental right, which is by hypothesis an element of this international public order, if not of *Jus Cogens*.[107]

The institutional logic may be all the more significant for the future that it meets with the political logic of the decision-making discussed above. It is to be noted that the decision to implement Article 33 in the ILC in June 2000 and in the Governing Body in November of the same year was taken with the support of a majority of the Employers' group. This is no accident. If employers have been critical towards the continued accumulation of new standards, and in some cases towards some aspects of the supervisory mechanisms, they have, by contrast, expressed a clear and consistent interest and support for the protection of fundamental rights at work. This interest and support seems to have broader implications as regards possible future applications of Article 33; the Employers' spokesman statement in connection with the examination of the Myanmar case before the ILC seems relevant in that respect.[108]

It seems more than doubtful by contrast that violations of more 'technical' conventions, in the unlikely case that they would be the subjects of a complaint, would ever lead to an Article 33 Resolution.[109]

---

[107] According to Art. 53 of the Vienna Convention of the Law of Treaties, the broadly accepted international law concept of *Jus Cogens* refers to: 'a norm accepted and recognized by the international community of States as a whole as a norm from which no derogation is permitted and which can be modified only by a subsequent norm of general international law having the same character.' See also R. Howse and M. Mutua, 'Protecting Human Rights in a Global Economy: Challenges for the World Trade Organization', International Center for Human Rights and Democratic Developments, Policy Paper, 2000.

[108] 'The Employer members added that they were aware of the gravity of the situation. They emphasized their support for the principles of labour law relating to the abolition of forced labour. There were no productive advantages, which were not based on the respect of these rights. States had to contribute to seeking solutions and to the application of all instruments of the ILO for the achievement of these goals. That is why they did not question the application of article 33 of the Constitution, . . . Employer members expressed their gratitude to the Liaison Officer, and for the appointment of a Facilitator, as well as for the adoption of the Plan of Action. This had to be implemented on the ground and immediately, since the case concerned *violations of fundamental human rights*' [emphasis added]. Intervention by M. Funes de Rioja, ILC, Provisional Record, 91st Session, Geneva, 2003, p. 13.

[109] It must be recognized that the shift from reciprocity to the protection of morality, if it gives a greater internal coherence for the application of Art. 33, may, through the possible linkage with Art. XX of GATT, result in the same type of institutional imbalance: violations of fundamental rights could be punished only in the case of countries having ratified and not the others. I will come back to this problem in the third part.

A more general lesson that is linked to the previous one is that, in a way, the question of the 'linkage' between international labour standards and rights, and the discipline of multilateral trade, does not necessarily need to be established to the extent that it already exists through the general exception provision of the GATT (and the GATS).[110] But this consideration goes even further. Thus the simplest and most coherent approach to the 'social clause' issue might be simply to ensure that all WTO members are bound by the relevant ILO Conventions. It is significant that nobody seems to have raised the question in those terms when it could have made a difference, for instance at the close of the Uruguay Round.[111]

B. Implementation beyond Enforcement

Subject to the qualifications previously indicated, the Myanmar experience does seem to show the capacity and potential of the ILO complaint procedure to force recalcitrant countries to honour—progressively if not spontaneously—their obligations, as the political and economic cost of denunciation or withdrawal is unbearable even for a 'closed' country like Myanmar—not to mention the fact that such steps would not even relieve them from a legal point of view.[112]

It would however be unwarranted to conclude that, with the new dimension added by Article 33, all possible gaps in the efficacy of the supervisory system have been filled. As already noted, the accumulation of evidence about 'cases of progress' recorded through the supervisory machinery, however important, relevant, and perhaps not sufficiently publicized outside the ILO,[113] cannot dispose of the issue of efficacy.

To be consistent with our general definition of efficacy of the system as its capacity to ensure not only that national legislations reflect the terms and meaning of the convention, but also that the realities within ratifying countries conform to the terms of the conventions. The efficacy of the mechanisms has to be established in terms of their overall impact and not only in terms of the number of cases solved (or the speed at which the result is obtained). Central to this overall assessment is the (prejudicial) question of how violations or inconsistencies, or at least the most serious of them, are brought to public notice and dealt with.

In view of the number of ILO members, its conventions, the limited time available for the political organs, and limited resources, it would be unrealistic to

---

[110] Joel P. Trachtman, 'Institutional Linkage: Transcending Trade and . . .', 96/1 *American Journal of International Law* (Jan. 2002) 77–93.

[111] One may wonder if this 'oversight' has something to do with the fact that certain eminent supporters of the social clause have not ratified some of the relevant conventions (in particular conventions No. 87 and No. 98) and apparently have no intentions to do so. Convention No. 87 Freedom of Association and Protection of the Right to Organise Convention 1948; Convention No. 98 Right to Organize and Collective Bargaining Convention 1949. http://ilolex.ilo.ch:1567/english/convdisp1.htm.

[112] As mentioned above, from a legal point of view, the withdrawal of a state from the ILO does not relieve this state from the international obligations it has accepted prior to its withdrawal. See Art. 1.5 of the ILO Constitution.

[113] This is basically the approach taken in the excellent book by E. Landy, *The Effectiveness of International Supervision: Thirty Years of I.L.O Experience* (London: Stevens; New York: Dobbs Ferry, 1966) 268.

think that the supervisory system can ensure conformity in all ratifying countries for all conventions, and in every detail of day-to-day working life.

Thus in the end, what counts, when assessing the overall efficacy of the ILO supervisory system, is whether such a system produces a balanced result, i.e. a result that reflects in a reduced format the global picture of violations and inconsistencies. The ILO supervisory system has a remarkable potential to produce such a balanced result because, as previously indicated, it combines the initiative from those who know better—i.e. those directly affected by the violations or inconsistencies—with supervision on the initiative of an independent body, the Committee of Experts. This complementarity was a key factor that made it possible, for instance, to bring up inconsistencies even in countries where workers or employers were not sufficiently independent to file a representation.

Due to various—and to some extent inevitable—factors, this potential does not yet seem to be fully exploited sometimes as a result of imbalances that have 'naturally' developed over time.

For a better understanding, I will enumerate the five main and largely interconnected imbalances.

First, the 'drop outs' from the supervisory system, which, in the ILO jargon, are known as 'automatic cases'. The so-called 'automatic cases' refer to situations in which members consistently fail to observe their reporting obligations under Article 22. Indeed, when no report is supplied or no reply is given to comments made by the supervisory bodies, the Committee of Experts may require the filing of non-periodic *detailed* reports. The ILC then 'automatically' proceeds to an examination of those cases.[114]

The second factor of imbalance refers to the *lopsided record as regards the object and nature* of the cases of discrepancies, which are discussed by ILO supervisory bodies. It is striking that the vast majority of cases discussed in the ILC or dealt with under Article 24 have to do with fundamental conventions, as if violations occurred only in these fields![115] This is due to the fact that, the ILC's Committee on the Application of Conventions and Recommendations has only a limited time to discuss a few selected cases. However it may be, it seems unfortunate that other violations, which may be of literally 'vital' importance, do not come up. The logical solution would be to deal with those 'secondary' violations through Article 24, but this is not the case in practice.

The third factor of imbalance has to do with the *overlap between Articles 22 and 24* to which the above-mentioned lopsided record may be linked. Whereas the two procedures naturally complement each other,[116] the practice has turned them into an almost complete duplication. Organizations can interchangeably trigger either

---

[114] It is not clear to what extent this corresponds to situations when the country was not ready to ratify, or the administrative requirements of the system are too heavy, or sheer bad will, but it would require further analysis.

[115] This concentration is becoming even more obvious with the follow-up to the Declaration, which by definition deals only with fundamental rights.

[116] This is because, *inter alia*, Art. 22 could help to deal with cases in countries where industrial organizations were not sufficiently free or developed to make representations.

Article 22 or Article 24 examinations by sending 'comments' to the Committee of Experts rather than a formal representation. Ultimately, the final outcome will be pretty much the same: if the 'comments' under Article 22 are found to be valid, publicity will be given to them through a special paragraph in the Applications Committee report at the ILC; under Article 24 the outcome will be the publication of the representation to which no convincing reply has been given by the government concerned in the Official Bulletin of the ILO.

The fourth factor of imbalance is the gap between Article 22 and Article 26 as there is no intermediary system to bring about additional pressure to what can be obtained with Article 22 before going to what may—especially with the possible linkage with Article 33—now appear as the 'overkill' solution of establishing a Commission of Inquiry under Article 26.

The case of Myanmar indeed suggests that Article 26 might be used only in cases sufficiently serious to ultimately lead to Article 33.[117]

The fifth factor relates to the gap between the rules and principles applicable to interpretation and the relevant practice.[118] The ILO Constitution provides for two formal systems of interpretation—not to mention the possibility of obtaining an advisory opinion from the ICJ, which is available to all UN specialized agencies. The paradox is, however, that none of these formal mechanisms has been used since WWII and that interpretation is informally dealt with through the Committee of Experts whose formal terms of reference do not include such responsibility.

This gap between the formal provisions and practice has implications from the viewpoint of efficacy. On the one hand, it may affect the authority of the Committee of Experts, whose 'informal interpretations' may be challenged by one group at the ILC all the more readily that they do not intend to draw the consequences of their objectives. On the other hand, the gap may leave the question of the real meaning of a Convention in the concrete realities of a country somewhat hanging in the air.

It is important to underline that all these imbalances (except the first one) are in no way inherent in the constitutional provisions. To the contrary, they are the result of a situation that has inevitably drifted away from the logic of the Constitution through successive layers of practices. There are of course technical solutions to the above-mentioned imbalances, which would involve a faithful return to the complementarity implied in the Constitution. It would be fairly easy for instance to reorganize Article 24 in such a way that representations would be sent to a tripartite Committee when they relate to matters in which the Committee of Experts has been

---

[117] Hesitations about the establishment of commissions of inquiry for the very serious violations in Colombia and subsequently Belarus (where a positive decision was finally taken in November 2003) have to be seen in that perspective.

[118] F. Maupain, 'L'Interprétation des conventions internationales du travail', *Droit et Justice* (Paris: Mélanges Valticos, Pedone, 1999) 567–83. A.-M. La Rosa, 'Links between the ILO and the ICJ: A Less than Perfect Match', in L. Boisson de Chazournes (ed.), *International Organizations and International Dispute Settlement* (New York: Transnational Publishers, 2002) 119–32. See also Governing Body, 256th Session, Geneva, May 1993, Document GB.256/SC/2/2.

unsuccessful in obtaining changes notwithstanding repeated direct requests and observations.

Interestingly, the ILO Governing Body has decided to engage in a review of these problems or at least some of them. However, experience has shown—e.g. the application of Article 33 to the Myanmar case—how difficult it is to make improvements on a piecemeal basis. For achieving long-term sustainability, the supervisory system has to be considered as a whole, and its parts need to be complementary to get maximum efficacy.

4. EFFICACY BEYOND IMPLEMENTATION OF STANDARDS: THE ILO'S CAPACITY TO MAKE THE COMMITMENT TO ITS OBJECTIVES AN EFFECTIVE PART OF THE GLOBAL ECONOMY

In the third part of my presentation, I intended to show that the supervisory system of the ILO has a great potential even though it may not be fully used, and that, contrary to a popular perception, it does have 'teeth' to ensure compliance with the obligations incurred through ratification.

At this stage, the question of the ILO's efficacy to achieve its objectives when members choose not to ratify conventions designed to implement these objectives has been raised. As briefly indicated in the second part, the initial hope was that countries, which voted for draft conventions, would feel morally bound to ratify them. It soon proved to be illusory. After the parenthesis of the 'thirty glorious years' of economic prosperity and the WWII, the globalization of the economy makes the dilemma of voluntarism and efficacy in promoting the ILO's objectives more acute.

Without attempting any exhaustive definition, it should be recalled that the phenomenon of globalization has been made possible by the combination of institutional factors (trade liberalization), and technological innovations (the computer revolution). This phenomenon is characterized by the free movement of goods, services, capital, and ideas across borders as well as by the cross-border organization of production and generalized competition. But this phenomenon also possesses a political and even ideological dimension—which is of course inseparable from the geo-strategic 'new deal' resulting from the fall of the Berlin wall.[119]

---

[119] This ideology was portrayed in the 1997 Director-General's report to the ILC: 'By a strange irony of history, the "dawning of a new age" is no longer expected to occur with the end of the class struggle, which finally reaches its fulfilment in the withering away of the state; this time will only come now once the state has been stripped of its social and economic prerogatives and a global civil society emerges which is answerable only to the laws of economic rationality, itself the sole guarantee of a future so full of promises that people forget the harshness of their present circumstances. Like all that have preceded it this new form of the ideology of progress assures that human progress is more important than actual human beings; and it might well, as the same causes engender the same effects, result in the same disillusions.' Report of the Director-General of the ILO, ILC, 85th Session, Geneva, June 1997. Document available at: http://www.ilo.org/public/english/standards/relm/ilc/ilc85/dg-rep.htm.

The effects of globalization on the production and ratifications of labour standards are twofold.

On the supply side, globalization has increased the imbalance between the cost and the reward attached to the ratification of conventions or the implementation of labour standards. In the 'thirty glorious years' the political, moral, and social stability and multiplayer-effect advantage of ratifying were not negligible, while the cost was not so important in view of the technological advantage of industrialized countries, which shifted in their favour the 'terms of trade'.

The objective impact of the change in the environment is further strengthened by the 'deregulation' orthodoxy that strikes at the heart of normative action by challenging the efficacy of its necessary support: state will and legislation.[120] While the view has recently lost its militancy, as a result of the excesses, disillusions, and failures it has created, the fact remains that even countries that were traditionally considered as the 'best clients' in terms of ratification of ILO conventions,[121] seem more and more reluctant to accept new international commitments for fear of their consequences on their competitive position or on foreign investment.

On the demand side, the phenomenon produces a diametrically opposed claim—even though it is sometimes expressed within the same countries and comes sometimes from the same people. As the social cost of globalization is getting much more readily identifiable than its more diffused benefits among consumers,[122] it creates a growing feeling of precariousness among workers, especially in industrialized countries.[123]

More basically perhaps, the contrast between the high mobility of capital (e.g. its capacity to freely move to places with cheap labour) and the relative immobility of

[120] It is argued that state legislation is becoming increasingly ineffective and can even be counterproductive in the new context of the free movement of capital as it inhibits productivity, deters investments and innovation and is ultimately detrimental to employment—in itself an essential social objective.
This aspect of the 'efficacy' of the ILO voluntary assumption would obviously require a separate treatment. It should simply be noted that, rather than being taken as hostage into this debate, the ILO is—or should be—in a position to act as the only possible judge or arbitrator. Leaving aside the fact that the ILO's objectives may be implemented by ways other than legislation (in particular through collective agreements), it should be emphasized that its tripartite structure combined with its supervisory mechanisms (in particular those covered by Art. 19, whose potential will be examined below) provides a unique framework in which to establish the validity of the pro and con arguments in the light of a critical tripartite assessment of the concrete evidence provided by the comparison of concrete national experiences.   [121] Northern European countries.

[122] Especially when it takes the form of 'relocation', i.e. the transfer of production lines across borders.

[123] See, for example, A. Parisotto, 'Economic Globalization and the Demand for Decent Work', in Roger Blanpain and Chris Engels (eds.), *The ILO and the Social Challenges of the 21st Century: The Geneva Lectures* (Boston: Kluwer, 2001).
A. Parisotto explains, 'There is growing concern that the benefits of globalization may be more volatile than expected and that they have accrued only to a very limited extent to those who need them the most. Growing economic insecurity and the failure to deliver significant development outcomes to a very large portion of the world's population—first and foremost enough work opportunities to meet people's aspiration to a decent life—is prompting many to question the policies, the institutional structures and the ideological stance that have governed the process of globalization so far.'

labour (e.g. the inability of workers to move across borders so as to seek better work conditions), definitely upsets the balance, in the negotiating position of the social partners, which had developed over the thirty glorious years within the framework of the 'Fordist model' in industrialized countries.[124] Hence the growing demand in developed countries for a 'social level playing field', i.e. a common basis of workers' rights among countries now part of the global market.

As the voluntarist option appears at an impasse for reasons previously indicated, the finalization of the Uruguay Round seemed to provide the forum in which the demand could logically be channelled: it did offer the solution to overcome the difficulty inherent in the voluntary option, which is essentially that ratification represents a cost and has no synallagmatic dimension in the context of globalization.

The possibility to link the respect of a certain 'floor' of workers' rights to the economic benefits expected from the further trade liberalization seemed to provide an obvious answer, especially as it had quickly and successfully been tested with intellectual property, a matter where World Intellectual Property organization's experience had been largely parallel to the ILO's.

This is the context in which, at a late stage before the establishment of WTO in 1994, a certain number of industrialized countries supported by national and international workers' organizations revived the—not so new—idea of 'social clauses' (already present in some form in the still-born Havana Charter[125]) to be inserted into the Charter of the new World Trade Organization designed to succeed the GATT.

This move was adamantly resisted by developing countries, which managed to block any substantive discussion on the subject. Some countries and in particular India thus suggested in Marrakech that the 'touching' concern and sense of solidarity shown by industrialized countries for the well-being of workers in developing countries could more convincingly express themselves by opening their borders to these workers as was done for goods and investments. In the WTO Third Ministerial Conference (Seattle), the opposition went so far as to prevent the WTO from even considering the possibility of discussing the issue in a joint forum as such a move would have been tantamount to acknowledging, to the social clause issue, some form of legitimacy within WTO.

---

[124] See, for example, Jean Michel Servais (regarding the issue of wages), 'Capital mobility destabilises the sheltered structure of wages that national industrial relations systems produced when market competition was largely a national matter' (J.-M. Servais, 'The Future of Work and Related Security: A Discussion of the Need to Place Matters in Perspective', in Roger Blanpain and Chris Engels (eds.), *The ILO and the Social Challenges of the 21st Century: The Geneva Lectures* (Boston: Kluwer, 2001) 11.

[125] Art. 7(1) of the Havana Charter states: 'The Members recognize that measures relating to employment must take fully into account the rights of workers under inter-governmental declarations, conventions and agreements. They recognize that all countries have a common interest in the achievement and maintenance of fair labour standards related to productivity, and thus in the improvement of wages and working conditions as productivity may permit. The Members recognize that unfair labour conditions, particularly in production for export, create difficulties in international trade, and, accordingly, each Member shall take whatever action may be appropriate and feasible to eliminate such conditions within its territory.'

The debate obviously raised issues of critical importance for the credibility of the ILO and its 'raison d'être' as it did put into question its claims to offer to all workers across the world a minimum of social protection notwithstanding international competition. It is an interesting—although fairly understandable—contrast that, contrary to the *non possumus* reaction in WTO, the ILO did not shy away from the debate.[126]

However, the real test of efficacy does not rest on the capacity of the ILO to simply engage in the debate, but indeed to provide a convincing answer.

The ILO did manage to provide such answer in a remarkably short period of time, even though this answer professes not to have anything to do with the social clause. This took the form of the ILO Declaration on Fundamental Principles and Rights at Work,[127] which was launched immediately after the first WTO Ministerial Conference of Singapore in December 1996[128] and was completed and adopted by the ILC at its June 1998 session.[129]

Although rightly hailed as a major development, it would be naïve to think that this Declaration could be the final answer to the demand for a uniform level playing field of workers' rights. This is especially true when one realizes, (i) that only half of the workers of the world are covered by the conventions on freedom of association and collective bargaining, Nos. 87 and 98;[130] and (ii) that international competition as it develops no longer leaves casualties solely among unspecialized workers in industrialized countries, but also among workers of developing

---

[126] Even though it would be an exaggeration to say that this debate went beyond a perfectly predictable exchange of conventional arguments in favour or against the social clause. Ultimately, however, this debate led, in the context of the Working Party on the Social Dimension of Globalization, to the conclusion that the issue of the social clause should be placed in abeyance as no agreement seemed possible, and that attention should focus on a critical assessment of empirical evidence concerning the concrete impact of globalization on social policy and progress, in particular through a series of in-depth country studies conducted among a representative sample of (voluntary) countries.

The ILO gave further evidence of its capacity to deal with this intractable subject when, in the wake of the breakdown of the Seattle Conference mainly around the central issue of establishing a 'forum' for the discussion of the issue, it managed to establish an ambitious World Commission composed of about 20 high-level personalities co-chaired by two heads of State to examine, report, and make appropriate recommendations on the 'social dimensions of globalization'. See http://www.ilo.org/public/english/wcsdg/index.htm.

[127] The text of the Declaration is published in the *Official Bulletin*, ILO, Vol. LXXXI, 1998, Series A, No. 2. It is also available at: http://www.ilo.org/public/english/standards/relm/ilc/ilc86/com-dtxt.htm.

[128] The First WTO Ministerial Conference was held in Singapore between 9 and 13 December 1996. See http://www.wto.org/english/thewto_e/minist_e/min96_e/min96_e.htm.

[129] For an in-depth presentation of the history of the Declaration, see H. Kellerson, 'ILO Declaration of 1998 on Fundamental Principles and Rights: A Challenge for the Future', 137/2 *International Labour Review* (1998) 223–35, also available at: http://training.itcilo.it/ils/foa/library/labour_review/1998_2/english/kellerson_en.html.

[130] Even though, Convention No. 87 has been ratified by 142 countries and Convention No. 98 by 154. Large countries such as China, Brazil, and India have not yet ratified these conventions. See http://ilolex.ilo.ch:1567/english/docs/declworld.htm.

countries which had benefited from the first 'wave' of trade liberalization in the 1980s.[131]

Anyhow, even if it cannot be considered as a final answer to the problem, the Declaration and its follow-up have made a definite contribution to the clarification of the confusing debate of the social clause. Three aspects of this contribution can thus be distinguished:

(1) the *delimitation* of which workers' rights deserve to be universally guaranteed and implemented and the reason for such guarantee and implementation;

(2) a *solution* (which is not necessarily exclusive of others) about how this universal recognition can be achieved;

(3) finally, through its follow-up, a *possible new model* for the monitoring of universal progress towards all other objectives and workers' rights compatible with the voluntary option.

I will quickly go through these three aspects.

A. Which of the Workers' Rights Call for Universal Recognition and Why?

The relationship between social progress and international competition has been pre-eminently recognized from the beginning in the ILO Constitution, more precisely in the famous preambular paragraph according to which, 'the failure of any nation to adopt humane conditions of labour is an obstacle in the way of other nations which desire to improve the conditions in their own countries'.[132]

It is necessary to point out that the subjects that were chosen for priority standard setting action immediately after the establishment of the ILO were among those that were perceived to have a direct bearing on the competitiveness of industrialized countries such as hours of work,[133] unemployment,[134] night work,[135] and minimum age.[136] More significantly, it was explicitly, albeit unsuccessfully, argued before the Permanent Court of International Justice on the basis of the above-mentioned preambular paragraph, that the ILO's mandate was limited to those issues that had a bearing on international competition.[137]

---

[131] Among other factors, the appearance of China as a major actor and competitor in particular as regards its capacity to attract the investments that were previously going to other developing countries and to supersede other competitors in some market niches like textiles is bound to reactivate the debate in a different perspective. [132] ILO Constitution, *supra* note 11.

[133] Hours of Work (Industry) Convention 1919 (No. 1).

[134] Unemployment Convention 1919 (No. 2).

[135] Night Work (Women) Convention 1919 (No. 4).

[136] Minimum Age (Industry) Convention 1919 (No. 5).

[137] This argument was developed by France in the framework of the PCIJ advisory opinion No. 2 mentioned above concerning the ILO's competence with respect to agricultural workers. The permanent Court did not follow this argument. *Advisory Opinion No. 2, Competence of the ILO to Regulate Agricultural Labor* (1922), PCIJ, *supra* note 19.

Surprisingly, the question of what aspects of workers' rights and protection could legitimately be the object of a 'trade linkage' has not been addressed as such at the Uruguay Round. The US formulation of the proposals broadly referred to internationally recognized labour standards.[138] Contrary to what a hasty reading may suggest, this phrase is however not deemed to refer to workers' rights recognized in ILO conventions, quite the contrary.[139] It may have more to do with the concept of 'internationally recognized workers' rights'—a language used under American federal statutes currently in effect, and which covers acceptable conditions of work as well as a decent salary.[140]

However it may be, the concept appears either arbitrary or largely open-ended, as it could conceivably cover minimum salary, the guarantee of hours of work and includes in the concept acceptable conditions of work as well as a decent salary to which reference is made in relevant American trade legislation.[141]

The 1994 report of the Director-General of the ILO (which was in fact published before the Marrakech Conference in April 1994) not only drew attention to the fact that this debate could not be ignored by the organization as it put into question its objectives and the efficacy of its voluntary method, but was also the first attempt to recast the issue in the ILO's perspective.[142]

This report triggered a process, which led to progressively focus the debate on the 'special significance' of certain 'fundamental' workers' rights. This process received decisive inputs from other sources, first and foremost from the Copenhagen Social Summit of 1995,[143] then from a more economic angle, from the OECD study in

---

[138] The United States has proposed adding the following language to the Uruguay Round text: 'The Ministers recognize that the more open multilateral trading system resulting from the Uruguay Round should benefit workers around the world through the impact of increased trade on employment and income. They also expressed the view that trade gains should not come from the relaxation of social objectives and, in this connection, have agreed to undertake early consideration of the relationship between the trading system and internationally recognized labour standards' ('Labour Standards Jeopardize Final Deal', *Trade Week in Review and Recent Publications*, Friday, 1 April 1994).

[139] 'The grammatically dubious phrase "workers rights" was created with a view to avoiding the use of terms such as "labour rights" or "labour standards" which might too readily have conjured up visions of existing ILO standards' (P. Alston, 'Labor Rights Provisions in US Trade Law', 15/1 *Human Rights Quarterly* (1993) 8.

[140] A rather sophisticated international law construction underlies the concept. L. Dubin, *La Protection des normes sociales dans les échanges internationaux* (Presses Universitaires d'Aix-Marseille, 2003) 56–9.

[141] See for recent examples, the Fair Trade in Pouch Tuna Act of 2003, the Haiti Economic Recovery Opportunity Act of 2003, the Middle East Trade and Engagement Act of 2003.

[142] '[T]he ILO should recognize both that its mandate requires that it be a party to this debate, and yet that it should not advocate either restrictions to trade or compulsory equalization of social costs' ('Defending Values, Promoting Change. Social Justice in a Global Economy: An ILO Agenda', Report of the Director-General of the ILO, ILC, 81st Session, Geneva, June 1994, p. 58).

[143] The 'Programme of Action' of the Copenhagen Summit made a decisive contribution at the political level by stressing the importance of these principles for 'achieving really sustained economic growth and truly lasting development'.

1996[144] and finally from the conclusions of the Ministerial Conference of Trade Ministers in Singapore in December 1996. In Singapore, trade ministers 'renewed' (*sic*) their 'commitment to the observance of internationally recognized core labour standards' and their support for the ILO's mandate and activities in this field while rejecting 'the use of labour standards for protectionist purposes, and agree that the comparative advantage of countries, particularly low-wage developing countries, must in no way be put into question. In this regard, we note that the WTO and ILO Secretariats will continue their existing collaboration'.[145]

The process culminated with the adoption by the ILO in June 1998 of the Declaration on Fundamental Principles and Rights at Work, which identifies four categories of principles or rights: '(a) Freedom of Association and the effective recognition of the right to collective bargaining; (b) the elimination of all forms of forced or compulsory labour; (c) the effective abolition of child labour; and (d), the elimination of discrimination in respect of employment and occupation', which, in 'seeking to maintain the link between social progress and economic growth', have a 'particular significance'.[146]

This rather succinct justification is however only the tip of the iceberg of a fairly comprehensive axiological construction. The elements of this construction were introduced at different times and are scattered in different documents produced between 1994 and 1998 but which complement each other and can conveniently be recapitulated as follows:

- The fact that the ILO Constitution clearly refers to the relevance of international competition for the achievement of its objective does not mean that its mandate is to remedy alleged distortions in trade resulting from differences in the level of social protection, and that its performance can be judged on its capacity to do so. The ILO is concerned about international competition to the extent that it affects the 'will' of its members to achieve social progress. Beyond Jenks' comments, this is the real flaw in the French argument before the Permanent Court of International Justice referred to above.

---

[144] *Trade, Employment and Labour Standards: A Study of Core Workers' Rights and International Trade* (Paris: OECD Publications, 1996), available at: http://www.oecd.org/LongAbstract/0,2546,en_2649_33705_1894458_1_1_1_1,00.html.

Its demonstration about the fact that there was no negative correlation between respect for fundamental rights and trade and economic performance of the countries concerned was sharply criticized by some scholars including Charnovitz.

[145] Para. 4 of the Ministerial Declaration reads as follows, 'We renew our commitment to the observance of internationally recognized core labour standards. The International Labour Organization (ILO) is the competent body to set and deal with these standards, and we affirm our support for its work in promoting them. We believe that economic growth and development fostered by increased trade and further trade liberalization contribute to the promotion of these standards.'

[146] The Declaration further states that these rights enable 'the persons concerned, to claim freely and on the basis of equality of opportunity, their fair share of the wealth which they have helped to generate, and to achieve fully their human potential' (ILO Declaration, *supra* note 129).

- The reaffirmation of the validity of the 'voluntary' approach to social progress: sustainable social progress cannot be imposed from the outside but must correspond to the idiosyncrasy, history, and preferences of each country and their people, based on the guidance offered by international standards.[147]
- This basically 'inner-directed' character of social progress and workers' protection does not mean that ILO members can arbitrarily decide on the level and specific content of workers' rights; not only do they have a commitment, as ILO members, to try to improve the lot of their workers in good faith and to all the extent of their possibilities, but their claim that the level and content has to take account of their history and preferences and alleged values is acceptable only to the extent that the said preferences and values can manifest themselves freely both on an individual and collective basis. This means that there are a certain number of rights whose universal guarantee *does not constitute an interference, but indeed the very condition for a credible exercise of national preferences and values*. The identification of the rights in question follows logically from the above premises. They cover all the rights, which relate to the individual or collective exercise of the 'autonomy of the will'.[148]
- Because these rights provide the workers concerned with the necessary leverage and tools to freely adjust their claims to the specific context of their respective countries, their universal guarantee has also special significance in the context of the global economy: they are 'enabling rights'—or to use the words of the Declaration's Preamble mentioned above—they are 'of particular significance in that they enable persons concerned to claim freely and on the basis of equality of opportunity, their fair share of the wealth they have helped to generate'.[149]
- This special nature also explains that their guarantee is not deemed to affect the comparative advantage of members. The last paragraph of the Declaration according to which, 'labour standards should not be used for protectionist trade purposes' and 'the comparative advantage of any country should in no way be called into question by this Declaration', has generated some criticisms and much misunderstanding.[150] This is not really surprising as it is the final outcome of a heated and sometimes confused debate.

---

[147] Two different examples illustrate this principle: the brutal collapse of the 'advanced system of social protection' in the Soviet bloc and the fact that, even in highly integrated regional integration systems, such as the EU, the content of social protection and rights remains largely a matter for each member to define.

[148] Even the protection of children whose will can be coerced. There was some fluctuation in this respect as initially child labour was, in some of its worst forms, assimilated to forced labour in accordance with the views expressed by the Committee of Experts itself.

[149] ILO Declaration, *supra* note 129.

[150] Steve Charnovitz and Brian Langille, in particular, have blamed the ILO for sheepishly following the WTO instead of defending its own principles and values. In their view, instead of repeating that protection of workers' rights must not serve as camouflage for protectionist designs, it should have stressed that free trade could not be used to encourage or excuse restrictions on basic rights. See B. Langille, 'The ILO and the New Economy', 15/3 *International Journal of Comparative Labour Law and Industrial Relations* (Fall 1999) 229–57. See also Charnovitz, 'The ILO in its Second Century', *supra* note 1.

However, when read carefully (the first part of the sentence in paragraph 5 refers to labour standards in general and not to fundamental rights) in the context of the preambular paragraph quoted above and the 'travaux préparatoires', its reference to the fact that 'the comparative advantage of any country should not be called into question by this Declaration and its follow up' cannot be read to mean that the non-respect of fundamental rights could be in some way considered as a comparative advantage or an acquired right. Quite on the contrary, *the only conclusion consistent with all the elements previously recapitulated, is that all Members have an obligation to work towards the ILO's objectives of social progress and that fundamental rights and principles, as 'enabling rights' are the necessary condition to prevent ILO Members from seeking a comparative advantage by maintaining an artificially low level of social protection.* This is the rationale behind the fact that some very important, indeed, 'vital' rights in the most literal sense such as safety and health at work are not included among fundamental rights.

B. How to Make the 'Enabling Rights' Effective?

It is clear that the recognition of the 'special significance' of fundamental workers' rights may remain of very little practical significance without some form of follow-up.

The more original and 'revolutionary' aspect of the Declaration is perhaps that it managed to overcome the dilemma of voluntary standards by establishing such a follow-up mechanism for all members irrespective of their ratification. However, the revolution could not obviously go so far as to subject members to the same obligations—and possible sanctions—as ratifying countries. It is of a promotional nature and thus can hardly close definitely the debate about how to ensure effectively the universal aspect of these rights, which have special significance.

Recognizing that the debate can hardly be considered as closed does not mean however that other solutions can readily be found as I will show by briefly examining two possible alternatives for making these rights universally effective.

The promotional solution of the Declaration and its limits

The general significance of the Declaration is that it has managed to overcome the dilemma between voluntarism and the universal protection of workers' rights. This was achieved by deriving certain obligations directly from the Constitution.

This approach was by no means a new idea. It was tried as early as 1927 but the only successful achievement—in extremely special circumstances—was the Freedom of Association procedure established in 1950.

The very success of the Freedom of Association precedent in fact explains the staunch resistance to its extension, even amongst Western democracies. Thus, at the beginning of the 1970s, the attempt to apply the Freedom of Association system to discrimination was a failure. And when former Director-General Hansenne suggested extending this procedure to other fundamental rights in his 1994 report, he faced determined opposition.[151]

The reason why it succeeded in 1998 is precisely that its legal justification was not sought in the contested Freedom of Association 'precedent'. Quite the contrary, great constitutional care and engineering was used to establish a 'sanitary cordon' between this scheme and the contested 'model'.

Substantive obligations were derived both from the preambular paragraphs of the ILO Constitution and the Declaration of Philadelphia[152] and were expressed in general terms: members 'have an obligation, arising from the very fact of membership in the organization, to respect, to promote and to realize, in good faith... the principles concerning the fundamental rights which are the subject of the ILO "fundamental conventions" '.[153]

The specific procedural elements of the follow-up were justified on the basis of the provisions in Article 19, paragraph 5(e) of the Constitution, which allow the organization to request reports from all members on unratified conventions.[154]

On that basis, a very comprehensive system was created. This new system combines annual reviews of the situation in countries that have not ratified the 'fundamental conventions', with four-yearly 'global reports' to review trends relating to each category of rights.

This 'revolution' being acknowledged, the limits of the exercise must be objectively recognized. The solution proposed by the Declaration is of a promotional nature and can only produce results over time. Its main success has been that, contrary to the prediction of those who considered that the promotional nature of the Declaration would constitute a disincentive to ratification; the follow-up has

---

[151] See the debates in the Governing Body on an extension of the Freedom of Association procedure to other fundamental rights. Governing Body, 265th Session, Geneva, March 1996. Document GB.265/8/2, paras. 46–76. See also Governing Body, 267th Session, Geneva, November 1996. Document GB.267/9/2, paras. 15–80.

[152] Sometimes in a rather indirect way as in the case of forced labour to which no reference whatsoever can be found in the constitutional provisions. (See 'Consideration of a possible Declaration of principles of the International Labour Organization concerning fundamental rights and its appropriate follow-up mechanism', Report VII, ILC, 86th Session, Geneva, June 1998. Available at: http://www.ilo.org/public/english/standards/relm/ilc/ilc86/rep-vii.htm.)

[153] e.g. the conventions covering the 'enabling rights', identified in the Declaration as (a) freedom of association and the effective recognition of the right to collective bargaining; (b) the elimination of all forms of forced or compulsory labour; (c) the effective abolition of child labour; and (d) the elimination of discrimination in respect of employment and occupation: ILO Declaration, *supra* note 129.

[154] To fend off the accusation of 'constitutional creep' expressed by some very vocal opponents to the project, Report VII introducing the proposal before the ILC in 1998 went as far as to explain that in fact the follow-up mechanism could have been developed without the Declaration whose importance was rather of a political and symbolic nature. 'Consideration of a possible Declaration of principles of the International Labour Organization concerning fundamental rights and its appropriate follow-up mechanism', Report VII submitted to the 86th Session of the ILC, *supra* note 152.

proven to be enough of a burden to non-ratifying states to contribute significantly to the increase in ratifications.[155]

There are obvious limits to this impact and the follow-up will have to prove that it does make a difference in the realities, and not only that it has enabled the ILO to channel technical cooperation to countries having difficulties in the implementation of the principle.

A key test in that respect should be the first report of the second cycle of global reports, which was due in 2003 and relates to Freedom of Association. This second report should be, in accordance with the logic of the follow-up, the occasion to evaluate beyond the description of technical cooperation projects, what has been the measurable impact of the follow-up towards the specific (even though modest) objectives established on the occasion of the first report.

There is however a more fundamental challenge to the promotional approach. Considering the 'special significance' recognized to these rights for achieving other rights and considering that they are stated in the Declaration to be an obligation inherent in membership, why should fundamental rights not be made enforceable *vis-à-vis* all members?

I have already mentioned the criticisms that were addressed to the last paragraph of the Declaration. In a recent article, Michael Trebilcock has very succinctly made the case. While rejecting the link between comparative advantage and the level of social protection, he points out, in the light of A. Sen's analysis, the contradiction between the recognition of the universal character of certain fundamental workers' rights, which are also human rights, and the *a priori* rejection of any form of linkage between trade policy and these rights. In his opinion, such a possibility is 'not only defensible but arguably imperative'.[156] However, the problem remains in how such linkage might be achieved.

The trade linkage 'quick fix'

Let us briefly consider first the 'quick fix' of the trade linkage for which the Agreement on Trade Related Aspects of Intellectual Property rights ('TRIPS') precedent is generally invoked. This may seem like beating a dead horse, as this

---

[155] Evolution in the number of ratifications (as of 13 October 2003)

	c.29	c.87	c.98	c.100	c.105	c.111	c.138	c.182
2003	163	142	153	161	161	159	130	145
2000	155	133	147	149	152	145	103	56
1998	146	121	137	136	129	129	46	—
1995	136	113	125	123	114	118	46	—

[156] Michael J. Trebilcock, 'The "Fair Trade" Debate: Protection of Labour Standards and International Economic Law', in S. Griller (ed.), *International Economic Governance and Non-Economic Concerns: New Challenges for the International Legal Order* (Vienna: Springer Wien New York, 2003) 299.

precedent is more than ever a political non-starter. However, this does not seem to be a sufficient reason to ignore its possible relevance. Indeed, there seems to be at least one angle under which the TRIPS has obvious relevance: the TRIPS allows/ requires a different treatment for products which, made under different working conditions, share exactly the same external intrinsic physical characteristics. The only difference between a counterfeited good and a 'genuine' one is based on the respect of some legally protected rights (in that case property),[157] which—contrary to other adjustments made to the 'processes and production methods' (PPM) distinction through case law—is not linked to any Article XX exceptions.[158]

However, this very relevance raises many difficult policy issues. Let me mention just two.

The first is the dilemma between increased efficacy and the respect for the integrity of the definition of the rights. There is an obvious risk that the possibility to attach trade measures to the implementation of fundamental rights would question the applicability of the praetorian extension of the definitions developed by the ILO's supervisory organs.[159]

The second is the dilemma between efficacy and the achievement of social justice and solidarity between workers. Goods made (or service rendered) in conditions contrary to the fundamental rights may in cases other than Freedom of Association represent a small fraction (around 5 per cent in the case of child labour) of traded goods. Closing national markets to goods made in those conditions would not, as such, bring about the social objective and would rather push the problem into the informal sector.

Certainly, these difficulties are not insurmountable. For instance, the unintended consequences of trade linkage could be avoided if the protection was linked (somewhat in line with the TRIPS model) to the application of national legislation to all workers in conformity with relevant ILO conventions. This would seem to confirm that the solution to establish a link, as indeed already suggested by the Myanmar case, would be quite simply to make ratification of relevant conventions a condition of membership in the WTO. Obviously, however, this solution seems even less likely today than when its membership was more limited.

---

[157] TRIPS 'requires Governments to establish a procedure enabling an intellectual property right holder to ask customs authorities to suspend the entry into the market of counterfeited or pirated goods. The only "unlikeness" between pirated and copyrighted or patented goods is situated on the level of their production process, which in the former case involves piracy, and which does not in the latter. No single Bilateral trade agreement ("BTA") or allied test criteria could ever distinguish both products, and yet a panel decision in the *United States—Section 337* Case did apply the national treatment standard where the measures in question related to intellectual property violations, not having anything to do with any physical characteristics', see P. Leenknegt, 'Domestic Regulations at the Global Crossroads of Trade and Labour: Social Labelling and the 2002 Belgian Law on Socially Responsible Production', paper submitted in partial fulfilment of the LLM degree at Harvard University Law School (Cambridge, 2003) 131.

[158] The Appellate Body in *US—Shrimp* has recognized that Art. XX may authorize certain PPM type policy. In *US—Shrimp* the right to protect the health of turtles justified the US measure, which made regulatory distinctions based on the way shrimp were fish. PPM seem now allowed under Art. XX.

[159] This is the case of the right to strike, not expressly dealt with in Convention No. 87.

A social label alternative for the universal enforcement of fundamental workers' rights?

In the light of the above, one may be tempted to conclude that reconciling the effective implementation of workers' rights, the integrity of their definition, and the universality of their application either in a binding or in a voluntary framework, is like trying to square the circle.

However, not only does such reconciliation appear technically possible, but the paradox is that it is possible in a voluntary framework, or more specifically in the framework of an ILO convention, which would be binding for those ratifying it. This is the sense of the solution of a 'global social label' mentioned in the Director-General's report of 1997.[160] This solution would provide the answer to the absence of real synallagmatical dimension in the ratification of ILO conventions (there would be an obvious advantage built in the ratification). The convention, which would be open to all members, would select ILO standards whose implementation would entitle ratifying members to authorize use of the label. Additionally, all states party to the convention would mutually recognize the labels attributed by others. All parties would be subject in addition to the normal supervisory procedures, to a system of direct international inspection in cases where a claim was made by another party that the attributions of the label was unjustified (as regards a particular good or service).

The 'global social label' initiative was met with great resistance and was promptly shelved. However, the idea was not completely lost. Some countries are in the process of introducing, or have introduced (in the case of Belgium), national legislation to create a label based on the rights recognized in the Declaration.[161] It is difficult at this stage to assess the viability of such national schemes but one may wonder if their possible proliferation could not paradoxically be the best manner to reactivate the option of an international system of mutual recognition.

C. From the Universal Implementation of Fundamental Rights to Universal Progress towards Workers' Rights other than Fundamental Ones

The emphasis placed on fundamental rights in the 1998 Declaration does not represent any 'retreat ' or disengagement of the ILO *vis-à-vis* its traditional objectives and the protection of other workers' rights as some comments suggested.[162] There is

---

[160] This somewhat inadequate description was in fact meant to cover a system of mutual recognition of labels within the framework of an ILO convention.

[161] See Belgian Parliament, 'Wet ter bevordering van sociaal verantwoorde productie/ Loi visant à promouvoir une production socialement responsable', 27 February 2002, *Belgisch Staatsbald / Moniteur Belge*, 26 March 2002. See also the paper submitted by Leenknegt, 'Domestic Regulations at the Global Crossroads of Trade and Labour', *supra* note 157. Belgium also notified this draft legislation to the TBT Committee.

[162] P. Alston and J. Heenan, 'The Role of International Labour Standards within the Trade Debate: The Need to Return to Fundamentals', First seminar, Geneva, 23–24 May 2002, p. 8 (publication forthcoming in *New York University Journal of International Law and Politics*, 2004).

enough evidence to the contrary. The contribution of the Declaration to universal protection in fact 'spills over' into the protection of all other rights not only from a substantive point of view (to the extent that, as previously explained, these fundamental rights are 'enabling rights'), but also as I shall now briefly explain, from a procedural point of view. The follow-up to the Declaration has brought to light the potential of Article 19 of the Constitution—on which the follow-up is based—for the promotion of all aspects of workers' protection covered by ILO conventions beyond the present limited practice of 'general surveys'.

This provision, which is indeed the imprint left from the initial supranational intentions of the ILO founders, has always been in the Constitution, though changes introduced on the occasion of the 1946 amendments extended it to apply to recommendations. It gives the ILO the right to request from member states, at appropriate intervals, reports on what they have done regardless of whether or not they have ratified the convention in question.

Such reports are to indicate 'the position of (the) law and practice (of member states) in regard to the matters dealt with in the Convention, showing the extent to which effect has been given . . . to any of the provisions of the Convention, . . . and stating the difficulties'.[163]

'General surveys' carried out under this provision have often turned in the past into comparative analyses of legislations rather than assessments of practical difficulties and the real impact of the instrument. But this practice is not inherent in the Constitution, quite the contrary. As I have indicated, the follow-up to the Declaration has shown the potential of this provision as an instrument to elicit information and indeed promote developments in non-ratifying states towards the general objectives that the relevant instruments (both conventions and recommendations) seek to achieve. In short, the Declaration illustrates the possibility of a universal system for assessing and promoting progress with respect to all the subjects of workers' protection covered by existing conventions and recommendations.

This being said, applying this instrument to each individual convention or recommendation would be unrealistic. However, the Declaration, combined with the Decent Work Strategy, opens a new perspective in this respect as well as the possibility of organizing the follow-up around what have been called 'families of instruments'.

D. Towards Greater Efficacy through the 'Privatisation' of Standards?

As can be seen from the above, there is no such a thing as an obvious 'quick fix' alternative to the ILO voluntary option to promote its objectives. The simplest and most readily available solutions to increase efficacy in the monitoring of progress towards the ILO's objectives for the many countries which are not bound by relevant conventions are ultimately to be found in the improvement of ILO

---

[163] Art. 19.5(e) of the ILO Constitution.

procedures or the imaginative use of the most traditional solution: an international labour convention that could be 'genetically modified' to build into its ratification the sort of reward that was inherent in the acceptance of the disciplines of international trade.[164]

Such a conclusion may however be hostage of the vision of social progress that is centred on the state,[165] and cannot be deemed final without at least briefly considering another type of alternative: the 'without toil' or 'do it yourself'[166] way to social progress through the development of private initiatives, codes of conduct, and social labels. This form of 'privatization' of international labour standards appears as an increasingly popular alternative, an almost 'magic formula' capable of bringing social progress without complicated standards and bureaucratic supervisory systems. All that it needs is some willingness from consumers to be selective and be ready perhaps to pay a little extra to have a clear social conscience.

Leaving aside the 'touching faith'[167] in the reliability of consumer choices that this new conventional wisdom seems to assume, there is no doubt that consumer choice is a potentially very powerful tool to induce good social practices. The loss of important markets is probably more effective than any other threat. The question, however, is whether this potentially enormous power can produce not only sporadic improvements—as it indeed does—but also a meaningful social progress. So far, the evidence does not seem really conclusive.[168]

---

[164] This idea was first introduced in the 1997 Director-General's report to the ILC, *supra* note 119. However, the model for this type of instrument, including a built-in reward, already existed in the form of convention on Merchant Shipping (Minimum Standards) 1976 (No. 147). It could take a more sophisticated form with the Consolidated Maritime instrument now under consideration, which would extend the protection of the instrument to ships flying the flag of non-ratifying countries through port state control.

Indeed, the first draft of the convention states: 'Every ship calling, in the normal course of its business or for operational reasons, in the port of a Member shall be subject to inspection by authorized officers of the Member for the purpose of reviewing compliance with the standards of this Convention relating to shipboard conditions of employment and shipboard living arrangements.' Such inspection must, in normal circumstances, be limited to an examination of the certificate required by the convention. Of course, only the ships from member states, which have ratified the convention, will possess the certificate. See http://www.ilo.org/public/french/dialogue/sector/techmeet/twgmls03/twgmls-r-2.pdf.

[165] F. Maupain, *L'OIT, la justice sociale et la mondialisation, supra* note 17, 223 *et. seq.*

[166] 'Do-it-yourself Labor Standards, While the WTO Dickers, Companies are Writing the Rules', *Business Week*, 19 November 2001. Available at: http://www.businessweek.com/magazine/content/01_47/b3758086.htm.

To use the description given by *Business Week* inherent to the ILO Constitution, but not necessarily 'efficient' in terms of present-day realities; as already noted the realities are those of the cross-border organization of production through MNEs. Not only MNEs 'emancipate' themselves from the will of the states, but they put those wills as expressed in national legislations on competition.

[167] To use Alston's words. Alston and Heenan, *supra* note 162, 8.

[168] In the wake of the pioneer study carried out by the ILO in 1998, it can be said that three objections to the privatization of standards are widely recognized. First, there are gaps in the subjects

Some have, however, argued[169] that this is a transitory state of things and that we may be moving towards a second more coherent generation of initiatives (for instance the Corporate Management Systems Standards under consideration in the International Organization for Standardization (ISO)).[170]

There are however some 'structural' reasons to doubt that the phenomenon will be able to effectively 'auto-regulate'.

Basically, the phenomenon of private initiatives and Corporate Social Responsibility appears to be largely a market phenomenon. As such it involves a demand, which emanates from consumers, and a supply, which is ensured by multinationals together with a quickly developing social auditing business. In view of the unreliability of consumer choices, it would seem that coherent guidance should be given in order to trigger coherent choices. Can the supply side, i.e. multinationals and the growing business of social auditing, provide for such coherent guidance? It can in fact be doubted that they have a real incentive to do so for reasons that would require more extensive analysis.[171]

The notion of codes of conduct raises a second question: even if coherent guidance could be given to industry, would that lead to coherent social progress?

---

covered by the codes of conduct (which often leave out essential aspects of social protection like Freedom of Association). Second, codes of conduct cause a sort of 'balkanization' of the standards of reference used for the subjects covered. Finally, there seems to be no comparability in the methods used to make sure that the standards or principles selected are respected along the production lines in the various countries where the firms operate. See Working Party on the Social Dimensions of the Liberalization of International Trade, 'Overview of the Global Developments and Office Activities Concerning Codes of Conduct, Social Labeling and Other Private Sector Initiatives Addressing Labour Issues', ILO Governing Body, 273rd Session, Geneva, November 1998, p. 18. Document GB.273/WP/SDL/1 (Rev. 1) Document available at: http://www.ilo.org/public/english/standards/relm/gb/docs/gb273/sdl-1.htm.

[169] See the article by Charles Sabel, Dara O'Rourke, and Archon Fung, 'Ratcheting Labor Standards: Regulation for Continuous Improvement in the Global Workplace', 23 February 2000. Available online at: http://www.lex.unict.it/dml-online/archivio/numero3/online/sabel.htm.

[170] See http://www.iso.ch/iso/en/commcentre/pressreleases/2002/Ref826.html. The ISO is recommending the adoption of an 'internationally agreed-upon framework for operationalization of corporate responsibility commitments, capable of producing verifiable, measurable outputs'. This system 'would build on the intellectual and practical infrastructure of ISO 9000 quality MSSs and ISO 14000 MSSs, and the momentum associated with close to one-half million firms certified as compliant with these standards'. Accordingly, 'firms could self-declare compliance with the proposed ISO CR MSSs [Corporate Responsibility Management System standards] or could seek certificates from authorized third parties. Key elements of the system proposed by the ISO 'include commitment to the concept of continual improvement . . . commitment to the concept of stakeholder engagement, and commitment to transparent, accountable reporting on CR initiatives to a firm's stakeholders and the greater public'.

[171] After all, the existing state of balkanization and confusion of the standards of reference does not necessarily represent a 'market failure' from the viewpoint of firms' objectives. The objective of multinational firms is not to produce social progress, as the ILO may understand it, it is rather to produce (or to claim to produce) improvements that will spare the firms concerned from consumers' attacks and vengeance. The fact that consumers are confused is not necessarily incompatible with that objective—this is not to deny that the ethical considerations are not relevant or genuine, but as an ILO Director-General

Again there can be some doubts for the same reason as has been mentioned with regard to the 'quick fix' solution of a compulsory social clause: the risk that the improvement may concern only workers involved in international trade and thus contribute to more sharply divided or 'dual' economy and society depending on whether or not the workers' conditions can benefit or not from the 'locomotive' of international trade. Again this may be avoided, but only to the extent that consumer choices were based on the application of relevant rights in the production of all goods made in the country and not only traded goods.[172]

This leaves us with a rather paradoxical conclusion. The two approaches that could be an alternative to the ILO's 'voluntary solution'—e.g. trade linkage and the privatization of standards—which start from radically different premisses, ultimately meet with the same type of difficulties.

First, in both cases it appears that specific sporadic improvements in favour of the workers directly concerned, even if they clearly represent a positive development, are not necessarily tantamount to social progress. The linkage solution, like the privatization solution, has the inherent risk of aggravating the 'dualization' of working conditions between activities that are fortunate enough to be pulled by the 'locomotive' of international trade and those in the rest of the economy.

Second, social progress to be sustainable cannot simply be imposed from the outside or granted by a benevolent employer. It needs the active involvement of those concerned, considering all relevant aspects. Fundamental rights and in particular Freedom of Association are essential as they are the tools whereby those concerned can express their choice and preferences, taking into account the culture and preferences of their country as well as its possibilities. It is certainly no accident from that point of view that Freedom of Association does not appear as the priority item in codes of conduct and other private initiatives. Despite the progress of international framework agreements concluded with unions' representatives[173] we are still far away from 'transnational collective bargaining' or agreements of an international character not less effective than national collective agreements that were envisaged as far back as 1944 when the ILO launched the idea of 'Industrial Committees'.[174]

observed, the ethics of trade have a tendency to quickly degenerate into the trade of ethics. See Report of the Director-General of the ILO, ILC, 86th Session, Geneva, June 1998.

As an economist recently put it, 'there is no example of good intentions which survived in the face of unfavourable circumstances'. See, for example, the recent article in *Le Monde*, 'Les Audits sociaux se multiplient dans les pays émergents', 22 September 2003, 22.

[172] Which would be the case with the 'global social label' solution previously examined. As we have noted this solution would link the social label to the respect of fundamental rights not only with respect to the goods wearing the label, but within the country of production and not only to the application.

[173] For analysis of these agreements, see the new Global Report on Freedom of Association which was presented at the 92nd Session of the ILC in June 2004.

[174] *Future Policy, Programme and Status of the ILO*, Report I, ILC, 26th Session, 1944, 75–7.

5. GENERAL CONCLUSIONS

This presentation has concentrated essentially on normative action, which has been traditionally—and rightly—considered as a main tool for achieving the ILO's objectives. In the light of recent developments, it seems clear that this tool has indeed an exceptional potential, which however, after more than eighty years of existence, is still not fully exploited. The Myanmar experience shows that the ILO may have 'a bite as well as a bark' with respect to ratified conventions. In addition, the Declaration opens new vistas about the use of non-binding instruments, such as the international labour recommendations to encourage and monitor progress of all members towards the different ILO's objectives whether or not they have ratified relevant conventions. It is important in this respect to underline the synergies between the Declaration and the Myanmar experience. This recent case places members that have not ratified fundamental conventions in the grip of the following dilemma: the burden that arises under the follow-up pushes them to ratify conventions; but at the same time, the ratification places them under the sword of Damocles hanging from Article 33.

The significance and potential of the ILO's normative action should not lead to underestimate ILO's 'stato-centric' limits as well as the importance of other means of action for achieving its objective.[175] To name a few, technical cooperation, research, 'clearing house', function for the exchange of information, the confrontation of ideas on a tripartite basis or otherwise are relevant tools in this respect. In its February 2004 report, the World Commission on the Social Dimension of Globalization[176] illustrated the importance of those non-normative means of action for the exploration of new paths and eventual invention of new tools to make these objectives effective.[177]

The natural conclusion is that the ILO does indeed have a strong capacity to promote, in a verifiable manner, its objectives. Yet its potential will remain inactive, unless there is a strong political will to activate it. This may seem like a convenient truism, but this truism covers some very concrete realities.

The first is the will to pay the price. The budgetary test of this will is a sobering one as it seems difficult to reach universal social justice with a yearly budget that represents the value of a Boeing 747.[178]

---

[175] See Art. 11 of the ILO Constitution.

[176] The World Commission on the Social Dimension of Globalization was established by the ILO Governing Body. It consists of about twenty very high-level personalities from academia, politics, and civil society, including two heads of states and a winner of the Nobel Prize for economics.

[177] Because of its representativity, the report of this commission, addressed not only to the ILO but also to all organizations concerned, could have an important impact on policies and perhaps future standards or rules by changing the very perception of, or approach to, the phenomenon of globalization.

[178] But it is also a sobering test for the real influence of tripartism at the national level.

The second is the will to 'integrate' the ILO's social objectives in the pursuit of other objectives. As the Great Depression of the 1930s should remind us, the ILO cannot, no matter how remarkable its potential might be, reach its social objectives alone, independently of other objectives and in particular of the objectives of 'production'—to use the pre-war language of the Permanent Court of International Justice.[179]

But reciprocally, the growing and more and more vocal contestation of the WTO and the IFIs[180] confirm that the capacity to ensure compliance with specific obligations is an illusory test of efficacy for any organization. The real test of efficacy, and ultimately of their capacity to survive, is the capacity to deliver the finalities or 'end results', referred to in their charters, and in particular employment and increased well-being for all.

Thus, the key to efficacy for both the ILO and other economic financial institutions is to develop a more coherent and complementary approach to their respective mandates. This cannot be achieved unless a change of mind takes place both among the international organizations and between their members.

As regards the organizations this change of mind involves a certain change in the 'sanitary cordon' vision of economic and trade objectives. In the case of the IFIs, this approach is justified in particular by the fact that, as stated in the International Monetary Fund's Articles of Agreement, 'only economic consideration shall be relevant' to their activities.[181] This has resulted for instance in a rather selective attitude towards fundamental workers' rights depending on whether or not in their judgment these rights are conducive to economic efficiency—with marked reticence towards freedom of association and collective bargaining. But this can also affect more trivial aspects such as the protection of workers in case of bankruptcy where advice can be given to governments that contradict ILO instruments.

The Articles of the Agreement, however, do not prohibit social considerations. As already noted the maintenance of high levels of employment and the 'raising of the standards of living and conditions of labour' is for instance mentioned in the first article of the IBRD's Articles of Agreement.[182] One may quibble as to whether it is an objective or an end-result, but in the end should not the result be the same?

This change in vision of the organization's mandate cannot however take place unless a parallel change occurs in the 'schizophrenic' attitude among their members and their propensity to leave at the IFIs' cloakroom their commitments towards other organizations objectives including ILO's. Obviously, this schizophrenia has deep and obvious political roots in national politics and cannot just be simply ruled out as 'unconstitutional'. Like the removal of the 'sanitary cordon' vision of the respective mandates, it can only come as a result of a process.

---

[179] Advisory Opinion No. 2, PCIJ, *supra* note 19.
[180] International Financial Institutions, hereinafter IFIs.
[181] Art. IV(10) of the Articles of Agreement of the IBRD.
[182] Art. I of the Articles of Agreement of the IBRD.

The ILO seems to be in a unique position to play a role in this process.

First, *it has a mandate*,[183] which gives it a special responsibility to judge, in the light of its objectives, 'all national and international policies and measures, in particular those of an economic and financial character'.[184]

Second, *it has a programme*, which is productive and decent employment. Not only does this programme fit perfectly, from a constitutional point of view, with the ultimate objective or end result to which all the constitutive agreements of the IFIs and WTO refer, but also from a practical point of view, employment is indeed the necessary 'transmission belt' between the increase in production and the raising of working conditions and living standards.[185]

Third, *its tripartite structure is a guarantee* that economic considerations are necessarily taken into account along with social objectives.

In the light of all of the above, it seems reasonable to finally conclude that not only does the ILO have the capacity to promote its objectives, but it also has the capacity to serve as a 'bridge' to promote a more integrated approach to economic and social objectives which is a *sine qua non* for sustainable economic and social progress in the future. If we must recognize that only a definite answer to the question of its efficacy for the past would require an investigation of what the situation would have been if the ILO had never existed, a somewhat parallel question must be considered before turning to better solutions for the future. Does the international community today have the creativity, vision, and will to devise a tool of such originality, flexibility, and potential? A potential still to be explored.

---

[183] Even if it is indeed the imprint of its failed attempt to establish itself in the words of E. B. Haas as the 'Master Agency' of the international system after WWII.

[184] Art. II(c) of the Declaration concerning the aims and purposes of the International Labour Organization (Declaration of Philadelphia).

[185] Indeed, and as the Director-General has pointed out before the last ILC, employment constitutes the 'missing link' in the global strategy to eradicate poverty. This may be due in part to the implicit conviction that the shedding of jobs is more often the inescapable casualty of increased productivity. Hence, the shift towards speaking of the eradication of poverty more and more often as an objective in itself rather than the by-product of an employment policy. However, as Mr Somavia puts it, 'The Millennium development goals are out of reach. But we have a solution—the way out of poverty is work.'

5

The Labor Dimension of the Emerging Free Trade Area of the Americas

STEVE CHARNOVITZ

Negotiations for a Free Trade Area of the Americas (FTAA) began over six years ago and are slated to be finished by 2005.[1] The nations of the Americas could certainly benefit from freer trade, as Latin America is afflicted with widespread poverty, high unemployment, and the most unequal income distribution in the world.[2] So far, no formal talks on labor have been held. That could change as the FTAA nears completion in 2004 or thereafter.

The purpose of this chapter is to explore a labor dimension for the FTAA. This study is divided into four parts: Part 1 provides context by reviewing the history of Inter-American economic cooperation, especially on labor and trade. Part 2 examines how labor has been addressed in the major free trade agreements of the Americas. Part 3 looks at the normative basis for international labor cooperation. Part 4 makes specific recommendations for addressing labor issues in the FTAA.

1. HISTORICAL CONTEXT

The significance of labor as an FTAA issue cannot be understood by looking only at the FTAA negotiations that commenced in April 1998. Although the official FTAA website traces the FTAA's 'antecedents' as far back as the 1st Summit of the Americas held in December 1994,[3] the story actually begins 170 years earlier—when Simon Bolívar inspired the first assembly of the American Republics. This 1824 Congress of Panama, as it became known, was convened to consider an agenda of political, collective security, and commercial issues. The Congress produced a Treaty of Perpetual Union, League, and Confederation which, although postponing the topic of commercial relations until the next assembly, dealt with a number of controversial issues,

---

[1] See generally José M. Salazar-Xirinaches and Maryse Robert (eds.), *Toward Free Trade in the Americas* (Brookings, 2001). The negotiations include all countries in the Americas except Cuba.

[2] Report of the ILO Director-General, *Globalization and Decent Work in the Americas*, 15th American Regional Meeting, December 2002, at 10–13. [3] http://www.ftaa-alca.org/View_e.asp.

such as the abolition of the African slave trade.[4] This Treaty did not go into force, however, and no follow-up assembly was held. Hemispheric cooperation puttered along over the next several decades in seeming perpetual discord.

The Western Hemisphere resurged in 1889 when the United States took the lead in convening and hosting the International American Conference.[5] The promotion of regional trade and dispute settlement were among the top goals for that endeavor. The Conference concluded that while free trade among the nations of the hemisphere was a premature idea, interested governments might seek partial reciprocity treaties with one or more countries as it may be in their interest to do.[6]

This First[7] Pan American Conference sparked new treaties and institutions that, in fits and starts, propelled continental economic and social cooperation over several decades. The International Bureau of American Republics was established in 1890 and became the Pan American Union in 1910. In 1948 the Pan American Union was transformed into the Organization of American States (OAS), which, together with the Rio Treaty for collective security, solidified the foundation for the Inter-American human rights system and many other fields of regional cooperation.

The Summit of the Americas of 1994 was not the first hemispheric summit, but it almost seems that way because it revitalized regional cooperation to promote democratic values and economic prosperity.[8] Today, the Inter-American system operates through a vibrant triad of: (1) formal institutions (the main ones being the OAS and the Inter-American Development Bank), (2) periodic transgovernmental Summits and conferences, and (3) partnerships with business and civil society organizations.

State participation in the system has been nearly universal with a few notable exceptions: Canada did not join the OAS until 1990. Cuba was made unwelcome at the OAS after 1962, a fate that did not befall other countries that suffered periods of dictatorship. The English-speaking Caribbean countries began entering the OAS in the 1960s.

The remainder of Part 1 will discuss the course of labor cooperation in the Americas during the past century. No comprehensive study of this topic has come to my attention, and my goal here is merely to highlight some of the key milestones.

---

[4] Peter Blanchard, 'Pan Americanism and Slavery in the Era of Latin American Independence', in David Sheinin (ed.), *Beyond the Ideal: Pan Americanism in Inter-American Affairs* (Praeger, 2000) 9, at 9–18; Josef F. Kunz, 'The Idea of "Collective Security" in Pan-American Developments', 6 *Western Political Quarterly* (1953) 658; Joseph Byrne Lockey, *Pan-Americanism: Its Beginnings* (MacMillan, 1920), at 312–45. The proposals to liberalize trade were blocked by Mexico. Samuel Guy Inman, *Inter-American Conference 1826–1954: History and Problems* (University Press and Community College Press, 1965), at 9.

[5] Javier Corrales and Richard E. Feinberg, 'Regimes of Cooperation in the Western Hemisphere: Power, Interests, and Intellectual Traditions', 43 *International Studies Quarterly* (1999) 1, at 5.

[6] *The International Conferences of American States 1889–1928* (Carnegie Endowment, 1931), at 33–4.

[7] In deference to tradition, I spell out the ordinal numbers denominating the early Pan American conferences. This will also distinguish them from the nomenclature of the recent conferences.

[8] See Robin L. Rosenberg, 'The OAS and the Summit of the Americas: Coexistence, or Integration of Forces for Multilateralism?' 43 *Latin American Politics and Society* (2001) 79.

Some commentators may dismiss this history as being inconsequential because of the seeming lack of governmental follow-up. A sound judgment needs to await new scholarship using both institutionalist and constructivist lenses.

Labor and social issues surfaced only occasionally in the early conferences. At the Second Pan American (Mexico City) Conference of 1901–1902, the governments formulated a Convention on the Practice of Learned Professions designed to make it easier for professionals in one country to practice in another.[9] The Fifth Pan American (Santiago) Conference of 1923 called on governments to promote vocational training through the exchange of teachers and workmen. The Conference further agreed that international questions relating to social problems should be included on the program of all future conferences.[10]

Alongside the hemispheric cooperation, there were also other efforts. For example, in 1923, a Conference of Central American Affairs approved a General Treaty of Peace and Amity, as well as some specialized treaties, including a Convention for the Establishment of Free Trade and a Convention on the Unification of Protective Laws for Workmen and Labourers.[11] The Unification Convention of 1923 was notably progressive—particularly with regard to prohibiting involuntary labor and providing for compulsory insurance—because similar norms were not achieved in the International Labour Organization (ILO) until years later.

The Pan American system was also remarkable for devoting attention to discrete social matters. The First American Child-Welfare Congress convened in 1916 with organizational assistance from the League of Women's and Child's Right.[12] Earlier child welfare and nutrition congresses had been held in Europe, and, as with much of the functional international networking of that era, the initiative and energy came from nongovernmental organizations (NGOs) working closely with technical experts and government officials. In 1927 the Fifth Pan American Child Congress established an International American Institute for the Protection of Childhood, which continues to operate today as the Inter-American Children's Institute, a specialized organ of the OAS.

Although there is some overlap between children's rights and labor rights, the two fields are distinguishable. The Pan American cooperation on children is noted here because it has been more active than the labor cooperation. One reason might be is that although the multilateral ILO existed for labor issues, children's issues lacked global institutions and therefore bloomed better at the regional level. The same point can be made about the Inter-American Commission on Women, founded in 1928, which preceded and inspired later developments at the global level.[13]

[9] Convention on the Practice of Learned Professions, 27 January 1902, 6 Martens (3d) 191.

[10] *The International Conferences of American States, supra* note 6, at 260–6.

[11] Manley O. Hudson (ed.), *International Legislation*, Vol. II, at 901 *et seq.*

[12] Seventh International Conference of American States, 'Fifth, Sixth and Seventh Committees' (1933), at 59–60.

[13] Myres S. McDougal, Harold D. Lasswell, and Lung-chu Chen, *Human Rights and World Public Order* (Yale 1980), at 644–5.

The Sixth Pan American (Havana) Conference of 1928 approved a resolution on Emigration and Immigration, which called for the principle of equality of civil rights as between nationals and foreigners.[14] The entire immigration issue proved controversial, however, as states jealously guarded their autonomy. For example, the United States insisted that 'the control of immigration is a matter of purely domestic concern'.[15] Yet some states saw a common interest in more open borders. For instance, El Salvador proposed no state not place obstacles to emigration and immigration among American states.

In 1933 the Seventh Pan American (Montevideo) Conference approved several labor-related resolutions. For example, the Conference called on governments to facilitate freedom of association, to adopt the principle of 'family income' in order to increase 'human capital', and to establish a register of immigration possibilities in each country.[16] Another resolution called for a 'Campaign Against Unemployment', including measures to facilitate local, national, and international commerce. The Conference also sought the establishment of an Inter-American Labor Institute with a mandate to develop recommendations and principles for the solution of American social problems, which were thought to have features 'distinctive from, if not in conflict with European problems' being dealt with by the ILO.[17] Among the valuable principles slated for discussion was 'that the machine must be considered as a helper of man and not as his substitute'. For various reasons, the hopes to establish the Institute proved unsuccessful.

Attention to labor issues continued during World War II. In 1942 a Meeting of Ministers of Foreign Affairs of the American Republics made a series of recommendations, one of which was that international agreements or long-term contracts should provide 'a fair standard of wages for the workers of the Americas, in which producers are protected against competition from products originating in areas wherein real wages are unduly low'.[18] The Ministers also asked for input regarding postwar problems from the Inter-American Juridical Committee. In response, the Juridical Committee put forward several recommendations, including the need to 'guarantee to each individual a degree of economic security . . . necessary to enable him to develop his personality'.[19] With regard to its social recommendations, the Committee observed that the 'realization of these objectives is primarily the task of each separate State, but only by parallel international action can they be adequately secured'.[20]

In early 1945 the Inter-American Conference on Problems of War and Peace (known as the Mexico City or Chapultepec Conference) approved an 'Economic

---

[14] *The International Conferences of American States, supra* note 6, at 378–81.   [15] *Ibid.*, at 380.

[16] *The International Conferences of American States. First Supplement 1933–1940* (Carnegie Endowment, 1940), at 92–3, 238–40, 270.

[17] *The International Conferences, First Supplement, supra* note 16, at 39–41.

[18] Final Act of the Third Meeting of Ministers of Foreign Affairs of the American Republics, January 1942, 36 *AJIL Supp.* (1942) 61, at 64.

[19] 'Preliminary Recommendations on Postwar Problems', *International Conciliation*, No. 387 (February 1943) 101, at 125.   [20] *Ibid.*

Charter of the Americas' containing ten guiding principles. The first principle was for governments to direct economic policies

toward the creation of conditions which will encourage, through expanding domestic and foreign trade and investment, the attainment everywhere of high levels of real income, employment and consumption, free from excessive fluctuations, in order that their peoples may be adequately fed, housed, and clothed, have access to services necessary for health, education, and well-being, and enjoy the rewards of their labor in dignity and in freedom.[21]

The Conference also approved a 'Declaration of the Social Principles of America', which called on every country in the region to adopt social legislation on a scale not lower than that indicated in ILO conventions, including the recognition of the right of workers to organize, bargain collectively, and to strike.[22] This Declaration was premissed on the axiom that 'man must be the center of interest of all efforts of peoples and governments', a thought that returned like a comet fifty years later at the United Nations (UN) Copenhagen Summit.[23] The extensive language on worker rights negotiated at Mexico City is astonishing and may be explainable in part by the fact that some of the national delegations contained nongovernmental advisers from labor, social, and educational movements.[24] This inclusive form of participation was not used in subsequent conferences and is not a feature of the current FTAA negotiations.[25]

Latin American attention to the problem of unfair labor competition was brought forward into the UN Conference on Trade and Employment. This Conference drafted the Charter of the International Trade Organization (ITO), but it did not go into force. As one of the drafters has chronicled, there was a demand from a number of Latin American countries that each government should be relieved of trade obligations toward countries having lower labor conditions.[26] Although this effort to

---

[21] Final Act of the Inter-American Conference on Problems of War and Peace (Pan American Union, 1945), Res. LI, 92, at 94–6. This was a conference of wartime allies that excluded Argentina because of its neutrality.

[22] Final Act, *supra* note 21, Res. LVIII, 102, at 104–5. This was three years before the adoption of the ILO Convention on Freedom of Association and the Right to Organise (No. 87).

[23] Compare: 'To this end, we will create a framework for action to: (a) Place people at the centre of development and direct our economies to meet human needs more effectively' (World Summit for Social Development, Copenhagen Declaration on Social Development, 12 March 1995, UN Doc. A/CONF.166/9, para. 26(a)).

[24] Inman, *supra* note 4, at 212. The nongovernmental advisers also sought to influence the negotiations on trade. For example, the US government's proposal for reciprocal tariff reductions was opposed by the Mexican trade unions who argued that the United States had relied upon tariffs to protect domestic industries during its own industrial development. *Ibid.*, at 215.

[25] Several years ago, Brazil sought a role for labor representatives in national delegations to the FTAA talks, but gave up after opposition by the Clinton Administration and other governments. Kevin G. Hall, 'Brazil Drops Demand for Labor at Trade Talks', *Journal of Commerce* (15 May 1997), 5A.

[26] Clair Wilcox, *A Charter for World Trade* (MacMillan, 1949), at 139.

adopt a labor escape clause failed, the ensuing ITO Charter did include a provision on fair labor standards.[27]

Labor has always been an OAS issue. The OAS Charter was drafted in 1948 at the Ninth Pan American (Bogotá) Conference.[28] The original OAS Charter contained two articles on Social Standards, one of which sought 'respect for freedom of association and for the dignity of the worker'.[29] The current Charter contains more elaborate provisions regarding labor.[30] For example, the governments have agreed to make the greatest possible efforts to harmonize social legislation of the developing countries, so that the rights of workers will be equally protected, and in order to facilitate the process of Latin American and Caribbean integration. In addition, the OAS spearheaded the American Convention on Human Rights of 1969, which features several labor rights provisions.[31]

The OAS has been very active in the period from 1994 onward. One key landmark was the adoption, on September 11, 2001, of the Inter-American Democratic Charter. Declaring that 'the peoples of the Americas have a right to democracy', the Charter contains numerous important commitments and statements, including that the strengthening of democracy 'requires the full and effective exercise of workers' rights and the application of core labor standards' recognized in the ILO.[32]

So far, my study has examined the labor facets of Inter-American political relations, but two other ongoing streams of regional labor cooperation should be considered. One has been carried out under the auspices of the ILO. The other operates within the framework of the Inter-American system.

One interesting footnote of ILO history is that the opening session of its inaugural 1919 conference was held in the ornate Hall of the Americas at the Pan American Union building in Washington, D.C. The Executive Officer of the Union welcomed the ILO and expressed hope that the thirty years of Pan American cooperation

---

[27] Havana Charter for an International Trade Organization, March 1948, Art. 7, available at: http://www.worldtradelaw.net. Susan Ariel Aaronson, *Taking Trade to the Streets: The Lost History of Public Efforts to Shape Globalization* (University of Michigan Press, 2001), at 52–3; Elissa Alben, 'GATT and the Fair Wage: A Historical Perspective on the Labor–Trade Link', 101 *Columbia Law Review* (2001) 1410, at 1427–41 (reviewing the negotiations and efforts to implement them).

[28] This Conference also approved the American Declaration of the Rights and Duties of Man that contains several provisions on labor and employment. See http://www1.umn.edu/humanrts/oasinstr/zoas2dec.htm. Among its provisions is the statement that 'It is the duty of every person to work, as far as his capacity and possibilities permit, in order to obtain the means of livelihood or to benefit his community.' *Ibid.*, Art. XXXVII.

[29] Charter of the OAS, 30 April 1948, 119 UNTS 3, Arts. 28, 29.

[30] Charter of the OAS, available at: http://www.oas.org, Arts. 34(g), 45, 46.

[31] See American Convention on Human Rights, 22 November 1969, available at: http://www.cidh.oas.org/Basicos/basic2.htm, Arts. XIV, XVI, XXII. Robert F. Drinan, *The Mobilization of Shame* (Yale, 2001), at 112–17 (discussing the Inter-American human rights regime).

[32] Inter-American Democratic Charter, available at: http://www.oas.org/charter/docs, Arts. 1, 10. The first initiative to promote democracy in Latin America may have been the effort of Pedro Felix Vicuña in 1837. Kathryn Sikkink, 'Reconceptualizing Sovereignty in the Americas: Historical Precursors and Current Practices', 19 *Houston Journal of International Law* (1997) 705, at 713.

would inspire the ILO.[33] At the 1919 Conference, there were delegations from sixteen Latin American countries.[34]

Since 1936, there have been fifteen Labour Conferences of the American States. Like all ILO activities, these were tripartite conferences with national participation by governments, workers, and employers. While many of the resolutions adopted were trained on industrial relations, some also covered international trade policy. For example, in 1939, a resolution on Economic and Financial Cooperation observed that 'an increase in international trade activity is calculated to promote an improvement in standards of life' and also recommended that 'credit arrangements concluded between nations of the American continent should make provision for the effective enforcement of fair labour standards upon all work financed in virtue of such agreements'.[35] The 1946 Conference approved a resolution on Vocational Training that went well beyond the existing ILO recommendation in addressing the need for 'training and retraining of adult workers'.[36] The 1949 Conference approved a resolution on the Social Aspects of Economic Development that called for measures to promote the expansion of markets by the development of international trade and urged the ILO to cooperate with the Economic Commission for Latin America and the International Trade Organization.[37] The resolution further stated that technical assistance directed to the social aspects of economic development should form an integral part of any program of technical assistance furnished through international organizations. In a survey of the first forty years of ILO work in Latin America, Jef Rens concluded that ILO conventions and technical assistance had an important influence on national law.[38]

The second stream of labor cooperation is transgovernmental.[39] In 1963 the labor ministers in the Americas began to hold conferences of their own as an outgrowth of the Alliance for Progress. The 1963 Conference agreed on several principles, including that financial aid and trade policy should be integrated, and that measures be taken to stabilize Latin America's foreign exchange earnings. Another principle enunciated was that there can be no effective economic and social development planning unless the legitimate rights of labor are recognized.[40] At the Fourth

---

[33] League of Nations, *International Labor Conference, First Annual Meeting* (GPO, 1920), at 11–12.

[34] Jef Rens, 'Latin America and the International Labour Organisation', 80 *International Labour Review* (1959) 1, at 2.

[35] *Second Labour Conference of the American States which are Members of the International Labour Organisation* (ILO, 1941), Res. XII, 262, at 263.

[36] *Third Labour Conference of the American States which are Members of the International Labour Organisation* (ILO, 1946), Res. 1, 270, at 274. Compare to the ILO Vocation Training Recommendation (No. 57), 1939.

[37] *Fourth Labour Conference of American States Members of the International Labour Organisation* (ILO, 1951), Res. 7, 263, at 268.

[38] Rens, *supra* note 34. He quotes a Colombian government official as saying in 1933 that legislative provisions for the protection of workers' rights in Latin America 'is due exclusively to Geneva'. *Ibid.*, at 19.

[39] The cooperation on labor is not formally part of the OAS. Similarly, the FTAA negotiations do not belong to the OAS. Based on interviews with OAS officials Eduardo Mendoza and José Manuel Salazar.

[40] Inter-American Conference of Ministers of Labor on the Alliance for Progress (OAS, 1963), at 48–9.

Conference in 1972, the labor ministers called attention to the 'gravity of the social problems affecting American countries and the urgency of social development that goes beyond the criteria of the economists'.[41] The Conferences over the next twenty years left little record.

Labor cooperation was reinvigorated by the 1st Summit of the Americas in 1994 and by the initiation of the FTAA process. These two developments breathed new relevance into the conferences of the Ministers of Labor by giving them an additional mission—to provide a channel for labor concerns outside of trade negotiations. The 10th Labor Conference, held in 1995, set up a working group to prepare a submission to the Ministers of Trade.[42] This declaration was presented to the 3rd FTAA ministerial in 1997. One of the suggestions made was that the FTAA should introduce 'a social dimension that guarantees, as a minimum, respect for basic labor standards'.[43] In 1998 the 2nd Summit of the Americas adopted a Plan of Action stating that the governments would exchange informational materials regarding their labor legislation and further secure the observance and promotion of internationally recognized core labor standards.[44] Shortly thereafter, the governments held the 11th Labour Conference, which stated that the policies that form the basis of economic growth, including free international trade, should be designed in a way that produces more jobs consistent with internationally recognized core labor standards.[45] In 2001 the 3rd Summit of the Americas adopted a Plan of Action with broad but general language on 'Labor and Employment'. Shortly thereafter, the 12th Labour Conference established two working groups—one on the Labour Dimensions of the Summit of the Americas Process and the other on Building Capacity of Labour Ministries.[46] The 13th Labor Conference of 2003 adopted the Salvador Declaration, which emphasizes the importance of considering the social and labor components of hemispheric integration during all stages of the FTAA negotiations process.[47]

Notwithstanding the repeated efforts of the labor ministers to signal that labor concerns should be addressed in FTAA talks, the most recent declaration adopted by the FTAA trade ministers (in November 2003) omits any labor dimension for the

---

[41] Fourth Conference, Final Act, OAS Doc. Ser.C/VI.16.4, November 1972, para. 5.

[42] The labor minister conferences benefit from two advisory committees, from trade unions and from business.

[43] Declaration of the Tenth Inter-American Conference of Ministers of Labor Presented at the Meeting of Ministers of Trade, Belo Horizonte, Brazil, May 1997, available at: http://www.sice.oas.org/FTAA/Belo/Minis/Cotpal_e.asp.

[44] Second Summit of the Americas, Plan of Action, April 1998. This and other Summit documents not specifically referenced here are available at: http://www.summit-americas.org.

[45] Declaration of Viña del Mar, 21 October 1998, OAS Trabadjo/doc.5/98 Rev. 2, para. 4.

[46] Declaration and Plan of Action of Ottawa, 2001, available at: http://www.oas.org/udse/ingles2004/frameset.html.

[47] 13th Inter-American Conference of Ministers of Labor, Salvador Declaration, 26 September 2003, para. 22, available at: http://www.summit-americas.org/Quebec-Labor/labor-eng.htm.

negotiations.[48] So far, no government has made a substantive labor proposal for the FTAA.

In summary, this historical glance back provides context for thinking about the labor and trade connection in the Western Hemisphere. Achieving an FTAA would be the fruition of efforts for trade integration that began in the early nineteenth century. Inter-American attention to employment and labor extends back to the early twentieth century, and the principle that there are common labor norms is well embedded. The idea that core labor standards should undergird trade liberalization has been part of trade discourse in the Americas since the 1940s. Nevertheless, consideration of labor as part of the FTAA negotiation has been resisted by nearly all countries, which have instead preferred to address labor via a network of labor ministries.[49] The inclusion of labor within an FTAA would be a dead letter were it not for the fact that gaining provisions on labor is one of the statutory trade negotiation objectives of the United States.[50]

2. HOW FREE TRADE AGREEMENTS ADDRESS LABOR

Any forthcoming labor dimension to the FTAA will be influenced by the existing law and practice of free trade agreements in the region. Part 2 will provide an overview of that varied experience. Some treaties, such as the recent Free Trade Agreement between Chile and South Korea, completely omit labor.[51] Yet many trade agreements do include labor, and this practice began with the North American Free Trade Agreement (NAFTA) which was accompanied by a side agreement on labor. The three parties in NAFTA are Canada, Mexico, and the United States.

The experience so far is summarized in Table One, 'Comparison of Key Labor Features of Selected Inter-American Free Trade Agreements'. The agreements are listed chronologically from left to right. One conclusion that can be drawn from Table One is that there is no optimal treatment of labor in the sense of an agreement that is more progressive than the others in every way. The purely American agreements do more on transparency and access to courts, while the agreement with

---

[48] 8th FTAA Ministerial Declaration, November 2003, available at: http://www.ftaa-alca.org. This Declaration expresses appreciation to the labor ministers for their input. An earlier FTAA ministerial declaration had stated that most ministers recognize that the issues of environment and labor should not be utilized as conditionalities nor be subject to disciplines. 6th FTAA Ministerial Declaration, April 2001, Annex I, para. 1, available at: http://www.ftaa-alca.org/Ministerials/BA/BA_e.asp.

[49] José Manuel Salazar-Xirinachs and Jorge Mario Martínez-Piva, 'Trade, Labour Standards and Global Governance: A Perspective from the Americas', in Stefan Griller (ed.), *International Economic Governance and Non-Economic Concerns* (Springer Verlag Wien, 2003) 315, at 336, 354.

[50] 19 USC § 3802(b)(11). See Robert B. Zoellick, 'When Trade Leads to Tolerance', *New York Times*, 12 June 2004, A13 ('The United States is the only nation pressing to include enforceable labor and environmental protections in its trade agreements').

[51] Free Trade Agreement between the Republic of Korea and the Republic of Chile, 15 February 2003, available at: http://www.sice.oas.org/Trade/Chi-SKorea_e.

Table One *Comparison of key labor features of selected inter-American free trade agreements*

	NAFTA Labor Side Agreement[1]	Canada–Chile Labour Side Agreement[2]	Canada–Costa Rica Labour Side Agreement[3]	Association Agreement between EC and Chile[4]	US–Chile Free Trade Agreement[5]
Requires public notice of national law	Yes[6]	Yes[7]	Yes[8]	No	Yes[9]
Requires access to justice in national court	Yes[10]	Yes[11]	Yes[12]	No	Yes[13]
Creates international commission to promote cooperation	Yes[14]	No[15]	No[16]	No[17]	No[18]
Creates transnational public labor advisory committee to treaty parties	No	No	No	Yes[19]	No
Nature of central labor obligation	Effectively enforce narrow range of national labor law[20]	Effectively enforce narrow range of national labor law[21]	Effectively enforce broad range of national labor law[22]	Engage in social dialogue, social cooperation, public administration cooperation, and cooperation to prevent illegal immigration[23]	Effectively enforce limited range of national labor law[24]
How central labor obligation is adjudicated	State-to-state dispute settlement[25]	State-to-state dispute settlement[26]	State-to-state dispute settlement[27]	None	State-to-state dispute settlement[28]
Compliance procedure following adjudication	Monetary enforcement assessment and trade sanction (with Canada exception)[29]	Monetary enforcement assessment and national court order[30]	None	N/A	Monetary assessment that can be collected through a trade sanction[31]

Individual right to seek investigation from international body	No[32]	No[33]	No[34]	No	No[35]

[1] The North American Free Trade Agreement (NAFTA) has a side agreement on labor called the North American Agreement on Labor Cooperation (NAALC), 14 September 1993. This and all the trade agreements discussed in this chart are available at: http://www.sice.oas.org/trade.

[2] Agreement on Labour Cooperation between Canada and Chile (Canada–Chile Side Agreement), 6 February 1997.

[3] Agreement on Labor Cooperation between Canada and Costa Rica (Canada–Costa Rica Side Agreement), 23 April 2001.

[4] Agreement Establishing an Association between the European Community and its Member States, of the one part and the Republic of Chile, of the other part (EC–Chile Association Agreement), 18 November 2002.

[5] United States–Chile Free Trade Agreement (US–Chile FTA), 6 June 2003.

[6] NAALC, 14 September 1993, Arts. 6, 7.

[7] Canada–Chile Side Agreement, Arts. 6, 7.

[8] Canada–Costa Rica Side Agreement, Arts. 7, 8.

[9] US–Chile FTA, Art. 20.3.

[10] NAALC, Arts. 4, 5.

[11] Canada–Chile Side Agreement, Arts. 4, 5.

[12] Canada–Costa Rica Side Agreement, Arts. 5, 6.

[13] US–Chile FTA, Arts. 18.3, 20.4, 20.5.

[14] NAALC, Art. 8.

[15] Creates a Commission, but in name only with no independent existence. Canada–Chile Side Agreement, Art. 8.

[16] Creates a Ministerial Council of Labor Ministers. Canada–Costa Rica Side Agreement, Art. 9.

[17] Creates an Association Committee of governmental representatives. EC–Chile Association Agreement, Art. 6.

[18] Creates a Labor Affairs Council at cabinet level and creates a Labor Cooperation Mechanism of Ministries of Labor. US–Chile FTA, Arts. 18.4, 18.5.

[19] EC–Chile Association Agreement, Arts. 9 (parliamentary cooperation), 10, 48.

[20] NAALC, Arts. 3, 29. Covered labor laws include only occupational safety and health, child labor, and minimum wage, and must be mutually recognized. The cause of action is a persistent pattern of failure to enforce that is trade-related.

[21] Canada–Chile Side Agreement, Arts. 3, 26. Covered labor laws include only occupational safety and health, child labor, and minimum wage, and must be mutually recognized. The cause of action is a persistent pattern of failure to enforce that is trade-related.

[22] Canada–Costa Rica Side Agreement, Arts. 4, 15. Covered labor laws broadly include freedom of association, the right to organize, the right to collective bargaining, the right to strike, prohibition of forced labor, labor protections for children, elimination of discrimination, and equal pay for women and men. Excludes minimum employment standards, occupational injury and illness, and worker compensation. Covered laws must be mutually recognized. The cause of action is a persistent pattern of failure to enforce that is trade-related.

[23] EC–Chile Association Agreement, Arts. 41.2(d), 43, 44, 46.

Table One (*continued*):

24 US–Chile FTA, Arts. 18.2(1). Covered labor laws include right of association, the right to organize and bargain collectively, prohibition of forced labor, labor protections for children, and acceptable conditions of work with respect to hours of work, occupational safety and health, and enforcement of minimum wage. Does not include the elimination of workplace discrimination. The cause of action is a sustained or recurring course of action to fail to effectively enforce labor laws in a manner affecting trade.

25 NAALC Arts. 23–29. Before invoking dispute settlement, a complaining party must first seek an analysis by an Evaluation Committee of Experts.

26 Canada–Chile Side Agreement, Arts. 21–26. Before invoking dispute settlement, a complaining party must first seek an analysis by an Evaluation Committee of Experts.

27 Canada–Costa Rica Side Agreement, Arts. 15–23.

28 US–Chile FTA, Art. 22.6.

29 NAALC, Arts. 39, 41. For Canada, treaty enforcement can be undertaken in national court. No trade sanctions are available against Canada.

30 Canada–Chile Side Agreement, Arts. 34–37. The provisions seem to suggest that a national court could order not only payment of the assessment but also improved national labor law enforcement.

31 US–Chile FTA, Art. 22.16. The assessment is an absolute amount not adjusted for the size of the economy and is limited to $15 million. If paid, the assessment is to expended to improve labor law enforcement in the violating country.

32 Each party shall create a National Administrative Office that may receive public communications. NAALC, Art. 16.3.

33 Each party shall create a National Secretariat that may receive public communications. Canada–Chile Side Agreement, Art. 14.3.

34 Each party shall receive public communications. Canada–Costa Rica Side Agreement, Art. 11.

35 Each party shall receive public communications. US–Chile FTA, Art. 18.4(7).

the European Community is more attentive to public participation and discourse. The only agreement to create an international commission to promote cooperation is the North American Agreement on Labor Cooperation (NAALC) in 1993. The other agreements promote cooperation through meetings of national officials.

As Table One shows, none of the provisions on labor is subject to adjudication except for the obligation that governments avoid a trade-related persistent pattern of failure to effectively enforce *national* labor law. The obligation to enforce national labor law is supervised through state-to-state dispute settlement rather than by giving victims a right of action. If a complaining government lodges a dispute and wins, the scofflaw government would be expected to improve its national enforcement and if it does not, a monetary assessment can be imposed. Two of the agreements provide for a trade sanction—a withdrawal of trade agreement benefits—to promote compliance.

A requirement to enforce national law is a puzzling objective in an international agreement. The traditional approach in conventional international law is to promote a convergence and uplifting of national law. Certainly, that is the stance taken by the ILO since 1919.[52]

The idea of using an international agreement to supervise the enforcement of national labor law began with the NAFTA side agreement in 1993. This agreement was orchestrated by the Clinton administration, which often pursued minimalist approaches to policy challenges. The proposition that Country A has an interest in whether Country B enforces its national labor law, irrespective of the content of Country B's labor law, is hardly self-evident. Certainly, one can imagine situations where B's law would be so repugnant to A that A might not want B to enforce it. B's law might also be inefficiently rigid, and so B may have a good reason not to enforce it. Many governments allow outdated laws to remain on the books.

Nevertheless, one should not controvert the possibility of constructive results from a process of reciprocal review of national enforcement. The actual results of the process need to be examined. No empirical study has come to my attention of changes in the quality of labor law enforcement in North America over the past ten years. But data are available about the implementation of the side agreement.[53]

The NAFTA labor side agreement has been in effect since January 1994, and in over ten years, no government has brought a case against another government's lack

---

[52] Nicolas Valticos, 'Droits de l'homme et droits du travail sur le plan international', in *Droits Syndical et Droits de l'homme à l'aube du XXIe siecle: Mélanges en l'honneur de Jean-Maurice Verdier* (Dalloz, 2001), at 473. See also ILO Convention Concerning Night Work in Bakeries (No. 20), 8 June 1925, Art. 5 (calling on parties to ensure that *its* prohibition 'is effectively enforced').

[53] No consensus exists about the value of the NAFTA labor agreement. Many analysts have commended it: see Frederick M. Abbott, 'The North American Integration Regime and its Implications for the World Trading System', J. H. H. Weiler (ed.), *The EU, the WTO and the NAFTA: Towards a Common Law of International Trade* (Oxford, 2001) 169, at 196–7; Ronald G. Ehrenberg, *Labor Markets and Integrating National Economies* (Brookings, 1994), at 98–9; William B. Gould IV, 'Labor Law for a Global Economy: The Uneasy Case for International Labor Standards', in Robert J. Flanagan and William B. Gould IV (eds.), *International Labor Standards* (Stanford University Press, 2003), 81, at 104–5; Marley S. Weiss, 'Two Steps Forward, One Step Back—Or Vice Versa: Labor Rights under Free Trade Agreements from NAFTA, through

of enforcement of the covered labor laws. Many informed observers have concluded that the NAFTA parties all live in glass houses with regard to labor rights, and so would be uninterested in throwing stones at the others. For that reason, the three governments are also uninterested in amending the side agreement to allow individuals to lodge complaints to an international tribunal.

The side agreement does allow individuals to send communications about national enforcement problems, and twenty-eight have been sent.[54] Little has happened as a result, however, except for some joint statements and remedial seminars. Of course, the fact that the enforcement provisions have proved a nullity does not mean that the side agreement is unsuccessful. Overall, the experiment has proved useful in creating an international commission to promote North American labor cooperation.

Unfortunately, that institutional centerpiece was omitted from the US–Chile Free Trade Agreement. All that free trade agreement (FTA) does is to copy the problematic enforcement provisions from the NAFTA side agreement. At the time of the NAFTA negotiation, the ILO Declaration on Fundamental Principles and Rights at Work did not yet exist.[55] The US–Chile FTA takes note of the Declaration, but does not mandate that governments follow it.[56]

The unratified US–Central America Free Trade Agreement (CAFTA) adopts the same approach of supervising the enforcement of national law.[57] Kimberly Elliott calls this the 'enforce-your-own-laws' standard and worries that it could discourage improvements in labor law if a government feels unable to enforce even its existing

---

Jordan, via Chile to Latin America, and Beyond', 37 *University of San Francisco Law Review* (2003) 689, at 700–7 (discussing the NAFTA 'innovation' of transposing domestic law into a trilateral agreement).

Others analysts have criticized the agreement: see 'Labor Agreement Process Criticized for Failure to Protect Workers' Rights', *BNA Daily Report for Executives*, 2 April 2004, A–10; William Dymond, 'Core Labour Standards and the World Trade Organization: Labour's Love Lost', 8 *Canadian Foreign Policy* (Spring 2001) 99, at 102; Pharis J. Harvey and Bama Athreya, 'Developing Effective Mechanisms for Implementing Labor Rights in the Global Economy', *Workers in the Global Economy* (Cornell University School of Industrial and Labor Relations, 2001) 1, at 13–16; Laura Okin Pomeroy, 'The Labor Side Agreement under the NAFTA: Analysis of its Failure to Include Strong Enforcement Provisions and Recommendations for Future Labor Agreements Negotiated with Developing Countries', 29 *George Washington Journal of International Law and Economics* (1996) 769; Katherine Van Wezel Stone, 'Labor and the Global Economy: Four Approaches to Transnational Labor Regulation', 16 *Michigan Journal of International Law* (1995) 987, at 1010 (noting that it is difficult to imagine any situation in which the side agreement's procedures for obtaining labor law enforcement would apply).

[54] Commission for Labor Cooperation, Summary of Communications, March 2004, available at: http://www.naalc.org/english/naalc.shtml.

[55] For a discussion of the 1998 Declaration, see Kari Tapiola, 'The ILO Declaration on Fundamental Principles and Rights at Work and its Follow-up', in Roger Blanpain (ed.), *Multinational Enterprises and the Social Changes of the XXIst Century* (Kluwer, 2000) 9.

[56] The US–Chile FTA calls on governments to 'strive to ensure' that municipal law is consonant with the ILO Declaration, but this provision is not subject to dispute settlement. US–Chile Free Trade Agreement, 6 June 2003, available at: http://www.ustr.gov, Art. 18.1.

[57] Central America Free Trade Agreement (CAFTA), 28 May 2004 (not in force), available at: http://www.ustr.gov, Chap. 16.

laws.[58] Senator John F. Kerry has pledged to revise the CAFTA's labor chapter if elected President.[59] Unlike NAFTA, CAFTA does not set up a labor commission.

The absence of aspirations for labor law harmonization in Inter-American FTAs can be contrasted with the pro-active approach taken with other economic objectives. This disparity is demonstrated by Table Two, a synoptic 'Comparison of Major Features of the North American Free Trade Agreement and Side Agreements'. NAFTA's provisions on market access, investment, and intellectual property commit the governments to follow NAFTA norms as prescribed or as incorporated by reference from other international treaties. For example, the commitment for intellectual property is not merely to enforce each country's own national law. Instead, the governments seek much deeper harmonization, by obliging each government to give rights to private parties in specified forms of intellectual property. By contrast, for labor and the environment, the NAFTA regime seeks only to reinforce the existing national law rather than to improve it.[60] Referring to this double standard in US trade agreements, Kimberly Elliott and Richard Freeman observe that 'If capital needs international protection from potentially corrupt and rapacious government officials, surely so does labor.'[61] The rationale for treating labor (and environment) differently from the other harmonization is not explained within the NAFTA side agreements or in newer FTAs with that same orientation, such as the US–Chile FTA. Perhaps revealing the insufficiency of the stated labor objectives of recent FTAs, US Trade Representative Robert B. Zoellick has sought public credit for coaxing other countries to raise their laws *during* the trade negotiations.[62]

The absence of any labor litigation under the NAFTA side agreement does not result from a lack of litigiousness among NAFTA's stakeholders. On the contrary, since the time that NAFTA went into force in 1994, there have been five commercial complaints brought by governments, ninety-four commercial complaints brought by private parties, and thirty-five investment complaints brought by private parties.[63] Thus, a reasonable hypothesis might be that if the NAFTA labor agreement

---

[58] Kimberly Ann Elliott, 'Labor Standards, Development, and CAFTA', *Institute for International Economics Policy Brief*, March 2004, at 6.

[59] Neil King Jr., 'Kerry Would Seek Tighter Standards Governing CAFTA', *Wall Street Journal*, 1 June 2004, A6.

[60] Both NAFTA side agreements contain hortatory provisions calling on parties to provide 'high levels of environmental protection' and 'high labor standards', and to strive for improvement. North American Agreement on Environmental Cooperation (NAAEC), 14 September 1993, Art. 3; NAALC Art. 2. Furthermore, the NAALC includes a list of 'Labor Principles' that parties are committed to promote, subject to each party's own domestic labor law. NAALC Annex 1.

[61] Kimberly Ann Elliott and Richard B. Freeman, *Can Labor Standards Improve under Globalization?* (Institute for International Economics, 2003), at 11.

[62] For example, Zoellick has stated that Chile repealed Pinochet-era labor laws during the course of the FTA negotiations and that Guatemala improved the implementation of labor laws in export processing zones. See Robert B. Zoellick, 'Helping Labor Through Trade', *Washington Post*, 19 April 2004, A19.

[63] Author's tabulations of data available on 30 May 2004 from: http://www.nafta-sec-alena.org and http://www.naftalaw.org.

Table Two *Comparison of major features of the North American Free Trade Agreement and Side Agreements*

	Market Access	Investment	Intellectual Property	Environment	Labor
Nature of central obligation(s)	Follow NAFTA norms[1]	Follow NAFTA norms and international law[2]	Follow NAFTA norms and designated treaties[3]	Effectively enforce national environmental law[4]	Effectively enforce narrow range of national labor law[5]
How central obligation is adjudicated	State-to-state dispute settlement and producer-to-state dispute settlement[6]	Investor-to-state arbitration (and state-to-state also possible)	State-to-state dispute settlement	State-to-state dispute settlement	State-to-state dispute settlement[7]
Individual right to seek enforcement of treaty obligations	No	Yes[8]	No	No, but individual may make submission to international commission[9]	No, but individual may make submission to National office[10]
Compliance procedure following adjudication	Trade sanction[11]	National court[12]	Trade sanction[13]	Monetary enforcement assessment and trade sanction (with Canada exception)[14]	Monetary enforcement assessment and trade sanction (with Canada exception)[15]

[1] North American Free Trade Agreement (NAFTA), 17 December 1992. The NAFTA and all the agreements discussed in this chart are available at http://www.sice.oas.org/trade/nafta. The obligations extend only to other parties, not vertically down to domestic persons who may want to import or export.

[2] NAFTA, Arts. 1104, 1105. The obligations extend only to investors of the other parties, not vertically down to domestic investors.

[3] NAFTA, chap. 17. The provisions are written vaguely but would seem to commit a government to provide rights to its own nationals as well as to nationals of the other parties.

[4] North American Agreement on Environment Cooperation (NAAEC), 14 September 1993, Arts. 5, 24, 45. Coverage excludes the management of commercial or aboriginal harvest of natural resources.

5 North American Agreement on Labor Cooperation (NAALC), 14 September 1993, Arts. 3, 29, 49. Covered labor laws include only occupational safety and health, child labor, and minimum wage, and must be mutually recognized.

6 NAFTA, chaps. 19, 20.

7 Before invoking dispute settlement, a complaining party must first seek an analysis by an Evaluation Committee of Experts. NAALC, Arts. 23–27.

8 NAFTA, Art. 1116.

9 NAAEC, Art. 14.

10 NAALC, Art. 16.3.

11 NAFTA, Art. 2019.

12 NAFTA, Art. 1136.4.

13 NAFTA, Art. 2019.

14 NAAEC, Arts. 34, 36. For Canada, treaty enforcement can be undertaken in national court. No trade sanctions are available against Canada.

15 NAALC, Arts. 39, 41. For Canada, treaty enforcement can be undertaken in national court. No trade sanctions are available against Canada.

contained a meaningful discipline and a private right of action, numerous cases would have been filed.

NAFTA is not the only Inter-American trade agreement with a labor dimension.[64] The Common Market of the South (Mercosur) also has given attention to social problems. The activities in Mercosur feature tripartite consultation and the collection and analysis of data. In the Andean Community, there are regular meetings of the ministers of labor.

The overall topic addressed by this study is whether the FTAA *should* contain rules on labor and, if so, what they ought to be. No optimal architecture exists for FTAs. Rather, the right design depends on what policymakers seek to achieve. Unless governments are willing to provide a private right of action to an international tribunal, however, no labor policy purpose is served by the current FTA approach of committing governments to enforce their own idiosyncratic labor laws. The only purpose being served by these labor provisions is to satisfy the political need of appearing to use the FTA to safeguard worker rights.

That an international commitment to enforce one's own domestic law makes little sense does not necessarily justify the alternative approach of including within an FTA an obligation to follow international labor standards. On the contrary, it would seem that if Countries A, B, C, etc. have an interest in upwardly harmonizing their labor policies, that goal might be better accomplished through a *labor* rather than a trade agreement. As Table One shows, some of the earlier Inter-American FTAs took the approach of having a separate labor agreement, but that configuration has now been abandoned (at least by the United States) in an effort to give trade agreements a holistic veneer. What seems to be driving the current US effort to incorporate labor provisions into FTAs is not to achieve benefits of labor cooperation, but rather to show that trade concessions will be withdrawable should the labor commitment be violated. That logic relates to political coalition building more than to economic coherence. Part 3 of this study will discuss the economic coherence of sole labor and trade-related labor cooperation, as well as the political foundations for intergovernmental labor cooperation.

Before moving to Part 3, this chapter will address one other matter, which is the tension between regional and multilateral initiative. If countries in the Americas want to foster worker rights and improve labor standards, then why not just do that through the ILO?[65] The answer is that international labor cooperation can be pursued on a dual track—globally at the ILO and regionally in various fora. The

---

[64] See American Center for International Labor Solidarity, *Justice for All: A Guide to Worker Rights in the Global Economy* (AFL-CIO, 2003), at 128–38; ILO, *Labour Standards and the Integration Process in the Americas* (2001); Marie-Claire Cordonier Segger, 'Inter-American Perspective: Sustainable Development in the Negotiation of the FTAA', 27 *Fordham International Law Journal* (2004) 1118, at 1140–56; Willi Momm (ed.), *Labour Issues in the Context of Economic Integration and Free Trade—A Caribbean Perspective* (ILO, 1999).

[65] Robert M. Stern, 'Labor Standards and Trade Agreements', University of Michigan Discussion Paper No. 496, 2003, at 21.

periodic ILO regional conferences are aimed at capacity building and strengthening of the multilateral system; they do not seek separate labor conventions.[66]

The orientation is different in the trade arena where regional efforts sometimes take the shape of preferential trade agreements. These are discriminatory regimes that may or may not be supportive of the multilateral World Trade Organization (WTO).[67] In general, a regional trade agreement can never rank higher than second best to a multilateral agreement.[68] The nature of trade and the need for cooperation is exactly the same in one region as in another.

By contrast, the rationale for a regional labor agreement can be stronger than for a regional trade agreement if a regional labor market exists or if a region has a distinctive pattern of industrial relations. In such instances, there may be a need for a discrete policy in one region that would not be appropriate in another region, or globally. More likely, however, the justification for including labor rules in a regional FTA will be to achieve a more balanced agreement. According to the World Commission on the Social Dimension of Globalization, 'if regional integration is to be a stepping stone towards a fairer globalization, a strong social dimension is required'.[69]

3. NORMATIVE BASIS FOR INTERNATIONAL LABOR COOPERATION

Part 3 discusses the conceptual underpinning of a labor dimension to the FTAA. Because labor law is so contested, this case will be constructed from the bottom up. First, I review the need for national labor law. Second, I explain the need for international labor law. Third, I consider whether labor objectives should be sought in a trade versus a labor agreement.

A. Why National Labor Law?

National labor law is aimed at achieving three distinct objectives—correcting market failure, protecting against government abuse, and enhancing equity. These concerns exist at the national level and would underlie labor law even in an imaginary world where countries shun transborder economic intercourse.[70] In the simplest vertical

---

[66] See Rens, *supra* note 34, at 6.

[67] See Jeffrey J. Schott, 'Free Trade Agreements: Boon or Bane of the World Trading System?' and the responses by Richard N. Cooper, Renato Ruggiero, and Guy de Jonquières, in Schott (ed.), *Free Trade Agreements* (Institute for International Economics, 2004), at 3–33.

[68] For a different perspective, see Sir James Goldsmith, *The Trap* (Carroll & Graf, 1993), at 43 (stating that 'We must start by rejecting the concept of global free trade and we must replace it by regional free trade').

[69] World Commission on the Social Dimension of Globalization, *A Fair Globalization* (ILO, 2004), para. 327.

[70] Contrasting autarkic with interdependent economies is helpful for analytical purposes, but there have been few instances in modern experience of autarkic economies.

model, the government regulates the private actors. In a vertical federal model, there are also allocations of authority between subnational governments and the national government.

Perhaps the most compelling reason for labor law is to correct market failures.[71] Such failures include: (1) poor information about workplace hazards, (2) imperfect competition in labor markets, (3) inadequate capital markets, which make it hard for workers to obtain education, training, and to relocate, (4) coercion of certain workers, such as children, and (5) an undersupply of quasi-public goods, such as labor–management harmony. Another problem is high unemployment, which might be considered a labor market failure in that there is a seller of labor without a buyer. Yet high unemployment also constitutes a government failure.[72] The unemployment may be caused by poor macroeconomic performance, excessive taxes or regulations on employment, or an economy inhospitable to new investment.

A second purpose of labor law is to protect individuals from mistreatment by government officials. The most serious abuses are forced labor, infringement on freedom of association, and discrimination against certain groups like indigenous persons and women. The prohibition of such behavior is often coupled with laws recognizing individual rights to be free from such practices. Governmental respect for those rights is a precondition for controlling similar abuses by private actors.

A third reason for labor law is to achieve the national conception of justice chosen through democratic processes. Labor markets are known to have inequalities in bargaining power between workers and employers.[73] This asymmetry is not necessarily a market failure—as markets are not established to achieve equity—but it is a social problem for which governments use law to remedy. For example, national labor law may provide a right to organize a labor union and to bargain collectively. Governments might also mandate a minimum quality of working conditions as a way to achieve income redistribution.

B. Why International Labor Law?

Why do governments cooperate and perceive a need to cooperate on labor issues?[74] The question is an important one and has not received the attention it

---

[71] Compare OECD, *Trade and Labour Standards: A Review of the Issues* (OECD, 1995), at 16 (stating that 'the literature on the labour standards question has not gone very far toward specifying what market failure is being corrected').

[72] Wallace McClure, *World Prosperity as Sought Through the Economic Work of the League of Nations* (Macmillan, 1933), at 65 ('The most vital national economic interest of every country is that its people shall always be efficiently at work').

[73] Lord Wedderburn, 'Common Law, Labour Law, Global Law', in Bob Hepple (ed.), *Social and Labour Rights in a Global Context* (Cambridge, 2002) 19, at 27.

[74] The question is somewhat ahistoric. The movement to enact national labor legislation does not significantly predate the movement to negotiate international conventions. See Ernest Mahaim, 'The Historical and Social Importance of International Labor Legislation', in James T. Shotwell (ed.), *The Origins of the International Labor Organization* (Columbia University Press, 1934), Vol. I, 3, at 5.

deserves.[75] Back in 1942, the Inter-American Juridical Committee acknowledged that the realization of labor objectives 'is primarily the task of each separate State', but then postulated that 'only by parallel international action can they be adequately secured'.[76] The Committee, however, did not explain why such parallel action proves useful.[77] This chapter seeks to do so.

In an autarkic economy, each nation would set its own labor law based solely on internal considerations; yet in an interdependent world economy, foreign conditions will also shape national welfare.[78] Typically, the effects of foreign conditions are transmitted through the market via cross-border trade and investment. Yet there are also some external effects that are transmitted physically.[79] For example, forced labor in Country A can send refugees to Country B; high unemployment in Country B can send migrants to Country C. Country D might be concerned about trafficking in women or children from Country E into D.

Before discussing the market-oriented factors and other rationales for international labor law, I should note that all of these explanations are state-centric. In other words, they try to explain why a government would seek coordination of labor law with another government, and would select modalities between soft norms and hard rules. Because hard rules restrict national autonomy, there is presumably a logic as to why a government would bind itself into such an arrangement. Yet sometimes, a clear logic may not be evident.

In reality, national policy may not be dictated by a rational sovereign. Instead, political processes may be driven by volitions of elites and technocrats and by pressures from interest groups. Thus, putting forward conceptual reasons why unitary governments might cooperate in labor policy may overemphasize top-down decision-making and underemphasize the economic and social actors that animate the political process.[80] Explanations of why states cooperate to liberalize trade often get stuck on the same flawed top-down orientation.

A central explanation for international labor cooperation is to prevent inefficient competition for trade and investment. This explanation is now called 'race to the

---

[75] Jan Klabbers, *An Introduction to International Institutional Law* (Cambridge, 2002), at 29 (noting that the explanation of international cooperation is one of the central questions of the social sciences).

[76] See text accompanying *supra* note 20.

[77] The proposition that the international economy necessitates international labor rules is often asserted without much explanation. For example, see J. F. Rischard, *High Noon* (Basic Books, 2002), at 146 (stating that 'the greater interdependence between countries created by the new world economy makes it more urgent to find a stronger and broader framework for labor rules than has evolved so far').

[78] See Chair's Conclusions, G8 Labor and Employment Ministers Conference, December 2003, para. 4, available at: http://www.g7.utoronto.ca ('Labor market development is shaped by many factors at both the domestic and international levels'); World Commission on the Social Dimension of Globalization, *supra* note 69, para. 493 ('Today, countries cannot achieve employment goals on their own').

[79] Compare Andrew T. Guzman, 'Trade, Labor, Legitimacy', 91 *California Law Review* (2003) 885, at 892 (stating that 'poor labor standards have virtually no harmful cross-border effects').

[80] See Richard E. Feinberg, 'The Political Economy of the United States' Free Trade Arrangements', 26 *World Economy* (2003) 1019, at 1037 ('A unitary actor model cannot explain contemporary US trade policy').

bottom'.[81] To wit, each government would like to propound good labor standards, but cannot because of competition against countries with lower labor standards. The optimal policy for each country of enjoying high standards is replaced by mutual defection, with all countries lowering their standards. The same story can be told in a less state-centric fashion by recounting the pressure that multinational corporations allegedly place on governments to lower their standards in order to attract or maintain investment.[82]

The traditional solution to this problem is that governments should agree to harmonize their core labor standards or agree on minimum standards. This is *mutually supportive cooperation* in the sense that a high labor standard in one country can help its trading partner maintain its own high standard. A bilateral agreement would make no sense if either of the two governments did not want the high standard in the first place. Mutually supportive cooperation can be distinguished from *essential cooperation*, which occurs when solving a problem requires joint action (e.g. cleaning up pollution in a border river).

The first champion of international labor law on mutually supportive grounds was the Swiss-Alsatian social reformer Daniel Legrand. In 1840 Legrand began calling for action to respond to labor 'abuses arising under the influence of competition through negotiations between the governments of industrial countries'.[83] Legrand's lobbying technique was to write a letter to a conference of the German customs union, the Zollverein, and then get the Prussian government to circulate the letter. No negotiations were undertaken by the Zollverein. Nevertheless, this episode has historical importance in showing that the earliest effort to secure international labor cooperation was linked to a trade agreement. Legrand worked nearly twenty years to promote international labor legislation, and his bust graces the lobby of the Geneva building housing the WTO.

The view that trade competition can undermine national labor standards has maintained its salience for over 160 years. In 1919 the Preamble to Part XIII (Labour) of the Treaty of Versailles famously intoned that 'the failure of any nation to adopt humane conditions of labour is an obstacle in the way of other nations which desire to improve the conditions in their own countries'.[84] As Herbert Feis

---

[81] Brian A. Langille, 'Eight Ways to Think about International Labour Standards', 31 *Journal of World Trade* (August 1997) 27, at 37–43. See also Christoph Scherrer, 'The Pros and Cons of International Labour Standards', in Norbert Malanowski (ed.), *Social and Environmental Standards in International Trade Agreements* (Westfälisches Dampfboot, 1997) 32, at 35 (stating that the threat to competitiveness is the reason why social standards have to be negotiated internationally).

[82] See Elliott and Freeman, *supra* note 61, at 23 (noting study of pressure placed on the United States).

[83] John W. Follows, *Antecedent of the International Labour Organization* (Oxford, 1951), at 28, 31, 42, 201. Before Legrand, there were others who had recognized the potential merit of international labor legislation, including Charles Hindley (then a British businessman, later a noted parliamentarian) and Jérôme Blanqui (a French economist).

[84] Treaty of Versailles, 28 June 1919, 112 BFSP 1, Part XIII preamble.

explained in 1927, the ILO was set up to help overcome the downward pressure on labor standards from international competition.[85] Similar explanations for international labor standards were offered in succeeding decades.[86]

The question of whether international competition presents a significant obstacle in reality was being debated by the 1920s.[87] Comprehensive empirical analysis did not begin until the mid-1990s, when a study by the Organisation for Economic Co-operation and Development (OECD) found no evidence that countries with low core labor standards enjoy better global export performance than countries with high standards.[88] Yet the fact that countries with high standards perform well in trade and economic growth does not mean that governments act accordingly. Governments may act irrationally. Or governments may be cowed by threats from multinational firms to relocate unless the government lowers its labor standards. Jagdish Bhagwati has pointed out that 'the evidence suggests that multinationals, generally speaking, do not go streaking to where labor rights are ignored or flouted'.[89] Yet even so, a government may still worry about the possibility that such a loss of investment could happen. As Brian Langille has observed, the threat of divestment may be much more important in labor relations than is evident in actual investment data.[90]

Fairness is another motivation for international labor standards. The fairness argument is related to, yet separable from, the efficiency argument that international competition constrains the proper setting of national labor standards. The fairness concern is that countries with high labor standards should not have to compete against countries with low standards.[91] This concern has been voiced against free

---

[85] Herbert Feis, 'International Labour Legislation in Light of Economic Theory', 1927, reprinted in Werner Sengenberger and Duncan Campbell (eds.), *International Labour Standards and Economic Interdependence* (International Institute for Labour Studies, 1994) 30, at 35.

[86] See, e.g., Miroslav Jirásek, *Principles of the Old and New Organization of the World: A Study in International Law* (Melantrich, 1945), at 195–6.

[87] See, e.g., Paul Perigord, *The International Labor Organization* (D. Appleton and Company, 1926), at 41–2.

[88] OECD, *International Trade and Core Labour Standards* (OECD, 2000), at 33. See also Toke Aidt and Zafiris Tzannatos, *Unions and Collective Bargaining* (World Bank, 2002), at 4 (noting that comparative studies reveal little systematic difference in economic performance between countries that provide for freedom of association and the right of collective bargaining, and those that do not); ILO, Report of the Director-General, *Organizing for Social Justice*, 2004, para. 50 ('A growing body of evidence suggests that freedom of association and the right to collective bargaining contribute to improving economic and trade performance and do not have the negative effects predicted by some economic theorists'), available on ILO website.   [89] Jagdish Bhagwati, *In Defense of Globalization* (Oxford, 2004), at 130.

[90] Langille, *supra* note 81, at 43. See also Terry Collingsworth, 'American Labor Policy and the International Economy: Clarifying Policies and Interests', 31 *Boston College Law Review* (1989) 31, at 45 (discussing threats to relocate).

[91] Rafael Caldera, '75 Years of ILO', in *Visions of the Future of Social Justice: Essays on the Occasion of the ILO's 75th Anniversary* (ILO, 1994) 55, at 57 (stating that 'Competition in international trade is unfair if it is based on a labour force that is ill-paid').

trade for over 150 years, and despite its incoherence—because unfairness is so subjective[92]—the fairness argument remains prominent today.

The reason why the claim of unfair trade stemming from sweated labor cannot be debunked is that the quest for fairness is a leitmotif of contemporary trade policy. Because current WTO rules seek to protect producers against injurious dumping and subsidies,[93] no way exists in principle to rule out parallel concerns about fairness to workers.[94] Brian Langille said it well: 'Fair trade is free trade's destiny.'[95]

Another problem with the unfairness claim is that Country A may have a valid reason to have a lower labor standard than Country B, and, furthermore, to use its labor standard as a way to compete against B. Deciding when regulatory labor competition is appropriate is a difficult challenge, particularly in a world in which worker exit (or more exactly, immigration) is sharply constrained.[96] An international harmonization of standards may not be better than continued diversity.[97]

The alleged unfairness of trade on labor grounds has long been used as a reason to block imports. In the nineteenth century, the concern was competition against 'pauper labor' or 'cheap labor'. In the 1920s the term 'social dumping' was applied to trade based on low labor conditions.[98] After World War II, when governments sought to establish a trading system, there were proposals to link market access to the level of labor standards. As noted above, several Latin American countries sought a labor escape clause, but this effort was resisted by the United States and others.[99]

A more refined version of the unfairness argument arose during the planning for the European common market. In 1956 the ILO established a Group of Experts to examine the social aspects of European integration. Among the Group's recommendations was that if a subset of countries agreed on the need to introduce some

---

[92] Michael J. Trebilcock, 'International Trade and International Labour Standards: Choosing Objectives, Instruments, and Institutions', in *International Economic Governance and Non-Economic Concerns, supra* note 49, 289, at 294–6 (explaining why the fairness argument is indeterminate).

[93] Douglas A. Irwin, *Free Trade under Fire* (Princeton, 2002), at 111–28 (discussing subsidies and dumping).

[94] OECD, *Regional Integration and the Multilateral Trading System* (OECD, 1995), at 22 (noting that trade liberalization agreements can no longer be concluded without taking account of sensitivities to environmental and social dumping).

[95] Brian Alexander Langille, 'General Reflections on the Relationship of Trade and Labor (Or: Fair Trade Is Free Trade's Destiny)', in Jagdish Bhagwati and Robert E. Hudec (eds.), *Fair Trade and Harmonization* (MIT Press, 1996), Vol. 2, 231, at 236.

[96] See David Charny, 'Regulatory Competition and the Global Coordination of Labor Standards', 3 *Journal of International Economic Law* (2000) 281 (discussing regulatory theory); Simon Deakin, 'Two Types of Regulatory Competition: Competitive Federalism Versus Reflexive Harmonisation', 2 *Cambridge Yearbook of European Legal Studies* (1999) 231, at 233; Gijsbert van Liemt, 'International Trade and Workers' Rights', in Brian Hocking and Steven McGuie (eds.), *Trade Politics: International, Domestic and Regional Perspectives* (Routledge, 1999) 111, at 113 (discussing labor immobility).

[97] For an early skeptical view of harmonization, see Leonard S. Woolf, *International Government* (Brentano's, 1916) 320.

[98] See Report and Proceedings of the World Economic Conference, May 1927, League of Nations Doc. C.356.M.129, 1927, Vol. II, at 100–1.   [99] See text accompanying *supra* note 26.

improvement in social or labor conditions, but, nevertheless, a minority of countries were to hold out against doing so, then a country whose interest was injured might be authorized to take steps to protect itself against competition from the holdout countries.[100] The Group further suggested that minimum labor standards be defined in an international agreement with reference to ILO conventions in order 'to eliminate international competition based on a country's failure to respect internationally agreed standards, and not to bring about a maximum of uniformity between countries'.[101] No action was taken on this recommendation.[102]

Although the concern about unfairness has been the principal rationale for a labor/trade link, there is a converse tradition of seeking to use trade liberalization as a way to induce countries to raise labor standards. The first champion was James T. Shotwell who, in 1933, proposed to US Secretary of State Cordell Hull that US tariffs be lowered against countries that were taking action to raise wages and standards of living.[103] Hull rejected the idea. Fifty years later, the idea was revived and made a feature of US trade preference programs.[104] The European Community also has incorporated a labor provision in its tariff preferences for developing countries. The Community makes available more favorable tariff treatment for countries deemed to be complying with the ILO's core labor standards.[105]

The labor provisions in contemporary FTAs are derivative of both traditions—the idea of positive incentives and the concern about trade unfairness. Yet the unfairness concerns seem more influential. After all, the cause of action in the US–Chile FTA is lax national enforcement that *affects trade* between the parties.[106] Inadequate labor law enforcement that lacks an impact on trade would not be actionable.

Another justification for international labor cooperation emphasizes the role of human resources in economic development.[107] Recall the attention to 'human

---

[100] *Social Aspects of European Economic Co-operation* (ILO, 1956), Studies and Reports, New Series, No. 46, paras. 218, 219. The Group of Experts was chaired by the Swedish economist and parliamentary leader Bertil Ohlin. For a tribute to Ohlin, see Jagdish Bhagwati, *Protectionism* (MIT Press, 1989), xi.

[101] *Social Aspects of European Economic Co-operation, supra* note 100, para. 220.

[102] Note that the Treaty of Rome of 1957 endorsed the harmonization of national social systems and established a European Social Fund. André Sapir, 'Who's Afraid of Globalization? Domestic Adjustment in Europe and America', in Roger B. Porter et al. (eds.), *Efficiency, Equity, and Legitimacy* (Brookings, 2001) 179, at 190 (discussing Arts. 117–25 of the Treaty).

[103] James T. Shotwell, *The Autobiography of James T. Shotwell* (Bobbs-Merrill, 1961), at 308.

[104] Steve Charnovitz, 'Caribbean Basin Initiative: Setting Labor Standards', 107 *Monthly Labor Review* (November 1984) 54.

[105] Council Regulation (EC) No. 2501/2001 of 10 December 2001 applying a scheme of generalized tariff preferences, OJ 2001 L 346/1.   [106] US–Chile FTA, *supra* note 56, Art. 18.2(1)(a).

[107] Sarah H. Cleveland, 'Why International Labor Standards?' in Flanagan and Gould, *supra* note 53, 129, at 139; Isobel Coleman, 'The Payoff from Women's Rights', *Foreign Affairs* (May/June 2004) 80; Ray Marshall, 'The Link between Labor Standards and Human Capital', in National Research Council, *Human Capital and Investment: Summary of a Workshop* (National Academies Press, 2003) 4; Peter Morici, *Labor Standards in the Global Trading System* (Economic Strategy Institute, 2001), at 43; Sandra Polaski, *Trade and Labor Standards: A Strategy for Developing Countries* (Carnegie Endowment for International Peace, 2003) 17.

capital' at the Pan American Conference of 1933. Promoting fuller employment and better working conditions in each country is in the interest of all because national prosperity has positive spillovers. Once best practices toward human resource development and workplace regulation are determined, then governments will benefit from widespread adoption of such practices.[108]

Note that this rationale may explain why governments cooperate, but does not fully explain why governments would bind themselves in international conventions. One explanation offered by political economists is that a breakdown in the domestic political process may prevent governments from enacting legislation to correct a market failure.[109] An international requirement to do so is therefore politically useful for a government to seek and accept. The Japanese term 'gaiatsu' is sometimes employed to describe this strategic use of foreign pressure for domestic reform. The same idea of an external normative push appeared in the 1956 report by the ILO Group of Experts, which explained that 'If international agreement can be reached that the introduction of certain types of social measures is desirable, this will strengthen the hands of those who, in the various countries, are pressing for the introduction of the measures in question.'[110]

The last rationale to be discussed is not based on a utilitarian purpose, but rather on the deontological ground that workers are to be respected as individuals.[111] In modern parlance, we capsulize this by saying that labor rights are human rights.[112] Yet one should also remember that labor rights were conceived as a form of international solidarity well before the modern human rights movement.

International law is premised on the dignity of the worker. As Paul O'Higgins has pointed out, the idea that 'Labour is not a commodity' is a fundamental precept of international labor law originated by the Irish economist, John Kells Ingram, in 1880.[113] The constitutional act of 1919 creating the ILO declared that 'labour should not be regarded merely as a commodity or article of commerce', and the ILO Declaration of Philadelphia of 1944 refined this proposition to state: 'labour is not a commodity.'[114] Besides the influence of Graham, that idea has a historical basis in

---

[108] See Werner Sengenberger, *Globalization and Social Progress: The Role and Impact of International Labour Standards* (Friedrich Ebert Stiftung, 2002), at 51 (describing international labor standards as international public goods).

[109] Drusilla K. Brown, Alan V. Deardorff, and Robert M. Stern, 'International Labor Standards and Trade: A Theoretical Analysis', in Bhagwati and Hudec, *supra* note 95, Vol. 1, 227, at 270–1.

[110] *Social Aspects of European Economic Co-operation, supra* note 100, para. 205.

[111] Guy Caire, 'Labour Standards and International Trade', in Sengenberger and Campbell, *supra* note 85, at 297 (discussing the two points of view, namely, the dignity of labor and the economic perspective).

[112] See, e.g., Hans-Michael Wolffgang and Wolfram Feuerhake, 'Core Labour Standards in World Trade Law', 36 *Journal of World Trade* (2002) 883, at 889 (discussing 'core labour standards as worker rights equivalent to human rights').

[113] Paul O'Higgins, ' "Labour is not a Commodity"—An Irish Contribution to International Labour Law', 26 *Industrial Law Journal* (1997) 225, at 233.

[114] Compare Treaty of Versailles, *supra* note 84, Art. 417 and Declaration of the Aims and Purposes of the International Labour Organization (Annex to the current ILO Constitution), sect. I.

religious doctrine, particularly Pope Leo XIII's encyclical of 1891, *Rerum Novarum*. This encyclical declares that 'It is neither just nor human so to grind men down with excessive labor as to stupefy their minds and wear out their bodies.'[115]

So far in Part 3, this chapter has sought to explain why governments intervene in the labor market, and why international harmonization is pursued. The next section in Part 3 discusses the choice of law. That is, should labor harmonization be pursued in labor agreements or in trade agreements?

C. Labor Versus Trade Agreements

Using a labor treaty to achieve common national objectives on labor would seem to be a more straightforward path than using a trade treaty. Certainly, that was the idea in 1919 when the ILO was created, many decades before a comparable international organization was established to promote common trade objectives. Nevertheless, the assumption underlying the longtime efforts to add social clauses to trade agreements is that the ILO is inadequate to achieving its purpose. Advocates of using the WTO to reinforce the ILO often contend that 'the ILO does not possess the international legal authority to enforce labour standards against recalcitrant states.'[116]

In the Inter-American context, no thought has been given to the idea of adopting regional labor treaties. The global-regional dynamic in labor policy is different than in trade policy, where it is thought that bilateral and regional agreements can play a useful role in supplementing multilateral agreements. Yet no one is arguing that the alleged inadequacies of the ILO should be remedied by a stronger regional labor agreement.[117]

Explaining why is a puzzle. The answer that governments are uninterested in regional labor policy is unsatisfying because, if so, then why would they seek to insert labor provisions in a regional trade agreement? It could be that governments lack frameworks for negotiating labor agreements in the same way that they negotiate trade agreements.[118] Or it could be that most governments do not want new international labor disciplines and can only be induced to accept them through linkage to highly desired trade agreements.

A theory of trade linkage has been developed by David Leebron who distinguishes between two claims—strategic versus substantive linkage.[119] In strategic linkage, the inclusion of labor in a trade agreement is dictated by political demands from

---

[115] *Rerum Novarum*, 15 May 1891, para. 42, available at: http://www.vatican.va/holy_father/leo_xiii/encyclicals.

[116] The quotation comes from Patrick Macklem, 'Labour Law Beyond Borders', 5 *Journal of International Economic Law* (2002) 605, at 638.

[117] Note that the General Agreement on Trade in Services (GATS) provides some deference to labor market integration agreements. GATS Art. V *bis*.

[118] This is certainly so in the United States, which has a fast-track process for approving trade agreements, but does not have one for approving labor agreements.

[119] David W. Leebron, 'Linkages', 96 *AJIL* (2002) 5, at 11–14.

particular countries. In substantive linkage, labor is included in a trade agreement either: (1) because labor and trade norms are related, or (2) because, without a linkage, the trade agreement might undermine labor norms. Leebron calls the first reason 'coherence' and the second 'consequentialist'.

So far, no analyst has taken Leebron's framework and applied it to a trade/labor linkage. All of the international concerns discussed above—a race to the bottom, fairness, and worker dignity—would seem to reflect either coherence or consequential aims. Are labor rights consistent with trading rights?[120] Would a trade agreement be more successful if accompanied by a baseline of core labor standards? These questions are important and deserve careful answers beyond the scope of this chapter.

However persuasive the rationale for including labor in a trade agreement, governments should also weigh the disadvantages of doing so.[121] One possible problem is that seeking labor provisions may discombobulate trade negotiations. Another is that the labor disciplines may lead to trade disputes that will undo trade liberalization. To be sure, these objections also apply to other topics of trade linkage, such as intellectual property rights.

Quite apart from any harm of labor linkage to the trade regime is the potential harm to the *labor* regime. Those who view the ILO and regional labor cooperation as ineffectual would probably not be concerned about such harm. Yet more thoughtful analysts have recognized the substantial benefits of the ILO, including how it helps governments through norm generation and capacity building.[122] Viewed in this way, the lack of FTA-style enforcement is a virtue of the labor regime rather than a weakness.

Most analysts who advocate the inclusion of labor disciplines in trade agreements prefer either the current US approach with FTAs or a more muscular approach that would incorporate ILO standards. In my view, neither path is optimal. In the current FTA approach, governments have crafted a labor discipline that is sufficiently vapid that it will not have any effect on trade flows. Yet if FTAs were to require compliance with core ILO conventions, that would affect trade flows, and

[120] See Christopher McCrudden and Anne Davies, 'A Perspective on Trade and Labour Rights', in Francesco Francioni (ed.), *Environment, Human Rights and International Trade* (Hart, 2001) 179, at 187 (suggesting that labor rights that serve to increase freedom of choice and contract are theoretically consistent with the ideology of free trade and may be required by it).

[121] See Philip Alston, 'Linking Trade and Human Rights', 23 *German Yearbook of International Law* (1980) 126, at 157 (noting that the potential costs of linking trade and human rights may be considerable and calling for a careful weighing process).

[122] Kofi Addo, 'The Correlation between Labour Standards and International Trade', 36 *Journal of World Trade* (2002) 285; Virginia A. Leary, 'Workers' Rights and International Trade: The Social Clause (GATT, ILO, NAFTA, U.S. Laws)', in Bhagwati and Hudec, *supra* note 95, Vol. 2, 177, at 189; Francis Maupain, 'International Labor Organization Recommendations and Similar Instruments', in Dinah Shelton (ed.), *Commitment and Compliance: The Role of Non-Binding Norms in the International Legal System* (Oxford, 2003) 372, at 392 (positing that bindingness is not the essence of international law); Salazar-Xirinachs and Martínez-Piva, *supra* note 49, at 332–4.

potentially make it harder for developing countries to expand their exports.[123] Furthermore, both paths are inadequate because they miss opportunities to zero in on a few important trade and labor connections. Part 4 will present my own recommendations for how to incorporate a labor dimension into the FTAA.

4. RECOMMENDATIONS FOR THE FTAA

A quarter century ago, the ILO annual conference passed a resolution requesting governments to:

see that the trade agreements concluded within the framework of appropriate institutions promote both the expansion of world trade and the local utilisation of the labour force available in various countries and make it possible to achieve a real improvement of the standard of living of the populations in accordance with the objectives of international labour standards in so far as they have been ratified.[124]

The resolution is noteworthy because it is a rare instance of an ILO pronouncement on trade agreements. The ILO's advice was well-crafted. The expansion of world trade can be good for workers,[125] but the actual outcome depends on the design of the trade agreement. Various features in a trade agreement can affect the amount of job creation, workplace conditions, and prospects for a rising standard of living.

If the FTAA is to have a labor dimension, its member governments should be bolder and more innovative than in existing Inter-American free trade agreements. Provisions are needed to do the following: (a) enhance the consumer role in the labor market, (b) promote worker adjustment, (c) disallow prohibitions of unions in export processing zones, and (d) expand protection for migrant workers. Part 4 presents these recommendations and then concludes the chapter.

A. Enhance the Consumer Role

Although government regulation and subsidies can play an important part in correcting labor market failures, they are not the only tools available. Governments can also facilitate efforts by consumers to seek more socially responsive practices by businesses. The consumer is empowered when he has reliable information about the employment conditions of the workers who produce the products that he buys. Such information can be facilitated by social labels, industry partnerships, and voluntary

---

[123] This is so whether compliance is induced through trade sanctions or monetary penalties. An FTAA labor provision enforced with monetary penalties is recommended by Bobbi-Lee Meloro, 'Balancing the Goals of Free Trade with Workers' Rights in a Hemispheric Economy', 30 *University of Miami Inter-American Law Review* (1998) 433, at 458.

[124] International Labour Conference, 65th Session, 1979, Record of Proceedings, Resolution Concerning the Follow-up to the World Employment Conference, lxxxiv, at xc.

[125] Recall the 1939 resolution of the American States which are Members of the ILO, see text accompanying *supra* note 35.

codes of conduct that are carefully monitored.[126] The worker is helped when her employer follows best practices in labor relations and seeks to invest in its employees.

How should a trade agreement catalyze such changes? Not through heavy-handed rules, but rather by improving regulatory transparency, encouraging national stakeholder dialogues, and using consultative mechanisms at the international level. As noted in Table One, the Association Agreement between the EC and Chile provides one example in its provisions on social dialogue.[127] The FTAA could adopt that approach and could also establish a network of the ongoing labor promotional activities in the NAALC, Mercosur, and other agreements of regional integration.

B. Promote Worker Adjustment

International trade will make a country better off as a whole, and yet some individuals may be left worse off. Therefore, governments should seek to broaden the distribution of the benefits from trade and deliver adjustment assistance to workers who suffer extended dislocations. That government role is sometimes called a 'safety net',[128] but that term seems too reactive. The aim of an adjustment program should not only be to protect workers from catastrophic impacts, but also to proactively help them find decent work in a changing economy. The instruments available include retraining, relocation allowances, and other employability assistance.

As noted in Part 1, the need for governmental efforts to accord 'economic security' in the Americas was perceived over fifty years ago, and the ILO regional conference of 1946 called for 'training and retraining of adult workers'. Yet despite these resolutions, very little has been done on a regional basis to promote worker adjustment. In 2002 the 7th FTAA Ministerial conference of 2002 (Quito Declaration) suggested the idea of a Hemispheric Cooperation Program that would, among other tasks, strengthen the capacity of countries in 'adjusting to

---

[126] Ian Graham and Andrew Bibby, 'Global Labour Agreements: A Framework for Rights', *World of Work* (December 2002) 4; Janet Hilowitz, 'Social Labelling to Combat Child Labour: Some Considerations', 136 *International Labour Review* (1997) 215; Vitit Muntarbhorn, 'International Commerce and the Rights of the Child', in Jean-François Flauss et al. (eds.), *World Trade and the Protection of Human Rights* (Bruylant, 2001) 151, at 167–74 (discussing catalytic role of stakeholders); Nick Robins and Liz Humphrey, *Sustaining the Rag Trade* (IIED, 2000); Christoph Scherrer and Thomas Greven, *Global Rules for Trade: Codes of Conduct, Social Labeling, Workers' Rights Clauses* (Westfälisches Dampfboot, 2001); Gijsbert van Liemt, 'Codes of Conduct and International Subcontracting: A "Private" Road Towards Ensuring Minimum Labour Standards in Export Industries', in Blanpain, *supra* note 55, at 167; Philip von Schôppenthau, 'Trade and Labour Standards: Harnessing Globalisation?' in Klaus Günter Deutsch and Bernhard Speyer (eds.), *The World Trade Organization Millennium Round* (Routledge, 2001) 224, at 232–4 (discussing codes of conduct); Robert Wai, 'Countering, Branding, Dealing: Using Economic and Social Rights in and around the International Trade Regime', 14 *EJIL* (2003) 35, at 73 (discussing branding).

[127] Recently, Robert Pastor proposed a North American interparliamentary group. Robert A. Pastor, 'North America's Second Decade', *Foreign Affairs* (January/February 2004) 124.

[128] Raymond Torres, *Towards a Socially Sustainable World Economy* (ILO, 2001), at 56 (discussing social safety nets).

integration'.[129] But to my knowledge, nothing concrete has been done to implement such a program or to improve the delivery of worker adjustment assistance.

Given that the benefits of a good national worker adjustment program would accrue primarily to that nation's own economy, governments should not need any fillip to carry out such programs. Sadly, though, many governments tend to be lackadaisical about responding to economic dislocations.[130] Even the US government, the biggest spender in the Americas, underinvests in such programs.

One idea for increasing governmental attention to worker adjustment would be to internationalize the issue. As Philip Alston has noted, ILO Director-General C. Wilfred Jenks gave an address to the UN Economic and Social Council in 1971 in which he posited an ILO role in the 'adoption of effective manpower adjustment measures calculated to facilitate trade liberalization measures by eliminating or reducing some of the grounds for opposition to them'.[131] Jenks was right to perceive labor adjustment as an international challenge and to see the connection to gaining public support for trade. In 1976 the ILO World Employment Conference advocated 'active manpower policies and adjustment assistance' and stated that 'Adjustment assistance is considered preferable to import restrictions.'[132]

Other stakeholders who recognized worker adjustment as an international problem suggested that it be taken up by the trading system. For example, in the early 1970s, the International Metalworkers' Federation proposed adding a 'social clause' to the General Agreement on Tariffs and Trade that would combine developing country job creation through new exports with industrial country efforts to give affected workers employment and income guarantees.[133] To my knowledge, the first proposal to include adjustment in a free trade agreement came in 1993, when Robert Howse suggested providing a 'right' to worker adjustment in the NAFTA.[134] Howse's proposal did not specify a package of benefits, but rather sought a commitment of the trading partners to deliver adjustment and to coordinate their efforts. His proposal was not adopted either in the NAFTA or in the labor side agreement.

---

[129] Ministerial Declaration, 1 November 2002, available at: http://www.ftaa-alca.org/Ministerials/Quito, Annex III.

[130] See C. Fred Bergsten, 'Foreign Economic Policy for the Next President', *Foreign Affairs* (March/April 2004) 88, at 96–7; Mack McLarty, 'Trade Paves Path to U.S. Prosperity', *Los Angeles Times*, 1 February 2004, 2; Jaime Saavedra, 'Labor Markets During the 1990s', in Pedro-Pablo Kuczynski and John Williamson (eds.), *After the Washington Consensus: Restarting Growth in Latin America* (Institute for International Economics, 2003), Chap. 9; Bruce Stokes, 'Rural Poor Need Trade and Aid', *National Journal*, 31 May 2003, 1710.

[131] Philip Alston, 'International Trade as an Instrument of Positive Human Rights Policy', 4 *Human Rights Quarterly* (1982) 155, at 176.

[132] ILO, Declaration of Principles and Programme of Action Adopted by the 1976 World Employment Conference, paras. 63, 69, reprinted in *Employment, Growth and Basic Needs: A One-World Problem* (Praeger, 1977) 189, at 202–3.

[133] Report of the ILO Director-General, 1976, reprinted in *Employment, Growth and Basic Needs: A One-World Problem, supra* note 132, 1, at 122.

[134] Robert Howse, 'The Case for Linking a Right to Adjustment with the NAFTA', in Jonathan Lemco and William B. P. Robson (eds.), *Ties Beyond Trade* (Canadian-American Committee, 1993) 79.

Howse's idea continues to have merit, however, and governments should include a basic commitment to worker adjustment within the FTAA. The richer governments in the region should provide financial assistance to adjustment programs in other countries, and all the governments should cooperate to develop quality standards for training programs. By making a commitment to worker adjustment, each country could, over time, lessen public opposition to trade agreements, and reduce the social and economic losses stemming from prolonged unemployment.

In 2003 the WTO Secretariat issued a study on 'Adjusting to Trade Liberalization' that devotes a chapter to how 'Governments can facilitate the adjustment process'. This chapter discusses social safety nets, labor markets, education and training, and other issues.[135] Although this WTO effort to delve into labor issues is commendable, the study was a disappointment because it ignored the opportunity for international cooperation. Indeed, the attention given to the international level is perverse, with the Secretariat instructing governments on how to delay trade liberalization by using lengthy transition periods and imposing temporary import protection.[136]

C. Disallow Bans on Unions in Export Zones

No one can seriously deny that the issue of worker rights in export processing zones (EPZs) is related to trade and can be properly addressed within a trade agreement. Nevertheless, no FTA contains standards for how workers are treated in such zones. Yet EPZs in many countries engage in severe abuses of fundamental worker rights.[137]

Crafting an FTAA rule for EPZs would be a challenge. The ILO lacks any conventions or recommendations on this topic. Surely it is too simplistic to say that EPZs should follow the same labor law that otherwise exists in a country, as that law could be too low to guarantee internationally recognized labor rights. On the other hand, prevailing law could be so restrictive that it inhibits investment. For a long time, many countries in Latin America suffered an enervating combination of excessive import protection combined with excessive *de jure* labor protection, with a consequent loss of investment and employment opportunities.[138]

My recommendation is that FTAA governments start with one basic rule—that EPZs must not forbid trade unions—and incorporate that into the FTAA. That rule would require some elaboration, of course, but governments should not try to import everything from the authoritative ILO conventions on freedom of association and collective bargaining. Any complaint raised would need to be premised on the FTAA rule, even against governments that are party to core ILO conventions.

The complaint procedure I envision is victim-to-state, not state-to-state. The rationale for a victim-to-state mechanism is that it depoliticizes the dispute system so

[135] WTO Secretariat, Adjusting to Trade Liberalization, Special Study 7, April 2003, Chap. V, available on WTO website.   [136] *Ibid.*, Chap. VI.

[137] International Confederation of Free Trade Unions, 'Export Processing Zones—Symbols of Exploitation and a Development Dead End', September 2003. See also Lori Wallach and Patrick Woodall, *Whose Trade Organization?* (New Press, 2nd edn. 2004), at 224 (discussing export promotion zones).

[138] See Roger Plant, *Labour Standards and Structural Adjustment* (ILO, 1994), at 85–90 (discussing the Latin American experience with inflexible labor markets).

that no government is saddled with having to espouse the claims of its citizens. Perhaps one reason why no NAFTA labor case was ever filed is that the target government might consider that an unfriendly act.

The complaint process would be similar to the investor-state arbitration in NAFTA except that an individual would also be able to lodge a complaint about the actions of its own government, rather than only a foreign government. Criteria would be needed to establish eligibility to lodge a complaint, and I favor a flexible procedure that permits complaints from individual victims, unions, and public interest groups. A valid complaint about an EPZ would lead to the appointment of an independent panel similar to the panels available for FTA commercial disputes. The worker would not have a right of action against the employer. Cases of that sort would need to remain in national tribunals. Even so, a screening mechanism should be set up to protect a company's reputation from being injured by frivolous complaints.

If the panel rules against the defendant government, the government would be given time to correct the violation, but if no correction ensues, the scofflaw government should be required to pay a fine until the matter is corrected. The fine would be paid to the independent FTAA commission, which could use the money for its regular programs.

Because the EPZ mechanism suggested here differs so much from the labor mechanism provided for in the CAFTA, it may be useful to summarize those differences. My proposal is based on an international rule (to be formulated in the FTAA), while CAFTA is based on each country's own domestic law.[139] My proposal provides for a private right of action, while CAFTA is state-to-state.[140] My proposal allows an individual to secure an independent panel, while in CAFTA, an individual submits a communication to an office in its country.[141] My proposal provides for a financial sanction in the event of non-compliance, while in CAFTA, the scofflaw government pays a monetary assessment to the CAFTA commission, with that money being used for labor initiatives *in the defendant country*.[142] My proposal is probably too bold to get enacted, but it would be an interesting experiment that could fructify a right to form and join a free trade union in EPZs.

D. Expand Protection for Migrant Workers

Although FTAs seek to liberalize the movement of goods, services, and capital, they have tended to given little attention to the movement of people. Yet worker mobility is logically a part of economic integration, and, like importing and exporting, can benefit both the sending and receiving countries.[143] This principle is recognized with regard to temporary entry for business executives and professionals, and the same need also exists for less-skilled workers.

---

[139] See CAFTA, *supra* note 57, Art. 16.2(1)(a).   [140] See *ibid.*, Art. 20.6.

[141] See *ibid.*, Art. 16.4. The government is obliged only to review the communication and to make it public, as appropriate.   [142] See *ibid.*, Art. 20.17(4).

[143] 'Trade Goes Global, Labour Remains Local', *Economiquity*, No. 26 (2003), at 1; Demetrios G. Papademetriou, 'The Shifting Expectations of Free Trade and Migration', in *NAFTA's Promise and Reality* (Carnegie Endowment, 2004) 39.

The issue of labor mobility has been addressed in some Inter-American trade agreements. Most notably, the Caribbean Community provides for the free movement of university graduates and those in listed occupations.[144] The NAFTA contains a chapter on Temporary Entry for Business Persons, as do the US and Canadian FTAs with Chile.[145] But the CAFTA does not because, in 2003, the US government got queasy from making immigration commitments in trade agreements.[146] For the United States, it seems that very little has changed since 1928 when it told the Pan American conference that the control of immigration 'is a matter of purely domestic concern'.[147] The ongoing FTAA talks have neglected even to set up a negotiating group for temporary entry.

If freer immigration cannot be achieved within the FTAA, then governments might instead try to negotiate provisions for greater protection of migrant workers. Relevant international norms already exist,[148] and key guarantees could be incorporated into the FTAA in the same manner that guarantees from intellectual property treaties will probably be incorporated. Establishing rules for the benefit of migrant workers in the FTAA would help individuals who are commonly exploited. Such rules would have synergies with ongoing regional cooperation on migration policy.[149]

E. Summary and Overall Conclusion

The ideas in Part 4 seek to stimulate practical, concerted action to address labor and employment problems of regional economic integration. My recommendations for the FTAA do not include an obligation to adhere to core ILO conventions. However one weighs the advantages and disadvantages of that course, such fusion is unlikely to be accepted by FTAA governments. As for the reciprocal obligation to enforce national law, it should be omitted unless governments are willing to replace the current window dressing with a private right of action.

Contemporary FTAs seem designed to assist global corporations and devote little attention to those without power or wealth. If governments were to get serious about helping vulnerable workers, then such action could help to humanize trade agreements and lead to more widely shared prosperity.

---

[144] See 'Free Movement of Skills', available on: http://www.caricom.org.

[145] North American Free Trade Agreement, 17 December 1992, chap. 16; US–Chile FTA, *supra* note 56, chap. 14; Free Trade Agreement between the Government of Canada and the Government of the Republic of Chile, 5 December 1996, chap. K.

[146] See Christopher S. Rugaber, 'Senate Judiciary Committee Members Criticize USTR on Temporary Entry Provision', *BNA International Trade Reporter*, 17 July 2003, 1216.

[147] See text accompanying *supra* note 15.

[148] See T. Alexander Aleinikoff and Vincent Chetail (eds.), *Migration and International Legal Norms* (Asser Press, 2003). Some of the key norms are protection against discrimination, access to health care, and a right to depart and re-enter.

[149] International Organization for Migration, 'Illustration of Multilateral, Regional and Bilateral Cooperative Arrangements in the Management of Migration', in Aleinikoff and Chetail, *supra* note 148, 305, at 310–15, 331–3.

6

Should the EU Have the Power to Set Minimum Standards for Collective Labour Rights in the Member States?

A. C. L. DAVIES

At present, the task of upholding freedom of association, the right to engage in voluntary collective bargaining, and the right to strike (hereafter 'collective labour rights') falls largely to the member states. Article 137(5) EC explicitly provides that the EU may not legislate on freedom of association or the right to strike. It will be argued in this chapter that EU law is heavily dependent on the effective protection of collective labour rights in the member states. Where that protection falls short, both the legitimacy and the effectiveness of EU law may be undermined. This should concern us even though the EU's involvement in the protection of collective labour rights is in fact more extensive than Article 137(5) appears to suggest. It will be concluded that the EU should be given the competence to set minimum standards for compliance with collective labour rights in the member states.

Part 1 will look at the potential problems that might arise as a result of the EU's reliance on the member states to protect collective labour rights. Part 2 will examine whether there is a real risk of a member state failing to protect collective labour rights. Part 3 will assess whether the EU's existing involvement in collective labour rights is sufficient to guard against the risks identified in Part 2 and thus to prevent the problems identified in Part 1 from arising. In Part 4, it will be argued that the EU ought to have the power to set minimum standards on collective labour rights in the member states. Part 5 will consider whether giving the EU this power would be consistent with the doctrine of subsidiarity.

1. EU LAW'S RELIANCE ON THE EFFECTIVE PROTECTION OF COLLECTIVE LABOUR RIGHTS IN THE MEMBER STATES

This part will highlight three potential problems with the EU's reliance on the member states to protect collective labour rights. First, the EU expects the member states to have thriving trade unions and employers' associations that can participate in the legislative process at the EU level. If these institutions are weak in some member states, the legitimacy of EU legislation may be undermined. Second, the EU expects the member states to have thriving trade unions and employers' associations that can help to implement directives at the national level. If these institutions are weak in some member states, directives may not be effectively implemented. Third, the EU places considerable importance on upholding human rights standards in its dealings with third countries. This may seem hypocritical if the EU does not have equivalent powers in relation to the member states.

A. Legitimacy Issues in EU Legislation

Trade unions and employers' associations have long been consulted in the formulation of Community social policy, largely on the initiative of the Commission and Parliament.[1] The involvement of the social partners first received formal recognition in 1986, when the Single European Act inserted a new Article 118b EC: 'The Commission shall endeavour to develop the dialogue between management and labour at European level which could, if the two sides consider it desirable, lead to relations based on agreement.' In 1992 the Agreement on Social Policy signed at Maastricht amplified this obligation considerably. Article 3 obliged the Commission to consult the social partners and Article 4 created the possibility that agreements reached by the social partners could be given effect as legislation. These provisions are now found in Articles 138 and 139 EC.

Article 138 obliges the Commission to engage in a two-stage consultation process with the social partners. First, under Article 138(2), it must consult them on 'the possible direction of Community action'. Then, if the Commission decides to take action on a particular issue, it must consult them 'on the content of the envisaged proposal'.[2] At this stage, the social partners may decide to reach an agreement on the issue themselves through the social dialogue procedure set out in Article 139. According to Article 139(2), 'Agreements concluded at Community level shall be implemented either in accordance with the procedures and practices specific to management and labour and the member states or, in matters covered by Article 137, at the joint request of the signatory parties, by a Council decision on a proposal from the Commission.' An agreement by the social partners on one of the labour law matters over which the Community has competence (a matter covered by Article 137) may be implemented as a directive. An agreement on a matter not covered by Article 137 could not be implemented as a directive because this would be outside the Community's powers. However, such agreements could be given effect through the collective mechanisms envisaged in the first part of Article 139(2).

---

[1] For history, see B. Bercusson, *European Labour Law* (1996), 72–4.   [2] Art. 138(3) EC.

As the Court of First Instance has pointed out, legislation which is enacted as a result of the social dialogue bypasses the European Parliament. It must therefore seek its legitimacy from another source:

However, the principle of democracy on which the Union is founded requires—in the absence of the participation of the European Parliament in the legislative process—that the participation of the people be otherwise assured, in this instance through the parties representative of management and labour who concluded the agreement which is endowed by the Council, acting on a qualified majority, on a proposal from the Commission, with a legislative foundation at Community level.[3]

The legitimacy of the social dialogue depends on the representativeness of the social partners. In turn, this depends on the existence of thriving collective bargaining structures at the national level. The problem is that if collective bargaining is weak in some member states, the legitimacy of Community law may be undermined.

The Commission has set out three criteria of representativeness. Social partner organizations should:

(1) be cross-industry or relate to specific sectors or categories and be organized at European level;

(2) consist of organizations which are themselves an integral and recognized part of member state social partner structures and with the capacity to negotiate agreements, and which are representative of all member states, as far as possible;

(3) have adequate structures to ensure their effective participation in the consultation process.[4]

The second criterion is of particular interest. Here, the Commission determines the representativeness of European organizations by looking at the *national* role of their constituent parts. The legitimacy of the social dialogue at European level thus turns on the representativeness of the social partners within each member state.

Workers are represented in the social dialogue by the European Trade Union Confederation (ETUC). A study conducted on behalf of the Commission found that the ETUC represented over 47 million workers drawn from all fifteen member states.[5] All ETUC members are involved in collective bargaining and consultation at the national level, and most are represented in the national delegation to the ILO. Its status as the sole representative of workers has been challenged by the European Confederation of Independent Trade Unions (CESI), but this organization has members in only six member states with the majority being concentrated in Germany and Italy.[6] It therefore seems unlikely that CESI would meet the

---

[3] Case T-135/1996, *UEAPME v. Council*, [1998] ECR II-2335, at 2371.

[4] Commission Communication of 14 December 1993, COM(93) 600 final, at para. 24, reaffirmed in Commission Communication of 20 May 1998, COM(98) 322, at para. 1.2.

[5] Institut des Sciences du Travail—Université Catholique de Louvain (IST), *Report on the Representativeness of European Social Partner Organisations* (1999), at 44–9.   [6] IST, *supra* note 5, at 51–4.

Commission's second criterion. However, even though the ETUC is clearly the most plausible candidate to represent workers at the European level, legitimacy problems remain. The ETUC's legitimacy is derived from the legitimacy of national trade union federations. To take the United Kingdom as an example, the TUC has some seventy-one affiliated unions representing just under 7 million workers. Although some unions are not affiliated to the TUC, the vast majority are. The TUC is therefore the organization that best represents *unionized* workers in the United Kingdom. But recent figures suggest that union density is around 36 per cent, a figure that is probably an overestimate because it excludes firms with fewer than twenty-five employees in which unionization is unlikely. Given that trade union members are a minority of the workforce as a whole, it becomes harder to argue that the TUC is a good representative of *all* workers. This problem could worsen with enlargement of the EU because some of the acceding countries have very low union density.

Employers are represented in the EU social dialogue by three main organizations: the Union of Industrial and Employers' Confederations of Europe (UNICE), the European Association of Craft Small and Medium-Sized Enterprises (UEAPME), and the European Centre of Enterprises with Public Participation and of Enterprises of General Economic Interest (CEEP). UNICE is the main employers' organization. Its members are, on the whole, the main cross-industry representative organization of private employers in each member state. These organizations have a strong claim to be considered social partners at the national level because of their involvement in social dialogue and representation at the ILO. However, the IST study found it difficult to obtain reliable information about the number of firms who are members of national organizations or the number of people they employ.[7] This makes it difficult to determine the representativeness of UNICE's members at the national level.

In the 1990s UNICE's role as the sole representative of private sector employers was challenged by UEAPME, an organization representing SMEs. UEAPME claims to represent 6.6 million businesses across the fifteen member states, but the IST study stated that it was difficult to obtain adequate data to verify this claim.[8] Although many UEAPME members are also affiliated to UNICE, UEAPME argued that UNICE did not adequately represent SMEs in the social dialogue. These arguments culminated in an action for annulment brought by UEAPME of the Parental Leave Directive,[9] which had been concluded through the social dialogue procedure.[10] In giving judgment, the CFI found that there was a duty on the Commission and Council to verify that the parties to an agreement reached under the social dialogue were representative. The CFI went on to find that the duty had been fulfilled in the case of the Parental Leave Directive. The Commission and Council were able to show that they had considered the question of representativeness. UNICE's general mandate to represent employers of all types was sufficient

---

[7] IST, *supra* note 5, at 39–43.   [8] IST, *supra* note 5, at 27–33.

[9] Council Directive 96/34/EC, OJ 1996 L 145/4.

[10] *Supra* note 3. For a fuller discussion of the case, see Bercusson, 'Democratic Legitimacy and European Labour Law', 28 *ILJ* (1999) 153.

to ensure that the interests of SMEs had been taken into account in the negotiations. UEAPME dropped an appeal against this decision when it too was accepted as a potential participant in the social dialogue. UNICE retains a leading role as the main private sector employer representative in the negotiations, but under an agreement between the two parties, it has undertaken to work in consultation with UEAPME.

The final employers' organization to be considered is CEEP. This body represents public sector organizations. It also includes private firms which provide public services, a substantial category after the wave of privatizations that have taken place in many member states, although in some countries such firms have chosen to join UNICE rather than CEEP. The available data on the representativeness of CEEP is, if anything, even thinner than that for UEAPME and UNICE.[11] For some countries, such as Ireland and the United Kingdom, almost no membership data is available. No other organization has challenged the representativeness of CEEP, and the importance of including it was stressed by the CFI in the *UEAPME* case, discussed above:

It is clear that if CEEP had not been one of the signatories to the framework agreement, this alone would have fundamentally affected the sufficiency of the collectively representational character of those signatories in view of the contents of that agreement, because then one particular category of undertakings, that of the public sector, would have been wholly without representation.[12]

Again, however, the fact that there is no alternative organization does not necessarily mean that CEEP itself is representative.

One obvious response to these concerns would be to argue that the social partners may be legitimate representatives even if they do not have widespread membership. For example, the ETUC could argue that it strives for the protection of non-unionized workers as well as unionized workers. Indeed, the role of the social partners in the series of directives on atypical forms of work in which workers are less likely to be unionized may be an illustration of this.[13] However, this 'NGO-style' role is highly problematic for organizations that are traditionally membership-based. The interests of non-unionized workers may come into conflict with the interests of unionized workers. In this situation, union leaders would have to represent the interests of unionized workers because unions are democratic organizations in which the leaders are accountable to the members. The same is true of employers' associations: the 'NGO' role can only be adopted where it does not conflict with members' interests.

Bercusson has argued that the concern with democratic legitimacy is misplaced.[14] He suggests that the social dialogue should be viewed in a labour law context rather than a constitutional one. From this perspective, scrutiny by the Council and Commission of the representativeness of the social partner organizations (which was confirmed as a legal obligation by the CFI in the *UEAPME* case, discussed above) is an infringement of their internal autonomy, an important value in labour law.

---

[11] IST, *supra* note 5, at 34–8.   [12] *Supra* note 3, at 2375.

[13] For example, Council Directive 97/81/EC, OJ 1998 L 14/9, on part-time work, and Council Directive 99/70/EC, OJ 1999 L 175/43, on fixed-term work.   [14] *Supra* note 10, at 159–65.

This argument might be persuasive if the social partners' agreements were only ever implemented through collective action in the member states. This would keep the process within the labour law sphere. But the possibility of enacting their agreements as legislation brings the social dialogue into the constitutional sphere.[15] Although it is common at the national level for legislation to be enacted after consultation with interested parties, such legislation usually requires a formal seal of approval from the legislature. Since the social dialogue does not allow for this, the insistence of the Commission and, more recently, the CFI, on the representativeness of the social partners is appropriate. It is therefore highly problematic that the Community has no power to ensure that the member states are encouraging the presence of active and representative trade unions and employers' associations at the national level.

B. The Effectiveness of EU Legislation

Community legislation commonly permits implementation of the obligations it contains, or derogation from those obligations, by collective bargaining in the member states. Again, therefore, it relies upon the existence of thriving collective bargaining structures at the national level.

The idea of implementing directives through collective agreements stemmed initially from the *de facto* use of this approach by the member states.[16] It was challenged in a number of cases before the ECJ. In an enforcement action, Italy argued that the Collective Redundancies Directive[17] had been implemented by a variety of measures including collective agreements.[18] The ECJ did not discuss the validity of this method of implementation and focused instead on the fact that the agreements relied on by the Italian government were not sufficient to implement all the obligations contained in the Directive in all relevant sectors of the economy. But in the later case of *Commission v. Denmark*, the ECJ explicitly acknowledged that it was legitimate for a member state to rely on collective agreements to implement Community legislation (in this case the Equal Pay Directive[19]) provided that they offered some other form of protection to workers who were, for whatever reason, not covered by a collective agreement.[20]

In the early 1990s the Commission responded by including an express provision in directives about implementation by collective agreement. One of the earliest examples stated:

member states shall adopt the laws, regulations and administrative provisions necessary to comply with this Directive no later than 30 June 1993 or shall ensure by that date that the

---

[15] See Obradovic, 'Accountability of Interest Groups in the Union Lawmaking Process', in P. Craig and C. Harlow (eds.), *Lawmaking in the European Union* (1998) 354.

[16] For a detailed discussion of the history, see Bercusson, *supra* note 1, chap. 9.

[17] Council Directive 75/129/EEC, OJ 1976 L 39/40.

[18] Case 91/81, *Commission v. Italy*, [1982] ECR 2133.

[19] Council Directive 75/117/EEC, OJ 1975 L 45/19.

[20] Case 143/83, *Commission v. Denmark*, [1985] ECR 427.

employers' and workers' representatives introduce the required provisions by way of agreement, the member states being obliged to take the necessary steps enabling them at all times to guarantee the results imposed by this Directive.[21]

On the positive side, this approach involves the social partners at the national level more fully in the implementation of Community law and respects the desire of member states to use collective agreements rather than legislation as a means of fulfilling their Community obligations. Indeed, implementation by the social partners might be more effective than legislation. The obligations can be tailored to fit particular firms and enforced more readily through collective pressure rather than individual litigation.

On the negative side, the social partners may be tempted to bargain over basic obligations rather than just the areas of discretion left to the member states. It may be hard to determine the relationship between collective implementation and the residual obligation to implement on the member state concerned. And it is particularly difficult for the Commission to police compliance when a member state's implementation measures consist of a number of collective agreements as well as legislation. Moreover, the ECJ may not be well-placed to scrutinize the efforts of the social partners. In *Commission v. France*,[22] the ECJ accepted an argument that implementation by the social partners had failed because only sixteen collective agreements had been renegotiated to take account of the Equal Treatment Directive.[23] Bercusson points out the flaw in the Court's reasoning: 'the figure of sixteen agreements amended has to be assessed not against the total number of agreements, but against those containing clauses requiring amendment.'[24] In short, the Community's acceptance of implementation through collective agreements may turn out to be a high-risk strategy because the Community cannot reinforce it with appropriate regulation of the collective bargaining process.

Another possibility is that a Directive may permit derogations by collective agreement from the obligations it contains. The Working Time Directive is a good example of this.[25] Article 17(3) permits derogations by collective agreement from several of the Directive's core obligations, including the obligations to provide: a minimum daily rest period of 11 hours,[26] a rest break in a working day of more than 6 hours,[27] and a minimum weekly rest period of 24 hours.[28] The only restriction on the social partners' power to agree derogations is that workers must be provided with compensating rest periods at other times. But this restriction need not be applied 'in exceptional cases where it is not possible for objective reasons to grant such periods', if the workers are granted 'appropriate protection' instead.[29]

Again, the possibility of derogating from the strict requirements of Community law has advantages and disadvantages. The main advantage is flexibility: one of the

---

[21] Council Directive 91/533/EEC, OJ 1991 L 288/32, Art. 9(1).
[22] Case 312/86, *Commission v. France*, [1988] ECR 6315.
[23] Council Directive 76/207/EEC, OJ 1976 L 39/40.   [24] Bercusson, *supra* note 1, at 124–5.
[25] Council Directive 93/104/EC, OJ 1993 L 307/18.   [26] *Supra* note 25, Art. 3.
[27] *Supra* note 25, Art. 4.   [28] *Supra* note 25, Art. 5.   [29] *Supra* note 25, Art. 17(3).

difficulties with general legislation on working time is that it may prove particularly burdensome to some firms, for example, where the level of business fluctuates dramatically over the course of the year. The employees may accept the need to work long hours at certain periods, knowing that they will be compensated with time off when business is slack. Indeed, the Working Time Directive has been criticized more for its rigidity than for its flexibility.[30] But the main disadvantage is inequality of bargaining power: how can we be sure that a collective agreement represents a genuine compromise between management and labour rather than the will of management imposed upon weak workforce representatives? The EU assumes that the member states can be relied upon to ensure that employers' associations and trade unions are thriving at the national level. But the effectiveness of EU law is put at risk if member states are not committed to this task.

C. External Relations

Promoting compliance with fundamental human rights, including collective labour rights, is an important element of the EU's foreign policy, particularly in relation to its trading partners. The EU makes trading agreements conditional on partner countries' compliance with human rights. It also offers additional trade incentives to those countries that can demonstrate a good record of compliance with particular rights. The difficulty is that these policies may seem somewhat hypocritical. The EU appears keen to enforce human rights against third countries but does little to keep its own house in order. This may lead third countries to question why they are being expected to comply with the relevant standards.

Since the early 1990s, the EU has included a human rights clause in its bilateral or multilateral trading agreements with third countries, making continuation conditional on respect for fundamental human rights and democratic principles.[31] Council guidelines adopted in 1995 set out a common form of clause and the procedures to be followed when implementing it.[32] The clause is controversial because it lacks a clear Treaty basis.[33] The only express reference to human rights in the external relations competences of the EU is in Article 177, which can be used in conjunction with Article 181 to conclude agreements with third countries for the purposes of development cooperation and to make those agreements conditional on respect for human rights.[34] However, agreements concerning development cooperation can *ex hypothesi* only be concluded with developing countries, so the scope of

---

[30] See Barnard, 'EC "Social" Policy', in P. Craig and G. de Búrca (eds.), *The Evolution of EU Law* (1999), at 488–92.

[31] See, generally, Linan Nogueras and Hinojosa Martinez, 'Human Rights Conditionality in the External Trade of the European Union: Legal and Legitimacy Problems', 7 *Colum. J. Eur. L.* (2001) 307; Riedel and Will, 'Human Rights Clauses in External Agreements of the EC', in P. Alston (ed.), *The EU and Human Rights* (1999) 723.   [32] *Bull. EU* 5-1995, at para. 1.2.3.

[33] For a fuller discussion of this issue, see Riedel and Will, *supra* note 31, at 732–7.

[34] This interpretation has been confirmed by the ECJ in Case C-268/94, *Portuguese Republic v. Council*, [1996] ECR I-6177.

this provision is limited. Article 310, which allows the EU to conclude association agreements, does not mention human rights. But association agreements involve particularly close cooperation with the EU, including harmonization of the third country's laws with the *acquis communautaire*. It is clear that the EU does have power to include human rights clauses in agreements of this type. The greatest difficulty is presented by Article 133, which empowers the EU to conclude agreements under the common commercial policy. This is the basis for the system of trade preferences as well as for certain trade agreements. One possible argument is that human rights clauses in trade agreements under Article 133 simply codify the EU's international law right to suspend a treaty for breach of *erga omnes* norms. But, as Riedel and Will point out, this would only permit the EU to use the clauses for treaty suspension, not for less serious measures. It would also limit the human rights that could be protected to those that have achieved recognition as *erga omnes* norms.[35] A broader argument that a human rights competence can be implied into Article 133 because of the EU's general support for human rights is superficially attractive but does not show proper respect for the fundamental principle of limited attribution. The validity of human rights clauses in agreements based solely on Article 133 therefore rests on uncertain foundations.

Leaving aside the question of competences, could a human rights clause ever be used to address violations of collective labour rights? We will take one of the most important external agreements, the Cotonou Agreement (2000), between the EU and the African, Caribbean, and Pacific (ACP) states, as our example.[36] This provides that 'respect for human rights, democratic principles and the rule of law, which underpin the ACP-EU Partnership, shall underpin the domestic and international policies of the Parties and constitute the essential elements of this Agreement'.[37] Article 96 provides that any party to the agreement may request consultations if it believes that another party is breaching this clause. If this fails, 'appropriate measures' can be taken. According to Article 96(2)(c), 'the "appropriate measures" referred to in this Article are measures taken in accordance with international law, and proportional to the violation. In the selection of these measures, priority must be given to those which least disrupt the application of this agreement. It is understood that suspension would be a measure of last resort.'

There are a number of difficulties with invoking this type of clause in practice. Where the offending country is a member of the World Trade Organisation (WTO), any attempt to suspend trading preferences may fall foul of Article 1 of the General Agreement on Tariffs and Trade (GATT), the 'most favoured nation' (MFN) clause. This requires the EU to extend trading preferences to all WTO members without discrimination. The only permitted exceptions to this rule are contained in Article XX of the GATT. Article XX refers to specific problems, such as the protection of public morals, the protection of human health, and the products of

---

[35] Riedel and Will, *supra* note 31, at 735.
[36] The Agreement is the successor to the Lomé Conventions.   [37] Art. 9(2).

prison labour, but does not contain any general reference to human rights.[38] Some commentators have suggested that it could be interpreted broadly to allow for the protection of human rights, including collective labour rights, but so far the WTO dispute resolution system has insisted on reading the clause narrowly.[39] Suspension may therefore be a realistic option only for non-WTO member countries.

However, even outside the WTO system, there are difficulties with suspending a bilateral relationship. One is that any action by the EU would doubtless be met with reciprocal action by the offending state. Thus, the EU must feel sufficiently strongly about the human rights violation in order to be willing to sacrifice its own access to the relevant state's markets. In a clash of the EU's political and economic interests, economic interests may well prevail. This leads to a further problem: which human rights violations would justify the use of the human rights clause? Article 9(2) provides:

The Parties refer to their international obligations and commitments concerning respect for human rights. They reiterate their deep attachment to human dignity and human rights, which are legitimate aspirations of individuals and peoples. Human rights are universal, indivisible and inter-related. The Parties undertake to promote and protect all fundamental freedoms and human rights, be they civil and political, or economic, social and cultural. In this context, the Parties reaffirm the equality of men and women.

This is commonly treated as a reference to the UN Universal Declaration of Human Rights, the International Covenant on Civil and Political Rights and the International Covenant on Economic, Social and Cultural Rights, instruments that have been expressly mentioned in other versions of the clause. The suspension of treaty obligations is, however, a serious step, and must be exercised in accordance with the principle of proportionality under Article 96(2)(c). This suggests that only grave breaches of fundamental rights—in situations in which civil war had broken out or democracy collapsed—would be likely to lead to the use of the clause. In these circumstances, freedom of association might be violated, but it seems unlikely that a breach of freedom of association alone would ever constitute grounds for treaty suspension.

Of course, treaty suspension is not the only 'appropriate measure' under the human rights clause. Breaches of collective labour rights could be addressed using lesser sanctions, such as a partial or temporary suspension of the treaty. But even this may be difficult to achieve in practice. The legitimacy of EU intervention in human rights issues in third states is reduced the less serious are the violations. This is true even if the sanctions proposed by the EU are proportionate. Therefore, it seems unlikely that a general clause such as that found in the Cotonou Agreement would be invoked to aid collective labour rights.

---

[38] Art. XX(a), (b), and (e), respectively.

[39] For an excellent introduction to the debate, see R. Howse and M. Mutua, *Protecting Human Rights in a Global Economy: Challenges for the World Trade Organisation* (2000), available at: http://www.ichrdd.ca/frame2.iphtml?langue=0&menu=m02&urlpage=english/about/hist.html.

The position is rather different in relation to the Generalized System of Preferences (GSP), the EU's main unilateral measure on trade.[40] Tariff preferences under the GSP scheme may be temporarily withdrawn in a range of situations, including 'serious and systematic violation of the freedom of association, the right to collective bargaining or the principle of non-discrimination in respect of employment and occupation, or use of child labour, as defined in the relevant ILO Conventions'.[41] This is an implicit reference to the ILO's Declaration on Fundamental Principles and Rights at Work 1998, which identifies these rights (along with freedom from forced labour, addressed in Article 26(1)(a) of the Regulation) as core labour rights to be observed by all ILO members by virtue of their membership, regardless of whether or not they have ratified the relevant Conventions. The fact that freedom of association and collective bargaining are expressly mentioned is highly significant. It overcomes the problem discussed above in relation to the general human rights clause that these rights may not seem sufficiently important to warrant punitive measures when considered in the context of all possible human rights violations. At the same time, the phrase 'serious and systematic' helps to ensure that the EU will not be tempted to intervene in respect of minor violations. If this condition is met, the EU's intervention is more likely to be regarded as legitimate.

The Regulation prescribes a complex procedure to be followed before temporarily withdrawing tariff preferences.[42] First, the situation must be investigated by the Commission, giving the beneficiary country 'every opportunity to co-operate' with the proceedings.[43] Findings of the ILO supervisory bodies must be taken into account in cases involving labour rights. If the Commission believes that temporary withdrawal is justified, the country is given a six-month period during which it may escape temporary withdrawal if it makes 'a commitment to take the measures necessary to conform, in a reasonable period of time, with the principles referred to in the 1998 ILO Declaration on Fundamental Principles and Rights at Work'.[44] If the country does not make this commitment, the Council may decide by a qualified majority to withdraw tariff preferences. This decision takes effect six months after it is made, 'unless it is decided before then that the reasons justifying it no longer prevail'.[45] These procedures give the offending country substantial periods of time within which to come into compliance with ILO standards. This may be highly beneficial. The purpose of sanctions is that they should promote compliance: when a sanction is invoked, it can be argued that it has failed. Lengthy procedures should give rise to considerable diplomatic pressure on the offending country to comply before the sanction is invoked. Moreover, EU member states may feel more willing to invoke the investigative process if it does not lead inexorably to the punishment of the offending state. But there are disadvantages. In the event of a clear breach on the

---

[40] Currently governed by Council Regulation 2501/2001 EC, OJ 2001 L 346/1, as amended.

[41] *Supra* note 40, Art. 26(1)(b).   [42] *Supra* note 40, Arts. 27–30.

[43] *Supra* note 40, Art. 28(2).   [44] *Supra* note 40, Art. 29(3).   [45] *Supra* note 40, Art. 29(5).

part of a recalcitrant state, complex procedures make it difficult for the EU to take swift, decisive action. This may create the impression that the EU supports states that violate collective labour rights.

GSP schemes are, in principle, contrary to the WTO's 'most favoured nation' principle,[46] because they grant preferences to developing countries without extending them to other WTO members. However, because of the benefits they bring to developing countries, the GATT contains an 'enabling clause', which permits developed countries to establish such schemes.[47] Paragraph 3(c) of the enabling clause states that preferences granted to developing countries must 'be designed . . . to respond positively to the development, financial and trade needs' of those countries. The EU argues that the temporary withdrawal provisions might need to be invoked 'where preferences provide incentives for maintaining unsustainable patterns of development'.[48] In other words, the possibility of withdrawing preferences, rather than being harmful to developing countries, is in fact designed to respond to their development needs. Developing countries might well see the issue differently. India's recent challenge to some aspects of the incentive provisions was upheld by the WTO Dispute Settlement Body.[49] The decision will be discussed fully below. It may also cast doubt on the compatibility of the withdrawal provisions with the GATT 'enabling clause'.

The GSP scheme contains incentives as well as sanctions. The beneficiary countries secure some tariff preferences automatically—unless they are withdrawn—under Article 7 of the Regulation.[50] But if they comply with environmental standards, tackle drug trafficking, or (most importantly for our purposes) uphold labour rights, they may ask to be granted additional preferences.[51] In the case of labour rights, the requesting country must demonstrate that its legislation 'incorporates the substance of the standards' laid down in ILO Conventions on the four core labour rights (freedom from forced labour, freedom from child labour, freedom from discrimination, and freedom of association and the right to collective bargaining), and that the legislation is 'effectively' applied.[52] The additional preferences may be granted to the country as a whole, or to particular sectors of the economy where the country cannot show that its entire economy meets the required standards. This is intended to make it more likely that countries will benefit from the additional incentives. The requesting country must supply information about its legislation and mechanisms for enforcement, and cooperate with an investigation by the Commission, which makes the final decision as to whether or not to grant the additional preferences.[53]

---

[46] GATT, Art. 1.   [47] GATT Contracting Parties, Decision of 28 November 1979 (L/4903).
[48] European Commission, *User's Guide to the European Union's Scheme of Generalised Tariff Preferences* (2003), at para. 15.
[49] WTO Panel, *European Communities—Conditions for the Granting of Tariff Preferences to Developing Countries* (2003) (WT/DS246/R).   [50] *Supra* note 40.
[51] *Supra* note 40, Arts. 8, 10, 14–25.   [52] *Supra* note 40, Art. 14(2).
[53] *Supra* note 40, Arts. 16–18.

Incentives are, inevitably, rather easier to use than sanctions. As we saw above, sanctions are seen as a measure of last resort because of the difficulties they create in the relationship between the EU and the offending state. They can only be used for serious violations of fundamental rights. Incentives form part of a more constructive relationship with third countries, in which the EU promises to *benefit* those that meet certain standards. This puts the EU in a persuasive, rather than aggressive, role. The standards do not have to be fundamental and the EU can require compliance with a detailed list of precise criteria. This is particularly relevant for freedom of association and collective bargaining. A state might be punished for serious breaches of this right, for example, if trade unionists were repeatedly attacked or imprisoned. But a state might fail to fulfil ILO Conventions in more subtle ways that could not be dealt with under the sanctions regime. Incentives give the EU a mechanism for addressing such problems.

However, the special incentive arrangements are not without their difficulties. First, some commentators have argued that the procedure for securing the preferences is unduly cumbersome.[54] The administrative burden of making the claim would be too great for those countries which would stand to gain most from the additional preferences. This seems to be borne out by the fact that so far, only Sri Lanka and Moldova have secured the additional preferences for compliance with labour rights.

Second, the compatibility of the special incentive arrangements with the GATT is a matter of some uncertainty. A panel has recently upheld a complaint by India that the special incentive arrangements applied to drug trafficking violate the GATT and the enabling clause.[55] The panel found that to be consistent with the enabling clause, a GSP scheme had to provide identical tariff concessions to *all* developing countries, not just to a small group of such countries. It held that references to 'developing countries' in the clause should be interpreted as references to 'all developing countries'. And it placed considerable weight on the fact that the original decision to make provision in the GATT for GSP schemes referred to such schemes as 'non-discriminatory'. The panel also rejected the EU's alternative argument that the scheme could be justified under Article XX(b) of the GATT. This obviously casts serious doubt on the legality of the labour rights provisions. Indeed, India's original complaint challenged the labour and environment arrangements as well as the drug arrangements. These aspects of the complaint were dropped because the labour and environment arrangements have hardly been invoked and have not therefore harmed India's trade.[56] But India has reserved the right to renew its claims if the labour incentives are granted to more countries. At the time of writing, the EU is appealing against the panel's decision on the drug trafficking provisions. The main difficulty facing the EU is the clash of values between its development policy and WTO

[54] Brandtner and Rosas, 'Trade Preferences and Human Rights', in P. Alston (ed.), *The EU and Human Rights* (1999), at 718–21.   [55] WTO Panel, *supra* note 49.
[56] *Supra* note 49, at para. 1.5.

norms. The EU invokes a concept of 'sustainable development' that includes progress on labour and environmental standards as well as increasing trade. But whilst this approach is uncontroversial within the EU, it is regarded with suspicion by trade theorists, who are keen to insulate the WTO from 'extraneous' non-trade issues.

To sum up, it is clear that there are various practical problems with invoking suspension clauses and even with offering incentives in order to promote collective labour rights. Nevertheless, these provisions have an important symbolic value. They show that the EU regards itself as having significant leverage over human rights issues in third countries. But this attitude can only be legitimate if the EU has similar control over its internal affairs.

2. IS THERE A REAL RISK THAT A MEMBER STATE MIGHT FAIL TO PROTECT COLLECTIVE LABOUR RIGHTS?

An obvious response to the arguments advanced in Part 1 is to point to the relatively good human rights record of the member states. Although it might be theoretically possible that EU law could be undermined in these various ways, such problems would never arise in practice because member states would always maintain an effective regime of protection for collective labour rights. This is particularly likely to be true of those member states in which collective labour rights are guaranteed under the constitution. Nevertheless, it will be argued here that this claim is not persuasive. The external safeguards that should guarantee that the member states are observing collective labour rights all suffer from various limitations and weaknesses.

One such external mechanism is the European Convention for the Protection of Human Rights and Fundamental Freedoms (ECHR). All EU member states are signatories. The great advantage of the ECHR is that individuals may bring a complaint to the European Court of Human Rights (ECtHR) if their rights are violated by a signatory state. The Court is highly regarded and states may come under considerable pressure to bring their law into compliance with its judgments. But the main disadvantage of relying on the ECHR to protect collective labour rights is that the content of Article 11 is limited. It provides that: 'Everyone has the right to freedom of peaceful assembly and to freedom of association with others, including the right to form and to join trade unions for the protection of his interests.' There are two important features to note about this right. First, the ECtHR has held that it includes a right to refuse to be a member of an association alongside the right to be a member.[57] Although this protects individuals' choices, it is unpopular with many trade unionists because it effectively outlaws the closed shop, one of the most effective ways of ensuring union strength in the workplace. Second, Article 11 does not specify any consequential rights, such as a right to

---

[57] See, for example, *Young, James and Webster v. UK*, [1981] 4 EHRR 38.

engage in collective bargaining or a right to strike. Applicants to the ECtHR have sought to argue that the phrase 'for the protection of his interests' implicitly includes these consequential rights, but despite early indications that this interpretation would be supported, later cases have been extremely cautious.[58]

The European Social Charter (ESC) offers a much fuller definition of collective labour rights. Article 5 protects the right to form and join trade unions and employers' associations, at the national and international levels. Article 6(2) requires signatories to 'promote, where necessary and appropriate, machinery for voluntary negotiations' between employers and unions, thus giving protection to collective bargaining. And Article 6(4) requires signatories to uphold the right to strike. But the difficulty with relying on the ESC is that states' acceptance of the obligations it contains is less comprehensive. Cyprus, Estonia, Finland, Sweden, France, Italy, Ireland, Lithuania, Portugal, and Slovenia have all ratified the revised ESC of 1996. The remaining member states have ratified the original ESC of 1961, but not the revised version. In relation to Articles 5 and 6, this does not matter in itself, since these provisions remain unchanged in the new Charter. However, there are some gaps in member states' acceptance of these key articles. Greece has not accepted either article, and Austria, Luxembourg, and Poland have not accepted Article 6(4), on the right to strike. Moreover, not all member states have signed up to the collective complaints procedure. Of course, all signatories are subject to the ESC's regular reporting requirements and reviews by the European Committee of Social Rights. But this procedure can only consider the rights at a high level of generality. Where the collective complaints procedure is in place, various bodies, including national trade unions and employers' associations, have the opportunity of drawing the Committee's attention to specific breaches of collective labour rights.

A third possibility is the ILO. Not surprisingly, the ILO places considerable emphasis on collective labour rights. There are two key conventions on freedom of association and collective bargaining, Conventions 87 and 98.[59] But states are deemed to support freedom of association by virtue of their membership of the ILO, regardless of whether or not they have ratified these conventions. Moreover, respect for freedom of association and collective bargaining are included in the ILO's Declaration on Fundamental Rights and Principles at Work of 1998, which also binds states as part of ILO membership. Although the ILO has not been able to agree a convention on the right to strike, it is accepted as a key aspect of collective labour rights in the ILO's practice.[60] All EU member states, including the acceding countries, have ratified Conventions 87 and 98.

---

[58] Compare *National Union of Belgian Police v. Belgium*, [1979–80] 1 EHRR 578, at 591, with *Swedish Engine Drivers' Union v. Sweden*, [1979–80] 1 EHRR 617 and *Schmidt and Dahlström v. Sweden*, [1979–80] 1 EHRR 637.

[59] ILO, *Freedom of Association and Protection of the Right to Organise Convention* (No. 87) (1948); *The Right to Organise and Collective Bargaining Convention* (No. 98) (1949).

[60] ILO, *Digest of Decisions and Principles of the Freedom of Association Committee* (1996), para. 447.

The main difficulty with relying on the ILO to ensure that states uphold collective labour rights is the weakness of its enforcement mechanisms.[61] One of the common criticisms of the ILO is that it is good at setting standards but in a weak position to enforce them. Under Article 22 of the Constitution, member states must submit an annual report that explains how they are implementing the Conventions they have ratified. If a state is failing to comply, another state may make a complaint or a trade union may make a representation to that effect.[62] The Governing Body refers complaints to a Commission of Inquiry where appropriate.[63] The Commission publishes its report and the Committee of Experts on the Application of Conventions and Recommendations follows up on implementation of the Commission's recommendations. Representations are reviewed by the Governing Body, which may decide to publish the representation along with any response received from the relevant government, or to appoint an ad hoc committee to investigate the matter further.[64] Freedom of association cases are dealt with by the Freedom of Association Committee, which also publishes its reports. The ILO does not have powers of enforcement, such as the ability to levy fines against governments.[65] All it can do is to persuade governments to comply. Phrases like 'moral suasion' or 'the mobilization of shame' are commonly used to describe the ILO's approach to enforcement. A truly recalcitrant government could simply ignore the ILO's views. And since states are under no obligation to ratify ILO Conventions in the first place, they can simply withdraw ratification if they are in breach.

This section has shown that the EU should not assume that other human rights regimes are protecting collective labour rights in the member states. All the obvious candidates suffer from weaknesses, either in terms of enforcement powers or in terms of the content of the rights they protect. Perhaps the member states do protect collective labour rights to a very high standard. It is not the purpose of this chapter to assess their records in detail. But Part 1 has established the potential for problems, and Part 2 has done nothing to dispel those problems.

3. WHAT POWERS DOES THE EU HAVE TO PROMOTE COMPLIANCE WITH COLLECTIVE LABOUR RIGHTS ON THE PART OF THE MEMBER STATES?

The presence of Article 137(5) in the Treaty creates the impression that the EU has no power to promote collective labour rights in the member states. In fact, this is

---

[61] For a more detailed account of the enforcement of ILO standards, see F. Maupain, 'The Settlement of Disputes within the International Labour Office', 2 *JIEL* (2000) 273.

[62] ILO Constitution, Arts. 26 and 24, respectively.   [63] *Supra* note 62, Arts. 26–9.

[64] *Supra* note 62, Art. 25.

[65] Under ILO Constitution, Art. 33, the 'Governing Body may recommend to the Conference such action as it may deem wise and expedient to secure compliance' with the recommendations of a Commission of Inquiry. This has been used only once, in 2000, to address the problem of forced labour in Burma/Myanmar.

misleading. The EU's social policy competences in the field of collective labour rights are more extensive than Article 137(5) implies. And because collective labour rights are fundamental human rights, the EU may be able to uphold them in the course of its general human rights activities. This section will explore the EU's true role in the promotion of collective labour rights. It will be argued in Part 4 that although this role is quite significant, it is not sufficient to guard against the problems identified in Part 1.

A. Social Policy Competences

In the social policy sphere, the position appears to be determined by Article 137(5) EC, which specifically excludes Community action in the fields of freedom of association and the right to strike. However, this leaves open a debate about whether or not the Community has competence over collective bargaining. Moreover, the Article only applies to legislation under Article 137, not to legislation enacted under some other Treaty basis.

1. Article 137(5) EC

The idea of explicitly excluding Community action in the field of collective labour rights first came about in 1992, in the Agreement on Social Policy annexed to the Maastricht Treaty. As is well-known, the Agreement represented a major advance in the Community's role in labour law. It provided a basis for legislation on various matters by qualified majority, including health and safety and information and consultation of workers. Legislation on 'representation and collective defence' of workers required unanimity. The European Works Councils Directive was enacted under the Agreement, and was subsequently extended to the United Kingdom.[66] But freedom of association and the right to strike (along with pay) were excluded altogether from the Agreement. This approach was followed when the Agreement was incorporated into the Treaty in 1997. The exclusion of collective labour rights is now to be found in Article 137(5) EC. As Ryan explains, although it seems plausible to suggest that these matters may have been excluded in the hope of persuading the United Kingdom to sign up to the Maastricht Agreement, the evidence indicates that there was no support from other member states for Community action in these fields.[67] The member states were keen to maintain exclusive control over collective labour rights.

An important point to note about Article 137(5) is that although it excludes freedom of association and the right to strike, it does not exclude collective bargaining. Thus, one of the three main collective labour rights is potentially included in the EU's competences. However, we need to find a basis for this within

---

[66] Council Directive 94/45/EC, OJ 1994 L 254/64, extended to the UK by Council Directive 97/74/EC, OJ 1998 L 10/22.

[67] Ryan, 'Pay, Trade Union Rights and European Community Law', 13 *IJCLLR* (1997) 305, at 308–9.

Article 137(1): according to the principle of limited attribution, the EU only has the competences which are expressly given to it by the Treaties. The most likely candidate is Article 137(1)(f), which covers 'representation and collective defence of the interests of workers and employers, including co-determination'. The Council may take two different types of action on this subject. One is to encourage cooperation between member states. The other is to enact directives setting out 'minimum requirements for gradual implementation'. The Council must act unanimously on a proposal from the Commission after consulting the European Parliament when it is invoking Article 137(1)(f).

To what extent does this provision cover collective bargaining? The reference to co-determination seems to be intended as a reference to the German tradition of worker participation through works councils (the German version of the Treaty uses the term 'Mitbestimmung'). This forms part of a 'dual channel' system. Although the trade union may play a role in getting the works council set up in the workplace, the two institutions coexist and perform different tasks. This phrase would not therefore seem to cover collective bargaining.

This leaves us with 'representation and collective defence'. This is a slightly odd phrase and is certainly not a term of art in English. Collective bargaining does involve the representation of workers' interests. It also involves the collective defence of workers' interests, since the bargainers are expected not just to express views to the employer but also to ensure that any deal they reach is beneficial for workers. The use of the term 'defence' is a little curious, since it might imply simply ensuring that workers' terms and conditions are not reduced, rather than seeking improvements in workers' terms and conditions (and collective bargaining usually involves both), but this interpretation seems unduly narrow.

However, there are three problems with interpreting this provision to cover collective bargaining. First, because Article 137(5) precludes Community action on freedom of association, the Community's competence over 'representation' might be limited in a trade union context. For example, would the Community be able to legislate on the procedures for the recognition of trade unions by employers, or on the protection against discrimination to be afforded to trade union representatives? Or are these matters of freedom of association for the member states to determine? Secondly, Article 137(5) excludes pay from the scope of Community competences. As Ryan points out, this could have a considerable impact on Community legislation on collective bargaining.[68] Pay is one of the main subjects for collective bargaining between workers and employers, so Community legislation on collective bargaining that did not cover this topic would be very largely emasculated. And thirdly, Article 140 contains an explicit reference to collective bargaining. This suggests that when collective bargaining is meant, the Treaty drafters were capable of referring to it in so many words. This may cast doubt on whether it is right to see Article 137(1)(f) in this light at all.

---

[68] Ryan, *supra* note 67, at 312.

Let us therefore examine some other possible interpretations of Article 137(1)(f). One possibility is that the phrase applies to consultation between the employer and worker representatives, hence the use of the term 'representation'. However, Article 137(1)(e) covers the 'information and consultation' of workers. This raises the question of how we could distinguish between the consultation referred to in sub-paragraph (e) and the consultation in sub-paragraph (f). One possibility is that the two paragraphs refer to the two different types of consultation in European law. There is a weaker version—the 'exchange of views and establishment of dialogue' typified by the European Works Councils Directive—which might be the one denoted by sub-paragraph (e).[69] And there is a stronger version—consultation 'with a view to reaching an agreement', as in the Collective Redundancies Directive— which might be denoted by sub-paragraph (f).[70] Another possibility is that (e) refers to the consultation of workers themselves, whereas (f) refers to consultation with worker representatives. This second interpretation is perhaps the more plausible of the two, since it explains the use of 'representation' in sub-paragraph (f). But both interpretations are problematic, since these various types of consultation could quite easily fall within the definition of 'information and consultation' in sub-paragraph (e). This seems to render (f) superfluous.

Another possible interpretation of sub-paragraph (f) is that it refers to forms of industrial action. This is an interpretation considered by Ryan.[71] He suggests that the phrase 'collective defence' implies collective action taken by workers to protect their interests. He goes on to point out that this creates a problem in respect of Article 137(5)'s exclusion of Community competence over the right to strike. On this theory, Article 137 could be used to set minimum standards in the field of action short of a strike, but not in respect of strike action itself. This is an odd result, particularly when one considers the difficulty of drawing a clear line between these two types of action.

It therefore seems that, although collective bargaining is not expressly excluded from the Community's competences under Article 137(5), it is difficult to find a clear Treaty basis for a directive on this subject. But Article 137 is not the only possible basis for legislation on collective labour rights. There are other possibilities, and it is to these that we will now turn.

2. Social Dialogue

The social dialogue was described in Part 1. An agreement reached by the social partners may be implemented in one of two ways: by enactment as a directive, or by collective bargaining within the member states. Where an agreement is to be enacted as a directive, it must relate to a matter over which the EU has competence. Thus, the exclusion of freedom of association and the right to strike in Article 137(5)

---

[69] *Supra* note 66, Art. 2(f).   [70] Council Directive 98/59/EC, OJ 1998 L 225/16, Art. 2(1).

[71] Ryan, *supra* note 67, at 312.

would be applicable. But no such constraints apply when the agreement is to be implemented through collective bargaining in the member states. This means that the social partners do have power to regulate collective labour rights through the social dialogue procedure. The recent Framework Agreement on Telework is the first agreement to be implemented through collective bargaining instead of legislation.[72] If it is successful, it may open up the possibility of using Article 139 to regulate collective labour rights at some point in the future.

The social partners are inherently likely to have an interest in collective labour rights. This is particularly true of the ETUC, which is committed in the Preamble to its constitution to the promotion of 'human and trade union rights'. But the social partners' record on collective labour issues is poor. They failed to reach an agreement on European Works Councils in 1993, and UNICE refused to negotiate on information and consultation in 1997. In relation to European Works Councils, there was strong support among the member states for legislation, so UNICE sought to use the social dialogue in the hope of securing an agreement which would be more favourable to businesses.[73] This placed the ETUC in a strong position: it did not need to make concessions because it was confident that legislation could be passed by the member states. The negotiations broke down when the CBI, the British member of UNICE, felt that too much ground had been given to the ETUC. In relation to information and consultation, UNICE refused to negotiate with the ETUC because it was strongly opposed to further European intervention in this area, arguing that legislation would cut across varied national practices to no real benefit.[74] This suggests that the ETUC does use the social dialogue procedure in order to advance collective labour rights, but that—not surprisingly—its interests diverge sharply from those of the employers.

The social dialogue has considerable potential as a mechanism for the promotion of collective labour rights. It avoids the formal limitation on the Community's competence and it is driven by organizations of employers and workers. This potential may, however, be difficult to realize in practice.

3. Articles 94 and 95

Articles 94 and 95 EC provide the Community with competence in relation to the development and functioning of the internal market. In the past, they have been used for legislation on social policy. The Collective Redundancies Directive is an example of this.[75] Could they be used for legislation on collective labour rights?

Article 95(1) EC allows for the adoption of measures 'for the approximation of the provisions laid down by law, regulation or administrative action in Member States which have as their object the establishment and functioning of the internal

---

[72] ETUC, UNICE–UEAPME, CEEP, *Framework Agreement on Telework*, 16 July 2002.
[73] Gold and Hall, 'Statutory European Works Councils: The Final Countdown?', 25 *IRJ* (1994) 177.
[74] UNICE, Press Releases of 16 March 1998 and 16 October 1998.
[75] *Supra* note 70, based on what is now Art. 94.

market'. Significantly, this Article permits the adoption of measures by qualified majority voting in the Council. However, its utility in relation to collective labour rights is limited by Article 95(2), which states that it cannot be used to enact provisions 'relating to the rights and interests of employed persons'. It has been argued that Article 95(2) could be interpreted narrowly, so that it would only preclude internal market measures that focused exclusively on the rights of employees, and would allow internal market measures that had some subsidiary impact on the rights of employees.[76] But even if this argument found favour with the ECJ,[77] it is difficult to see how a directive setting minimum standards for the protection of collective labour rights could be presented in these terms.

Article 95 operates as a derogation from Article 94 EC, so where the former is not available, the latter still applies. Article 94 EC provides for 'directives for the approximation of such laws, regulations or administrative provisions of the member states as directly affect the establishment or functioning of the common market'. The wording of Article 94 is broader than that of Article 95, and the reference to the 'common market'[78] is more general than the reference to the 'internal market'[79] in Article 95. However, the major disadvantage of using Article 94 is that it requires unanimity in the Council. In any event, it seems doubtful whether Article 94 could be used as the basis for a directive setting out minimum standards for collective labour rights in the member states. In the *Tobacco Advertising* case, the ECJ held that a directive which set minimum standards could not be regarded as removing obstacles to free movement in the internal market.[80] This was because the member states remained entitled to set higher standards if they wished. And it was the variation in standards between the member states that was most likely to constitute an obstacle to free movement. Syrpis has pointed out that this has significant implications for social policy.[81] Because of the differences in traditions between the member states, directives that set minimum standards are a common tool in this field. A directive of this type would certainly be the most attractive option for collective labour rights, because the member states' approaches are particularly diverse. But the *Tobacco Advertising* case casts doubt on the possibility of using Article 94 in this way. Moreover, the ECJ is likely to be particularly alert to attempts to 'evade' specific prohibitions in the Treaty by using Articles that grant relatively general legislative competences.[82] Thus, the use of Article 94 for a directive on collective labour rights might be regarded as an evasion of Article 137(5).

---

[76] See, for example, Vogel-Polsky, 'What Future is There for a Social Europe', 19 *ILJ* (1990) 65, at 70–3.

[77] For discussion, see J. Kenner, *EU Employment Law: From Rome to Amsterdam and Beyond* (2003), at 82–8.   [78] See Art. 2 EC.

[79] Defined in Art. 14(2) EC.

[80] Case C-376/98, *Germany v. European Parliament and Council*, [2000] ECR I-8419.

[81] Syrpis, 'Smoke without Fire: The Social Policy Agenda and the Internal Market', 30 *ILJ* (2001) 271, though cf. Kenner, *supra* note 77, at 86–7.

[82] The preference for specific over general Treaty articles is expressed in a number of cases, including Case C-84/94, *UK v. Council*, [1996] ECR I-5755.

4. 'Soft Law'

The social policy chapter of the Treaty grants a 'softer' competence for the Commission to 'encourage cooperation between the member states and facilitate the co-ordination of their action in all social policy fields' under Article 140.[83] This Article explicitly refers to 'the right of association and collective bargaining'. It allows the Commission to engage in research, to produce reports and to encourage consultation on both national and international dimensions of these issues. Although this provision does not grant legislative competence, it does justify Commission activity that relates to two of the three collective labour rights: freedom of association and collective bargaining.

In fact, Article 140 is only one element in a broader trend towards the use of 'soft law' in social policy. The Commission's Social Policy Agenda sets out a series of 'objectives' for the EU and the member states, and then identifies various types of 'action' to be taken in pursuit of these objectives.[84] Although some parts of the Agenda are to be implemented through legislation, the vast majority of 'actions' do not involve changes to the law. For example, under the objective of developing the social dialogue at EU and national level, the actions include: 'launch a reflection group on the future of industrial relations' and 'promote interaction between social dialogue at European and national level through national round tables on issues of common interest (work organisation, future of work, new forms of work)'.[85]

An important feature of the 'soft law' approach is use of the 'open method of coordination', initially developed in relation to the European Employment Strategy and now used in many areas of European activity, including social policy.[86] The underlying idea is that the EU should set the goals for social policy, but the member states should have discretion as to how they work towards those goals. To give more precision to the process, targets are set for the member states and monitored on a regular basis. However, there are no sanctions for failure to meet targets and considerable emphasis is placed on the idea that member states can learn from each other during the monitoring process.

The wider use of soft law approaches has clear advantages. It overcomes the common criticism that Community law was unduly rigid and inflexible, failing to respond to differing national conditions and industrial relations traditions.[87] It may also overcome resistance on the part of the member states to new Community initiatives: if they are not legally binding, they may not seem so threatening. It can therefore be portrayed as a 'smart' regulatory technique, because it maximizes the likelihood that the subjects of regulation—the member states—will accept the

---

[83] The Council also has a 'soft law' competence under Art. 137(2)(a) but this is subject to the exclusion of freedom of association and the right to strike by Art. 137(5).

[84] Commission Communication on the Social Policy Agenda of 28 June 2000, COM(2000) 379 final.

[85] *Supra* note 84, at 23–4.   [86] For discussion, see Kenner, *supra* note 77, chap. 11.

[87] Barnard, *supra* note 30, at 487–93.

regulation and find it easy to comply with.[88] But soft law approaches have disadvantages too. One problem is vagueness. The various 'actions' designed to promote the social dialogue do not involve any clear targets against which to assess the progress of the Community and the member states. For example, the Commission undertakes to 'closely monitor and continuously update the study on representativeness of social partners at European level'.[89] This could have been coupled with targets for the member states to increase the membership of trade unions and employers' associations at the national level. But instead, the Commission prefers to keep the process at a high level of generality.[90] In turn, this means that the member states can safely ignore much of what the Commission is doing.

More generally, soft law competences are not particularly suitable for setting *minimum* standards. The purpose of a minimum standard is to identify a level of protection below which the member states should not be allowed to fall. Such a standard necessarily entails strict enforcement procedures. Once a legally-binding minimum standard is in place, soft law competences can be used to encourage the member states to implement a more generous level of protection. Thus, soft law cannot take the place of a directive setting out minimum standards for the protection of collective labour rights.

B. Human Rights

Collective labour rights are, of course, not just a matter of social policy. They also form part of the corpus of internationally recognized fundamental human rights. This means that general Community law on fundamental rights may be used to promote compliance with collective labour rights on the part of the member states.

1. The ECJ's Jurisprudence

The Community institutions, and the member states when they are implementing Community law, are under an obligation to respect human rights. This obligation has been developed by the ECJ. The court's jurisprudence on this issue grew out of its development of the doctrine of the supremacy of Community law over inconsistent national law.[91] At first, some national constitutional courts resisted supremacy. They argued that their role was to uphold the human rights guarantees contained in national constitutions. This meant scrutinizing Community law, as well as national law, for its compliance with these rights, rather than applying it unquestioningly in accordance with the principle of supremacy. Such scrutiny would

[88] For a discussion (in the context of employer compliance), see Barnard and Deakin, 'In Search of Coherence: Social Policy, the Single Market and Fundamental Rights', 31 *IRJ* (2000) 331, at 340–4.

[89] *Supra* note 84, at 23.

[90] This is reflected most clearly in Commission Communication on the Scoreboard on Implementing the Social Policy Agenda of 6 February 2003, COM(2003) 57 final.

[91] Case 6/64, *Costa v. Enel*, [1964] ECR 585.

have defeated the ECJ's objective of ensuring the uniform application of Community law. The Court therefore undertook to perform human rights scrutiny itself.[92] The ECJ's jurisprudence on fundamental rights has gradually been given formal acknowledgement in the treaty architecture. This process began with the Single European Act of 1986, which included a brief reference to human rights in the Preamble. The Treaty on European Union of 1992 drew more heavily on the existing case law. Article F(2) provided that 'the Union shall respect fundamental rights, as guaranteed by the European Convention for the Protection of Human Rights and Fundamental Freedoms signed in Rome on 4 November 1950 and as they result from the constitutional traditions common to the Member States, as general principles of Community law'. In a bizarre twist, this provision was expressly excluded from the jurisdiction of the ECJ.[93]

The most significant developments came with the Treaty of Amsterdam in 1997. Article F(2) of the TEU became Article 6(2), and was brought within the ECJ's jurisdiction, and a new Article 6(1) provided that 'the Union is founded on the principles of liberty, democracy, respect for human rights and fundamental freedoms, and the rule of law, principles which are common to the Member States'. The EU Charter of Fundamental Rights, proclaimed in 2000, gives further guidance as to the content of the human rights to be respected by the EU and has been incorporated into the new EU Constitution. Article 7(2) of the Constitution proposes that the EU should seek accession to the ECHR, a move which would inevitably strengthen the role of the ECtHR's jurisprudence in EU law, with mixed consequences for the protection of collective labour rights.

Let us begin by considering the place of collective labour rights in the EU Charter. Article 12(1) protects freedom of association, including the right to 'form and to join trade unions'. This right is very similar to Article 11 of the ECHR, so its interpretation is governed by Article 52(3) of the Charter. This requires the EU institutions to interpret the right in the same way as its ECHR equivalent, although EU law may provide more extensive protection. This is unfortunate because the ECtHR's jurisprudence on Article 11 is particularly narrow, focusing on the freedom to form and join associations and largely excluding related rights such as the right to engage in collective bargaining or the right to strike.[94] However, this problem is substantially mitigated by the presence in the EU Charter of Article 28. This provides that:

Workers and employers, or their respective organisations, have, in accordance with Community law and national laws and practices, the right to negotiate and conclude collective agreements at the appropriate levels and, in cases of conflicts of interest, to take collective action to defend their interests, including strike action.

Thus, the Charter offers protection to all three collective labour rights: freedom of association, collective bargaining, and the right to strike. At present, the Charter is

---

[92] Case 11/70, *Internationale Handelsgesellschaft*, [1970] ECR 1125.   [93] Art. L.
[94] *Supra* note 58.

simply a 'proclamation' of the Council, Commission, and Parliament that has been 'approved' by the member states. It has been considered in some decisions of the CFI,[95] but not so far by the ECJ. In view of its uncertain status, it is also necessary to consider the existing case law of the ECJ, to which we will now turn.

Two main sources of rights have been identified in the ECJ's case law: international human rights treaties of which the member states are signatories, and the constitutional traditions of the member states.[96] In the former category, the ECHR has been given particular importance.[97] This is highly significant because Article 11 of the ECHR protects freedom of association, including the right to form and join trade unions, though it does not appear to protect the right to engage in collective bargaining or the right to strike.[98] Article 11 has been accepted by the ECJ as one of the fundamental rights recognized in Community law in several cases, albeit not in a trade union context.[99] In construing Article 11, the ECJ has regard to the jurisprudence of the ECtHR. In the *Albany* case, the Advocate-General reviewed the ECtHR case law and concluded that:

> The Community legal order protects the right to form and join trade unions and employers' associations which is at the heart of freedom of association. In my view, the right to take collective action in order to protect occupational interests in so far as it is indispensable for the enjoyment of freedom of association is also protected by Community law. However, it cannot be said that there is sufficient convergence of national legal orders and international legal instruments on the recognition of a specific fundamental right to bargain collectively.[100]

The ECJ rejected a claim that the collective agreement at issue in the case was a breach of competition law, thus upholding the role of collective bargaining, but it did not comment on the Advocate-General's conclusions on the human rights point.

It may be possible to incorporate a wider range of collective rights into EU labour law through the other main source of fundamental rights, the constitutional traditions of the member states. For example, the right to strike is explicitly guaranteed by the constitutions of France, Italy, Portugal, Spain, Greece, and Sweden.[101] In several other countries, such as Germany and Luxembourg, the courts have been willing to extend the constitutional guarantee of freedom of association to include a right to strike. However, Britain, Austria, and Denmark do not use the mechanism of a right—whether explicit or implicit—to protect strikes. This raises an interesting question as to what exactly is meant by the 'common constitutional traditions' of the member states. A reference to a particular right in the constitution of just one member state does not seem sufficient, since this would allow a Community act to be judged in the light of a member state's constitutional law, contrary to the

---

[95] Case T-177/01, *Jégo-Quéré v. Commission*, [2002] ECR II-2365, later overruled.

[96] Case 4/73, *Nold v. Commission*, [1974] ECR 491, and see Art. 6(2) TEU.

[97] Case 36/75, *Rutili v. Minister of the Interior*, [1975] ECR 1219, and see Art. 6(2) TEU.

[98] *Supra* note 58. [99] For example, Case C415/93, *Bosman*, [1995] ECR I-4921, at 5065.

[100] Case C-67/96, *Albany International*, [1999] ECR I-5751, at 5793.

[101] See Jacobs, 'The Law of Strikes and Lockouts', in R. Blanpain and C. Engels (eds.), *Comparative Labour Law and Industrial Relations in Industrialized Market Economies* (2001) 585.

principle of supremacy itself.[102] The right to strike has much more widespread recognition, but could its status as a Community fundamental right be denied because it does not appear in some constitutions? If the states concerned recognized the right to strike by non-constitutional means, it could be argued that their failure to include the right in their constitutions was simply a reflection of the haphazard nature of constitutional drafting or the difficulties of constitutional amendment. It would be more difficult for the ECJ to recognize the right to strike if the member states argued that they did not include it in their constitutions because they did not consider it fundamental or because they did not consider it to be a right at all. However, the better view seems to be that recognition in the constitutions of a majority of the member states would be sufficient to achieve the status of a Community fundamental right.

If collective labour rights were recognised by the ECJ, they would, of course, be qualified. Article 11 of the ECHR is subject to numerous qualifications which would be applied by the ECJ as part of its respect for the jurisprudence of the ECtHR. And the ECJ's own case law is beginning to develop a notion of justified limits on fundamental rights. This is evidenced by cases such as *Wachauf*, in which it was stated that:

The fundamental rights recognized by the Court are not absolute, however, but must be considered in relation to their social function. Consequently, restrictions may be imposed on the exercise of those rights, in particular in the context of a common organization of a market, provided that those restrictions in fact correspond to objectives of general interest pursued by the Community and do not constitute, with regard to the aim pursued, a disproportionate and intolerable interference, impairing the very substance of those rights.[103]

A similar point can be made about the rights contained in the EU Charter. Article 12 of the Charter would be interpreted in the light of the qualifications contained in Article 11 ECHR. Article 28 is qualified by the phrase 'in accordance with Community law and national laws and practices'. This gives the member states and Community institutions a considerable discretion in implementing the right to collective bargaining and the right to strike. Presumably, the ECJ would only find a violation of those rights if the limits imposed by Community law or national law were such as to substantially interfere with their protection.

But the most important feature of fundamental rights in EU law is their limited role in the legal order. Fundamental rights are seen as a condition of the lawfulness of Community acts. In other words, the doctrine is used to control the Community institutions or the member states when implementing Community law, not to give them new competences.[104] This position has not changed even though the Charter forms part of the new EU Constitution. Article 51 of the Charter sums up the approach very neatly. According to Article 51(1), the Charter is 'addressed to the

---

[102] Case C 234/85, *Staatsanwaltschaft Freiburg v. Keller*, [1986] ECR 2897, at 2912.
[103] Case 5/88, *Wachauf v. Germany*, [1989] ECR 2609, at 2639.
[104] Opinion 2/94, *Accession by the Community to the ECHR*, [1996] ECR I-1759.

institutions and bodies of the Union . . . and to the Member States only when they are implementing Union law'. And under Article 51(2), the Charter 'does not establish any new power or task for the Community or the Union'.

Of course, it is important for the effective protection of collective labour rights in the member states that the EU institutions should be prevented from interfering with them. It is also important that the member states should not be able to use EU law as an excuse for lowering the level of protection they afford to collective labour rights. However, the doctrine of fundamental rights does not require the member states to promote collective labour rights. Nor does it enable the EU to take action if a particular member state is failing to uphold such rights in its domestic law.

2. Article 7 TEU

The Treaty of Amsterdam introduced a new Article 7 TEU (ex Article F(1)) which provides the EU with a means of punishing a member state in the event of a 'serious and persistent' breach of the obligation under Article 6(1) to respect human rights. The member state concerned would remain bound by its obligations under Community law, but its rights under the treaties—including its voting rights in the Council—could be suspended. In theory, this provision could be used to tackle breaches of collective labour rights, but its use in this regard is, in practice, unlikely.

A first difficulty is that Article 7 is hedged about with procedural constraints.[105] When determining whether or not a 'serious and persistent' breach has taken place, the Council must act unanimously, with the assent of the European Parliament, after hearing representations from the member state concerned. Once such a determination has been made, the Council may act by qualified majority to suspend the member state's rights, but it must take account of 'the possible consequences of such a suspension on the rights and obligations of natural and legal persons'.[106] The suspension of a member state's treaty rights is, of course, a serious step, and should only be made on the basis of clear evidence and widespread agreement. However, these procedural requirements make it less likely that Article 7 will be used.

A second issue is whether a breach of collective labour rights could ever be sufficiently serious or persistent to warrant the use of Article 7. Nowak argues that the phrase 'serious and persistent' can be equated to the concept of 'gross and systematic violations' as applied in the UN human rights system.[107] The notion of a 'persistent' or 'systematic' violation is clearly designed to indicate a practice that is widespread, as opposed to an isolated case. The notion of a 'serious' or 'gross' violation is much harder to interpret. Obvious examples include genocide, slavery, apartheid, or torture. The 'disappearance' of trade union activists might fall within this category. But it is unclear whether breaches of freedom of association per se would do so. Moreover, although Nowak is keen to assert the indivisibility of human

---

[105] The details of the procedure were slightly amended by the Treaty of Nice.   [106] Art. 7(3).

[107] Nowak, 'Human Rights "Conditionality" in Relation to Entry to, and Full Participation in, the EU', in P. Alston (ed.), *The EU and Human Rights* (1999) 687, at 694–6.

rights, he is forced to acknowledge that it is more difficult to include breaches of economic and social rights (with the exception of education and extreme poverty) in the category of 'gross' violations.[108] Of course, a state that fell foul of Article 7 because of an obviously 'gross' violation of human rights would probably not be a respecter of collective labour rights, but it seems unlikely that a breach of collective labour rights alone would in practice lead to the use of Article 7.

As many commentators have pointed out, however, Article 7 has a significant symbolic value. By showing that there are conditions attached to continuing EU membership, it raises the profile of human rights concerns within the EU. This may contribute in an indirect way to greater compliance with human rights—including collective labour rights—on the part of member states.

C. Accession

A third way in which the EU might be able to promote compliance with collective labour rights in a particular country is when the country is a candidate for membership of the EU. Various conditions are imposed on countries seeking to accede to the EU, including respect for fundamental human rights and compliance with the '*acquis*', the existing body of Community law. Collective labour rights are of relevance in both these areas.

In 1997 the Treaty of Amsterdam amended Article 49 TEU (ex Article O) to provide that 'any European State which respects the principles set out in Article 6(1) may apply to become a member of the Union'. Thus, the reference to respect for human rights in Article 6(1) was made a condition of EU membership. In fact, Article 49 gives a treaty basis to one of the 'Copenhagen criteria' for accession, set out at the Copenhagen European Council in 1993: 'stability of institutions guaranteeing democracy, the rule of law, human rights and respect for and protection of minorities.'[109] In 1997 the Commission published its Opinions on the progress of each of the candidate countries towards meeting the Copenhagen criteria, including their compliance with human rights.[110] These are updated annually by the Commission in a series of Regular Reports. Collective labour rights are considered in these assessments. Under the heading of civil and political rights, the Commission examines freedom of association in general, and under the heading of economic and social rights, the Commission focuses on trade union rights, including collective bargaining and industrial action.

On the whole, the Commission has expressed satisfaction with the candidate countries' legislation in this field, although some countries have experienced difficulties. For example, in the case of Lithuania, the Commission noted in its 1997 Opinion that there were low levels of trade union membership,[111] and by 2001 the

---

[108] *Supra* note 107, at 695–6.   [109] European Council, *Bull. EC* 6-1993, at para. 1.13.

[110] Commission, *Agenda 2000: For a Stronger and Wider Union*, COM(97)2000 final.

[111] Commission, *Agenda 2000: Commission Opinion on Lithuania's Application for Membership of the European Union* (DOC 97/15), at 17.

position did not seem to have changed significantly.[112] Nevertheless, the Commission's criticism remains muted: 'There are concerns that legislation on union rights is not duly enforced in all cases.'[113] Nowak has commented, with some justification, that 'the analysis seems . . . rather superficial and relates more to the *de jure* than the *de facto* situation'.[114] Perhaps more worrying is that where the Commission *is* critical, its comments do not seem to prompt improvements over time, perhaps because they are not very strongly worded.

The third Copenhagen criterion is the 'ability to take on the obligations of membership, including adherence to the aims of political, economic and monetary union'.[115] This requires candidate countries to show that they have implemented existing Community legislation, the '*acquis communautaire*'. Again, the Commission is supposed to look beyond formal enactment of legislation and to consider whether it is effective in practice. This criterion is relevant to collective labour rights because one of the issues that receives particular attention in the Commission's comments on social policy is whether or not there is an effective social dialogue with employers' associations and trade unions within each candidate country. The Commission's strategy paper in 2002 reveals that the social dialogue is a problem area for several countries, including Estonia and Lithuania, although some countries, notably Hungary, had made improvements in this area.[116]

It is clear that collective labour rights do play a role in the accession process, because they feature in two of the Copenhagen criteria. Their significance is inevitably limited by the fact that they form a small part of the law on human rights and an even smaller part of the *acquis*. Moreover, the Commission's scrutiny is relatively weak, perhaps reflecting strong political pressure not to place obstacles in the way of enlargement. Nevertheless, their presence does show the Community's expectation that member states will respect collective labour rights.

4. ARE THE EU'S CURRENT POWERS TO PROMOTE COLLECTIVE LABOUR RIGHTS SUFFICIENT?

To overcome the problems identified in Part 1, the EU needs to be able to do two things. First, it needs to be able to demonstrate to third countries that its enforcement of human rights against them is matched by equivalent powers to enforce those rights internally. Second, it needs some mechanism for ensuring that there is a thriving social dialogue within each member state. Are the powers discussed in Part 3 sufficient for these purposes?

The introduction of Article 7 TEU has gone some way towards addressing the first problem. The EU's ability to suspend a member state's voting rights in the event

[112] Commission, *2001 Regular Report on Lithuania's Progress towards Accession* (SEC(2001) 1750), at 23.
[113] Commission, *2002 Regular Report on Lithuania's Progress towards Accession* (SEC(2002) 1406), at 29.
[114] Nowak, *supra* note 107, at 691.   [115] *Supra* note 109.
[116] Commission, *Towards the Enlarged Union*, COM(2002)700 final, at 48, 60, and 52, respectively.

of a serious breach of human rights is the equivalent of its power to suspend a trade treaty or trade preferences on that ground. As we have seen, Article 7 is unlikely to be invoked in practice (except in an extreme case) because it is a very serious step and is hedged about with procedural constraints. It is unlikely to be used to tackle a breach of collective labour rights alone. But the same is true of the suspension provisions in trading agreements. A decision to invoke those provisions would have serious political consequences and would clearly be a measure of last resort. The incentive provisions in the GSP have no obvious internal equivalent. An assessment of their legitimacy must therefore turn on the more general, second question of whether or not the EU has the power to promote a thriving social dialogue within the member states.

One problem is that the EU does not have a clear legislative power to set minimum standards for freedom of association, collective bargaining, and the right to strike in the member states. As we have seen, it may be possible for the EU to legislate on collective bargaining, because this is not expressly excluded by Article 137(5) EC, but the Treaty basis for such legislation is unclear. In any event, legislation on collective bargaining would do nothing to protect freedom of association or the right to strike. Articles 94 and 95, which are not directly affected by Article 137(5), might possibly provide a basis for legislation on collective labour rights, but the ECJ might not be sympathetic to their use for this purpose. Another option is the social dialogue. This is not constrained by Article 137(5) EC where the social partners are willing to implement the standards themselves through collective bargaining in the member states. But again, there are problems. Collective bargaining is inherently voluntary, and Article 139 EC is carefully drafted to ensure that the social partners have the choice of whether or not to pursue negotiations on any particular topic. Moreover, if collective labour rights are weak in a particular member state, standards about such rights which are to be implemented through collective bargaining are, *ex hypothesi*, unlikely to be very effective. Finally, although the EU's 'soft law' competence covers collective bargaining and freedom of association, it does not cover the right to strike and would not be likely to have much impact on a truly recalcitrant member state.

As we have seen, the fact that collective labour rights are also human rights adds another dimension to their protection. During the accession process, a country's human rights record is an important part of the negotiations, as well as its ability to comply with the *acquis communautaire*. However, even if the Commission's scrutiny at this stage is highly rigorous (and some argue that it is not), the fact that a state respects human rights, including collective labour rights, at the time of accession is no guarantee that it will continue to do so in the future. Perhaps the most important aspect of the Community's human rights activities is the legal obligation on the Community institutions and on the member states when they are implementing Community law to refrain from interfering with human rights, an obligation that seems likely to include collective labour rights. This ought to ensure that Community law itself does not damage collective labour rights in the member states.

But it is of no assistance where a member state's own domestic law fails to uphold those rights.

To conclude, the EU's patchwork of powers over collective labour rights is not sufficient to ensure that member states are observing minimum standards. A situation could arise in which a member state did not have an adequate system of collective bargaining at the national level. As a result, the legitimacy and effectiveness of EU legislation could be put at risk. Moreover, there is some force in the argument that the EU's human rights policy in its external relations is hypocritical, despite the introduction of Article 7 TEU. The EU should therefore be granted the competence to set minimum standards of freedom of association, collective bargaining, and industrial action to be observed by the member states.

5. SUBSIDIARITY

The main task of this paper has been to show that the current exclusion of collective labour rights from the competence of the EU is unhelpful. But this argument might not be seen as sufficient, in itself, to justify extending the EU's competence to include these rights. It might be objected that EU intervention in collective labour rights would infringe the principle of subsidiarity. This section will assess the validity of this objection.

The principle of subsidiarity in Community law operates at a number of different levels. At the lowest level, it is used to determine whether the Community or the member states should take action on a particular issue where their powers are concurrent.[117] At the highest level, it is a general political principle that plays an important part in debates about whether or not the member states should grant further powers to the Community. It is expressed in Article 1 TEU, which refers to the principle that 'decisions [should be] taken . . . as closely as possible to the citizen'. In the second *Defrenne* case, the ECJ identified two factors that justify action at the Community level in the field of social policy: preventing unfair competition and promoting social progress.[118] It will be argued here that both these factors could be used to justify Community action in the field of collective labour rights.

Let us begin by examining the prevention of unfair competition. In *Defrenne*, the ECJ explained this principle in the following way, in the context of a discussion of what is now Article 141:

First, in the light of the different stages of the development of social legislation in the various member states, the aim of Article 119 is to avoid a situation in which undertakings established in states which have actually implemented the principle of equal pay suffer a competitive disadvantage in intra-Community competition as compared with undertakings established in states which have not yet eliminated discrimination against women workers as regards pay.[119]

[117] Art. 5 EC.   [118] Case C43/75, *Defrenne v. SABENA*, [1976] ECR 455, at 472.
[119] *Supra* note 118, at 472.

The Court's focus in this quotation is on the protection of firms in member states with strong social regulation. Underlying this is the desire to prevent a 'race to the bottom' among states themselves. In an attempt to attract investment, national governments might be tempted to reduce social policy legislation to the 'lowest common denominator'. But Community law should step in to prevent this.

The first question we need to ask is whether firms might be reluctant to invest in member states that offer strong protection to collective labour rights. On the one hand, it is arguable that firms might welcome employee participation in decision-making. They might regard unions as important intermediaries between management and employees, conveying employees' ideas and suggestions to management, and informing employees about future developments in the firm. On the other hand, firms might be hostile towards unions because of their goal of securing better terms and conditions of employment through collective bargaining, and because of their ability to organize disruptive strike action in the event of a disagreement. One interesting empirical indicator of firms' attitudes towards unions is what happens when firms set their own labour standards. Many multinational enterprises have devised their own codes of conduct to set minimum standards for their global operations. These codes often include labour standards. A survey by the ILO of 215 such codes found that a mere 15 per cent included freedom of association and collective bargaining.[120] This may be explained in various ways.[121] A code may be intended to help the firm to avoid adverse publicity. Breaches of collective labour rights—in contrast to the use of child labour or breaches of health and safety standards—may not attract widespread criticism in the media. But the sheer reluctance of firms to promote collectivism at work may also be an important factor. Firms may not want powerful challenges to their authority from independent organizations of workers.

If firms are thought to be hostile towards trade unions, member states might be tempted to reduce the protection they offer to collective labour rights in order to attract investment.[122] As discussed above, some member states protect collective labour rights in their constitutions. This makes it difficult for them to deregulate this area to any great extent. For those member states with no constitutional guarantees, the position is very different. In the United Kingdom, a succession of Conservative governments from 1979 to 1997 pursued an explicit policy of deregulating the labour market.[123] Attacks on the trade union movement formed an important part of this policy. The closed shop was made unenforceable, trade unions were required to overcome a number of procedural hurdles before they could take lawful industrial action, and the scope of lawful industrial action was restricted. The election of a Labour government in 1997 did not bring about any major changes in the law on

---

[120] Diller, 'A Social Conscience in the Global Marketplace?: Labour Dimensions of Codes of Conduct, Social Labelling and Investor Initiatives', 138 *ILR* (1999) 99, at 112.

[121] Diller, *supra* note 120, at 112–13.   [122] See, generally, Ryan, *supra* note 67, at 317–19.

[123] For discussion, see P. Davies and M. Freedland, *Labour Legislation and Public Policy* (1993), chap. 9.

collective labour rights, apart from the introduction of a statutory procedure to compel employers to recognize a trade union for collective bargaining where this is supported by a majority of the workforce.[124] This indicates that the 'race to the bottom' among EU member states is a real threat in the case of collective labour rights.

In recent years, some theorists have argued that deregulation is a mistaken strategy in economic terms.[125] They suggest that high labour standards may make workers more productive, leading to greater profit for firms and greater prosperity for states. For example, workers who are given a say in important decisions through collective bargaining might feel more valued by the firm and might therefore be more loyal towards it. This would give a government with high labour standards an incentive to retain such standards, and might even lead to a 'race to the top' among other states. While this argument is persuasive, it seems more likely to yield results over the longer term. In the short term, governments may be tempted to deregulate. This could be prevented if the EU had the competence to set minimum standards for collective labour rights.

In the *Defrenne* case, the ECJ identified a second justification for Community action in the field of social policy. Referring to Article 119 (now Article 141), the Court stated:

Secondly, this provision forms part of the social objectives of the Community, which is not merely an economic union, but is at the same time intended, by common action, to ensure social progress and seek the constant improvement of the living and working conditions of their peoples, as is emphasized by the preamble to the Treaty.[126]

Thus, Community intervention may be justified on non-economic grounds, where it is necessary to ensure that citizens reap tangible benefits from European integration. It will be argued here that greater protection of collective labour rights would bring tangible benefits to workers, in several respects.

Collective labour rights empower workers in their dealings with employers. Most significantly, workers are able to choose which claims they wish to pursue and which they are prepared to compromise. They are not tied to any particular agenda set by a distant legislator with a limited understanding of the specific needs of their workplace. Of course, collective labour rights could not simply replace statutory guarantees of minimum protection for workers, such as minimum wage levels or the right not to be unfairly dismissed. But statutory guarantees are just that—a *minimum*—on which workers might be able to build. It hardly needs saying that workers as individuals are rarely in a position to bargain with their employer. Collective labour rights are vital if the floor of minimum rights is not to become a ceiling of maximum protection.

---

[124] Department of Trade and Industry, *Fairness at Work* (1998) (Cm 3968).

[125] See, for example, Deakin and Wilkinson, 'Rights vs Efficiency: The Economic Case for Transnational Labour Standards', 23 *ILJ* (1994) 289.   [126] *Supra* note 118, at 472.

Collective labour rights also empower workers in the political sphere. Dictator-ships are rarely willing to tolerate strong labour movements because they provide a forum for open political debate and a potential centre of opposition. In democracies, trade unions have an important role to play in political life. They campaign for improvements in labour legislation and reforms to social policy. And more generally, they encourage individuals to join an organization and to take an interest in political issues. This role is highly relevant in an era of declining voter turnout for elections and growing disillusionment with politics. Moreover, it could be of particular significance in the EU context, because—as is well known—many citizens feel distanced from the Union and confused by its structure and functions. Trade unions could play a useful role in involving individuals more fully in the political process at the EU level as well as within the member states.

These practical benefits of collective labour rights are reflected in the strong protection they are afforded at international level. As we have seen, freedom of association and collective bargaining are included alongside freedom from forced labour, freedom from child labour, and freedom from discrimination in the ILO's 1998 Declaration on Fundamental Rights and Principles at Work. Although it is important not to be complacent, forced labour and child labour are not major issues in the member states. Where these problems do exist, it is largely due to a lack of compliance with existing law rather than an absence of legal regulation. Indeed, the EU itself has made some effort to regulate the number of hours worked by children and young people.[127] Freedom from discrimination is, obviously, a key area of EU activity. This is particularly significant after treaty amendments to broaden the scope of the EU's competence beyond sex discrimination to include discrimination on grounds of age, race, sexual orientation, disability, and religion or belief.[128] The missing piece of the jigsaw is freedom of association and collective bargaining. If the EU could intervene in these areas, it would be protecting one of the most important rights a worker can claim.

Experience with Article 141 EC has shown that the Community can benefit citizens by enabling them to turn fundamental human rights guarantees into a practical, legally enforceable reality. As we saw in Part 2, where national law falls short, workers have few other avenues to pursue. The position would be very dif-ferent if the EU had competence over collective labour rights and agreed a directive setting out minimum standards. A member state that failed to implement the directive correctly would face infringement proceedings by the Commission with the prospect of a penalty if it did not respond to an adverse judgment of the ECJ. Under the doctrine of direct effect, public sector workers would be able to rely on the directive as against their employer. And private sector workers would be able to invoke the directive as an aid to the interpretation of national law, under the *Marleasing* principle, in an action against their employer,[129] or bring a *Francovich*

---

[127] Council Directive 94/33/EC, OJ 1994 L 216/12.   [128] See Art. 13 EC.
[129] Case C106/89, *Marleasing*, [1990] ECR I-4135.

action against the national government for damages for any losses caused by its failure to implement the directive.[130] This would indeed be a tangible improvement in the living and working conditions of ordinary citizens of the Union.

6. CONCLUSION

There are powerful arguments in favour of giving the EU competence over collective labour rights. First, this would help to overcome the problems inherent in the current situation, in which the legitimacy and effectiveness of EU law may be undermined by weak protection of collective labour rights in the member states. Second, it would protect firms established in member states with a strong tradition of collective labour rights from unfair competition from firms in member states with a lower level of protection. It would also help to prevent governments from reducing their protection of these rights in order to attract investment from firms. Third, EU competence over collective labour rights would help to improve the living and working conditions of EU citizens, by empowering them both in the workplace and in the broader political sphere.

It would, of course, be foolish to ignore the fact that simply granting competence over collective labour rights to the EU would not be the end of the story. Many difficulties would arise when the EU sought to exercise that competence. The most obvious problem is that the member states have very different industrial relations traditions.[131] As we have already seen, some member states accord constitutional protection to collective labour rights whereas others do not. Some countries place a distinction between disputes of right and disputes of interest at the heart of their industrial action law; in others, it is irrelevant. Some permit solidarity strikes; others ban them completely. These examples could easily be multiplied. Harmonization of collective labour laws across the member states is out of the question. It is no accident that this chapter has only advocated a power for the EU to set *minimum* standards for collective labour rights.

A good source of inspiration for these minimum standards would be the core ILO Conventions on freedom of association and collective bargaining, Conventions 87 and 98.[132] All member states have already accepted the obligations they contain. The Conventions include basic rights for workers to join a trade union and to be protected from discrimination by the employer for this reason, and basic obligations on the state to promote voluntary collective bargaining between trade unions and employers or employers' associations. An explicit right to strike might have to be added for completeness. A directive setting out these minimum standards would,

---

[130] Case C6&9/90, *Francovich and Bonifaci v. Italy*, [1991] ECR I-5357.

[131] For an overview, see R. Blanpain and C. Engels (eds.), *Comparative Labour Law and Industrial Relations in Industrialized Market Economies* (2001).

[132] A solution also advocated by Ryan, *supra* note 67, at 320–4.

of course, give member states a discretion to implement them in a way that would mesh with national traditions.

It is not the purpose of this chapter to set out a draft directive. But it is important to convey some idea of the difficulties that would arise during the negotiation of such a directive. Let us take freedom of association as our example. A directive that required member states to uphold individuals' right to freedom of association instantly raises the issue of the legality of 'closed shop' arrangements. Does the right to join a trade union also include a right to refuse to join? Could the right to refuse to join be limited to certain circumstances, for example, when the individual has a conscientious or religious objection to trade union membership?

The international human rights instruments vary in their treatment of this issue. The clearest stance is that taken by the Universal Declaration, which simply states in Article 20(2) that 'no-one may be compelled to belong to an association'. In the case of the ECHR, there is some evidence from the *travaux préparatoires* that the drafters intended to adopt a neutral approach so that signatory states could decide the issue for themselves.[133] However, this approach has not found favour with the Court. Although it has never clearly held that there is a right not to join a trade union which has equal status with the right to join, it has condemned closed shops in a number of cases.[134] ILO Convention No. 87 is silent on the question of the closed shop. This has been interpreted to mean that states have a discretion to prohibit or permit the closed shop as they choose.[135] The ILO Committee of Experts has stated that 'systems which prohibit union security practices in order to guarantee the right not to join an organisation, as well as systems which authorise such practices, are compatible with the Convention'.[136] The main qualification to this is that a closed shop will only be permitted where it results from a voluntary agreement between unions and employers. States are not allowed to impose closed shops through legislation.

Ryan suggests that 'the more controversial question of the right not to join a trade union could be omitted, or member states given the option of excluding the right in some circumstances'.[137] This proposal is attractive because it conforms to ILO practice and leaves discretion to the member states, thus respecting the diversity of their national systems. However, it leaves open the possibility that the ECJ might be called upon to interpret the right to freedom of association as set out in the directive, and to decide whether the right not to join a union is included. This would be a very difficult task for a court which is not familiar with collective labour rights issues. Moreover, because the right to freedom of association is contained in the ECHR,

---

[133] 'Report of 19 June 1950 of the Conference of Senior Officials', in Council of Europe, *Collected Edition of the 'Travaux Préparatoires'* (1975–85), Vol. IV, at 262.

[134] *Young, James and Webster v. UK*, [1981] 4 EHRR 38; *Sigurjonsson v. Iceland*, [1993] 16 EHRR 462.

[135] International Labour Conference, 43rd Session, 1959, Report of the Committee of Experts, Report III (Part IV), para. 36.

[136] ILO, *General Survey on Freedom of Association and Collective Bargaining* (1994), para. 100.

[137] Ryan, *supra* note 67, at 322.

it seems likely that the ECJ would have regard to the ECtHR's case law. As we have seen, this case law is relatively hostile to the closed shop. Thus, the ECJ's decision might curtail the member states' freedom in this respect. It therefore seems that, despite the difficulties of negotiation that would ensue, the directive would have to specify, at the very least, whether or not member states were permitted to protect such a right, even if they were not obliged to do so.

There are many other well-known controversies surrounding collective labour rights. Would member states be permitted to place limits on secondary industrial action? To what extent would they be permitted to ban strikes in essential services? A directive on collective labour rights would have to address these issues in order to avoid creating confusion and putting undue pressure on the ECJ. But it is important to acknowledge that the more precise the directive sought, the more difficult it would be to negotiate.

In practice, the prospects for the extension of Community competence to cover collective labour rights seem, at present, somewhat remote. The deliberate exclusion of these rights from the Maastricht Agreement on Social Policy indicates that hostility to Community competence over them is not just the preserve of governments that are sceptical of Community social policy as a whole. Nevertheless, the arguments in favour of some Community action are powerful ones, and the history of Community social policy is littered with developments that seemed impossible for many years and then suddenly became possible. It is to be hoped that collective labour rights will follow the same pattern.

7

The European Union and International Labour Standards: The Dynamics of Dialogue between the EU and the ILO

TONIA NOVITZ

1. INTRODUCTION

International labour standards consist of workers' rights that have been recognized by international instruments. Historically, the most influential of these have been those promulgated by the International Labour Organization (ILO). This is an organization, established by the Treaty of Versailles in 1919, which has survived to exert a measure of influence today as a United Nations (UN) agency.

This chapter focuses, in particular, on those international labour standards identified as being 'core' in meetings of the ILO Governing Body,[1] the 1995 Copenhagen World Summit on Social Development,[2] and the 1998 ILO Declaration on Fundamental Principles and Rights at Work.[3] They are:

(1) freedom of association and the effective recognition of the right to collective bargaining;
(2) the elimination of all forms of forced or compulsory labour;
(3) the effective elimination of child labour; and
(4) the elimination of discrimination in respect of employment and occupation.

These principles correlate broadly to certain 'fundamental' ILO Conventions, namely: Conventions Nos. 87 and 98 on Freedom of Association and Collective Bargaining (1948 and 1949), Conventions Nos. 29 and 105 on the Elimination of All Forms of Forced and Compulsory Labour (1930 and 1957), Convention No. 138

---

[1] Certain 'fundamental' Conventions were identified by the ILO Governing Body at its 264th Session (November 1995) as a priority for ratification by ILO member states and this prioritization has since been reiterated, for example, at the discussions of the Governing Body in its 282nd Session (November 2001).

[2] World Social Summit held at Copenhagen, 6–12 March 1995. See Final Declaration, Commitment 3.

[3] ILO Declaration on Fundamental Principles and Rights at Work 1998, Art. 2.

on the Minimum Age for Admission to Employment (1973), Convention No. 182 on the Worst Forms of Child Labour (1999), and ILO Conventions Nos. 100 and 111 on the Elimination of Discrimination in Respect of Employment and Occupation (1957 and 1958). This prioritization of a very few Conventions is a relatively recent phenomenon, but there is no doubting the importance of these selected standards as a focus for policy-making in the international community.[4]

The ILO has been recognized as 'the competent body to set and deal with such standards',[5] but the substance of ILO constitutional norms, conventions, and recommendations have long been reflected in instruments adopted by the UN, such as the International Covenant on Civil and Political Rights 1966 and the International Covenant on Economic, Social and Cultural Rights 1966. They are also echoed in the content of the Council of Europe's European Social Charter 1961 and the 'San Salvador' Additional Protocol to the American Convention on Human Rights in the Area of Economic, Social and Cultural Rights 1988.

The relationship between the EU and ILO is currently described by the European Commission and Council as one of 'cooperation' and constructive dialogue.[6] Such a conception of this relationship is alert to the creative aspects of discourse. It also summons up a vision of a deliberative process, in which those formulating EU social policy can benefit from information relating to the treatment of international labour standards in other organizations, while making a reciprocal positive contribution to the formulation of such standards and their enforcement internationally. This is a view which seems to be informed by that expressed by Jürgen Habermas's model of deliberative democracy and can be linked to his argument that the EU should play a role in resisting the neo-liberal pressures of globalization.[7] This chapter examines the extent to which this notion of constructive and disinterested dialogue does indeed characterize the relationship between the EU and the ILO as regards enforcement of international labour standards, suggesting that such a characterization may be naive in present circumstances.

[4] See endorsement of these core labour standards again by the ILO World Commission on the Social Dimension of Globalization Final Report, *A Fair Globalization: Creating Opportunities for All* (2004), xiii.

[5] Singapore Ministerial WTO Declaration, 13 December 1996, WT/MIN96/DEC/W, para. 4. This would seem to also follow from the principle of 'speciality'. For a statement of the latter principle, see *Legality of the Use by a State of Nuclear Weapons in Armed Conflict (Request by the World Health Organisation for an Advisory Opinion)* (1998) 110 ILR 1.

[6] See the 'Exchange of Letters' between the EU Commissioner for Employment and Social Affairs, Anna Diamantopoulou, and the ILO Director-General, Juan Somavia, which is available at: http://europa.eu.int/comm/employment_social/news/2001/jun/letter1_en.html and http://europa.eu.int/comm/employment_social/news/2001/jun/letter2_en.html. See also the Commission Communication, *Promoting Core Labour Standards and Improving Social Governance in the Context of Globalization*, COM(2001)416 final, Conclusions, at paras. 21–3.

[7] See, for example, Habermas, 'The European Nation-State and the Pressures of Globalization' 235 *New Left Review* (1999) 46; for comment, see Grewal, 'The Paradox of Integration: Habermas and the Unfinished Project of the European Union' 21(2) *Politics* (2001) 114. For a broader vision of the deliberative democratic process, see J. Habermas, *Between Facts and Norms: Contributions to a Discourse Theory of Law and Society*, trans. W. Rehg (1996).

There are two key means by which the European Union might recognize core international labour standards set by the ILO. The first is *via* internal regulatory action, designed to govern the conduct of EU Member States. This can be achieved in a variety of ways, such as protection of workers' rights through Treaty articles, EC directives relating to social policy, soft law initiatives, and the fundamental rights jurisprudence of the Court. The second is *via* EU external relations, which can make trade and aid preferences conditional on compliance with international labour standards.

It will be demonstrated here that implementation of ILO norms within the Union was initially minimal and is still far from comprehensive. It is externally, as an international actor, that the EU has taken a more emphatic interest in the promotion of such standards, especially as a condition for access of third countries to trade and aid. In this context, specific reference is made to ILO Conventions as the justification for imposition of certain conditions.

The European Commission has also stated its intention to assist in the reform of the ILO, to ensure the effective application of core workers' rights.[8] This intention is consistent with statements made by the Commissioner for Employment and Social Affairs, Anna Diamantopoulou, to the effect that the EU could contribute further to the wider international debate on social governance.[9] The desire for extended international influence in the sphere of social policy was recently endorsed by the Council in 2003.[10] Moreover, we shall see that in this context, the ILO Director-General seems appreciative of the interest and support of the EU, rather than critical of its conduct. This chapter concludes by considering the reasons why ILO officials might take such a stance.

2. INTERNAL EU REGULATORY ACTION

The EU has, despite an initial dearth of interest in international labour standards, sought to correct this by various means. This part considers the bases for regulatory action in the field of social policy, the forms such action has taken, the role of social dialogue in EC policy-making, and the extent to which labour rights have been recognized as fundamental constitutional rights within the EU. It is evident that while protection of core workers' rights has been enhanced over the years, there is no mechanism to ensure that all basic ILO norms are implemented by EU Member States. Moreover, in the policy documents produced by EU institutions, there is little

---

[8] *Promoting Core Labour Standards, supra* note 6.

[9] See, for example, her comments at the meeting on The European Social Agenda and the EU's International Partners, Brussels, 20–21 November 2001, 2; more recently, see the summary of discussions in B. Brunhe, *Report on the High Level Seminar Organised by the European Commission to Contribute to the Work of the World Commission on the Social Dimension of Globalisation, 3–4 February 2003* (Brussels: European Commission, 2003).

[10] Council Conclusions on the Commission Communication on Promoting Core Labour Standards, Brussels, 17 July 2003, 11555/03, para. 1.

evidence of concern arising from ILO condemnation of labour practices in EU Member States.

A. Treaty Bases for Regulatory Action

In 1957, when the Treaty of Rome was signed, there was scant enthusiasm for the promotion of international labour standards through the medium of a European Economic Community (EEC). Curiously, this was indicative of ILO influence in the formation of the Community, rather than its absence. ILO experts were called in, but stated in the 'Ohlin Report' that it was unnecessary for the nascent EEC to play such a role. The Ohlin Report expressed the view that different labour standards were unlikely to distort competition within a European common market. Special measures to harmonize social policies were considered to be largely impracticable, especially if all the states concerned were members of the ILO, already obliged to abide by their obligations under ILO conventions.[11] It is probable that ILO experts at this time did not anticipate the future significance of Community law through principles developed by the European Court of Justice, such as 'direct' and 'indirect' effect. Moreover, they saw the EEC as primarily a market-oriented endeavour, which should not impinge on workers' rights, but which need not be utilized to provide active protection of international labour standards. This view was accepted by the drafters of the Treaty and was reflected in the Treaty's content.[12]

It was declared in the Preamble to the 1957 Treaty of Rome that one of the essential objectives of the EEC was to improve the living and working conditions of its people. Article 117 of the Treaty restated this commitment, but made no provision for the Council to make regulations or directives to achieve this end. Article 118 contemplated that the Commission would promote 'close co-operation between Member States in the social field'. Such cooperation was, however, apparently only to entail 'making studies, delivering opinions and arranging consultations'. Concessions were made to the French lobby, so as to include Article 119 (now Article 141 of the current EC Treaty), which provided for equal pay for men and women, but set out no means for implementation. No Treaty article dealt specifically with freedom of association, protection from forced and child labour, and prevention of discrimination generally, or appeared to envisage legal measures being taken to promote the same.

There has since been considerable extension of the competence of the now European Union, due to the subsequent amendment of the EC Treaty and the Treaty on European Union. Notable developments include the incorporation of the 'Agreement on Social Policy', originally appended to the Treaty on European Union, into the body of the EC Treaty, following the Treaty of Amsterdam 1997.[13]

---

[11] Report of a Group of Experts, *Social Aspects of European Economic Co-operation* (ILO: Geneva, 1956) 40.

[12] Discussed in Davies, 'The Emergence of European Labour Law', in W. McCarthy (ed.), *Legal Intervention in Industrial Relations* (1992) 319 and Barnard, 'EC "Social Policy"', in P. Craig and G. de Burca (eds.), *The Evolution of EU Law* (1999) 480.

[13] Now amended again, although not significantly, by the Treaty of Nice 2000.

Article 136 of the current EC Treaty does not mention ILO standards explicitly, but does refer to two instruments that reflect their significance, namely the Council of Europe instrument, the European Social Charter 1961, and the Community's own Charter of the Fundamental Social Rights of Workers 1989. Article 137 contemplates measures relating to such matters as health and safety, working conditions, social protection, information and consultation of workers, representation and collective defence of workers and employers, social inclusion, and combating sexual discrimination. The potential to address sex discrimination bolsters further what is now Article 141 (ex Article 119). The adoption of measures to address other forms of discrimination is dealt with under Article 13.

Some core labour standards are regarded as appropriate for qualified majority vote; others are not. Discrimination on grounds other than sex falls within the latter category. Predictions that this would pose an insuperable barrier to the adoption of directives in this field proved incorrect.[14] Yet, while the requirement of unanimous voting did not, in the end, prevent the adoption of directives under this treaty base, it is arguable that this led to dilution of their content, their broad 'framework' style approach making significant the manner of national level implementation (and the extent to which this is then scrutinized by the European Court of Justice).[15]

Still excluded from EC competence in the sphere of social policy are 'pay, the right of association, the right to strike [and] the right to impose lock-outs' under Article 137(5). According to the Commission (and presumably the Member States in Council), this is an inappropriate matter for EC intervention. The reasons would seem to be that systems of collective bargaining in EU Member States are too distinctive to be subjected to shared norms, and that therefore the matter is better regulated by national legislation or custom, according to the principle of subsidiarity.[16]

This leaves a core international labour standard without the prospect of EC regulation. It is possible that a directive addressing freedom of association could be adopted under Article 94 (ex Article 100) or Article 308 (ex Article 235) of the EC Treaty, but the principle that a specialized treaty base should prevail makes this course of action unlikely and potentially open to challenge by Member States.[17]

---

[14] Bell, 'The New Art. 13 EC Treaty: A Sound Basis for European Anti-discrimination Law', 6 *MJ* (1999) 5; and Flynn, 'The Implications of Art. 13 EC—After Amsterdam Will Some Forms of Discrimination be More Equal Than Others?' 36 *CMLRev* (1999) 1127; and Waddington, 'Testing the Limits of the EC Treaty Art. on Non-discrimination', 28 *Industrial Law Journal* (1999) 133.

[15] For example, see as regards implementation of provisions relating to disability, Whittle, 'The Framework Directive for Equal Treatment in Employment and Occupation: An Analysis from a Disability Rights Perspective', 27 *ELRev* (2002) 303. See also discussion of these directives *infra*, at 222.

[16] Discussed by Ryan, 'Pay, Trade Union Rights and European Community Law', 13 *International Journal of Comparative Labour Law and Industrial Relations (IJCLLIR)* (1997) 305 at 310–16.

[17] Cf. Case C-84/94 *UK v Council*, [1996] ECR I-5755. See also Dashwood, 'The Limits of EC Powers', 21 *ELRev* (1996) 113.

For this reason, particular concern has been raised relating to the right to strike, recognized by the ILO as a vital aspect of freedom of association.[18]

The case has long been made that, if solidarity between workers across the Union is to be made possible, some European provision for the right to strike is necessary.[19] In particular, fears have been expressed that EC rules relating to free movement of goods would prevent industrial action being taken by workers.[20] This has, to some extent, been addressed by the 'Monti' Regulation,[21] which recognizes the right to strike as an exception, but does not provide a European-level definition of the scope of legitimate industrial action.[22] It is arguable that in such circumstances, there is little to protect this entitlement from progressive erosion.[23]

It seems that the Commission does not regard the absence of a treaty base for protection of freedom of association as problematic. When discussing EU external relations, the Commission has stated that 'the fundamental principles and rights at work identified by the International Labour Organization of course apply in their entirety to the countries of the EU'.[24] What is not spelt out is that this is by virtue of the independent commitments of EU member states as members of the ILO, rather than EU regulation. The Commission will not intervene, except to recommend ratification of certain ILO Conventions.[25]

The Commission seems to assume that EU members do comply with their international obligations to respect freedom of association, but evidence from the ILO indicates that this assumption may be misguided. For example, the United Kingdom is notorious for its continued breach of Convention Nos. 87 and 98.[26]

---

[18] *Freedom of Association: Digest of Decisions and Principles of the Freedom of Association Committee of the Governing Body of the ILO* (4th edn., 1994), para. 477; *Committee of Experts on the Application of Conventions and Recommendations: General Survey on Freedom of Association and Collective Bargaining* (1994), paras. 175 and 179.

[19] For the history of debates in the European Parliament on this issue, see T. Novitz, *International and European Protection of the Right to Strike* (2003) 156–7 and 162.

[20] Cox, 'Social and Labour Policy in the EEC', 1 *BJIR* (1963) 5 at 9; Jacobs, 'Towards Community Action on Strike Law', 15 *CMLRev* (1978) 133; L. Betten, *The Right to Strike in Community Law: The Incorporation of Fundamental Rights in the Legal Order of the European Communities* (1985), chap. 8.

[21] Council Regulation 2679/98 [1998] OJ L337/8, Art. 2.

[22] See the concerns raised in this regard by Orlandini, 'The Free Movement of Goods as a Possible "Community" Limitation on Industrial Conflict', 6 *ELJ* (2000) 341.

[23] Germanotta and Novitz, 'Globalisation and the Right to Strike: The Case for European-Level Protection of Secondary Action', 18 *IJCLLIR* (2002) 67.

[24] *Promoting Core Labour Standards*, *supra* note 6, at 11.

[25] See 2000/581/EC Commission Recommendation of 15 September 2000 on the ratification of ILO Convention No. 182 of 1999 concerning the prohibition and immediate action for the elimination of the worst forms of child labour (notified under document C(2000) 2674).

[26] See, for example, *Case No. 1852 (UK)*, 309th Report of the ILO Governing Body Committee on Freedom of Association (CFA) (1998), para. 308. The capacity for trade union discrimination highlighted in this case was addressed in the decision of the European Court of Human Rights in *Wilson and the NUJ v. UK* [2002] IRLR 128, and is apparently to be tackled in the Employment Relations Bill 2003. Other outstanding UK violations of the principle of freedom of association were highlighted in the ILO Committee of Experts on the Application of Conventions and Recommendations (CEACR) Individual Observations Concerning Convention No. 87 (UK) in 2003 and Concerning Convention No. 98 in 2002.

In addition, Austria has breached Convention No. 87 by virtue of its reluctance to allow foreign workers to be eligible for election to works councils;[27] concerns have been raised as regards the rules for access of occupational organizations to the National Labour Council in Belgium;[28] the failure of Denmark to allow non-nationals to engage in collective bargaining when employed on Danish ships has only recently been remedied;[29] and Germany's refusal to allow public servants to strike has long been the subject of criticism.[30] Two recent cases concerning Spain were brought before the ILO Governing Body Committee on Freedom of Association. One related to the failure of the Spanish government to negotiate with trade unions over public sector terms and conditions. The other concerned new legislation that prohibits strikes by foreign workers unless 'they obtain authorisation for their stay or residence'. In both instances, the Committee was critical of the government's conduct.[31] The Committee has also criticized the actions of the Greek government in issuing a civil mobilization order to end a lawful strike.[32]

The views of the ILO supervisory bodies indicate that much more needs to be done to ensure that EU member states comply with their international obligations as regards at least one core labour standard, namely freedom of association. Moreover, the attempt made by the ILO to communicate these failings to the states does not seem to have met with great success. The reluctance of EU institutions to respond, or even acknowledge such findings, would seem to suggest that they are less interested in 'dialogue' than they might have us believe. It may be that this fundamental workers' right is excluded from EU competence, not because EU member states are already in compliance, but because so much would need to be done to ensure compliance.

B. Regulatory Measures Taken

Initially, the limited competence of the European Economic Community in the sphere of social policy meant that few regulatory measures were taken to ensure EU implementation of ILO standards. As noted above, standards relating to freedom of association remain expressly excluded from consideration. Nevertheless, it is useful to consider what has been accomplished as competence in other fields has been extended. Recent EU emphasis on 'soft' as well as 'hard' regulatory measures suggests that not only directives, but other declaratory instruments and programmatic initiatives may also require recognition in this regard.

---

[27] CEACR Individual Observation concerning Convention No. 87 (Austria) 2003.

[28] CEACR Individual Observation concerning Convention No. 87 (Belgium) 2003.

[29] CEACR Individual Observation concerning Convention No. 87 (Denmark) 2003.

[30] CEACR Individual Observation concerning Convention No. 87 (Germany) 2003.

[31] *Case No. 2121 (Spain)*, 327th Report of the CFA (2002), para. 548; *Case No. 2123 (Spain)*, 329th Report of the CFA (2002), para. 512.

[32] *Case No. 2212 (Greece)*, 330th Report of the CFA (2003), para. 721, at para. 752.

The first initiatives of note were the directives adopted in the 1970s relating to equal pay and equal treatment for men and women.[33] These were to give effect to the principles that underlay the provision for equal pay set out in Article 119 (now Article 141) of the Treaty of Rome. They also followed from the case law of the European Court of Justice (ECJ), which sought expressly to give effect to the international standards enshrined in ILO Conventions Nos. 100 and 111.[34]

It was later acknowledged by EU institutions that the content of the 1970s sex equality directives was inadequate, and that their revision or elaboration was required; the result being the adoption of supplementary directives, such as that relating to maternity[35] and that changing the burden of proof in discrimination cases.[36] More importantly, the 2002 'Amending Directive on Equal Treatment' has elaborated upon and developed protection.[37]

The sum total of these regulatory instruments are more detailed in their requirements than ILO Conventions relating to discrimination on grounds of sex. They are also supplemented within the EU by policies relating to 'gender mainstreaming', that is, incorporating equal opportunities for women and men into all Community policies and activities. This has led to the expression of Community concern with, for example, gender-related issues in the implementation of the European Employment Strategy (EES), the use of Structural Funds, and participation and representation in political decision-making.[38]

As Kenner points out, although the term 'gender mainstreaming' stems from a UN initiative, this has long been an EC policy, as is evident from the Third Equalities Action Programme of 1991–1995. The concern he expresses (and one which others share) is that the objectives of 'gender mainstreaming' may, in the context of the EES, have more connection to promotion of employment and economic restructuring than the welfare of women per se. In the European Union, the risk is that, for as long as social and economic objectives are described in official policy statements as being entirely compatible and the tensions between them are not addressed, a hidden prioritization in favour of a market-oriented perspective may remain.[39]

---

[33] Council Directive 75/117/EEC [1975] OJ L 45/19; Council Directive 76/207/EEC [1976] OJ L 39/40.

[34] Case 43/76 *Defrenne v. Sabena* [1976] ECR 455 at 472, paras. 27–8; and Case 149/77 *Defrenne v. Sabena (No. 3)* [1978] ECR 1365, paras. 26–7. The ILO concept of equal pay for work of equal value (rather than merely equal work) as expressed in ILO Convention No. 100 was also influential in the subsequent interpretation by the European Court of Justice of Council Directive 75/117/EEC. See Case 61/81 *Commission v. UK* [1982] ECR 2601.

[35] Council Directive 92/85/EEC [1992] OJ L 348/1.

[36] Council Directive 97/80/EC [1998] OJ L 14/6.

[37] Council Directive 2002/73/EC [2002] OJ L 269/15.

[38] See, for example, Communication from the Commission *Towards a Community Framework Strategy on Gender Equality (2001–2005)* COM(2000)355 final, 7 June 2000.

[39] J. Kenner, *EU Employment Law: From Rome to Amsterdam and Beyond* (2003), chaps. 7 and 11.

ILO Convention No. 111 does not only relate to equal treatment of men and women, but also 'any distinction, exclusion or preference made on the basis of race, colour, sex, religion, political opinion, national extraction or social origin, which has the effect of nullifying or impairing equality of opportunity or treatment in employment or occupation' and 'such other distinction, exclusion or preference which has the effect of nullifying or impairing equality of opportunity or treatment in employment or occupation as may be determined by the Member concerned after consultation with representative employers' and workers' organizations, where such exist, and with other appropriate bodies'.[40] In this respect, the protection envisaged by the ILO Convention goes further than that at first envisaged as appropriate for action by the European Commission and Council, which was restricted to sex discrimination.

It was only in 2000, that the EC began to address discrimination not only on grounds of sex, but on grounds of race. The 'Race Directive' adopted in 2000[41] means that EC law therefore now comes closer to the broad prohibition of discrimination set out in Convention No. 111. Indeed, it might even be claimed that the EU now goes further than this definition, by providing protection from discrimination on grounds of age, disability, religious belief, and sexual orientation under the new 'Framework Directive' of 2000.[42] The protection lent by the latter compares favourably also with the limited protection provided for workers on these grounds under other ILO conventions. For example, workers with a disability receive express protection under Article 6(1) of ILO Convention No. 168 on Employment Promotion and Protection against Unemployment Convention (1988) and Article 5(1) of Convention No. 181 on Private Employment Agencies (1998), but this is fairly piecemeal in nature, relating only to state provision for protection from unemployment and the conduct of private employment agencies. It seems appropriate for a regional organization to elaborate upon bare international standards, and the EU's extension of interest in the anti-discrimination field will be welcome to many.

As regards other 'core' rights identified by the ILO, the 1994 directive relating to the minimum age of workers makes explicit reference in the Preamble to 'the principles of the International Labour Organization regarding the protection of young people at work, including those relating to the minimum age for access to employment or work'.[43] This intention seems to be borne out by differentiation of treatment of workers under the ages of 13 years, 15 years, and 16 years, which corresponds broadly to that in ILO Convention No. 138 of 1973.[44]

No specific EC legislation has been adopted relating to forced labour, even though there would seem to be competence to adopt a directive on this subject matter by qualified majority vote under Article 137(1)(b) of the EC Treaty, insofar as its content could be said to relate directly to 'working conditions'. The assumption

---

[40] ILO Convention No. 111, Art. 1.   [41] Council Directive 2000/43/EC [2000] OJ L 180/22.
[42] Council Directive 2000/78/EC [2000] OJ L 303/16.   [43] EC Directive 94/33 OJ L216/12.
[44] See ILO Convention No. 138, Arts. 2(3), 2(4), 3(1), and 7.

appears to be that all EU Member States, as members of the UN and ILO would not allow such practices, and that therefore such action is unnecessary. Once again, as in the case of freedom of association, the findings of the ILO Committee of Experts on the Application of Conventions and Recommendations (CEACR) indicate that such an assumption would be mistaken. The CEACR has recently expressed concern at the use of forced labour in prisons in Austria,[45] France,[46] Germany,[47] and the United Kingdom,[48] which it considers do not comply with the requirements of ILO Convention No. 29. Greece has also been criticized for breach of ILO Convention No. 105, by virtue of sanctions imposed on seafarers for collective action.[49]

The importance, in principle, of prohibition of forced labour is recognized in both the Community Charter of the Fundamental Social Rights of Workers 1989 and the EU Charter of Fundamental Rights 2000. Both, however, have only declaratory effect at present, as opposed to the legal effect of a directive.[50] They cannot therefore be used to remedy the concerns expressed by the ILO CEACR in this regard.

While there is no competence to adopt a directive explicitly protecting freedom of association, there is indirect recognition of the potentially important role of the 'social partners' (that is, management and labour) in managerial decision-making and the implementation of European labour standards. National level information and consultation was advanced in the 1970s through directives (since amended) relating to transfers of undertakings and collective redundancies.[51] Davies has identified the limitations inherent in such provisions and the inability of labour to veto structural change in the enterprises concerned.[52] It has been questioned whether there is genuine 'dialogue' through information and consultation (or 'works councils'), without EU protection of freedom of association or a right to strike.[53] Nevertheless, there has been no change of policy in response to such concerns. Instead, there seems to be a trend towards expanding the scope of dialogue beyond management and labour to other key actors in civil society, such as appropriate non-governmental organizations (NGOs). This trend is arguably exemplified by the provision for involvement of NGOs included in the 2000 'Race Directive'.[54]

---

[45] CEACR Individual Observation concerning Convention No. 29 (Austria) 2002.

[46] CEACR Individual Observation concerning Convention No. 29 (France) 2003.

[47] CEACR Individual Observation concerning Convention No. 29 (Germany) 2002.

[48] CEACR Individual Observation concerning Convention No. 29 (UK) 2002.

[49] CEACR Individual Observation concerning Convention No. 105 (Greece) 2003.

[50] See *infra,* at 228–9.

[51] Council Directive 75.129/EEC [1975] OJ L 45/19, Council Directive 77/187/EEC [1977] OJ L 61/26, Council Directive 92/56/ EEC [1992] OJ L 245/3, Council Directive 98/50/EC [1998] OJ L 201/88, Council Directive 98/59/EC [1998] OJ L 225/16, Council Directive 2001/21/EC [2001] OJ L 82/16.

[52] Davies, 'Acquired Rights, Creditors' Rights, Freedom of Contract and Industrial Democracy', 9 *Yearbook of European Law* (1989) 21.

[53] Lord Wedderburn, 'Consultation and Collective Bargaining in Europe: Success or Ideology', 26 *Industrial Law Journal* (1997) 1.

[54] Council Directive 2000/43/EC [2000] OJ L 180/22, Arts. 11, 12, and 16. See the discussion of these provisions in Bell, 'Beyond European Labour Law? Reflections on the EU Racial Equality Directive', 8 *ELJ* 384 (2002), at 395–6.

The desire to extend consultation also reflects a recent general concern of the European Commission and Council with 'good governance' and thereby greater involvement of civil society in EU decision-making and the implementation of EU policy.[55] This is not an entirely new initiative, given the long-standing role of the Economic and Social Committee in the EC. The difficulty is that the Economic and Social Committee has not been overly successful in its representation of societal interests or in wielding influence, and this may also be true of consultation of a broad band of 'civil society'.[56]

C. Provision for Involvement of Management and Labour in the Formation of Social Policy

The EC Treaty currently contemplates the involvement of European-level representatives of management and labour in deliberation on the content of EC directives. Under Article 138, the Commission is obliged to consult management and labour at Community level, in particular, prior to submitting proposals in the social policy field. If, after consultation, the measure still seems to the Commission to be 'advisable', it must further consult the social partners on the content of the proposal. At this stage, management and labour may inform the Commission of their desire to initiate a procedure known as 'social dialogue' under Article 139. This enables them to take the matter away from deliberation by the Commission (usually only for a period of nine months, unless all parties agree that the time limit should be extended) and seek to reach an agreement on the type and content of regulation that would be appropriate in the circumstances. This may lead to contractual relations between the parties. The agreement can then be implemented either by the social partners at member state level or by a Council decision on a proposal from the Commission. Once again, these provisions would seem to assume adequate protection of freedom of association in EU member states, which is in itself questionable.

The social dialogue procedure is relatively novel, not being replicated by any other international or regional organization. If anything, it comes closest to the 'tripartite' decision-making structure of the ILO, in which worker and employer representatives are given the opportunity to vote alongside government representatives on the adoption of ILO Conventions at the International Labour Conference and to play a key role in determining the agenda of the Conference through a voice on the ILO Governing Body.[57] Tripartism has been viewed as a strength of the ILO, for it can create a balance of bargaining power between two distinct factions that might otherwise seek to influence the adoption and content of legislative acts through

---

[55] See the Commission White Paper on *European Governance* COM(2001)428, 25.7.2001.

[56] For a useful critique of the Economic and Social Committee's role and this policy trend, see respectively, Smismans, 'An Economic and Social Committee for the Citizen, or a Citizen for the Economic and Social Committee', 5 *European Public Law* (1999) 557, and Smismans, 'European Civil Society: Shaped by Discourses and Institutional Interests', 9 *ELJ* (2003) 473.

[57] ILO Constitution, Arts. 3, 7, 14, and 19.

covert means. It also ensures that the practical implications of any measures taken are not overlooked. The social consensus required for the adoption of any measure might also be thought to lend any regulatory action a degree of authority.[58] By analogy, the EU could be said to have taken steps, not only to promote protection of core labour standards, but also to incorporate these values within its legislative process. However, various commentators have cast doubt on the legitimacy of the selection of representatives and procedures, and thereby the merits of EU social dialogue.[59]

First, there is no guarantee that all interested social partners will be given the opportunity to participate in the EU social dialogue process; the issue of representativity only being determined after the fact at the stage at which the Commission recommends adoption of a directive giving legal effect to the collective agreement.[60] Moreover, where, as in the case of the recent Telework Agreement agreed through social dialogue on 16 July 2002, there is no proposal for implementation by means of an EC directive, but only by the social partners through collective agreement, there would seem to be no scope for any such scrutiny.[61] This can be contrasted with the approach taken within the ILO. A standing feature of the ILO International Labour Conference is the tripartite Credentials Committee, which assesses at the outset whether employer and worker delegates are sufficiently representative of employers and workers in the state concerned. The Committee then reports back to the plenary meeting of the Conference, which may vote on proposals made. The Conference can, by two-thirds of the votes cast by the delegates present, refuse to admit any delegate or adviser whom it deems not to have been nominated in accordance with Article 3 of the ILO Constitution.[62]

Secondly, in the EU context there is no regulation of the process by which decisions are reached in social dialogue. There is no official record of debates or engagement of management and labour with government representatives, as exists in the ILO International Labour Conference and Governing Body minutes. There is

---

[58] For an early statement of the advantages of tripartism, see Thomas, 'Preface', in *The International Labour Organization: The First Decade* (1931).

[59] See, for example, Betten, 'The Democratic Deficit of Participatory Democracy in Community Social Policy', 23 *ELRev* (1998) 20; Schmidt, 'Representativity—A Claim Not Satisfied: The Social Partners' Role in the EC Law-Making Procedure for Social Policy', 15 *IJCLLIR* (1999) 259.

[60] This was demonstrated by the finding in Case T-135/96 *Union Européenne de l'Artisan et des Petits et Moyennes Enterprises (UEAPME) v. Council* [1998] ECR II-2335. See also Dorssemont, 'Some Reflections on the Origin, Problems and Perspectives of the European Social Dialogue', in M. De Vos (ed.), *A Decade Beyond Maastricht: The European Social Dialogue Revisited* (2003) 22.

[61] For the voicing of this concern, see Syrpis, 'Social Democracy and Judicial Review in the Community Order', in C. Kilpatrick, T. Novitz, and P. Skidmore (eds.), *The Future of Remedies in Europe* (2000) 253, at 263–5; as regards its realization in the context of the Telework Agreement, see Deinart, 'Self-executing Collective Agreements in EC Law', in De Vos, *supra* note 60.

[62] For further discussion of the working of this process, see L. Betten, *International Labour Standards: Selected Issues* (1993) 17–18. For review of the workings of the Credentials Committee and the necessity for it to change its criteria in the post-Cold War period, see ILO Governing Body policy document, *The Role of the Credentials Committee* GB 286/LILS/3 (2003); see also *infra*, at 236 and 239–40.

only informal engagement between European-level social partners. It has been suggested that the lack of formality reflects an essentially voluntarist industrial relations approach to collective bargaining.[63] Such an approach would seem to overlook the public regulatory aspect of these proceedings, which may lead to or preclude law-making by EU institutions.[64] It also appears inappropriate in a context where the bargaining power of the social partners is not what it would be in the national industrial context, there being no European-level entitlement to call industrial action,[65] and arguably no practical means by which to do so. In these circumstances, it may well be management rather than labour that possesses the greater bargaining power, leading one commentator to observe that the introduction of social dialogue into standard-setting was merely replacing the prior veto of any one member state under unanimous voting with the potential for a veto by employers.[66] To this extent, the accountability and transparency linked to tripartism in the ILO appear to be lost in EU social dialogue.

D. Recognition of International Labour Standards as Fundamental Rights

Core international labour standards that do not receive protection through the adoption of EC directives may still be incorporated into the fundamental rights jurisprudence developed by the European Court of Justice. These 'general principles' recognized by the Court have been applied to limit the scope of EC law, circumscribe the activities of EC institutions, and restrict the actions of member states when implementing EC law.[67] While market integration might take priority, the jurisprudence of the Court tempers its dominance.

The Court has, for some considerable period of time, appreciated that international labour standards can constitute fundamental rights. The ECJ has, for example, made reference to the prohibition of discrimination on grounds of sex set out in ILO Convention No. 111.[68] More recently, in the *Bosman* case, the Court noted that the principle of freedom of association was 'one of the fundamental rights which, as the Court has consistently held . . . are protected under the Community legal order'.[69]

---

[63] Bercusson, 'Democratic Legitimacy and European Labour Law', 28 *Industrial Law Journal* (1999) 153.

[64] This public regulatory aspect is discussed by Fredman, 'Social Law in the European Union: The Impact of the Law-Making Process', in P. Craig and C. Harlow (eds.), *Lawmaking in the European Union* (1998). [65] See *supra*, at 218–20.

[66] Rhodes, 'The Social Dimension After Maastricht: Setting a New Agenda for the Labour Market', 9 *IJCLLIR* (1993) 297, at 300.

[67] See as to the potential extension of its jurisdiction, D. S. Binder, *The European Court of Justice and the Protection of Fundamental Rights in the Community: New Developments and Future Possibilities in Expanding Fundamental Rights Review to Member State Action* (1995) Jean Monnet Working Paper Series 4/95.

[68] See *supra*, at 221; also Szyszczak, 'Social Rights as General Principles of Community Law', in N. Neuwahl and A. Rosas (eds.), *The European Union and Human Rights* (1995) 211.

[69] Case C-415/93 *Union Royale Belge des Sociétés de Football Association and Others v. Bosman and Others* [1995] ECR I-4921, Judgment, para. 79.

It was therefore perhaps not surprising that the Court found in *Albany International* that 'the social policy objectives pursued by [collective] agreements' would be seriously undermined if management and labour were to be subject to EC competition law provisions when adopting measures to improve conditions of work and employment, even if there was no explicit recognition by the ECJ that this was required by protection of freedom of association as a fundamental right.[70] In these ways, the Court would seem to have sheltered international labour standards from encroachment by other EU objectives.

There are, however, three important limitations to the Court's approach. The first is inherent in the function of the fundamental rights jurisprudence of the Court, which is that such entitlements constitute only an exception to the standard application of Community law, and cannot provide the basis for a proactive effort to enforce workers' rights. A second limitation follows from the influence of other EU institutions. The outcome of the 'night work' litigation, in which EC law relating to equal treatment came into conflict with national implementation of an ILO Convention, revealed that, whatever the formal legal view taken as regards prior international obligations, the Commission's recommendation as to denunciation of an ILO Convention would in practice prevail.[71] The third limitation is not inherent, but is observable from the Court's practice. This is the Court's preference for reference to the civil and political rights set out in the European Convention on Human Rights, as opposed to socio-economic entitlements recognized by the ILO.[72]

An emphasis on civil and political rather than socio-economic entitlements is also evident in the Treaty of European Union. Article 6(1) states that 'the Union is founded on the principles of liberty, democracy, respect for human rights and fundamental freedoms', while Article 7 states that, in the event of 'a serious and persistent' violation of Article 6, the Council may suspend the rights of the Member State in question. To the extent that international labour standards may be viewed as human rights and fundamental freedoms, they would seem to come within the ambit of this provision, but Article 6(2), refers only to 'fundamental rights, as guaranteed by the European Convention on Human Rights . . . and as they result from the constitutional traditions of Member States as general principles of Community law'. As the European Convention on Human Rights is ostensibly devoted

---

[70] Case C-67/96 *Albany International BV v. Stichting Bedrijfsfonds Textielindustrie* [1999] ECR I-5751, even if AG Jacobs did not consider that this could be justified on the basis of the fundamental rights jurisprudence of the Court (Opinion, paras. 130–65).

[71] See Case C-345/89 *Stoeckel* [1991] ECR I-4047; Case C-151/91 *Levy* [1993] ECR I-4287; Case C-13/93 *Office National de l'Emploi v. Minne* [1994] ECR I-371. For analysis of these cases, see Kilpatrick, 'Production and Circulation of EC Nightwork Jurisprudence', 25 *ILJ* (1996) 169.

[72] See Report of the Expert Group on Fundamental Rights, *Affirming Fundamental Rights in the European Union: Time to Act* (European Commission DG for Employment and Social Affairs, 1999) 14; and Betten, 'The EU Charter on Fundamental Rights: A Trojan Horse or a Mouse', 17 *IJCLLIR* (2001) 151.

to civil and political rights only, protection of socio-economic rights being relegated to a separate instrument, the European Social Charter,[73] much depends on what is understood by the constitutional traditions of member states.

A more significant shift in orientation might be expected following the recent adoption of a Charter of Fundamental Rights in 2000, which provides significant recognition of socio-economic rights, including labour standards. Article 5 of the Charter stresses the importance of 'prohibition of slavery and forced labour', which can be linked to the 'freedom to choose an occupation and right to engage in work' set out in Article 15 and the requirement of 'fair and just working conditions' under Article 31. Prohibition of child labour and provision for protection of young people at work is elaborated upon in Article 32. There is a general provision relating to non-discrimination in Article 21, and specific treatment of 'equality between men and women . . . in all areas, including employment, work and pay' in Article 23. 'Integration of persons with disabilities' is promoted under Article 26. 'Freedom of assembly and of association' are recognized in Article 12, while Article 27 states a right to information and consultation of worker representatives and Article 28 a right of collective bargaining and action. Article 28 is apparently limited in substance, as is evident from the reference to 'national laws and practices' in the provision. The explanatory text indicates that this means, for example, that the scope of any right to strike is to be defined entirely at the national level, which would ensure that no EU standard is set as regards scrutiny of compliance with the right. Nevertheless, generally, the content of the 2000 Charter looks promising in terms of recognition of core labour standards; and Article 53 indicates that the instrument is not intended to limit or adversely affect human rights and fundamental freedoms recognized in other international instruments.

The chief stumbling block is the Charter's lack of legal effect. Formally, the Charter is merely a solemn proclamation by the European Parliament, Council and Commission. Moreover, significant limitations are placed on its effect by Articles 51–54.[74] For example, Article 51 makes it clear that the Charter 'does not establish any new power or task for the Community or Union, or modify powers or tasks defined by the Treaties'. It was at one point hoped that, although the instrument is not as yet legally binding, it could provide a new source of reference for the courts in the exercise of its fundamental rights jurisprudence. This aspiration has abated

---

[73] There is obviously some overlap between these different categories of rights, as observed by Ewing, 'Social Rights and Constitutional Law', *Public Law* [1999] 105; see also Novitz, 'Are Social Rights Necessarily Collective Rights? A Critical Analysis of the Collective Complaints Protocol to the European Social Charter', *European Human Rights Law Review* [2002] 50.

[74] See as to the stress the United Kingdom placed on the lack of legal effect, Lord Goldsmith, 'A Charter of Rights, Freedoms and Principles', 38 *CMLRev* (2001) 1201. See generally as to its legal implications, Betten, 'Human Rights', 50 *ICLQ* (2001) 690; Gijzen, 'The Charter: A Milestone for Social Protection in Europe?', 8 *MJ* (2001) 33, at 45–7; and Curtin and van Ooik, 'The Sting is Always in the Tail: The Personal Scope of the Application of the EU Charter of Fundamental Rights', 8 *MJ* (2001) 102.

following the judgment of the European Court of Justice in the *UPA* case.[75] Instead we are waiting for inclusion of the Charter into the Treaties. The Convention on the Future of Europe, envisaged incorporation of the Charter verbatim into Part II of the proposed Draft Treaty Establishing a Constitution for Europe.[76] Nevertheless, the final terms of any new Constitution have yet to be agreed by member states and remain the subject of negotiation. The content of the instrument will be finalized only (if at all) at the 2004 Inter-government Conference. The result is that, for the time being, the Charter of Fundamental Rights is likely to have limited impact on the domestic policies of EU member states.

3. EU EXTERNAL RELATIONS AND THE USE OF CONDITIONALITY IN TRADE AND AID

By 1994 the Council was advocating EU promotion of core labour standards not within, but outside the Union. In this section, the content of the relevant 1994 Council Resolution is examined, as is its outcome, namely the attempt to enforce compliance with international labour standards in third countries through social conditionality in trade and aid agreements. The legal validity and ethical defensibility of this policy is also considered.

A. A Change of Policy in the 1994 Council Resolution

The 1994 Council Resolution concerned not only external but internal policies relating to core labour standards. The instrument stated explicitly that regulation on matters such as freedom of association was considered unnecessary as regards EU member states, for 'the national identity of the Member States is particularly defined by their individual paths to solidarity within society and social balance'. However, no contradiction was seen in expressing the Council's ambition to set fair rules of international competition 'for the future organization of world trade and above all for combating forced labour and child labour and securing freedom of association and collective bargaining'.[77]

Previously, the promotion and acceptance of international instruments pertaining to workers' rights had been regarded as a matter for the foreign policy of member

---

[75] Case C-50/00 *Unión des Pequeños Agricultures (UPA) v. Council* [2002] ECR I-6677, in which an argument for reform of the requirements for standing of 'non-privileged applicants' based on Art. 47 of the Charter was rejected by the European Court of Justice, despite enthusiasm for change voiced previously by AG Jacobs and the Court of First Instance in Case T-177/01 *Jégo-Quéré et Cie SA v. Commission* [2002] ECR II-2365. See for a useful discussion of these cases, Hunt, 'Legal Developments', 41 *JCMS* (2003) 79 at 81–3.　　　　　　　　　　　　　　　　　　[76] CONV 850/03 18 July 2003.

[77] Council Resolution of 6 December 1994 on certain aspects of a European social policy: a contribution to economic and social convergence in the Union [1994] OJ C 368/6, Preamble, especially paras. 3 and 9.

states, subject to the constraints of EC law.[78] The 1994 Resolution suggested that EU Heads of State were coming to realize the utility of collective representation in relation to the links between international trade, aid, and labour standards.

This was the precursor to Commission attempts to persuade WTO members of the merits of linking compliance with core ILO standards to trade access under the General Agreement on Tariffs and Trade (GATT).[79] Fears of protectionism meant that developing and newly industrialized states were not persuaded.

In the absence of international agreement, the EU has nevertheless acted to require compliance with international labour standards in various preferential trade and aid agreements.[80] An important example is the 2000 Cotonou Agreement, the successor to the Lomé Conventions. This states that the parties are committed to protection of 'core labour standards' and announces that one of the aims of cooperation is to respect 'basic social rights'.[81] Perhaps even more significant has been the strategy adopted under the EU 'Generalized System of Preferences' (GSP).

B. Protection of ILO Standards under the EU GSP

The GSP is a mechanism under which industrialized states can grant non-reciprocal preferences to 'developing' nations. The European Community first implemented its own GSP in 1971, but first introduced preferences relating to labour standards in 1998,[82] which were elaborated further in 2001.[83]

These measures are positive, in that they offer third countries special incentive tariffs where they can demonstrate compliance with certain labour standards, as opposed to the approach taken by the US administration, which is solely punitive, focusing on withdrawal of preferences for violation. The approach taken by the

---

[78] See *Opinion 2/91 regarding ILO Convention No. 170 on Chemicals at Work*, Decision of 19 March 1993 [1993] ECR I-1061, which concerned the struggle for competence to determine ratification of ILO Conventions by member states. The decision indicated that where EC law harmonized national laws, the EC could maintain exclusive competence to represent the EC internationally in the social field. However, where the EC merely set minimum standards competence was shared by the EC and member states.

[79] For background to the role played by the EU and the United States in this regard, see Summers, 'The Battle in Seattle: Free Trade, Labor Rights and Societal Values', 22 *University of Pennsylvania Journal of International Economic Law* (2001) 61; and Charnovitz, 'Trade, Employment and Labour Standards: The OECD Study and Recent Developments in the Trade and Labor Standards Debate', 11 *Temple International and Comparative Law Journal* (1997) 131 at 154–63.

[80] To this extent, the EU has been described as acting 'unilaterally'. See McCrudden and Davies, 'A Perspective on Trade and Labour Rights', 21 *Journal of International Economic Law* (2000) 43 at 53–4.

[81] Cotonou Agreement 2000, Arts. 25 and 50.

[82] See Council Regulation 3281/94 L 348/1 and Council Regulation 1256/96 L 160/1, which envisaged the introduction of social conditionality, but which required a further measure, Council Regulation 2820/98 [1998] OJ L 357/1, in order for such provisions to have effect. See Nogueros and Martinez, 'Human Rights Conditionality in the External Trade of the European Union: Legal and Legitimacy Problems', 7 *Columbia Journal of European Law* (2001) 307, at 322–3.

[83] Council Regulation 2501/2001 [2001] L346/1. Note the subsequent amendment of this Regulation by Council Regulation 814/2003 L116/1 and Council Regulation 815/2003 L116/3, but these amendments are not significant for our purposes.

United States has also been described as 'idiosyncratic', for it seeks to enforce what the United States regards as 'core labour standards' according to its own definitions, as opposed to those established through the medium of the International Labour Organization.[84] By contrast, the EU GSP operates with reference to ILO standards.

Previously, under the EU GSP Regulation of 1998, ILO Conventions Nos. 87, 98, and 138 were a basis for application for preferential trade access, while provision was made for withdrawal of such preferences where the country in question allowed slave labour, permitted forced labour, or sought to export goods made by prison labour. The disparity between grounds for granting and withdrawing preferential trade access was an obvious basis for concern.[85]

Under the new Regulation of 2001, which governs the operation of GSP until 31 December 2004, 'special incentive arrangements for the protection of labour rights' may be granted to a country the national legislation of which incorporates the substance of the standards laid down in *all* the 'fundamental' ILO Conventions.[86] The third country in question must make a formal request for such incentive arrangements to be made, in the appropriate form accompanied by sufficient evidence.[87] The Commission will give other interested parties notice of the request and the opportunity to make their views known in writing before deciding whether to grant the request.[88] This creates the potential for improved transparency, but does not require the Commission to give public reasons for their final decision.

There may be temporary withdrawal of these preferential arrangements for 'practice of any form of slavery or forced labour' and/or 'serious and systematic violation of the freedom of association, the right to collective bargaining or the principle of non-discrimination in respect of employment and occupation, or use of child labour, as defined in relevant ILO Conventions', as well as 'export of goods made by prison labour'.[89] In this manner, the parity of grant and withdrawal of special preferences is apparently achieved.

The decision on withdrawal is not to be taken lightly and is more complicated than the initial grant of preferences. The current Regulation requires, first, a decision by the Commission to investigate and then a thorough investigation, giving the beneficiary country 'every opportunity to cooperate'.[90] What is significant, as an elaboration on the previous Regulation, is that reference is to be made to 'the available assessments, comments, decisions, recommendations and conclusions of the various supervisory bodies of the ILO', which 'shall serve as the point of departure for the investigation'.[91] Whereas the conclusions of ILO supervisory

---

[84] For analysis of the operation of the US GSP as regards labour standards, see Compa and Vogt, 'Labor Rights in the Generalized System of Preferences: A 20-Year Review', 22 *Comparative Labor Law and Policy Journal* (2001) 199, especially at 234.

[85] Discussed by Tsogas, 'Labour Standards in the Generalized Systems of Preference of the European Union and the United States', 6 *European Journal of Industrial Relations* (2000) 349. See also *Promoting Core Labour Standards, supra* note 6, 16–17.

[86] Council Regulation 2501/2001 [2001] L346/1, Art. 14.   [87] *Ibid.*, Art. 15.

[88] *Ibid.*, Arts. 16–18.   [89] *Ibid.*, Art. 26.   [90] *Ibid.*, Art. 28(2).   [91] *Ibid.*, Art. 28(3).

bodies are not regarded as sufficient grounds for action by the Commission when they concern the conduct of EU member states, they may be more significant in relation to the conduct of third countries.

Ultimately, if the report following the investigation indicates that temporary withdrawal is not justified, the investigation shall be terminated and notice of its conclusions shall be made available in the *Official Journal*. If withdrawal is found to be justified, the Commission will monitor and evaluate the situation in the beneficiary country for a further six months and a notice will appear in the *Official Journal* announcing that a proposal will be made to the Council for withdrawal 'unless, before the end of the period, the beneficiary country concerned made a commitment to take the measures necessary to conform in a reasonable period of time, with the principles referred to in the 1998 ILO Declaration on Fundamental Principles and Rights at Work'.[92] In this way, once again, EU conduct in trade relations is to be justified by reference to ILO standards. The decision as to withdrawal shall, however, finally be taken by the Council by qualified majority vote and is certainly not delegated to the ILO or the Commission. There is thereby some risk that, ultimately, political considerations will prevail.[93]

Various applications were made under the 1998 Regulation for special preferences relating to labour rights. Of these various are still pending, but at least one, that of Moldova, was successful.[94] It is interesting that the Commission's decision on the request by Russia has been officially postponed, on the basis that Russia needed additional time to comply with the requirements for special preferences. The reasons for Russia's request for a postponement were not evident on the face of the Commission decision.[95] Applications for special preferences have also been formally made under the 2001 Regulation by China,[96] Sri Lanka,[97] and Uzbekistan.[98] There has been no apparent decision on these and therefore no initiation of the process for withdrawal. It is therefore difficult to assess how the procedures will operate in practice. We do know that the EU is sometimes prepared to terminate preferences, an example being the termination of GSP benefits for Burma/Myanmar following findings relating to that country's forced labour practices in 1996.[99]

---

[92] Council Regulation 2501/2001 [2001] L346/1, Art. 29(2) and (3).

[93] See for concern as regards this phenomenon as regards 'human rights' conditionality, K. Smith, *The Use of Political Conditionality in the EU's Relations with Third Countries* (1997) EUI Florence Working Paper SPS No. 97/7.

[94] The official position is set out at: http://europa.eu.int/comm/trade/issues/global/social/index_en.htm.

[95] Commission Decision of 13 November 2002 on postponing the decision on the request of the Russian Federation for the special incentive arrangements for the protection of labour rights L 312/27.

[96] Notice regarding the request submitted by the People's Republic of China in order to benefit from the special incentive arrangements for the protection of the environment 15 June 2002 C 143/6.

[97] Notice regarding the request submitted by the Democratic Socialist Republic of Sri Lanka in order to benefit from the special incentive arrangements concerning labour rights 19 April 2002 C 95/14.

[98] Notice regarding the request submitted by the Republic of Uzbekistan in order to benefit from the special incentive arrangements for the protection of labour rights 9 August 2002 C 189/21.

[99] For the significance of this measure, see Charnovitz, *supra* note 79, at 151.

C. The Legal Validity and Ethical Value of GSP Measures

The use of ILO standards as a reference point in the EU GSP is interesting, given the ILO's own ambivalent official stance on social conditionality. It would be going too far to say that the EU is acting with the ILO's blessing when making reference to ILO standards in the EU GSP. This is apparent from the background to discussions concerning trade conditionality held in the ILO context.

In 1994 the ILO Governing Body established a working party on the social dimension of the liberalization of international trade, which later became known as the 'Working Party on the Social Dimension of Globalization'.[100] This ILO Working Party initially considered whether the inclusion of a social clause in trade agreements (such as GATT) was feasible, but swiftly recognized that no consensus could be reached on this matter, there being too stark a difference of opinion between Western states, such as EU members who supported such measures, and other states who tended to regard these as a form of disguised protectionism. Instead, a World Commission on the Social Dimension of Globalization was established in 2002[101] to reach consensus on strategies for the effective protection of international labour standards, given the challenges posed by market-led globalization. The final report of the Commission in 2004 stated that 'core labour standards as defined by the ILO provide a minimum set of global rules for labour in the global economy and respect for them should be strengthened in all countries',[102] but does not seem to endorse current policy under the EU GSP. Rather, it considers that 'the policies of international organizations and donor countries must . . . shift more decisively away from external conditionality to national ownership of policies'.[103]

A further crucial issue is whether the inclusion of social conditionality in the EU GSP will be regarded as in compliance with GATT. The GSP was originally recommended by the United Nations Conference on Trade and Development (UNCTAD) as a measure that could be taken by industrialized states to assist developing countries. An 'enabling clause' was agreed by GATT Contracting Parties in 1971 so that GSP could constitute an exception to the 'most favoured nation' (MFN) principle, initially for a period of ten years, which was extended indefinitely in 1979.[104]

It would therefore seem that it has been assumed that the GSP is immune from scrutiny under Article XX of GATT, which is the bedrock for justification of *ad hoc* exceptions to the MFN principle. This assumption was recently challenged by India in an application made to a WTO panel relating to EU GSP concerning drug enforcement, labour standards, and environmental measures and may be open to

---

[100] See Governing Body Working Party on the Social Dimension of Globalization, *Enhancing the Action of the Working Party on the Social Dimension of Globalization: Next Steps* GB.282/WP/SDG/1 (2001). [101] http://www.ilo.org/public/english/wcsdg/index.htm.

[102] See *supra* note 4, xiii. [103] *Ibid.*, xii.

[104] GATT, *Decision on Differential and More Favorable Treatment, Reciprocity and Fuller Participation of Developing Countries*, 28.11.1979, GATT BISD (26th Supp.) (1980), available at: http://www.wto.org/english/docs_e/legal_e/enabling1979_e.htm#fntext1.

question.[105] The arguments relating to labour standards were ultimately not pursued and at least one commentator, Howse, has concluded that the imposition of conditions pertaining to compliance with ILO Conventions is defensible under both the enabling clause and Article XX.[106] Nevertheless, there may be more potential scope for concern under Article XX than he allows.

The application of Article XX entails a two-tier test, the second limb of which may not be satisfied by the EU GSP. The first test requires assessment as to whether protection of 'core labour standards', as endorsed by the ILO, comes within the list of legitimate exceptions set out in Article XX. This could arguably be achieved under (a) 'public morals', (b) protection of human life or health, and (e) measures taken 'relating to the products of prison labour'. The second test arises from the 'chapeau' to Article XX, namely whether the preference in question is 'a means of arbitrary or unjustifiable discrimination between countries' or 'a disguised restriction on international trade'. Howse considers that this test is also satisfied, given the application of transparent criteria and flexibility envisaged as to implementation of the conditions.[107] However, he does not consider the risk that EU practice can be regarded as arbitrary or discriminatory if it requires of third states standards which it does not require of its own member states. For example, reference to ILO standards or the findings of ILO supervisory bodies can arguably serve only to justify the grant or withdrawal of trade preferences if these standards or findings are also respected by EU members.[108] There is therefore some doubt as to the justification for the EU GSP as it operates at present, given the lack of compliance by certain EU member states with recommendations made by ILO supervisory bodies.[109] Nevertheless, this argument has yet to be pursued in the WTO and we cannot therefore know what the outcome would be if this were done.

The Council does not seem unduly concerned by the potential for such a challenge, having concluded in 2003 that 'the possibility to use GSP incentives to promote core labour standards has proven to be an important feature of the EU's GSP scheme and should be considered as part of the EU's GSP scheme for the period 2005–2014'.[110] Furthermore, the Council continues to stress the role of ILO standards in this process.[111]

---

[105] European Communities—Conditions for Granting of Tariff Preferences to India, Request for the Establishment of a Panel by India, WY/DS246/4 9.12.2002.

[106] Howse, 'India's WTO Challenge to Drug Enforcement Conditions in the European Community Generalized System of Preferences: A Little Known Case with Major Repercussions for "Political" Conditionality in US Trade Policy', 4 *Chicago Journal of International Law* (2003a) 385; and Howse, 'Back to Court After *Shrimp/Turtle*? Almost But Not Quite Yet: India's Short Lived Challenge to Labor and Environmental Exceptions in the European Union's Generalized System of Preferences', 13 *American University International Law Review* (2003b) 1333.

[107] See Howse (2003b), *supra* note 106, 1367–73 and 1374–5.

[108] Discussed in T. Novitz, *Promoting Core Labour Standards and Improving Global Social Governance: An Assessment of EU Competence to Implement Commission Proposals* (2002) EUI Florence Working Paper RSC No. 2002/59, 29–30.   [109] *Supra*, at 219–20 and 223.

[110] Council Conclusions, *supra* note 10, para. 9.   [111] *Ibid.*, paras. 10 and 11.

4. THE DYNAMICS OF DIALOGUE BETWEEN THE EU AND THE ILO

The view expressed at present by both the EU Commissioner for Employment and Social Affairs and the ILO Director-General is that the approaches of the ILO and EU are very similar, and that they are 'acting in concert on the global stage'.[112] This raises questions as to the terms of such cooperation. This part analyses the dynamics of dialogue between the EU and the ILO as regards protection of international labour standards. It begins by considering the relative influence of these two institutions in the post-Cold War period, which seems to be slanted more in favour of the EU than was previously the case. The formal role that the EU now plays within the ILO is then outlined, having regard to the manner of EU representation within the organization. It is suggested that this is well-established and is unlikely to change. Instead, what may be more significant is the subtle influence of the EU on future ILO constitutional change and policy-orientation.

A. The Relative Influence of the EU and ILO in the Post-Cold War Period

There is little doubt that the EU has grown in significance as an international actor in the post-Cold War period.[113] This may be attributed to its economic strength as a regional organization, as well as its ability to attract former Eastern bloc states as potential members through 'enlargement'. In this manner, the EU has been able to 'export' certain standards through the '*aquis communitaire*'. In her address at the Seminar on the Social Dimension of Globalization, Commissioner Diamantopoulou observed that 'enlargement offers us the opportunity to renew the European approach' to social policy.[114] At a later meeting in Prague she made the even bolder claim that: 'The European Union is emerging as a new World model of development. Not just for candidates joining the EU. But for Southern America. Asia. Africa. The countries of the ILO in general.'[115] Similar statements have been made in other settings.[116]

---

[112] See the 'Exchange of Letters', *supra* note 6 above; and also the statement made by the ILO Director-General, Juan Somavia at the meeting on The European Social Agenda and the EU's International Partners, *supra* note 9, at 4.

[113] For discussion of this phenomenon, see, for example, J. Weiler (ed.), *The EU, the WTO and the NAFTA* (2000); and Meunier and Nicolaidis, 'Who Speaks for Europe? The Delegation of Trade Authority in the EU', *JCMS* (1999) 477.

[114] A. Diamantopoulou, Address at the Seminar on the Social Dimension of Globalisation organised by the European Commission and the World Commission on the Social Dimension of Globalisation, Brussels, 3.2.2003.

[115] A. Diamantopoulou, 'Making Europe Work For People', 10th ETUC Statutory Congress, 26.5.2003.

[116] For example, the meeting on The European Social Agenda and the EU's International Partners, *supra* note 9, at 2.

While the EU can be bold in its assertion of its new-found influence, the ILO has struggled to maintain its position as a prominent UN agency. One aspect of its initial function was to prevent the spread of Communism by promising 'social justice' to working people, as is evident from the deliberations of those who drafted the first ILO Constitution in 1919.[117] In the Cold War era, Communist states were admitted as members and the ILO International Labour Conference became a significant forum for debate between the West and the Eastern bloc.[118] When the Cold War ended, the role of the ILO in the international community had to change and the organization faced an 'identity crisis'.[119]

By 1990 free market values appeared to have been vindicated by the collapse of the Soviet Union, and radical deregulation of labour markets was now envisaged by certain Western governments, the United Kingdom being a notable example.[120] The position of the employers' group as a lobby seemed to be strengthened by this turn of events; and previously accepted ILO norms were questioned by employer representatives at the International Labour Conference.[121] Government representatives also took this opportunity to challenge past assumptions as to the relative priority of certain ILO standards.[122] Meanwhile, academic commentators expressed concern at the 'overproduction' of ILO Conventions.[123] The response of the then ILO Director-General, Michel Hansenne, was to take these threats to the established function of the ILO seriously, and to initiate a study into the viability of ILO standards.[124]

In 1995 a working party was established by the ILO Governing Body to advise as to which Conventions should be given priority and which should be regarded as defunct. There followed in 1997 an amendment to the ILO Constitution, making provision for abrogation of outdated Conventions.[125] The International Labour

---

[117] G. Barnes, *History of the International Labour Organisation* (1926) 80. See also M. Imber, *The USA, ILO, UNESCO and IAEA: Politicization and Withdrawal the Specialized Agencies* (1989) 43.

[118] A. Alcock, *History of the International Labour Organisation* (1971) 318–37. See also V.-Y. Ghebeli, *The International Labour Organization: A Case-Study on the Evolution of UN Specialised Agencies* (1989). On the difficulties this posed for the ILO Credentials Committee, see *The Role of the Credentials Committee, supra* note 62.

[119] Langille, 'The ILO and the New Economy: Recent Developments', 15 *IJCLLIR* (1999) 229.

[120] Discussed by K. Ewing, *Britain and the ILO* (2nd edn., 1994).

[121] For an example relating to the right to strike, see *Record of Proceedings* (1994) International Labour Conference (ILC) 81st Session, 25/31–41.

[122] See the request made by M. Barrot, Minister of Labour, Social Dialogue and Participation in France, that priority be given to employment promotion rather than collective bargaining, see *Record of Proceedings* (1995) ILC 82nd Session, 8/11–8/12. See also the comments of Mr Melkert, Minister of Social Affairs of the Netherlands, at the same conference.

[123] An example was Cordova, 'Some Reflections on the Overproduction of International Labour Standards', 14 *Comparative Labor Law Journal* (1993) 138.

[124] See *Report of the Director-General: Defending Values: Promoting Change* (1994); and *Report of the Director-General: Promoting Employment* (1995).

[125] The result was what is now Art. 19(9) of the ILO Constitution. See *Report of the Committee on the Application of Standards* (2001), especially at paras. 57–61; and http://www.ilo.org/public/english/standards/norm/comefrom/uptodate/revise2.htm.

Office, which is the Secretariat of the ILO, found itself having to justify the utility of other Conventions and workers' rights in economic terms, as opposed to its past emphasis on social justice and human rights.[126] A campaign was launched by the ILO Governing Body focusing on ratification of the 'fundamental' ILO Conventions, which was followed by a restatement of those workers' rights to be regarded as 'fundamental' in the 1998 ILO Declaration on Fundamental Principles and Rights at Work. The attempt to give priority to four 'core' entitlements has given the ILO a basis for promoting its international profile, and in this way has achieved some success.[127] However, this shift in orientation also reflects the pressure to which the organization was subjected to narrow its ambitions. For example, the exclusion of health and safety from the list may be regarded as questionable.[128]

The lack of any palpable sanction for non-compliance with ILO Conventions now arguably poses more difficulties than it did in the past. Incentives for compliance with even core labour standards are minimal. A follow-up procedure attached to the 1998 Declaration monitors compliance, but has not had full cooperation from recalcitrant states.[129] By contrast, the conditions under which financial assistance is provided by organizations such as the World Bank and the International Monetary Fund have had a palpable influence on national socio-economic policies, sometimes to the detriment of workers' rights. The International Labour Office, the secretariat of the ILO, has sought to counteract this trend and now contributes to the drafting of Poverty Reduction Strategy Papers used by these organizations, but has not been as successful in collaboration on social security and other objectives.[130]

It therefore seems that despite its proactive approach to the continuing promotion of international labour standards, the influence of the ILO is not what it was. The strength of the employer lobby has increased, which means that the workers' group is likely to be more defensive and less confident in its ability to shape the content of new Conventions for the protection of workers' rights.[131] There is instead a

---

[126] See also the research carried out under the auspices of the International Institute for Labour Studies (IILS) attached to the ILO in Geneva, such as D. Campbell and W. Sengenberger (eds.), *Creating Economic Opportunities: The Role of Labour Standards in Industrial Restructuring* (1994). These findings were also bolstered by OECD reports, *Trade, Employment and Labour Standards: A Study of Core Workers' Rights and International Trade* (1996) and *International Trade and Core Labour Standards* (2000).

[127] See, for example, the World Summit on Social Development and endorsement of its role by the WTO Ministerial Meeting at Singapore referred to *supra* note 5, 1–2.

[128] Fields, 'International Labour Standards and Economic Interdependence', 49 *Industrial and Labor Relations Review* (1996) 571, at 572; and Hepple, 'New Approaches to International Labour Regulation', 26 *Industrial Law Journal* (1997) 353, at 358.

[129] See for discussion of this problem, *Review of the Annual Reports under the Follow-up to the ILO Declaration on Fundamental Principles and Rights at Work* (2001) GB 280/3/2.

[130] *Report of the Director-General: Reducing the Decent Work Deficit: A Global Challenge* (2001), chap. 2.

[131] See, for example, the resistance of the workers' group to any proposed Convention on the settlement of labour disputes that would demarcate the scope of a right to strike. Discussed in Novitz (2003) *supra* note 19, 120–3.

tendency to consolidate existing norms rather than create new ones; and to narrow its focus to ensure protection of the most basic workers' rights. Even extant standards now have to be justified in economic as well as social terms. Moreover, the lack of efficacy of ILO Conventions and supervisory procedures are illustrated by EU member states' often nonchalant response to non-compliance with even core ILO standards.[132] This suggests that in its dialogue with the EU, the ILO is likely to be less influential than was possible hitherto.

B. Representation of the EU in the ILO

EU member states are members of the ILO, but the EU itself is not. The ILO respects this distinction, which means that the EU is not held to account for any breach of standards by EU member states. That is not to say that there is no recognition of the significance of the EC (and now the EU) as a regional organization. This began with the conclusion of a cooperation agreement in 1958, which has been supplemented at various junctures, the most recent of which is the 'Exchange of Letters' that took place between the ILO Director-General and the Commissioner for Employment and Social Affairs in 2001.[133]

At present, the Commission's representative may speak for the EU as an 'observer' at the International Labour Conference, but cannot vote and is not subjected to criticism. The statements made by the Commission in this forum also tend to be bland, consisting of endorsements of action taken by the ILO or policies pursued in the EU, and often stressing the potential link between the two.[134] There are also informal but 'high level' meetings that take place between representatives of the two organizations.[135] There are, however, no records of such discussions and it is therefore difficult to assess their effect.

The tendency within the International Labour Conference and committees is not for the EU to openly meet or speak as a bloc. This may, however, be done behind the scenes. At one point the Commission was, it seems, frustrated by the lack of co-operation by certain member states, but they are now apt to speak with one voice in circumstances where standards have been set and harmonized under EC law.[136] More commonly, EU member states form part of a larger group of states with industrialized market-oriented economy countries, known as 'IMEC', which have broader shared aims.

---

[132] See *supra* 219–20 and 223.   [133] See *supra* note 6.

[134] See that made by Ms Quintin in the *Record of Proceedings* (2003) ILC 91st Session, 8/15, which stresses the convergence of objectives of the ILO and EU, and states how current European policies concerning the European Employment Strategy and social dialogue in the EU achieve these goals. Note also the statement made on behalf of the European Economic and Social Committee by Mr Briesch at 7/30.   [135] Referred to in the 'Exchange of Letters' of 2001, see *supra* note 6.

[136] See *Opinion 2/91 regarding ILO Convention No. 170 on Chemicals at Work*, Decision of 19.3.1993 [1993] ECR I-1061, discussed *supra* at note 78.

C. Potential for EU Influence in ILO Constitutional Reform and Formulation of Future Policy Objectives

The EU may well have budgetary significance for the ILO,[137] given the statement by the Commission and Council that they plan to contribute more financial support to technical assistance provided through the ILO.[138] Yet its importance may be more likely to turn on the stated intention of the EU to promote the 'fundamental' ILO Conventions and designated core labour standards. Arguably, use of ILO standards as a reference point for its trade and aid provision is likely to raise the profile of the ILO at a time when it most requires recognition and support. This may be why ILO officials have not publicly criticized EU use of GSP, despite the current controversy over social conditionality within the ILO. Indeed, the current Director-General, Juan Somavia, seems to have cautiously given support to the Commission Communication on *Promoting Core Labour Standards*, which states the EU's continued ambitions in this regard.[139] My intention here is to consider not merely how it may be that the EU is immune from influence from the ILO, but also the extent to which the EU may itself influence either ILO constitutional structures or policy objectives.

EU participation in ILO constitutional reform is an objective set out in a Commission Communication of 2001,[140] and in the Council Resolution of 2003.[141] These policy documents envisage chiefly change to the supervisory processes within the ILO, an objective that reflects concerns already raised elsewhere as to their efficacy.[142] There may, however, also be more subtle ways in which the EU has an impact on ILO constitutional norms and policy orientation.

For example, the principle of 'tripartism' has recently come into question, it being argued that a broader representation of society beyond management and labour will be necessary for the formation of appropriate social policy.[143] This is reminiscent of the emphasis on participation to be found in current debates concerning European governance.[144] The ILO Director-General has stated, in response, that tripartism 'is

---

[137] For the current budget, see http://www.ilo.org/public/english/standards/relm/ilc/ilc89/pdf/rep-ii.pdf.

[138] *Promoting Core Labour Standards, supra* note 6, at 15; and Council Conclusions, *supra* note 10, at para. 7.

[139] See, for example, the statement made by the ILO Director-General, Juan Somavia, at the meeting on The European Social Agenda and the EU's International Partners, *supra* note 9, at 4.

[140] *Promoting Core Labour Standards, supra* note 6, at 13–16.

[141] Council Conclusions, *supra* note 10, at paras. 5 and 6.

[142] Oates, 'International Labour Standards: Challenges of the 21st Century', in R. Blanpain and C. Engels (eds.), *The ILO and the Social Challenges of the 21st Century: The Geneva Lectures* (2001) 100; Cooney, 'Testing Times for the ILO: Institutional Reform for the New International Political Economy', 20 *Comparative Labor Law and Policy Journal* (1999) 365; and Ewing, 'Modernising International Labour Standards: Globalisation, Multinational Companies and International Trade Union Rights', 50 *Federation News* (2000) 109.

[143] See Cooney, *supra* note 142, 371–3 and 390–3; and Vosko, ' "Decent Work": The Shifting Role of the ILO and the Struggle for Global Social Justice', 2(1) *Global Social Justice* (2002) 19 at 38–9.

[144] Discussed briefly *supra*, at 224.

under no threat' but that he does envisage extending opportunities for civil society organizations to be included in deliberation on matters where they have expertise.[145] This form of 'tripartite-plus' representation[146] has already been recognized and utilized in the EU, as noted above.[147]

Another example of potential EU influence is the increasing emphasis on 'soft' as opposed to 'hard' law. Within the ILO, the employer lobby has suggested that adoption of international instruments may be less appropriate than 'campaigns to raise public awareness, declarations, codes of conduct and technical assistance'.[148] Such a strategy has led to alarm on the part of the workers' group, who have expressed concern at the 'proliferation of initiatives seeking to call into question the universal scope, the application, even the existence of standards'.[149] The response of the current ILO Director-General, Juan Somavia, has been to say that he will not abandon the protection of standards, which he regards as a 'stern indicator of progress towards the achievement of ILO objective, not through lip-service but in law and practice'.[150] Nevertheless, he also seems to embrace alternative mechanisms for promotion of international labour standards. His praise for the International Programme for the Elimination of Child Labour (IPEC) is indicative of the importance of a programmatic approach to implementation of labour standards.[151] Also, soft law measures familiar to the EU, such as 'gender main-streaming', have now been introduced.[152] Moreover, in a manner comparable to the EU 'open method of co-ordination', the follow-up procedure to the 1998 ILO Declaration involves not only disclosure of information relating to non-compliance, but the sharing of best practice and the setting of new goals and objectives for states.[153]

---

[145] *Report of the Director-General: Reducing the Decent Work Deficit: A Global Challenge* (2001), chap. 3.2.

[146] Blackett, 'Global Governance, Legal Pluralism and the Decentered State: A Labour Law Critique of Codes of Conduct', 8 *Indiana Journal of Global Legal Studies* (2001) 401, at 438.

[147] See Smismans (1999), *supra* note 56.

[148] *Report of the ILO Governing Body Committee on the Application of Standards* (2000), paras. 37–8.

[149] *Report of the ILO Governing Body Committee on the Application of Standards* (2001), para. 42.

[150] *Report of the Director-General: Reducing the Decent Work Deficit: A Global Challenge* (2001), chap. 3.2.

[151] See www.ilo.org/public/english/standards/ipec/index.htm. For discussion of the importance of such programmes, see *Report of the Director-General: ILO Programme Implementation 2000–1* (2002).

[152] See as to the priority given to gender mainstreaming within the EU as early as 1996, Commission Communication, *Incorporating Equal Opportunities for Women and Men into All Community Policies and Activities* COM(96)67; and *Progress Report from the Commission on the Follow-up of the Communication: Incorporating Equal Opportunities for Women and Men into All Community Policies and Activities* COM(98)122. This policy is discussed briefly *supra*, at 221. By contrast, the ILO Action Plan on Gender Equality and Mainstreaming in the ILO was presented to the ILO Governing Body only in March 2001. See http://www.ilo.org/public/english/bureau/gender/.

[153] See, for example, *Time for Equality at Work: Global Report under the Follow-up to the ILO Declaration on Fundamental Principles and Rights at Work* (2003), ILC, 91st Session.

5. CONCLUSION

EU institutions seem eager to represent their relationship with the ILO as one of mutual cooperation and constructive dialogue. Moreover, the ILO seems to have been loathe to contradict statements made by the Commission to this effect. This chapter has examined the extent to which the EU has actually sought to promote international labour standards and has investigated the dynamics of dialogue between the two organizations.

One obvious problem with the Commission's representation of recent events is the failure of the EU to make provision for internal enforcement of all core ILO standards. There is also some danger that the notion of disinterested discussions between organizations could be employed to gloss over the internal workings of those organizations and, in particular, those who wield influence within them. It is, for example, worth considering the mechanisms available for influence by employer and worker groups within each organization, and how the balance of power may have shifted over time. In addition, such a vision of the relationship between the ILO and the EU has the potential to ignore the broader dynamics of international relations within which this relationship is situated, namely the relative power of the institutions.

It has been argued here that the enhanced economic power of the EU, when combined with the struggle of the ILO for influence in a post-Cold War climate, has allowed the EU to maintain a double standard. As an organization, the EU can evade responsibility for implementation of international labour standards in member states, while requiring that third states do so if they wish to receive certain trade and aid benefits. This casts doubt on EU attempts to legitimize its external relations policies with reference to ILO standards. Indeed, the capacity of the ILO to influence the conduct of EU member states would appear to have declined, while pressure on the ILO to respond to EU initiatives has increased. This might explain why, in various respects, we may now see the ILO following the lead of the EU, rather than the other way around.

The World Commission on the Social Dimension of Globalization has stated that organizations like the EU should 'assume their part' in promoting core labour standards.[154] The policy statements of EU institutions presume that this has been achieved. However, on the basis of the evidence presented here, there is reason to question the claim to this achievement, given the continuing disjuncture between EC social policy and EU external conditionality. The disjuncture can be explained by the current dynamics of dialogue between the EU and the ILO, but cannot so easily be excused. It is only when EU institutions 'ensure that no aspect of their policies and programmes impedes implementation of [workers'] rights',[155] that we will be able to applaud their protection of international labour standards.

---

[154] *Supra* note 4, xiii.   [155] *Ibid.*

Index

accountability, 23–4
ACP–EU Partnership, 185
adjustment assistance. *see* worker
    adjustment
AFL–CIO, 7
Agreement on Social Policy (EU), 19, 178,
    193, 213, 217
Agreement on Trade Related Aspects of
    Intellectual Property Rights
    (TRIPS), 133–4
Albany case (ECJ), 20, 78–9, 227
Alliance for Progress, 149
Alston, Philip, 173
American Convention on Human Rights,
    1969, 148, 215
American Society of International Law, 85
American states. *see also* FTAA; inter-American
    trade agreements; OAS; Pan American
    conferences
  Alliance for Progress, 149
  children, cooperation on, 145
  Declaration of Social Principles, 147
  free trade agreements. *see* FTAA;
    inter-American trade agreements;
    NAFTA
  labour conferences, 149–50
  labour cooperation, 144–51
    free trade agreements, 151–61
  worker adjustment, 172–4
Amsterdam Treaty, 79–80, 200, 203, 217
Arthurs, Harry, 21, 82
association, freedom of. *see* freedom of
    association
Association Agreement between the
    European Community and Chile, 17
Austria, 220

Belgium, 220
Bentham, Jeremy, 31
Bercusson, B., 181
Berlin wall, collapse of, 91, 123
Beveridge, William, 12, 32, 34, 35
Bhagwati, Jagdish, 6, 7, 165
Bolivar, Simon, 143
Bolsheviks, 89
Booth, Charles, 32

Britain
  industrial revolution, 27–31, 37
  poor law, 12, 27–38
  welfare state, 31–5
Burma. *see* Myanmar
Burmese Freedom and Democracy Act,
    2003, 107, 112–15

CAFTA, 156–7, 175
Canada, 3, 21, 66, 67, 73, 144
Canada–Chile Labour Side Agreement, 17
Canada–Costa Rica Labour Side
    Agreement, 17
capability approach, 13, 52, 55–6, 60
  uses and limits of, 58–60
capital mobility, 124
capitalism, 28, 36
Caribbean countries, 144. *see also* American
    states
casualization, 32, 33
CBI (Britain), 196
CEEP, 50, 180–1
Centros case (ECJ), 45–7
CESCR, 71–2, 83
CESI, 179–80
CFA, 65–8, 71, 192
CFI, 180, 181, 182, 201
Charnovitz, Steve, 17–18, 21, 86–7, 109
Charter of Fundamental Rights of the EU, 20,
    25, 80–2, 228
  collective labour rights, 200–1, 202
  labour standards, 228
  legal effect, 228
Charter of Fundamental Social Rights for
    Workers (EU), 80, 81, 218
Charter of the International Trade
    Organization, 147
child labour, 2, 3, 9, 214–15, 240
Chile, 17, 73
  US–Chile Free Trade Agreement, 156, 157
China, 6, 232
citizenship, 26, 35, 36
civil rights, 26, 36, 59, 83, 227–8
closed shops, 212
co-evolution, 42
codes of conduct, 18, 21, 139